Special educational needs and disability discrimination in schools

a legal handbook

Sarah Hannett is a barrister at Matrix where she practises in public law and human rights. Her education law clients include parents and young people, schools, local authorities and the Secretary of State for Education. In 2013 she was awarded the Bar Pro Bono award for her work on the School Exclusion Project (which provides free representation for the parents of children permanently excluded from school).

Aileen McColgan is a barrister at Matrix and professor of human rights at King's College London. One of her areas of specialism is education law including that relating to SEN and disabilities, and she has a particular interest in disability discrimination.

Elizabeth Prochaska is a barrister at Matrix, where she specialises in public and human rights law. She enjoys representing parents and local authorities in education cases and she has been a governor of a special school.

Available as an ebook at www.lag.org.uk/ebooks

The purpose of the Legal Action Group is to promote equal access to justice for all members of society who are socially, economically or otherwise disadvantaged. To this end, it seeks to improve law and practice, the administration of justice and legal services.

Special educational needs and disability discrimination in schools

a legal handbook

Sarah Hannett, Aileen McColgan and Elizabeth Prochaska

Legal Action Group
2017

This edition published in Great Britain 2017
by LAG Education and Service Trust Limited
National Pro Bono Centre, 48 Chancery Lane, London WC2A 1JF
www.lag.org.uk

British Library Cataloguing in Publication Data
a CIP catalogue record for this book is available from the British Library.

Print ISBN   978 1 908407 76 4
ebook ISBN   978 1 908407 77 1

Typeset by Regent Typesetting, London
Printed in Great Britain by Hobbs the Printers, Totton, Hampshire

Foreword

by Jane McConnell
Judge of the First-tier Tribunal (Health, Education and
Social Care Chamber) and Lead Judge SEND

Since the introduction of the Children and Families Act 2014, the
SEND (special educational needs and disability) legislative framework
has been undergoing its biggest change in over 30 years. As children
and young people supported on School Action/School Action Plus
or with a statement of SEN are moved from the old law under the
Education Act 1996 into the new legal landscape of SEN Support or
education, health and care (EHC) plans it is important for all those
affected to understand the difference in the approach the law now
requires to be taken.

The trigger point for this change came following the Lamb Inquiry
into parental confidence in the SEN System which reported in 2009.
I was a professional adviser to the inquiry and the overwhelming
evidence we heard was that the then legal system was not working
for the children and young people it sought to protect. It was considered outdated as it failed to see a child or young person with SEND
holistically. Instead it supported local authorities to identify silos of
need in the areas of education and social care, whilst health needs
and provision were dealt with by an additional, completely separate,
system. The green paper issued by the government in 2011, which
set the development of new legislation into motion, proposed a new
approach which would put children and young people at the heart
of the process. It looked to establish new legal rights requiring local
authorities and health providers to join up their approaches and
work collaboratively. All agencies would be required to work in co-
production with parents and young people.

The final legislation, as enacted by Parliament, reflects this goal
to an extent. It widened the legal framework to include children and
young people from 0 to 25 years old. Whilst the threshold for getting a
higher level of support than an education placement can provide from
its own resources is still based on educational need, the EHC assessment process that must then be followed by a local authority has a
wider remit. It must include the local authority seeking information

and advice from not just educational professionals, but in addition health and social care practitioners. Though the legislation as originally drafted did not give the First-tier Tribunal the powers to consider and decide issues concerning health and social care, a pilot of powers to make recommendations in these areas across all local authorities for a minimum period of two years starting in 2018 will bring the process closer towards the original goal of a child or young person being considered as a 'whole' individual.

As with any new law, we are in a period where the true scope of what it requires still has to be tested and clarified through the development of case-law. While this is happening the legal framework has to be made to work to provide appropriate support for the vulnerable children and young people it seeks to protect and empower.

Whether you are a legal practitioner, a local authority, early years provider/school/further education college, professional working with children and young people with SEND, parent of a child with SEND or young person with SEND, it is vital that you have reliable resources on which you can rely to help you to understand and unpick what might be otherwise be considered a tangled web of legal rights, policy and practice. This publication seeks to do this in a way which divides areas of the SEND legal framework into the specific legal steps in the process of identifying and making provision to support our children and young people with SEND. It is a legal handbook so provides an in-depth level of legal research and comment. It is not intended to be a simple guide to this area of practice. However, it is written in a style which I consider will be accessible to many different audiences.

Consistent application of the SEND legal framework will ensure good practice in local authorities and ultimately be a safety net to catch children and young people on occasions where the system fails to do so successfully. As always the ultimate advice to those seeking to ensure this legislation is effective has to be 'know the law and apply the law'. This publication will help to do this.

Tribunal Judge Jane McConnell MBE
March 2017

Preface

This is a book for and about children and young people with special educational needs or a disability. It is a book aimed primarily at helping them, or their parent, bring a SEN appeal or a disability discrimination claim.

It is also a book for representatives who appear on behalf of children and young people in the First-tier Tribunal (FTT). Education law can be daunting, for lawyers and non-lawyers alike, and we want to make our knowledge and experience accessible to anyone who has to deal with it. Frequent requests from junior colleagues and our trainees for the 'muppet's guide' to FTT proceedings convinced us that there is a real need for a specialist text in this area. We intended the book to be all things to all women and men (and to be as helpful to parents as to specialist counsel). We hope that we have achieved that rather ambitious goal, at least in part.

We also hope that the book is timely as well as useful. The Children and Families Act 2014 has been in force since 1 September 2014 and has now bedded in. Whilst the book makes reference where appropriate to the Education Act 1996, it focuses on the Children and Families Act 2014 given that local authorities must, by 2018, transfer children and young people with statements of SEN and LDAs to EHC plans.

As ever in an undertaking of this type, friends and colleagues have helped along the way. Anna Bicarregui, Tracey Eldridge-Hinmers, Paul Greatorex, Darryl Hutcheon, Aidan Wills and David Wolfe QC have each read one or more chapters of the book and we are grateful for their comments and insights (and particularly Darryl and Aidan who road-tested chapters of the book for sense and accessibility). We are also grateful to the Legal Information Team at Matrix who provided research assistance at the start of this project. Throughout the writing period, our practice teams kept us in paying work and good humour.

Our publisher, Esther Pilger, has been the model of patience, even when the news on progress was inevitably bad, and remained in good cheer even when the manuscript was delivered more than a year after we had confidently predicted that it would be finished.

We are grateful to Judge McConnell for taking the time to contribute the foreword, and for her generous comments.

We thank our families for their support and encouragement (Kirsty, Lois and Joseph; Chris and Rionach; Duncan, Eva and Anton).

Finally, each of us has enjoyed the writing of this book immensely, and the act of collaboration even more. A few grammatical skirmishes aside, it has been a huge privilege to write with colleagues who are also good friends.

We welcome feedback and corrections, which should be sent to sarahhannett@matrixlaw.co.uk. We have endeavoured to set out the law as it stands at January 2017 although some additions were possible at the proof stage.

Sarah Hannett
Aileen McColgan
Elizabeth Prochaska
March 2017

Contents

Table of cases

Table of statutes

Table of statutory instruments

Table of European and international legislation and conventions

Abbreviations

AAC	Administrative Appeals Chamber
ADHD	attention deficit and hyperactivity disorder
ASD	autism spectrum disorder
AWPU	Age-Weighted Pupil Unit
CA 1989	Children Act 1989
CA 2004	Children Act 2004
CA 2014	Care Act 2014
CC	County Council
CCGs	Clinical Commissioning Groups
CFA 2014	Children and Families Act 2014
CHAT	Comprehensive Health Assessment Tool
CJEU	Court of Justice of the European Union
Code	Special Educational Needs and Disability Code of Practice (May 2015)
CSDPA 1970	Chronically Sick and Disabled Persons Act 1970
DDA 1995	Disability Discrimination Act 1995
EA 1996	Education Act 1996
EAPSB Regs	Education (Areas to which Pupils and Students Belong) Regulations 1996 SI No 615
EAT	Employment Appeals Tribunal
ECHR	European Convention on Human Rights
ECJ	European Court of Justice
EHC	education, health and care
EHRC	Equality and Human Rights Commission
EIA 2006	Education and Inspections Act 2006
EqA 2010	Equality Act 2010
FTT	First-tier Tribunal
FTT Rules	Tribunal Procedure (First-Tier Tribunal) (Health, Education And Social Care Chamber) Rules 2008 SI No 2699
HRA 1998	Human Rights Act 1998
HSCA 2012	Health and Social Care Act 2012
IARE Regs	Inter-authority Recoupment (England) Regulations 2013 SI No 492
LBC	London Borough Council
LA	local authority
LDAs	Learning Difficulty Assessments

LSA 2000	Learning and Skills Act 2000
MBC	Metropolitan Borough Council
MCA 2005	Mental Capacity Act 2005
PCC	provision, criterion or practice
PSED	public sector equality duty
SEN	special educational needs
SENCO	SEN co-ordinator
SEND	special educational needs and disability
SEND Regs	Special Educational Needs and Disability Regulations 2014 SI No 1530
SENDDP Regs	Special Educational Needs and Disability (Detained Persons) Regulations 2015 SI No 62
SEND (Pilot) Regs	Special Educational Needs and Disability (First-tier Tribunal Recommendation Power) (Pilot) Regulations 2015 SI No 358
SENPB Regs	Special Educational Needs (Personal Budgets) Regulations 2014 SI No 1652
SENT	Special Educational Needs Tribunal
SSFA 1998	School Standards and Framework Act 1998
TCEA 2007	Tribunals, Courts and Enforcement Act 2007
TSP Order	Children and Families Act 2014 (Transitional and Saving Provisions) (No 2) Order 2014 SI No 2270
UNCRC	United Nations Convention on the Rights of the Child
UNCRPD	United Nations Convention on the Rights of Persons with Disabilities
UT	Upper Tribunal
UT Rules	Tribunal Procedure (Upper Tribunal) Rules 2008 SI No 2698
YJB	Youth Justice Board
YOT	youth offending team

CHAPTER 1

General principles

Key points

Legal framework

- The legal framework for special educational needs (SEN) in the Children and Families Act (CFA) 2014 transformed the law on SEN. It introduced new requirements to improve the participation of children, parents and young people in the SEN system and the integration of SEN with health and social care.
- There is now one system for assessing children and young people with SEN. Statements of SEN and learning difficulty assessments (LDAs) have been replaced by education, health and care (EHC) plans for children and young people from 0 to 25.
- The Special Educational Needs and Disability Regulations 2014 SI No 1530 (SEND Regs) are the principal regulations dealing with the process for EHC needs assessment and the creation of EHC plans.
- Statutory guidance for all the institutions involved in SEN provision is contained in the *Special educational needs and disability code of practice*.
- Human rights principles in international conventions have informed the development of the SEN regime and will be used by the courts to interpret SEN legal provisions.

General duties imposed by the Children and Families Act 2014

- The CFA 2014 imposes general duties on local authorities, schools and other institutions involved in SEN provision.
- The duties reflect the legislative objectives of greater participation, integration and cooperation in the SEN system.
- Some of the duties are aspirational and will not translate directly into enforceable legal rights, while others impose specific legal obligations on local authorities.
- Local authorities are under a duty to publish a 'local offer' that sets out the education, health and social care provision that they expect to be available for children and young people with SEN and disabilities in their area.
- The CFA 2014 imposes an obligation on schools to support children with medical conditions.

Children with SEN but without an education, health and care plan

- All children with SEN are entitled to support in schools, regardless of whether or not they have an EHC plan.

- Children who do not have an EHC plan must be educated in mainstream school. There are very limited exceptions to this presumption.
- Schools are under an obligation to use their 'best endeavours' to secure SEN provision to meet the needs of children with SEN.
- If a school cannot provide adequate SEN support, it may mean that the child needs an EHC plan.

Legal framework

1.1 The legal framework for identifying, assessing and supporting children and young people with special educational needs (SEN) in England is contained in:

- Part 3 of the CFA 2014;
- the regulations made under that Act; and
- the *Special educational needs and disability code of practice* ('the Code').[1]

Children and Families Act 2014

1.2 The CFA 2014 transformed the law on special educational needs, which had previously been addressed in the Education Act (EA) 1996 and the Learning and Skills Act (LSA) 2000. In its proposals for reform, the government stated that the previous legal regime was 'no longer fit for purpose',[2] describing the SEN system as fragmented and bureaucratic. The government explained that its motivation for the reforms stemmed from its desire to give children and their parents more involvement in planning the SEN support that they receive. Another central ambition of the CFA 2014 is to promote local authority co-operation with their partners in health and social care to plan and commission provision for children with SEN.

---

1 Department for Education and Department of Health, *Special educational needs and disability code of practice: 0 to 25 years. Statutory guidance for organisations which work with and support children and young people who have special educational needs or disabilities*, current version published 2015.

2 Department for Education, *Support and aspiration: a new approach to special educational needs and disability. A consultation* Cm 8027 ('SEN green paper'), The Stationery Office, March 2011, para 9. Available at http://webarchive. nationalarchives.gov.uk/20130401151715/https:/www.education.gov.uk/ publications/eorderingdownload/green-paper-sen.pdf.

1.3   The CFA 2014 establishes a single system for children with SEN and disabilities from birth to the age of 25. It introduced the following significant changes:

- The views, wishes and feelings of the child or young person, and his or her parent, and his or her participation in decisions, are mandatory considerations for local authorities when they are exercising their powers under the CFA 2014.[3]
- Statements of SEN[4] and learning difficulty assessments (LDAs)[5] are replaced by education, health and care (EHC) plans for children and young people from birth to the age of 25.
- Local authorities must publish a 'local offer', setting out information about the provision they expect to be available across education, health and social care for children and young people in their area who have SEN or are disabled, including those who do not have EHC plans.[6] Children and young people are expected to be involved in the development and review of the local offer.
- Parents' right to express a preference for the school they wish their child to attend is extended to young people in further education.[7] In addition, the institutions for which parents can express a preference are widened to include academy schools, further education colleges and sixth form colleges, non-maintained special schools and independent special schools and independent specialist colleges.[8]
- The CFA 2014 imposes a new requirement on health commissioners to deliver the healthcare services specified in EHC plans.[9]
- The right to appeal against the institution named in the EHC plan is extended to young people in education and training.[10] In addition, the CFA 2014 includes the power to pilot giving children the right to make appeals to the First-tier Tribunal (FTT) themselves, rather than appealing through their parents.[11]
- Parents of children with an EHC plan and young people with an EHC plan are given the option of personal budgets which will

---

3 CFA 2014 s19.
4 Made under EA 1996 s324.
5 Made under LSA 2000 s139A.
6 CFA 2014 s30.
7 CFA 2014 s38(3).
8 CFA 2014 s38(3).
9 CFA 2014 s42(3).
10 CFA 2014 s51(3)(iii).
11 CFA 2014 s58.

enable them, or a third party, to purchase and manage services set out in their EHC plans.[12]

- 'School Action' and 'School Action Plus' – school-based intervention schemes for children without a statement – have been removed in the Code. Instead, schools must identify children who need extra specialist provision and take a 'graduated approach' to their SEN support.[13]

1.4　The CFA 2014 came into force on 1 September 2014. There was concern at the time of its introduction that local authorities were not prepared for a major overhaul of SEN law and would struggle with the new obligations that the CFA 2014 imposed. To give local authorities time to implement the changes and transition children and young people from statements and LDAs to EHC plans, the government introduced a lengthy transitional period from 1 September 2014 until 1 April 2018. During this time, local authority decisions about existing statements and EHC plans are governed by transitional provisions in the Children and Families Act 2014 (Transitional and Saving Provisions) (No 2) Order 2014 SI No 2270. Further guidance for local authorities was provided by the Department for Education in *SEN and disability: managing the September 2014 changes to the system*. This guidance is currently in its fourth edition, and will be reviewed periodically until the end of the transition period on 1 April 2018. The system for transferring children and young people from statements and LDAs to EHC plans is dealt with in detail in chapter 2.

The regulations

1.5　In addition to the transitional provisions described above, three sets of regulations have so far been made under the CFA 2014.

1.6　The Special Educational Needs and Disability Regulations 2014 SI No 1530 (SEND Regs) are the principal regulations under the Act and deal with the detail of the local authority's obligations for assessing children and drawing up EHC plans, discussed further in chapter 2. The SEND Regs also impose obligations on schools and SEN co-ordinators (SENCOs) to identify children with SEN and secure appropriate services for them.[14] Schools' responsibilities are dealt with in paras 1.48–1.54 below.

12　CFA 2014 s49.
13　Code, para 6.44 and following.
14　SEND Regs Part 3.

1.7   The Special Educational Needs (Personal Budgets) Regulations 2014 SI No 1652 (SENPB Regs) set out the legal framework for dealing with requests for personal budgets by parents of children with EHC plans and young people with EHC plans. Personal budgets are addressed in detail in chapter 2 at para 2.120 onwards.

1.8   The Special Educational Needs and Disability (Detained Persons) Regulations 2015 SI No 62 (SENDDP Regs) concern SEN assessment and support for children and young people in custody. Detained children have very high levels of SEN – approximately 18 per cent of children and young people in custody have a statement, compared to three per cent in England overall – and these provisions fill a critical gap in the SEN system.[15] Further details of SEN provision for children in custody are set out in paras 2.126–2.151.

The SEN code of practice

1.9   The SEN code of practice came into force on 1 September 2014, replacing the SEN code of practice published in 2001.[16] The old code applies during the transition period to children who still have a statement under Part 4 of the EA 1996 and who have not yet transferred to an EHC plan. An updated version of the Code was published in May 2015 to provide guidance on SEN support for children and young people in youth custody.

1.10   The Code is published under the CFA 2014 and it therefore has the status of statutory guidance.[17] This means that local authorities, schools, healthcare commissioners and all other agencies with responsibilities under the Code *must* follow it unless there are exceptional reasons not to do so.[18] In *Manchester City Council v JW*,[19] the Upper Tribunal (UT) commented that the Code was guidance to which the local authority and the FTT must have regard. However, where the statute (in this case the EA 1996, but the comments apply with equal force to the CFA 2014) sets out a general test, there may be factors additional to those in the Code to take into account.[20]

---

15   SENDDP Regs, explanatory memorandum.
16   Department for Education and Skills, *Special educational needs code of practice*, DfES/581/2001.
17   CFA 2014 s77.
18   *R v Islington LBC ex p Rixon* (1997–98) 1 CCLR 119. The full list of bodies which must have regard to the Code is set out in CFA 2014 s77(1).
19   [2014] UKUT 168 (AAC).
20   [2014] UKUT 168 (AAC) at para 17.

1.11   The Code is intended to be a comprehensive guide to the duties, policies and procedures relating to children and young people with SEN or disabilities. The government anticipated that it should be used by both agencies and individuals, including parents and young people. It should be consulted as a first step whenever a question about provision for a child or young person's SEN or disability arises. Prior to its publication, the Code was criticised by a House of Lords scrutiny committee for its length and complexity, and the chapter dealing with personal budgets was deemed particularly inaccessible.[21] We explain any complications and ambiguities in the Code when necessary in this text.

Human rights

1.12   The overhaul of the SEN regime was inspired, in part, by the development of human rights obligations in international conventions, including the United Nations Convention on the Rights of the Child (UNCRC) and the United Nations Convention on the Rights of People with Disabilities (UNCRPD).[22] The UNCRC provides that 'the best interests of the child shall be a primary consideration' in all the actions of parliament, public and private social welfare institutions, administrative authorities and the courts.[23] Article 23(1) provides that children with mental or physical disabilities should 'enjoy a full and decent life, in conditions which ensure dignity, promote self-reliance and facilitate the child's active participation in the community'. Article 28(1) guarantees the right to education, which must be achieved on the basis of equal opportunity.

1.13   These international obligations have not been incorporated into English law, which means that it is not possible to bring a legal claim based directly on violation of one of their provisions. However, parliament is expected to legislate consistently with its international obligations and the courts are increasingly using international human rights law to inform their interpretation of domestic law.[24] While the

---

21 House of Lords, Secondary Legislation Scrutiny Committee, Third Report of Session 2014–15, 24 June 2014.

22 See para 1.17 below.

23 UNCRC Article 3. This principle has been incorporated directly into some areas of English law. For example, it is reflected in Children Act 1989 s1, which states that the child's welfare is the paramount consideration in proceedings brought under the Act.

24 See *SG v Secretary of State for Work and Pensions* [2015] UKSC 16, [2015] 4 All ER 939.

impact of the UNCRC has not yet been felt in judicial decisions relating to SEN, the principles are now well integrated into the Code and government guidance concerning children with disabilities.

1.14   Human rights are directly protected by the Human Rights Act (HRA) 1998, which incorporates the rights in the European Convention on Human Rights (ECHR) into the law of the UK. There is specific protection for the right to education.[25] Other ECHR rights are also relevant to SEN, including Article 14, the right to non-discrimination.

1.15   There have been very few human rights claims relating to children with SEN. This is partly because the SEN legal regime offers the most appropriate means for challenging decisions which have an effect on children's rights, but also because the courts have taken a restrictive view of the right to education. In *A v Essex CC*,[26] the Supreme Court found that the fact that it took a local authority 18 months to secure a placement for a child with severe disabilities and SEN did not breach his ECHR rights. Children's rights are a fast-developing area of the law and international conventions and the HRA 1998 may evolve to offer children with SEN and disabilities greater protection in the future.

Definitions

1.16   Many of the terms used in the SEN system have a specific legal meaning. We set out the main definitions here:

- **Child:** Surprisingly, 'child' is not defined in the CFA 2014 or in the Code. However, it is clear from the statutory provisions that 'child' is intended to cover a person aged 0 until the end of the academic year in which he or she turns 16, at which point they become a 'young person' for the purposes of the SEN regime.[27]
- **Young person:** A person over compulsory school age (the end of the academic year in which he or she turns 16) but under 25.[28] From this date, the right to make decisions about matters covered

---

25 ECHR Protocol 1 Article 2 provides that 'no person shall be denied the right to education' and obliges the state to respect the 'right of parents to ensure such education in conformity with their own religious and philosophical convictions'.

26 [2010] UKSC 33, [2010] 3 WLR 509.

27 The definition of 'child' in EA 1996 s312(5) includes children up to age 19 who are registered pupils at a school. This section now only applies to children in Wales with SEN.

28 CFA 2014 s83(2). Compulsory school age is defined in EA 1996 s8(3).

by the CFA 2014 applies to the young person directly, rather than to the young person's parents, subject to the young person's mental capacity.

- **Special educational needs (SEN):** A child or young person has SEN if he or she has a learning difficulty or disability which calls for special educational provision to be made for him or her. A child of compulsory school age or a young person has a learning difficulty or disability if he or she has a significantly greater difficulty in learning than the majority of others of the same age, or has a disability which prevents or hinders him or her from making use of educational facilities of a kind generally provided for others of the same age in mainstream schools or mainstream post-16 institutions.[29] A child under compulsory school age has a learning difficulty or disability if the child is likely to meet the test applicable for those of compulsory school age when of compulsory school age (or would be likely, if no special educational provision were made).[30] 'Special educational needs' do not include needs that arise as a result of the child speaking a language other than English in his or her home.[31]

- **Special educational provision:** Special educational provision is provision that is different from or additional to that normally available to pupils or students of the same age, which is designed to help children and young people with SEN or disabilities to access the national curriculum at school or to study at college. It also includes healthcare provision or social care provision which educates or trains a child or young person.[32] Special educational provision for a child under two means educational provision of any kind.[33]

- **Healthcare provision:** There are three types of healthcare provision identified in the CFA 2014. First, healthcare provision that educates or trains a child. This is treated under the CFA 2014 as SEN provision.[34] Second, healthcare provision reasonably required by the learning difficulties and disabilities which result in him or her having special educational needs.[35] Third, other healthcare provision reasonably required by the child, for example provision for 'a

---

29 CFA 2014 s20; Code, p285.
30 CFA 2014 s20(3).
31 CFA 2014 s20(4); Code, para 5.30.
32 CFA 2014 s21(1); Code, p285.
33 CFA 2014 s21(2).
34 CFA 2014 s21(5).
35 CFA 2014 s37(2)(d).

long-term condition which might need management in a special educational setting'.[36]

- **Social care provision:** A reference to social care provision means any provision made by the local authority in the exercise of its social services functions.[37] Four different kinds of social care provision are identified in the legislation: First, social care provision which educates or trains a child; this is to be treated as SEN provision.[38] Second, any social care provision that must be made for the child under Chronically Sick and Disabled Persons Act 1970 (CSDPA 1970) s2, such as practical assistance in the home.[39] Third, any social care provision reasonably required by the learning difficulties and disabilities which result in the child having SEN, for example provision identified through early help and children in need assessments and safeguarding assessments.[40] Fourth, any other social care provision reasonably required by the child, for example provision identified in child in need or child protection plans.[41]

- **Maintained school:** Schools in England that are maintained by a local authority. This includes any community, foundation or voluntary school, community special or foundation special school.[42]

- **Mainstream school:** A maintained school that is not a special school, or an academy school that is not a special school.[43]

- **Post-16 institution:** An institution which provides education or training for those over compulsory school age, but is not a school or other institution which is within the higher education sector or which provides only higher education.[44]

- **Mainstream post-16 institution:** A post-16 institution that is not a special post-16 institution.[45]

---

36 CFA 2014 s37(3); Code, p165.
37 CFA 2014 s21(4).
38 CFA 2014 s21(5).
39 CFA 2014 s37(2)(e); Code, p168.
40 CFA 2014 s37(2)(f); Code, p168.
41 CFA 2014 s37(3); Code, p169.
42 CFA 2014 s83(2) and (5), which defines these by reference to such a school within the meaning of the School Standards and Framework Act (SSFA) 1998. See SSFA 1998 ss20, 21 and 142. See the Code, p282.
43 CFA 2014 s83(2).
44 CFA 2014 s83(2).
45 CFA 2014 s83(2).

- **Special post-16 institution:** A post-16 institution that is specially organised to make special educational provision for students with SEN.[46]
- **Independent school:** A school that is not maintained by a local authority and is registered to admit children with an EHC plan under CFA 2014 s41.[47]
- **Academy:** A state-funded school in England operating under the Academies Act 2010. Academies are self-governing, directly funded by the Department for Education and independent of local authority control.[48]
- **Free school:** A type of academy. Like academies, they are directly funded by the Department for Education and are independent of local authority control.[49]
- **Special school:** A school which is specifically organised to make special educational provision for pupils with SEN. Special schools maintained by the local authority comprise community special schools and foundation special schools.[50]
- **Non-maintained special school:** Schools in England approved by the secretary of state under EA 1996 s342 as special schools which are not maintained by the state but charge fees on a non-profit-making basis. Most non-maintained special schools are run by charitable organisations.[51]

General duties imposed by the Children and Families Act 2014

Introduction

1.17   The CFA 2014 establishes general principles and duties on local authorities, schools, healthcare providers and others to ensure that a child-centred and integrated approach is taken to SEN provision. This new approach to SEN law reflects the increasing acceptance of the principles contained in the UNCRC and the UNCRPD, which

---

46   CFA 2014 s83(2).
47   Code, p281. Note that the Code erroneously refers to the old statutory provisions on registration in EA 1996 s464.
48   Code, p278.
49   Code, p280.
50   Code, p285.
51   Code, p283.

emphasise participation by children and their parents in decision-making and information-sharing.[52]

1.18   Some of these general duties are 'target duties'. This means that the duty is owed to society at large, or a specific section of it, and sets a target for local authorities, such as the duty on local authorities to identify all children in its area with SEN. A target duty does not generally create legal rights for individuals.[53] As a result, it may be difficult for a person to bring a legal challenge solely on the basis of failure to satisfy a target duty, but the existence of the duty will inform scope of the specific obligations on the public authority set out in the CFA 2014 and relevant regulations.

1.19   We deal below with the main duties relating to SEN provision on local authorities, schools and health authorities.

Duty of participation and support

1.20   The government's desire to put children and young people at the centre of SEN planning is reflected in CFA 2014 s19. This provides that local authorities must pay particular attention to the following matters when exercising their powers under the Act:

- the views, wishes and feelings of the child or young person, and the child's parents;
- the importance of the child or young person, and the child's parents, participating as fully as possible in decisions;
- the importance of the child, young person or parent, being provided with the information and support necessary to enable participation in those decisions;
- the need to support the child or young person, and the child's parents, in order to facilitate the development of the child or young person and to help him or her achieve the best possible educational and other outcomes, preparing him or her effectively for adulthood.

1.21   These general principles translate into specific duties on local authorities to ensure that children and young people are actively involved in the SEN process, such as the obligation to consult a child's parent or a young person about the content of an EHC plan.[54] The Code

---

52 Code, para 1.6 refers explicitly to Articles 12 and 13 of the UNCRC on respect for children's views and the right to freedom of expression.
53 See *R (Ahmad) v Newham LBC* [2009] UKHL 14, [2009] 3 All ER 755.
54 CFA 2014 s38(1), discussed in chapter 2.

explains and expands on these duties in detail, and we set out relevant sections in following chapters.

1.22 The duty to support children, young people and parents to achieve the best possible educational outcomes in section 19(d) has already attracted the attention of the courts. In the case of *Devon CC v OH*[55] the UT considered whether section 19(d) imposed a duty on local authorities to achieve the best possible educational outcomes for children with SEN.[56] It considered provisions of the Code dealing with the concept of 'best possible' outcomes. In chapter 5, on early years education, the Code states:[57]

> All children are entitled to an education that enables them to:
> - achieve the best possible educational and other outcomes, and
> - become confident young children with a growing ability to communicate their own views and ready to make the transition into compulsory education

1.23 In chapter 6, on schools, the Code states:[58]

> All children and young people are entitled to an appropriate education, one that is appropriate to their needs, promotes high standards and the fulfilment of potential. This should enable them to:
> - achieve their best
> - become confident individuals living fulfilling lives, and
> - make a successful transition into adulthood, whether into employment, further or higher education or training

1.24 The court concluded that the section 19(d) duty was limited to supporting children, young people and their parents to achieve these outcomes and that the likelihood of actual achievement of outcomes was not itself a mandatory consideration for local authorities. While local authorities, and the courts, could consider what the best possible educational outcomes might be for a child, they could only do so in the context of supporting children and young people and should not use the likelihood of achieving good outcomes as the legal test to determine whether SEN provision was appropriate for a child. The UT emphasised that the Code could not override the provisions of the CFA 2014.

1.25 This case reveals the reluctance of the courts to use aspirational language in the Code to supplement or enhance the legal duties in the CFA 2014. These duties are likely to be carefully interpreted by

---

55 [2016] UKUT 292 (AAC), [2016] ELR 377.
56 *Devon CC v OH* [2016] UKUT 292 (AAC), [2016] ELR 377.
57 Code, para 5.1.
58 Code, para 6.1.

the courts so that they do not impose an unpredictable or unmanage-
able burden on local authorities.

Duty of identification

1.26   CFA 2014 s22 places a duty on local authorities to identify all the
children and young people in their area who have or may have SEN,
and all the disabled children and young people in their area. This is a
positive duty – it means that local authorities will actively need to put
systems in place for obtaining relevant information from other agencies, such as schools and healthcare bodies. The Code notes that local
authorities do not have an obligation to assess all home-educated
children for SEN.[59]

1.27   CFA 2014 s23(3) imposes a corresponding obligation on Clinical
Commissioning Groups (CCGs) and NHS trusts to bring children
who they believe have SEN or a disability to the attention of local
authorities, after they have informed children's parents and given
them an opportunity to discuss their opinion.

1.28   Schools are also under an obligation to consider whether children
have SEN and to inform parents when they believe that they do.[60]
The Code expects class teachers, in collaboration with the SENCO, to
assess whether a child whose progress is slower than expected may
have SEN.[61]

Duty of integration and co-operation

1.29   One of the central aims of the CFA 2014 is to promote integrated
working across education, healthcare and social care. To that end,
CFA 2014 s25 places a duty on local authorities to promote integration between educational, health and social care provision. This duty
builds on existing statutory co-operation duties, including those in
the Children Act (CA) 2004[62] and the Health and Social Care Act
(HSCA) 2012.[63]

---

59   Code, para 10.30.
60   SEND Regs reg 50; Code, para 6.14.
61   Code, para 6.19.
62   CA 2004 s10 provides that local authorities must make arrangements to
     promote co-operation with local partners to promote, among other things,
     children's physical and mental health and education.
63   National Health Service Act 2006 (as amended by the Health and Social Care
     Act 2012) s13N imposes a duty on NHS England to promote integrated services
     with local authorities.

1.30   CFA 2014 s26 places a duty on local authorities and 'partner commissioning bodies' to put in place joint commissioning arrangements. 'Partner commissioning bodies' are NHS England and individual CCGs which provide services to children in their areas. The purpose of the joint commissioning arrangements is to plan and jointly commission the education, health and care provision for disabled children or young people and those with SEN. The Code envisages that joint commissioning arrangements 'should enable partners to make best use of all the resources available in an area to improve outcomes for children and young people in the most efficient, effective, equitable and sustainable way'.[64]

1.31   Joint commissioning arrangements must deal with the following issues:[65]

- the education, health and social care provision needed by disabled children and young people and those with SEN, how this provision will be secured and by whom;
- how complaints about education, health and social care provision are dealt with;
- the procedures for ensuring that disputes between local authorities and CCGs are resolved as quickly as possible; and
- how education, health and care assessments should be secured.

1.32   The Code provides examples of the specialist support and therapies that should be covered in joint commissioning arrangements, including clinical treatment and medication, speech and language therapy, assistive technology, personal care, equipment, occupational therapy, physiotherapy and highly specialist services, such as alternative communication technologies.[66] The joint commissioning arrangements should be reflected in the services that are set out in local authorities' local offer, discussed below.

1.33   The provisions on integration are complemented by CFA 2014 ss28, 29 and 31, which mandate cooperation between local authorities and their local partners. The local partners include maintained schools and nurseries, academies, non-maintained special schools, further education institutions, NHS England, CCGs and youth offending teams. The governing bodies of schools are required to co-operate with local authorities in all circumstances.[67] Other local partners must co-operate with requests from the local authority unless it

---

64 Code, para 3.7.
65 CFA 2014 s26(3)–(5).
66 Code, para 3.9.
67 CFA 2014 s29(1)–(3).

would be incompatible with their duties or otherwise have an adverse effect on their functions.[68]

1.34   The integration of social care, health and education is part of a broader government programme of strategic collaboration led by health and wellbeing boards, which have been established to provide leadership across health and social care. The boards carry out a joint strategic needs assessment of their local populations, which inform the commissioning decisions made in the joint commissioning arrangements. The Code explains the relationship between these processes in detail.[69]

Duty of review

1.35   The obligation to keep SEN provision under review is a fundamental element of the SEN regime. It applies both to SEN provision for individual children and young people and to general local authority decisions about the provision of SEN.

1.36   CFA 2014 s27 requires local authorities to keep under review the education, training and social care provision made for children and young people with SEN or disabilities for whom it is responsible both within and outside its local area. In carrying out its review of local services, the local authority must consider the extent to which the provision is sufficient to meet the needs of children and young people.[70] It must consult with children and young people with SEN and disabilities, and their parents, as well schools, post-16 institutions and youth offending teams.[71] The review process must be integrated with the joint strategic needs assessment by the local health and wellbeing board.[72]

1.37   At an individual level, CFA 2014 s44 guarantees the right to review of the EHC plan every 12 months or at the request of the child, young person or parent, or the educational institution he or she attends.[73]

1.38   Local authorities are empowered to access the premises of any institution where a child or young person receives education in pursuance of an EHC plan in order to monitor the education that is being provided.[74] The Code does not give guidance about the exercise

68   CFA 2014 s31.
69   Code, chapter 3.
70   CFA 2014 s27(2).
71   CFA 2014 s27(3).
72   CFA 2014 s27(4); Code, chapter 3.
73   See paras 2.55–2.78 for discussion of reviews of EHC plans.
74   CFA 2014 s65.

of this power, but if a local authority has concerns about SEN provision, or a parent believes that it is not adequate, the local authority should consider using it. If SEN provision is disputed in an appeal, the FTT may expect the local authority to have exercised this power.

The local offer

1.39 The CFA 2014 introduced the concept of the 'local offer'. Section 30 requires local authorities to publish and maintain a local offer that sets out the education, health and social care provision that the authority expects to be available for children and young people with SEN and disabilities in its area. It must also specify provision available outside its area for children for whom it is responsible and for children within its area who have a disability.[75]

1.40 By publishing information on SEN and disability provision, the local offer is intended to increase the transparency and accessibility of the support that local authorities make available for children and young people, as well as making provision more responsive to local needs by involving the community in its development.[76] It should be produced alongside the joint strategic needs assessments and the joint commissioning arrangements, and reflect the provision agreed in those documents. The local offer must be kept under review.[77]

1.41 Local authorities must consult a wide range of people, including children, young people and parents, and organisations before they publish a local offer.[78] The Code provides detailed guidance on the manner in which local authorities must consult, suggesting that they hold events to increase participation by children and young people.[79] Local authorities have a duty to publish comments from children, young people and parents on the local offer and any actions they intend to take in response.[80] Comments should be published annually.[81]

1.42 The local offer must set out education, health and care provision, training provision and information about travel arrangements to and from schools, nurseries and post-16 institutions.[82] It must also

---

75 CFA 2014 s30(1)(b).
76 Code, para 4.2.
77 CFA 2014 s30(5).
78 SEND Regs reg 54.
79 Code, para 4.12.
80 CFA 2014 s30(6).
81 Code, para 4.24.
82 CFA 2014 s30(2).

specify provision that will help children and young people prepare for adulthood, including finding employment, accommodation and participation in society.[83] The SEND Regs describe the information that must be contained in the local offer in greater detail. For example, the SEND Regs require that local authorities provide extensive information on the SEN provision available in schools, such as the approach to teaching children with SEN, how outcomes are assessed, expertise in the school, activities that are available and how emotional, mental and social development of children with SEN is supported and improved.[84] The local offer should also include a policy on personal budgets, including a clear statement of eligibility criteria and the decision-making process.[85]

1.43   In the case of *R (L) v Warwickshire CC*,[86] the High Court considered the adequacy of the local offer produced by the local authority. The court considered the 'huge range' of information which had to be included in a local offer and found that the draft publication produced by the local authority fell short of the statutory requirements. The judge noted that the local offer was an iterative document that had to be kept constantly under review. He also emphasised that the section 30 obligation was simply to publish details of what the local authority expects to be available; it is not a guarantee of any particular service.[87]

1.44   In addition to the local offer, local authorities must directly provide children, parents and young people with SEN and disabilities with 'advice and information' about matters relating to SEN and disabilities.[88] This will include sources of information, advice and support in the authority's area, which ought also to be found in the local offer.[89]

Children with medical conditions

1.45   Schools are under an obligation to support students with medical conditions.[90] The CFA 2014 does not expand on the nature of the obligation, but instructs schools to have regard to the statutory guidance

---

83   CFA 2014 s30(3).
84   SEND Regs Sch 2.
85   See paras 2.120–2.151 below.
86   [2015] EWHC 203 (Admin), [2015] LGR 81.
87   [2015] EWHC 203 (Admin), [2015] LGR 81 para 51.
88   CFA 2014 s32; Code, para 9.12.
89   SEND Regs reg 15.
90   CFA 2014 s100.

produced by the Department for Education.[91] As the guidance recognises, there will very often be an overlap between students with SEN and students with a medical condition, and many students with a medical condition will be disabled under the EA 2010.[92] The line between SEN provision and support for a child's medical needs may not be easy to draw. Schools should have regard to the Department for Education guidance in any case where a child appears to have a medical condition, whether or not it has been formally diagnosed.[93]

1.46 Schools are expected to produce a policy explaining how they support children with medical conditions.[94] In some cases, schools should create an individual healthcare plan for a child with a long-term or complex condition.[95] The healthcare plan should set out the steps that are needed to manage the child's condition, how they can overcome potential barriers to education and how they work with other statutory agencies. If the child has SEN but does not have an EHC plan, this must be mentioned in the healthcare plan; if the child has an EHC plan, the healthcare plan must be linked to it.

1.47 Schools must take steps to ensure that students with a medical condition have full access to education, including school trips and physical education. As the guidance anticipates, some students may not be able to attend school full-time, and will need a combination of education at school and alternative provision by the local authority.[96]

Children with SEN but without an EHC plan

Introduction

1.48 The majority of children who have SEN will not have an EHC plan. Their needs may be met in mainstream education without the need for an EHC assessment, or they may have been assessed and the local authority concluded that their needs can be met without the creation of an EHC plan. The obligations on local authorities and schools are directed at all children with SEN, and while children with an EHC

---

91 Department for Education, *Supporting children at school with medical conditions: Statutory guidance for governing bodies of maintained schools and proprietors of academies in England*, December 2015.

92 *Supporting children at school with medical conditions*, para 3.

93 *Supporting children at school with medical conditions*, para 11.

94 *Supporting children at school with medical conditions*, para 9.

95 *Supporting children at school with medical conditions*, para 13.

96 *Supporting children at school with medical conditions*, para 5.

Plan have specific statutory rights to appropriate provision, any child with SEN is entitled to appropriate support. The general duties under the CFA 2014, discussed in paras 1.17–1.38 above, apply to children with SEN regardless of whether or not they have an EHC plan.

Presumption of mainstream education

1.49   After generations of stigmatisation, discrimination and exclusion from education, it is now widely recognised that children with SEN and disabilities should be able to access mainstream education. The UK has ratified the UNCRPD, which commits states to ensuring that children with disabilities are not excluded from the general education system and can access 'an inclusive, quality and free primary education and secondary education on an equal basis with others in the communities in which they live'.[97]

1.50   On the basis of this commitment, the CFA 2014 provides that children without an EHC plan must be educated in maintained nursery school, mainstream school or mainstream post-16 institution.[98] Their parents may choose to send them to an independent school or non-maintained special school if the cost is not met by the local authority.[99]

1.51   There are limited exceptions to the presumption of mainstream education for children and young people without an EHC plan. They may only be educated in a special school or special post-16 institution in the following circumstances:

- They have been admitted for the purposes of an EHC needs assessment and consent has been obtained from the local authority, the head teacher of the special school, the child's parent or young person and any other person whose advice is required for the assessment.[100] They can remain at the special school for ten days following the assessment, if the local authority has decided not to make a plan, and until the plan is finalised, if the authority has chosen to make a plan.[101]
- They are admitted following a change in their circumstances and the local authority, the head teacher of the school and the child's

97   UNCRPD Article 24.
98   CFA 2014 s34(2).
99   CFA 2014 s34(3).
100 CFA 2014 s34(5). The list of individuals and organisations that must be contacted for advice in an EHC assessment is set out in SEND Regs reg 6.
101 CFA 2014 s34(6); SEND Regs reg 48.

parent or young person agrees.[102] These are known as 'emergency placements' and the Code states that the local authority should immediately commence an EHC needs assessment as soon as such a placement is made.[103]

- They are admitted to a special school in a hospital.[104]
- They are admitted to a special school or a special post-16 institution that is an academy, if the academy arrangements agreed with the secretary of state permit it to admit children with SEN without an EHC plan.[105] The Code makes it clear that academies that have been authorised by the secretary of state to take children with SEN but without a plan, can only be placed there at the request of their parents or their own request and with the support of professional advice. Academies can only admit children who have the type of SEN for which the academy has been designated.[106]

1.52   An autism spectrum disorder (ASD) unit within a mainstream school is a mainstream school placement, even if the unit is in a separate building and there is limited integration with other children.[107]

1.53   The presumption in favour of mainstream education is reflected in the *School admissions code*.[108] Schools are obliged to consider applications for admission from parents of children without SEN as part of the normal admissions process and in accordance with their admissions criteria. They cannot refuse to admit a child with SEN but who does not have an EHC plan because they cannot cater for the child's needs.[109]

Duties on schools

1.54   The CFA 2014 places maintained nurseries, mainstream schools, post-16 institutions and pupil referral units under a general duty to use their 'best endeavours' to secure SEN provision to meet the needs of any child or young person with SEN.[110] Where SEN provision is

---

102 CFA 2014 s34(7).
103 Code, para 1.29.
104 CFA 2014 s34(8).
105 CFA 2014 s34(9).
106 Code, para 1.30.
107 *MA v Kensington and Chelsea RLBC* (SEN) [2015] UKUT 0186 (AAC).
108 Department for Education, *School admissions code. Statutory guidance for admission authorities, governing bodies, local authorities, schools adjudicators and admission appeals panels*, December 2014.
109 *School admissions code*, paras 1.9(h) and 3.13. See paras 6.10 and following.
110 CFA 2014 s66.

made for a child or young person who does not have an EHC plan, the school must inform the child's parent or the young person that SEN provision is being made.[111]

1.55 The concept of 'best endeavours' is taken from the old law under the EA 1996.[112] It has been interpreted by the courts to mean the same thing as 'reasonable endeavours'.[113] It is not an absolute obligation to make SEN provision available, and permits competing demands on the school to be taken into account. The Code suggests that schools should do all that they can to secure SEN provision.[114] Whether or not a school has met its obligation will depend on multiple factors, including the individual child's needs, the nature and extent of the steps the school has taken, whether it has appropriate policies in place and has followed them, whether the school has sought appropriate professional advice and whether it has properly consulted with parents. If a school has failed to use its best endeavours, or refused to do so, it is likely to be necessary for the local authority to assess the child and issue an EHC plan.[115]

1.56 The best endeavours duty is complemented by a power on local authorities to supply goods and services to schools for the purposes of assisting them to fulfil their duty to children with SEN.[116] It enables schools to buy in specialist provision from the local authority, such as speech and language therapy and occupational therapy, for children regardless of whether they have an EHC plan.

1.57 Schools and nurseries must designate a member of staff as SEN co-ordinator (SENCO) to have responsibility for co-ordinating SEN provision.[117] The details of SEN provision that schools must make available are not specified in the CFA 2014, but the Code gives guidance on the approach schools should adopt. It describes a 'graduated approach' to identifying and supporting students with SEN led by the SENCO that replaces the previous two-tiered support known as 'School Action' and 'School Action Plus'.[118] The graduated approach

---

111 CFA 2014 s68.
112 EA 1996 s317(1)(a).
113 *SC and another v Worcestershire CC* [2016] UKUT 267 (AAC), [2016] ELR 537, para 25.
114 Code, para 6.2.
115 See para 2.5 below.
116 CFA 2014 s64.
117 CFA 2014 s67. SEND Regs reg 49 sets out the prescribed qualifications and experience that are required by the SENCO. SEND Regs reg 50 sets out the duties of the governing body of the school in respect of the SENCO.
118 Code, para 6.44 and following.

involves four stages of action: assess, plan, do and review. The Code sets out the process schools are expected to follow for each of these stages, emphasising the need to involve parents and keep them informed of the child's progress.

1.58   The CFA 2014 also imposes a specific obligation on mainstream schools and maintained nurseries educating children with SEN to ensure that the child engages with the activities of the school together with children who do not have SEN.[119] The school only has to meet this obligation insofar as it is reasonably practicable, and it must be compatible with the child receiving SEN provision, the provision of efficient education for other children and the efficient use of resources. This obligation applies regardless of whether or not the child has an EHC plan.

1.59   Maintained schools and nurseries, including academies and special schools, must prepare a 'SEN information report', which explains their approach to children with SEN and disabilities.[120] The SEND Regs set out a comprehensive list of the information that must be published, including:

- the kinds of SEN for which the school makes provision;
- information about identification and assessment of pupils with SEN;
- the school's policies for making SEN provision available whether or not pupils have EHC plans, including evaluation of effectiveness, assessment and review, approach to teaching and additional support provided by the school;
- information about the expertise and training of staff and how specialist expertise will be secured;
- arrangements for consulting parents, young people, health service and other public bodies about the school's provision.[121]

1.60   The report must be available on the school's website and updated annually, or as soon as possible after any information changes.[122]

---

119 CFA 2014 s35.
120 CFA 2014 s69.
121 SEND Regs reg 51 and Sch 1.
122 Code, para 6.79.

CHAPTER 2

EHC assessments and making plans

continued

Key points

EHC needs assessments

- The child's parent, the young person or the school (or anyone else) may request an education, health and care (EHC) needs assessment for a child or young person.
- A local authority is responsible for a child or young person while he or she (a) is in the authority's area and (b) has been identified as someone who has or may have special educational needs (SEN), or has been brought to the authority's attention as someone who has or may have SEN.
- The local authority must determine whether or not to undertake an EHC needs assessment; it must make that decision as soon as practicable, but in any event within six weeks.
- If the local authority refuses to undertake an EHC needs assessment, the child's parent or the young person must be notified. They have a right of appeal to the First-tier Tribunal (FTT).
- If the local authority undertakes an EHC needs assessment, it must seek advice and information from specified professionals, as well as the child's parent or the young person.
- Having undertaken an EHC assessment, the local authority must determine whether or not to issue an EHC plan. This decision must be made and notified to the child's parent or young person as soon as practicable, but in any event within 16 weeks of the local authority receiving a request for an EHC needs assessment.
- Where, in the light of an EHC needs assessment, it is necessary for special educational provision to be made in accordance with an EHC plan, the local authority must prepare a plan. A finalised EHC plan must be issued within 20 weeks of the initial request for an assessment.

EHC plans

- The SEND Regs and the SEN code of practice require an EHC plan to include sections A–K.
- The local authority must send the EHC plan in draft to the child's parent or young person, who have 15 days to make representations about the content and to request that a particular school be named.

continued

- If the child's parent or the young person requests a particular type of school or institution, the local authority must name it in section I of the EHC plan unless (a) the school or institution is unsuitable for the age, ability, aptitude or SEN of the child or young person concerned, or (b) the attendance of the child or young person at the school or institution would be incompatible with the provision of efficient education to others, or the efficient use of resources.
- The local authority must send a copy of the final EHC plan to the parent or the young person and notify them of their rights of appeal.
- The local authority must secure the special educational provision specified for the child or young person in the plan (ie that in sections F and I).
- If the EHC plan specifies healthcare provision, the responsible commissioning body must arrange the specified healthcare provision for the child or young person.
- Where particular types of schools are named in section I of a child or young person's EHC plan, the governing body or principal of the school or institution must admit the child or young person.

Review and reassessment

- A local authority must review an EHC plan within 12 months of it having been made, and must review the EHC plan in at least 12 month intervals after that.
- There are particular requirements of review when the child or young person is moving from one phase of education to another.
- In respect of children under five, an EHC plan should be reviewed every three to six months (although these can be streamlined reviews).
- Local authorities have the power to undertake interim reviews when the child or young person has been (or is at risk of) being permanently excluded, or where the school or institution is struggling to meet the child's needs or where circumstances have changed such that the EHC plan is no longer meeting the child's needs.
- The SEND Regs and the SEN code require reviews to be conducted in a particular manner.

- After a review, the local authority must decide to continue to maintain the EHC plan in its current form, amend it or cease to maintain the EHC plan. The parent or young person has a right to appeal any of these decisions to the FTT.
- The local authority may (and in some circumstances, must) carry out a reassessment of the child or young person's educational, health and social care needs.

Transfers from statements of SEN and LDAs to EHC plans

- Local authorities must complete transfers from statements of SEN to EHC plans by 1 April 2018.
- EHC plans must have been prepared by 1 September 2016 for all young people who had received support as a result of a Learning Difficulty Assessments (LDA) and who continue in further education or training and need SEN provision beyond that date.
- Children and young people who had statements and LDAs at the time of transfer will almost always be entitled to EHC plans.
- Transition plans published by every local authority in consultation with children and young people should set out the timetable and process for transfer.
- Children should be transferred to an EHC plan whenever there is a significant review of their statement during the transition period and at specific stages in their education.
- Transfer reviews must be carried out before a child moves from a statement to an EHC plan.
- Transfer reviews consist of EHC needs assessments under the SEND Regs. They follow the same process as a needs assessment and give rise to the same appeal rights.
- Parents will be given a minimum of two weeks' notice before a transfer review is carried out.
- The local authority must complete the transfer review process and send a final EHC plan to parents within 18 weeks of giving the parents notice of the review.

Ceasing to maintain an EHC plan and transfer to another local authority

- A local authority may cease to maintain an EHC plan for a child or young person if (a) the local authority is no longer responsible for the child or young person, or (b) the local authority determines that it is no longer necessary for the plan to be maintained.

continued

- A parent or young person has a right of appeal against a decision to cease to maintain an EHC plan. The local authority must not implement the decision to cease to maintain the EHC plan until after the appeal has been determined.
- Where a local authority is considering ceasing to maintain a child or young person's EHC plan, it must inform the parent or young person, consult them, and consult the headteacher or equivalent at the institution named in section I of the EHC plan.
- A local authority is responsible for a child or young person while he or she (a) is in their area and (b) has been identified as someone who has or may have SEN, or has been brought to the local authority's attention as someone who has or may have SEN.
- SEND Regs and the SEN code make provision for the transfer of the responsibility for the EHC plan from one local authority to another (and for the transfer for the responsibility for securing the health care provision from one responsible commissioning body to another).

Personal budgets (including direct payments)

- Personal budgets are 'an amount of money identified by the local authority to deliver provision set out in an EHC plan where the parent or young person is involved in securing that provision'.
- Personal budgets are optional but, if the local authority maintains an EHC plan (or is preparing one), it must prepare a personal budget for the child or young person if asked to do so by the parent or young person.
- A direct payment is one way of delivering a personal budget: there is no right to a direct payment, rather the local authority must satisfy itself of certain matters prior to making a direct payment.
- The local authority has a duty to make available information and advice and support in respect of personal budgets (and this information should be provided as part of the 'local offer').
- A request for a personal budget (including a direct payment) can be made at any time during the period in which the draft EHC plan is being prepared or the plan is being reviewed or reassessed.
- A direct payment must be sufficient to secure the provision it covers.
- Section J of the EHC plan must set out the special educational provision to be secured by a direct payment, and the outcomes to be met by a direct payment.

- Before agreeing to make a direct payment, the local authority must satisfy itself (a) that the recipient is a person to whom direct payments can be made, (b) that it is satisfied of the matters set out in Special Educational Needs (Personal Budgets) Regulations 2014 SI No 1652 (SENPB Regs) reg 6(1), and (c) that the recipient will comply with the conditions imposed under SENPB Regs reg 8.
- Where a local authority makes a direct payment in respect of special educational provision, it is to be treated as having secured the special educational provision for the child or young person for the purposes of CFA 2014 s42(2).
- The local authority must monitor and review the use of direct payments.
- Direct payments can also be made in respect of healthcare and social care provision.
- Provision must cease to be made by way of direct payment if the recipient of the direct payments withdraws consent to this method of delivery.

EHC needs assessments

Definitions

2.1　The first stage in the process of obtaining an education, health and care (EHC) plan is an EHC needs assessment. An 'EHC needs assessment' is an assessment of the educational, health care and social care needs of a child or young person.[1]

2.2　An EHC needs assessment may (but will not always) lead to the preparation of an EHC plan. An EHC plan is a plan specifying:[2]

    (a) the child or young person's special educational needs (SEN);

    (b) the outcomes sought for him or her;

    (c) the special educational provision required by him or her;

    (d) any healthcare provision reasonably required by the learning difficulties and disabilities which result in him or her having SEN;

---

1 CFA 2014 s36(2). This can be contrasted with the position under EA 1996 s323, in which the local authority was to make an assessment of the 'child's educational needs' only. CFA 2014 s83(2) defines a 'young person' as being aged between 16 and 25.

2 CFA 2014 s37(2).

    (e) in the case of a child or a young person aged under 18, any social care provision which must be made for him or her by the local authority as a result of CSDPA 1970 s2;

    (f) any social care provision reasonably required by the learning difficulties and disabilities which result in the child or young person having SEN, to the extent that the provision is not already specified in the plan under paragraph (e) above.

2.3   An EHC plan may also specify other health and social care provision reasonably required by the child or young person.[3]

2.4   A local authority is responsible for a child or young person if (a) he or she is in the local authority's area, and (b) has been identified by the local authority as someone who has or may have SEN, or has been brought to the local authority's attention by any person as someone who may have SEN.[4]

Initiating an assessment

2.5   The child's parent, the young person or a person acting on behalf of a school or other educational institution may request a local authority to secure an EHC needs assessment for a child or young person.[5] If a person acting on behalf of a school or other educational institution requests an EHC needs assessment, this should ideally be with the knowledge and agreement of the child's parent or the young person where possible.[6]

2.6   The Code emphasises, however, that anyone else can bring a child or young person who has (or may have) SEN to the attention of the local authority, particularly where they think an EHC needs assessment may be necessary.[7]

2.7   The local authority's decision whether to undertake an EHC needs assessment is a two-stage determination:

---

3 CFA 2014 s37(3).

4 CFA 2014 s24(1).

5 CFA 2014 s36(1).

6 Code, para 9.8.

7 Code, para 9.9 (reflecting CFA 2014 s24(1)(b)). The Code gives the examples of foster carers, health and social care professionals, early years practitioners, youth offending teams or probation services, those responsible for education in custody, school or college staff or a family friend. The Code notes that this should be done with the knowledge, and where possible, agreement of the child's parent or the young person.

- **Stage one:** An initial determination of whether or not special educational provision may be necessary (this is best understood as a screening decision).
- **Stage two:** A decision whether or not to conduct an EHC needs assessment.[8]

2.8 Both decisions must, however, be taken within six weeks of the initial request for an EHC needs assessment.[9]

Initial determination

2.9 When the local authority receives a request for an EHC assessment, it must first take the screening decision to determine whether it *may* be necessary for special educational provision to be made for the child or young person in accordance with an EHC plan.[10] In reaching this initial determination, the local authority must consult the child's parent or young person[11] as soon as practicable after receiving the request (or becoming responsible for the child or young person pursuant to section 24 of the CFA 2014).[12] As the Code notes, this is particularly important where the request was not made by the child's parent or the young person, so they have sufficient time to provide their views.[13] The local authority must also notify:

(a) the responsible commissioning body;
(b) the local authority officers responsible for social care for children or young people with SEN;
(c) where a child attends an early years setting, the manager of that setting;
(d) where a child or young person is registered at a school, the headteacher (or equivalent); and
(e) where the young person attends a post-16 institution, the principal (or equivalent).[14]

---

8 The two-stage process is apparent from the structure of the legislation: see in particular CFA 2014 s36(3) and (4), as compared to CFA 2014 s36(6) and (7), and SEND Regs reg 4 as compared to reg 5 (and see also *Cambridgeshire CC v FL-J* [2016] UKUT 225 (AAC) per UT Judge Jacobs at para 3). The Code, however, does not properly reflect the fact that the legislation contemplates two separate decisions by the local authority.
9 SEND Regs regs 4(1) and 5(1).
10 CFA 2014 s36(3).
11 CFA 2014 s36(4).
12 SEND Regs reg 3.
13 Code, para 9.12.
14 SEND Regs reg 4(2).

2.10   If an EHC plan is maintained already for the child or young person, or the child or young person has been assessed during the previous six months, the local authority does not need to go on to consider stage two (although it may do so) (see below at paras 2.12–2.20).[15]

2.11   Where the local authority determines that it is not necessary for special educational provision to be made in accordance with an EHC plan, it must notify the child's parent or the young person of that determination, and of the reasons for that determination.[16] The notification should be as soon as practicable, but in any event within six weeks of receiving a request for an EHC needs assessment (or becoming responsible for the child or young person in accordance with CFA 2014 s24).[17]

Decision whether to conduct an EHC needs assessment

2.12   Having determined that it *may* be necessary for special educational provision to be made for the child or young person in accordance with an EHC plan, the local authority must notify the child's parent or the young person:

- that it is considering securing an EHC needs assessment for the child or young person; and
- that the child or young person has the right to express views to the local authority (orally or in writing), and submit evidence to the local authority.[18]

2.13   The local authority must secure an EHC needs assessment for the child or young person if, after considering any views expressed and/or evidence provided, the local authority is of the opinion that the child or young person has or may have SEN, and that it may be necessary for special educational provision to be made for the child or young person in accordance with an EHC plan.[19]

2.14   The Code states that, in considering whether an EHC needs assessment is necessary, the local authority 'should consider whether there is evidence that despite the [educational institution] having

---

15   CFA 2014 s36(6).

16   CFA 2014 s36(5).

17   SEND Regs reg 4(1). Regulation 4 does not require notification of a right of appeal, but there can be no doubt that a right of appeal arises from a negative screening decision as it is a decision that the local authority 'has decided not to secure an EHC needs assessment for the child or young person' (CFA 2014 s36(5)(b)) which triggers a right of appeal to the FTT under CFA 2014 s51(2)(a).

18   CFA 2014 s36(6) and (7).

19   CFA 2014 s36(8).

taken relevant and purposeful action to identify, assess and meet the special educational needs of the child or young person, the child or young person has not made expected progress'.[20] The Code directs the local authority to consider specific evidence as follows:[21]

- evidence of the child or young person's academic attainment (or developmental milestones in younger children) and rate of progress;
- information about the nature, extent and context of the child or young person's SEN;
- evidence of the action already being taken by the early years provider, school or post-16 institution to meet the child or young person's SEN;
- evidence that, where progress has been made, it has only been as the result of much additional intervention and support over and above that which is usually provided;
- evidence of the child or young person's physical, emotional and social development and health needs, drawing on relevant evidence from clinicians and other health professionals and what has been done to meet these by other agencies, and
- where the young person is over the age of 18 a local authority must, in making a determination or forming an opinion in respect of an EHC assessment, consider whether he or she requires additional time, in comparison to the majority of others of the same age who do not have special educational needs, to complete his or her education or training.[22]

2.15 The UT has considered the test to be applied by the local authority in determining whether to undertake a statutory assessment on two occasions (in both cases in the context of the predecessor legislation: EA 1996 s323).[23]

---

20 Code, para 9.14.
21 Code, para 9.14.
22 CFA 2014 s36(10); Code, para 9.14.
23 The test in CFA 2014 s36(3) and (6) ('whether it may be necessary for special educational provision to be made for the child or young person in accordance with an EHC plan') is different to that previously applied in EA 1996 s323(1) which provided that the local authority had to conduct an assessment where they are 'of the opinion ... that the child falls, or probably falls, within subsection (2)'. A child fell within subsection (2) if: '(a) he has special educational needs; and (b) it is necessary for the authority to determine the special educational provision which any learning difficulty he may have calls for'.

2.16   In *NM v Lambeth LBC*[24] UT Judge Mark emphasised that the question of whether a child had made progress was not the only criterion to be applied in considering whether or not an EHC assessment was necessary. He emphasised that a local authority (and the FTT on appeal) also had to ask whether such progress had been achieved as a result of effort and instruction above what would normally be provided. Further, the local authority and FTT ought to consider that a statement of SEN would 'provide some protection to a child where additional funding ceased to be available in the absence of a statement. It could also assist a child if he moved school or if there was a change in relevant teaching staff'.[25]

2.17   In *MC v Somerset CC*[26] UT Judge Ward posed the question of when it might be necessary 'for the authority to determine the special educational provision which any learning difficulty he may have calls for'. He gave two examples (while accepting that there were other possibilities): (a) where there was insufficient awareness of the special educational provision which a child requires, and (b) where the child needed to have a statement of SEN to access the relevant provision.[27]

2.18   Further, UT Judge Ward accepted that the amount of money delegated by the local authority to the school may be a material factor: the more money a local authority delegated to schools, the more a school may be reasonably be able to provide without the need for an EHC plan.[28]

2.19   The local authority may develop criteria as guidelines to help them decide when it is necessary to carry out an EHC needs assessment (and following assessment, whether it is necessary to issue an EHC plan).[29] The criteria must be capable of being departed from, however, and must not be applied as a blanket policy to certain groups of children or certain types of need.[30]

---

24 [2011] UKUT 499 (AAC), [2012] ELR 224.
25 [2011] UKUT 499 (AAC), [2012] ELR 224 at paras 16–17. UT Judge Ward made the same point in *MC v Somerset CC* [2015] UKUT 461 (AAC), [2016] ELR 53 at para 22.
26 [2015] UKUT 461 (AAC), [2016] ELR 53.
27 [2015] UKUT 461 (AAC), [2016] ELR 53 at para 19.
28 [2015] UKUT 461 (AAC), [2016] ELR 53 at para 23 (and see the case-law at para 2.29 below).
29 Code, para 9.16.
30 Code, para 9.16.

2.20   The local authority must notify the child's parent or the young person as soon as practicable and in any event within six weeks[31] of receiving a request for an assessment (or becoming responsible for the child or young person in accordance with CFA 2014 s24) of its decision whether or not it is necessary to secure an EHC needs assessment for a child or young person.[32] The local authority must also notify the responsible commissioning body, the local authority officers responsible for social care for children or young people with SEN, the manager of any early years setting attended by a child, the headteacher (or equivalent) of any school at which a child or young person is registered and the principal (or equivalent) of any post-16 institution which a young person attends.[33]

Conducting an EHC needs assessment: information and advice to be obtained by the local authority

2.21   When it undertakes an EHC needs assessment, the local authority must seek the following advice and information[34] on the needs of the

---

31 There are circumstances in which the local authority does not have to comply with the time limit, see SEND Regs reg 5(4). The child's parent or young person should be informed if exemptions apply so that he or she is aware of, and understands, the reasons for the delays. Local authorities should aim to keep delays to a minimum and as soon as the conditions that lead to an exemption no longer apply, the local authority should endeavour to complete the process as quickly as possible. All remaining elements of the process must be completed within their prescribed periods, regardless of whether exemptions have delayed earlier elements. See Code, para 9.43.

32 SEND Regs reg 5(1). The local authority must also notify the parent or the young person about his or her right to appeal the decision, the time limits for doing so, provide information concerning mediation and the availability of disagreement resolution services and information and advice about matters relating to the special educational needs of children and young people: see SEND Regs reg 5(3).

33 SEND Regs reg 5(2).

34 Where a local authority requests the co-operation of the bodies specified in CFA 2014 s31 (namely another local authority, a youth offending team, the person in charge of any relevant youth accommodation, the National Health Service Commissioning Board, a Clinical Commissioning Group (CCG), a Local Health Board, or an NHS trust or NHS foundation trust) in securing an EHC needs assessment, the body must comply with such a request within six weeks of receiving it, SEND Regs reg 8(1) (there are exemptions to this time limit in reg 8(2)). The child's parent or young person should be informed if exemptions apply so that they are aware of, and understand, the reasons for the delays. local authority should aim to keep delays to a minimum and as soon as the conditions that lead to an exemption no longer apply, the local authority should endeavour to complete the process as quickly as possible. All remaining elements of

child or young person, on what provision may be required to meet such needs, and on the outcomes that are intended to be achieved by the child or young person receiving that provision:[35]

- advice and information from the child's parent or young person;
- educational advice and information from the headteacher or principal of the school or post-16 institution that the child or young person is attending;[36]
- medical advice and information from a health care profession identified by the responsible commissioning body;
- psychological advice and information from an educational psychologist;[37]
- advice and information in relation to social care;[38]
- advice and information from any other person the local authority thinks is appropriate;[39]
- advice and information in relation to provision to assist any child or young person in or beyond year 9 in preparation for adulthood and independent living; [40]

the process must be completed within their prescribed periods, regardless of whether exemptions have delayed earlier elements. See Code, para 9.43.

35 SEND Regs reg 6(1). The local authority is not required to seek the advice above (except for advice from the child's parent or the young person) if such advice has previously been produced for any purpose and the person providing the advice, the local authority and the child's parent or the young person are satisfied that it is sufficient for the purposes of an EHC needs assessment: SEND Regs reg 6(4).

36 SEND Regs reg 6(1)(b) contemplates alternative sources of advice and information where this is not available. Further, where it appears to the local authority that the child or young person in question is either or both hearing impaired or visually impaired, if the teacher from whom advice is sought is not qualified to teach hearing or visually impaired pupils, the advice sought shall be given after consultation with a person who is so qualified: SEND Regs reg 6(2).

37 The Code notes that the educational psychologist should normally be employed or commissioned by the local authority. The educational psychologist should consult any other educational psychologists known to be involved with the child or young person: see Code, para 9.49.

38 The Code notes that in some cases, a child or young person may already have a statutory child in need or child protection plan, or an adult social care plan, from which information should be drawn for the EHC needs assessment. See Code, para 9.49.

39 The Code suggests Early Help Assessments; in the case of children of members of the Armed Forces advice from the Children's Education Advisory Service; and in the case of a looked after child, advice from the Virtual School Head in the local authority that looks after the child and the child's Designated Teacher and the Designated Doctor and Nurse for looked after children: Code, para 9.49.

40 SEND Regs reg 2 defines 'year 9' as 'the year of compulsory schooling in which the majority of pupils in the class attain the age of 14'.

- advice and information from any person the child's parent or young person reasonably requests the local authority seek advice from.[41]

2.22 The Code also adds that in certain circumstances the local authority should seek advice from a youth offending team.[42]

2.23 The local authority must provide the person from whom advice is being sought with copies of any representations made by the child's parent or the young person and any evidence submitted by or at the request of the child's parent or the young person.[43]

2.24 Advice and information must be provided within six weeks of the request, or more quickly if possible to enable a timely process.[44]

2.25 When conducting an EHC needs assessment, the local authority must:[45]

- consult the child and the child's parent, or the young person, and take into account their views, wishes and feelings;[46]
- consider any information provided to the local authority by or at the request of the child, the child's parent or the young person;
- consider the information and advice obtained from the persons listed in para 2.21 above;
- engage the child and the child's parent, or the young person and ensure they are able to participate in decisions: the Code states that local authorities should support and encourage the involvement of children, young people and parents or carers by providing them with access to the relevant material in accessible format,

41 The Code notes that parents might suggest consulting a GP or other health professional: Code, para 9.49.

42 The Code notes that where the child or young person is detained in a Young Offender Institution, the local authority should seek advice from his or her youth offending team. Where the young person is serving his or her sentence in the community, the local authority should seek such advice where it considers it appropriate. Code, para 9.49.

43 SEND Regs reg 6(3).

44 SEND Regs reg 8(1) and Code, para 9.52. There are exemptions to this time limit in reg 8(2)). The child's parent or young person should be informed if exemptions apply so that they are aware of, and understand, the reasons for the delays. Local authorities should aim to keep delays to a minimum, and as soon as the conditions that lead to an exemption no longer apply, the local authority should endeavour to complete the process as quickly as possible. All remaining elements of the process must be completed within their prescribed periods, regardless of whether exemptions have delayed earlier elements. See Code, para 9.43.

45 SEND Regs reg 7.

46 Code, paras 9.21–9.23 and 9.49.

giving them time to prepare for discussions and meetings and dedicating time in discussions and meetings to hear their views.[47] The Code also acknowledges that some children or young people will require support from an advocate where necessary (which could be a family member or a professional) to ensure that their views are heard and acknowledged;[48]

- minimise disruption for the child, the child's parent, the young person and their family: the Code provides that local authorities must work with parents and children and young people to understand how best to minimise disruption for them and family life. The Code notes that multiple appointments should be coordinated or combined where possible and appropriate.[49]

2.26   The Code notes that information-sharing is vital to support an effective assessment and planning process, but that local authorities must discuss with the child and young person and his or her parents what information they are happy for the local authority to share with other agencies. A record should be made of what information can be shared and with whom.[50]

2.27   Importantly, the Code emphasises that where particular services are assessed as being needed (eg under the Children Act (CA) 1989), their provision should not be delayed pending the completion of an EHC plan. Rather, help and support should be given to the child and family as soon as a need is identified.[51]

Outcome of the EHC needs assessment: deciding whether to issue an EHC plan

2.28   Having carried out an EHC needs assessment, a local authority must determine whether or not to issue an EHC plan. The statutory test, contained in CFA 2014 s37(1), is that the preparation of an EHC plan should be secured where 'in the light of an EHC needs assessment, it is necessary for special educational provision to be made for a child or young person in accordance with an EHC plan'. The wording

---

47 Code, paras 9.24; and see also paras 9.27–9.29.
48 Code, para 9.25.
49 Code, para 9.28, and see also paras 9.30–9.31.
50 Code, paras 9.32–9.34.
51 Code, para 9.35.

is similar, although not identical, to the wording used in EA 1996 s324,[52] which stated:

> If, in the light of an assessment ... of any child's educational needs and of any representations made by the child's parent ... it is necessary for the local authority to determine the special educational provision which any learning difficulty he may have calls for, the authority shall make and maintain a statement of his special educational needs.

2.29 There is no statutory definition of 'necessary'.[53] In *NC and DH v Leicestershire CC*, UT Judge Pearl held that a local authority (and the FTT on appeal) must ask two questions when determining whether it was 'necessary' to issue a statement of SEN: (a) whether the special educational provision identified as necessary for the child in the assessment is in fact available within the resources normally available to a mainstream school; and (b) if so, can the school reasonably be expected to make such provision from within its resources.[54] UT Judge Pearl accepted that the resources 'normally available' will differ from case to case and from local authority to local authority, but that it was proper for a local authority to take account of the money and personnel provided to a school by a delegated budget.[55] In *SC and MS v Worcestershire CC*,[56] UT Judge Mitchell agreed with this

---

52 The Code provides, however, that the 'legal test of when a child or young person requires an EHC plan remains the same as that for a statement under the Education Act 1996' (p15, para (xi)).

53 In *Buckinghamshire CC v HW* [2013] ELR 519, UT Judge Jacobs stated that it meant somewhere between indispensable and useful, but that he would not define it more precisely (at para 16). He added that it is a word in common usage and it is that usage that a local authority or the FTT must apply. In *Manchester City Council v JW* [2014] UKUT 168 (AAC) UT Judge Mark observed that 'if a thing is needed it is necessary' and that the need 'may be clear or it may involve a value judgment' (at para 14). In *Hertfordshire CC v MC* [2016] UKUT 385 (AAC) UT Judge Lane stated that what was 'necessary' is 'a matter to be deduced rather than defined. Its determination will vary according to the circumstances of a particular case and may well involve a considerable degree of judgment' (at para 36).

54 [2012] UKUT 85 (AAC), [2012] ELR 365 at para 32. Similarly, in *Islington LBC v LAO* [2008] EWHC 2297 (Admin), HHJ Waksman QC, sitting as a Deputy Judge of the High Court, derived from the code of practice then in force three stages to a decision whether to issue a statement of SEN: the first was to ascertain the degree of the child's learning difficulties and the SEN that resulted; the second was to determine what provision was required; and the third was to determine whether that provision was available in the normal resources available to the local authority (at paras 6–7).

55 [2012] UKUT 85 (AAC), [2012] ELR 365 at paras 35–38. See also *LS v Oxfordshire CC* [2013] UKUT 135 (AAC), [2013] ELR 429 per UT Judge Wikeley (at paras 23–27).

56 [2016] UKUT 267 (AAC), [2016] ELR 537.

test, but suggested that it could be more practically stated by asking whether 'without a statement, the decision maker can be satisfied, to a reasonable degree of certainty, that the required educational provision will be delivered'.[57]

2.30   The Code reflects the decision in *NC and DH v Leicestershire CC.* The Code suggests the local authority should consider whether, in the light of the EHC needs assessment, the existing special educational provision is well matched to the SEN of the young person.[58] Further, where despite appropriate assessment and provision, the child or young person is not progressing, or not progressing sufficiently well, the local authority should consider what further provision may be needed. The local authority should take into account:

- whether the special educational provision required to meet the child or young person's needs can reasonably be provided from within the resources normally available to mainstream educational institutions; or
- whether it may be necessary for the local authority to make special educational provision in accordance with an EHC plan.[59]

2.31   In *Manchester City Council v JW*,[60] UT Judge Mark commented (in respect of EA 1996 s324, but the comments apply with equal force to CFA 2014 s36) that the Code, being guidance only, does not affect the generality of the statutory test so as to exclude the possibility that a statement may be necessary for some other reason, for example, where a school or local authority, despite having the necessary resources, simply refused to use their best endeavours to provide the requisite special educational provision.[61]

2.32   One relevant factor in considering the meaning of 'necessary' is that the local authority must provide the provision in an EHC plan, while in respect of children and young people without EHC plans the governing body of the school (or other appropriate authority in respect of the institution) must only use its best endeavours to secure the special educational provision called for by the child or young

---

57 [2016] UKUT 267 (AAC), [2016] ELR 537 per UT Judge Mitchell at para 49. This test had the advantage, stated the judge at para 50, of reducing the likelihood of the FTT having to spend time dealing with local school financing arrangements. It also simplified matters where the child did not attend a maintained school.

58 Code, para 9.54.

59 Code, para 9.55.

60 [2014] UKUT 168 (AAC), [2014] ELR 304.

61 [2014] UKUT 168 (AAC), [2014] ELR 304 at para 17.

person's SEN is made.[62] So if there is a realistic doubt that the operation of the 'best endeavours duty' would result in the required provision, that favours a conclusion that the duty to make and maintain a statement of SEN arises because it is a case where it is 'necessary' to determine special educational provision.[63]

2.33 A further relevant factor is the status of the school. In *LS v Oxfordshire CC*,[64] the local authority determined not to issue a statement of SEN after carrying out an assessment. The FTT dismissed the parent's appeal. One week after the FTT's hearing, the school attended by the child converted to become an academy. The UT held, first, that the FTT needed to know that the school was about to become an academy as the local authority relied on the delegated funding available to the school to say that a statement was unnecessary to meet the child's needs. That the system of funding was about to alter was a material consideration for the FTT.[65] Second, the change in status to an academy *could* have made a difference to the FTT's decision.[66] The UT quashed the FTT's decision and remitted it back for reconsideration.

2.34 Finally, in both deciding whether an assessment is necessary and in the process of carrying out an assessment, the local authority must look to the future (even if that would require assessment of what special educational provision will be required in a different school).[67]

Notification of the decision on whether to issue an EHC plan

2.35 After the EHC needs assessment has been carried out, the local authority must notify the child's parent, or the young person, of the outcome of the assessment, whether it proposes to secure that an EHC

---

62 See paras 1.54–1.55 above. Compare CFA 2014 ss42(2) and 66(2). The UT held this to be relevant in *SC and MS v Worcestershire CC* [2016] UKUT 267 (AAC), [2016] ELR 537 per UT Judge Mitchell at paras 41–42, and *MC v Somerset CC* [2015] UKUT 461 (AAC), [2016] ELR 53 per UT Judge Ward at para 22.

63 *SC and MS v Worcestershire CC* [2016] UKUT 267 (AAC), [2016] ELR 537 per UT Judge Mitchell at para 42. See also *Manchester City Council v JW* [2014] UKUT 168 (AAC), [2014] ELR 304 per UT Judge Marks at para 17.

64 [2013] UKUT 135 (AAC), [2013] ELR 429.

65 [2013] UKUT 135 (AAC), [2013] ELR 429 per UT Judge Wikeley at paras 47–49.

66 [2013] UKUT 135 (AAC), [2013] ELR 429 per UT Judge Wikeley at paras 53–58.

67 See paras 3.33–3.34 below. In particular, see *Wilkin v Goldthorpe and Coventry City Council* [1998] ELR 345; *Buckinghamshire CC v HW* [2013] UKUT 470 (AAC), [2013] ELR 519 per UT Judge Jacobs at paras 19–22; and *OR v Ealing LBC* [2012] UKUT 211 (AAC), [2012] ELR 436 per UT Judge Williams at paras 31–34.

plan is prepared for the child or young person, and the reasons for that decision.[68] The local authority must also notify the headteacher of the school at which the child is a registered pupil (or the person identified as having responsibility for SEN at a provider of relevant early years education, or the principal of a post-16 institution).[69]

2.36   If the local authority decides that it is not necessary for special educational provision to be made for a child or young person in accordance with an EHC plan, the notification to the child's parent or the young person must be given as soon as practicable, and in any event within 16 weeks[70] of the local authority receiving a request for an EHC needs assessment (or becoming responsible for the child or young person in accordance with CFA 2014 s24).[71] The local authority must also notify the child's parent or the young person of their right to appeal the decision.[72]

2.37   The local authority should also provide feedback collected during the process of considering whether an EHC needs assessment is necessary, including advice from professionals, which the parent, young person or educational institution may find useful.[73]

EHC plans

Introduction

2.38   The Code describes the purpose of an EHC plan as being 'to make special educational provision to meet the special educational needs

---

68   CFA 2014 s36(9).

69   SEND Regs reg 10(2).

70   SEND Regs reg 10(4) contains exemptions to the time limit. The child's parent or the young person should be informed if exemptions apply so that he or she is aware of, and understands, the reasons for the delays. Local authorities should aim to keep delays to a minimum and as soon as the conditions that lead to an exemption no longer apply, the local authority should endeavour to complete the process as quickly as possible. All remaining elements of the process must be completed within their prescribed periods, regardless of whether exemptions have delayed earlier elements. See Code, para 9.43.

71   SEND Regs reg 10(1).

72   SEND Regs reg 10(3). The notification must also include the following information: (a) the time limits for an appeal; (b) the requirement to consider mediation should the parent or young person wish to appeal; (c) the availability of information, advice and support and disagreement resolution services; and (d) the FTT's power to make social care recommendations under a pilot scheme (on which, see paras 4.25–4.29 below).

73   Code, paras 9.19, 9.59.

of the child or young person, to secure the best possible outcomes for them across education, health and social care and, as they get older, prepare them for adulthood'.[74] This section describes the process by which an EHC plan is made. An overview of what is expected by way of content is set out at paras 2.39–2.40 below. Chapter 3 contains a more detailed analysis of the content of EHC plans.

Contents of an EHC plan: an overview

2.39 The plan must, at the least,[75] set out the following:[76]

- Section A: The views, interests and aspirations of the child and his or her parents or the young person.
- Section B: The child or young person's SEN (equivalent to Part 2 in statements of SEN).
- Section C: The child or young person's healthcare needs which relate to his or her SEN.
- Section D: The child or young person's social care needs which relate to his or her SEN or disability.
- Section E: The outcomes sought for the child or young person.
- Section F: The special educational provision required by the child or young person (equivalent to Part 3 in statements of SEN).
- Section G: Any healthcare provision reasonably required by the learning difficulties or disabilities which result in the child or young person having SEN. The healthcare provision specified must be agreed by the responsible commissioning body.[77]
- Section H1: Any special care provision which must be made for the child or young person as a result of CSDPA 1970 s2.
- Section H2: Any other social care provision reasonably required by the learning difficulties or disabilities which result in the child or young person having SEN.
- Section I: The name of the school, maintained nursery school, post-16 institution or other institution to be attended by the child or young person, and the type of that institution or, where the name of the school or other institution is not specified in the EHC plan, the type of school or other institution to be attended by the child or young person (the equivalent of Part 4 in statements of SEN).

---

74 Code, para 9.2.
75 The Code provides that the format of the EHC plan can be agreed locally, but as a statutory minimum sections A–K must be included, Code, para 9.62.
76 SEND Regs reg 12(1).
77 SEND Regs reg 12(2).

- Section J: Where any special educational provision is to be secured by a direct payment, the SEN and outcomes to be met by the direct payment.

2.40   The advice and information obtained in accordance with SEND Regs reg 6(1) must be set out in appendices to the EHC plan.[78] The Code describes this as 'section K'.[79] Further, where the child or young person is in or beyond year 9, the EHC plan must include within the special educational provision, healthcare and social care provision specified, provision to assist the child or young person in preparation for adulthood and independent living.[80]

Preparing the EHC plan

2.41   When preparing a child or young person's EHC plan, a local authority must take into account the evidence received when securing the EHC needs assessment, and consider how best to achieve the outcomes to be sought for the child or young person.[81]

2.42   The local authority must first produce the EHC plan in draft. It must consult the child's parent or the young person about the content of the plan during a preparation of a draft of the plan.[82] The local authority must then send the draft plan to the child's parent or to the young person.[83] The draft plan must not name a school or other institution, or specify a type of school or other institution (this is to allow for the parent or young person to request a school – see paras 2.43–2.46 below).[84]

2.43   When the local authority sends a draft plan to the child's parent or young person it must give them at least 15 days (beginning with the day on which the draft plan was served) in which to make representations about the content of the draft plan, to request that a particular school or other institution be named in the plan and to require the local authority to arrange a meeting between them and an officer of

---

78 SEND Regs reg 12(4).

79 Code, para 9.62.

80 SEND Regs reg 12(3); Code, para 9.63. The Code identifies four 'preparing for adulthood outcomes', namely: (i) moving into paid employment and higher education, (ii) independent living, (iii) having friends and relationships and being part of their communities, and (iv) being as healthy as possible, see Code (Introduction to Chapter 8).

81 SEND Regs reg 11.

82 CFA 2014 s38(1); Code, para 9.77.

83 CFA 2014 s38(2); Code, para 9.77.

84 CFA 2014 s38(5); Code, para 9.77.

the local authority at which the draft plan can be discussed.[85] The local authority must also advise the child's parent or the young person where they can find information about the schools and colleges that are available for the child or young person to attend.[86] Further, the local authority should seek agreement of any personal budget specified in the draft plan.[87] Personal budgets and direct payments are dealt with in more detail in paras 2.120–2.154 below.

2.44   A parent or young person can only request that certain types of school (described below as 'qualifying schools') be named in the plan, namely a maintained school, a maintained special school, an academy, a further education institution, a non-maintained special school or an independent special school or special post 16 institution approved by the secretary of state.[88] If the parent or young person names a qualifying school, the CFA 2014 contains a presumption in favour of parental preference in that the local authority must secure that the EHC plan names the requested educational institution unless the criteria in CFA 2014 s39(4) apply: (a) the school or other institution is unsuitable for the age, ability, aptitude, or SEN of the child or young person concerned; or (b) the attendance of the child or young person at the requested school or other institution would be incompatible with the provision of efficient education for others or the efficient use of resources.[89] The exercise of parental preference is dealt with in more detail at paras 3.35–3.65 below.

2.45   If, before the end of the 15-day period, the parent or young person requests the local authority to name a qualifying school in the EHC plan, the local authority must consult the governing body, proprietor or principal of the school or other institution requested and if the school is maintained by another local authority, that local authority.[90]

---

85 SEND Regs reg 13(1)(a); Code, para 9.77.
86 SEND Regs reg 13(1)(b); Code, para 9.77.
87 Code, para 9.77.
88 For definitions of schools, see para 1.16 above. See CFA 2014 s38(3); Code, para 9.78. CFA 2014 s83(2) defines a 'maintained school' as '(a) a community, foundation or voluntary school, or (b) a community or foundation special school not established in a hospital'. Section 83(5) further defines reference to a community, foundation or voluntary school or to a community or foundation special school to be a reference to such a school within the meaning of the School Standards and Framework Act (SSFA) 1998 (on which see SSFA 1998 ss20, 21 and 142). CFA 2014 s41 and SEND Regs regs 58–62 make provision for independent special schools and special post-16 institutions to be approved by the secretary of state.
89 CFA 2014 s39(3) and (4).
90 CFA 2014 s39(1) and (2); Code, para 9.80.

2.46   Where CFA 2014 s39(4) applies, or where the parent or young person makes no request to name a qualifying school to the local authority before the end of the 15-day period, the local authority must secure that the plan names a school or other institution which the local authority thinks would be appropriate for the child or young person, or specifies the type of school or other institution which the local authority thinks would be appropriate for the child or young person.[91] If the parent or young person has requested that a non-qualifying school be named (for example, an independent mainstream school), the local authority must have regard to the preference.[92] Before naming any school or other institution in an EHC plan, the local authority must (if it has not done so already) consult the governing body, proprietor or principal of any school proposed to be named in the plan, and if the school is maintained by another local authority, that local authority.[93]

Finalising the EHC plan

2.47   If, following consultation:

a) the parent or young person proposes changes to the draft EHC plan which the local authority agrees, then the EHC plan can be amended and issued as soon as possible. The final EHC plan must differ from the draft EHC plan only as a result of the representations made; if the local authority wishes to make any further amendments, it must re-issue the draft plan to allow the parent or young person to comment;[94]

b) the parent or young person proposes changes that are not agreed, then the local authority may proceed to issue the final EHC plan without the requested changes.[95]

2.48   The local authority must send a copy of the finalised EHC plan to the child's parent or to the young person,[96] to the governing body, proprietor or principal of any school or other institution named in the plan[97] and to the responsible commissioning body[98] as soon as

---

91 CFA 2014 ss39(5), 40(1) and (2); Code, paras 9.88–9.90.
92 See EA 1996 s9, and for the correct approach see paras 3.44–3.47, 3.52–3.65 below.
93 CFA 2014 ss39(6) and 40(3).
94 Code, para 9.125.
95 Code, para 9.126.
96 CFA 2014 ss39(8), 40(5) ; SEND Regs reg 13(2).
97 CFA 2014 ss39(8), 40(5); SEND Regs reg 13(2).
98 SEND Regs reg 13(2).

practicable and in any event within 20 weeks of the local authority receiving a request for an EHC needs assessment (or becoming responsible for the child pursuant to CFA 2014 s24).[99]

2.49 When sending a copy of the finalised EHC plan to the child's parent or to the young person, the local authority must notify them of their right to appeal.[100]

Maintaining an EHC plan

2.50 An EHC plan imposes duties on a local authority and (where relevant) on the responsible commissioning body, specifically:

- The local authority must secure the special educational provision specified for the child or young person in the EHC plan (specifically in sections F and I).[101] This includes a duty to pay any fees payable in respect of the provision of education at a school or institution.[102]
- If the EHC plan specifies healthcare provision, the responsible commissioning body must arrange the specified health care provision for the child or young person.[103]

2.51 In the context of the EA 1996, the courts held that the requirement on the local authority to 'arrange' special educational provision is a mandatory one, and that financial or other practical difficulties in giving effect to the terms of the statement of SEN provide no excuse.[104] Given the materially similar wording of the CFA 2014, the courts are likely to follow the pre-existing case-law.

---

99 SEND Regs reg 13(2). The exemptions to the time limits set out in reg 10(4) apply, see SEND Regs reg 13(3).

100 SEND Regs reg 14(2); Code, paras 9.126–9.128. The notification must include the time limits for making an appeal, the requirement to consider mediation should the parent or young person wish to appeal, the availability of information, advice and support and disagreement resolution services and the FTT's powers to make social care recommendations under a pilot scheme, on which see paras 4.25–4.29 below.

101 CFA 2014 s42(1) and (2).

102 CFA 2014 s63(1) and (2).

103 CFA 2014 s42(3) and (4); Code, para 9.141.

104 See *R v Harrow LBC ex p M* [1997] ELR 62, per Turner J; *R (N) v North Tyneside BC* [2010] EWCA Civ 135, [2010] ELR 312, per Elias LJ (at paras 9–11). EA 1996 s324(5) stated that the local authority 'shall arrange' the special educational provision in the statement of SEN. CFA 2014 s42(2) states that the local authority 'must secure' the special educational provision; section 42(3) states that the responsible commissioning body 'must arrange' the healthcare specified in the EHC plan.

2.52   Neither the duty on the local authority, nor the duty on the responsible commissioning body, arises if the child's parent or the young person has made suitable alternative arrangements.[105] The Code provides that the local authority must satisfy itself that any alternative arrangements made by the parent or young person are suitable before it is relieved of its duty to secure the provision.[106] Suitable alternative arrangements must include arrangements which are financially secure (at least for a reasonable period of time).[107]

2.53   The CFA 2014 contains no equivalent duty on social care to secure the provision of any social care provision set out in an EHC plan. In many (but possibly not all) cases the duty to secure any services provided will arise under CSDPA 1970 s2 (in respect of children under the age of 18) or under Care Act 2014 (CA 2014) s18. The Code requires the local authority to state in section H1 of the EHC plan which services (if any) are provided under the CSDPA 1970 or under CA 2014 s18.[108]

Duty on schools to admit where named in section I of an EHC plan

2.54   Where certain types of school[109] are named in an EHC plan, the governing body or principal of the school or other institution must admit the child or young person for whom the EHC plan is maintained.[110]

---

105 CFA 2014 s42(5).

106 Code, para 9.133 (and see further, paras 9.134–9.136). On an application for judicial review, the question of whether suitable alternative arrangements have been made is not a question of fact for the court to determine, but a question for the local authority, subject to *Wednesbury* unreasonableness (ie so unreasonable that no reasonable decision maker could have reached that conclusion) and other public law arguments; see *White v Ealing LBC* [1997] EWHC 651 (Admin), [1998] ELR 203 per Dyson LJ (this conclusion was not challenged in the Court of Appeal, [1998] ELR 319).

107 See *R v Hackney LBC ex p GC* [1995] ELR 144, 153B per Auld J; *R v Kent CC ex p W* [1995] ELR 362, 370F per Turner J; and *White v Ealing LBC* [1997] EWHC 651 (Admin), [1998] ELR 203 per Dyson LJ.

108 Code, para 9.137.

109 By CFA 2014 s43(1): a maintained school, a maintained nursery school, an academy, an institution within the further education sector in England, a non-maintained special school and an institution approved by the secretary of state under CFA 2014 s41.

110 CFA 2014 s43(2); Code, para 9.130.

Review and reassessment

Reviews

Introduction

2.55   The Code states that 'EHC plans should be used to actively monitor children and young people's progress towards their outcomes and longer term aspirations'.[111] Reviews are an essential part of this process.

2.56   The Code describes the purposes of a review to be as follows:

- gather and assess information so that it can be used by early years settings, schools or colleges to support the child or young person's progress and their access to teaching and learning;
- review the special educational provision made for the child or young person to ensure it is being effective in ensuring access to teaching and learning and good progress;
- review the health and social care provision made for the child or young person and its effectiveness in ensuring good progress towards outcomes;
- consider the continuing appropriateness of the EHC plan in the light of the child or young person's progress during the previous year or changed circumstances and whether changes are required including any changes to outcomes, enhanced provision, change of educational establishment or whether the EHC plan should be discontinued;
- set new interim targets for the coming year and where appropriate, agree new outcomes; and
- review any interim targets set by the early years provider, school or college or other education provider.

Timing

2.57   A local authority must review an EHC plan that it maintains in the period of 12 months starting with the date on which the plan was first made, and in each subsequent period of 12 months starting with the date on which the plan was last reviewed.[112]

---

111 Code, para 9.166.
112 CFA 2014 s44(1).

2.58   Further, there are particular requirements of review when a child is about to transfer between phases of education.[113] Where a child or young person is within 12 months of a transfer between phases of education, the local authority must review and amend (where necessary) the child or young person's EHC plan before 31 March (in the calendar year of the child or young person's transfer from secondary school to a post-16 institution) or 15 February (in the calendar year of the child's transfer in all other cases). Where necessary, the local authority must amend the EHC plan so that it names the school or institution the child will attend following the transfer.[114] Where it is proposed that a young person transfers from one post-16 institution to another post-16 institution at any other time, the local authority must review and amend where necessary the young person's EHC plan at least five months before the transfer takes place so that it names the post-16 institution the child will attend following the transfer.[115]

2.59   In respect of children under the age of five, the Code suggests that local authorities consider reviewing an EHC plan at least every three to six months to ensure that the provision continues to be appropriate. The Code proposes that, depending on the needs of the child, these can be streamlined reviews (ie that they may not necessarily require the attendance of all of the professionals).[116]

2.60   Neither the legislation nor the Code refers to emergency (or interim) reviews. Nevertheless, where a child is at risk of being (or has been) excluded from the school named, or where a school is struggling to meet a child's needs, or where circumstances have changed significantly such that it would be appropriate to review the provision contained in the EHC plan, a child's parent or a young person, or the head teacher of a school, should consider asking the local authority to convene an emergency (or interim) review.[117]

---

113 The Code describes the phase transfers as: (i) early years provider to school; (ii) infant school to junior school; (iii) primary school to middle school; (iv) primary school to secondary school; and (v) middle school to secondary school; see Code, para 9.179.

114 SEND Regs reg 18(1).

115 SEND Regs reg 18(2).

116 Code, para 9.178.

117 The previous Code, *Special educational needs code of practice* (2001) referred to 'interim reviews' and stated that these should take place 'where a school identifies a pupil with a statement of special educational needs who is at serious risk of disaffection or exclusion, an interim or early review should be called. It will then be possible to consider the pupil's changing needs and recommend amendments to the statement, as an alternative to the pupil being

2.61   When the local authority is transferring a child or young person with a statement of SEN to an EHC plan, the local authority must conduct a transfer review. This will often replace the annual review of the statement of SEN in the year in which the local authority intends to transfer the child or young person. Transfer reviews, and the transfer of children and young people from statements of SEN to EHC plans, are dealt with in para 2.80–2.98 below.

Conduct

2.62 When undertaking a review of an EHC plan, a local authority must:[118]

- consult the child and the child's parents or the young person, and take account of their views, wishes and feelings;
- consider the child or young person's progress towards achieving the outcomes specified in the EHC plan and whether these outcomes remain appropriate for the child or young person;
- consult the school or other institution attended by the child or young person.

2.63 SEND Regs reg 20 sets down the process to be followed where the child or young person attends a school or institution.[119]

2.64   There must be a meeting held to conduct the review.[120] The following must be invited:

(a) the child's parent or the young person;
(b) the headteacher or principal of the school or institution attended;
(c) an officer from the local authority's SEN department;
(d) a healthcare professional identified by the responsible commissioning body to provide advice about healthcare provision in relation to the child or young person; and
(e) an officer from the local authority's social services department.[121]

At least two weeks' notice of the date of the meeting must be given.[122] The person arranging the review meeting must obtain advice or

---

    excluded' (at para 9.44). It is unfortunate that reference to interim reviews is absent from the current code.

118 SEND Regs reg 19. See also CFA 2014 s44(6) which requires a local authority to consult the parent of the child or the young person during a review.

119 SEND Regs reg 21 sets out a slightly modified process where a child does not attend a school or other institution. See also the Code, at paras 9.173–9.177.

120 SEND Regs reg 20(1).

121 SEND Regs reg 20(2).

122 SEND Regs reg 20(3).

information from the invitees and circulate this to all other invitees at least two weeks in advance of the meeting.[123]

2.65   The meeting must consider the child or young person's progress towards meeting the outcomes specified in the EHC plan.[124] Further, where the child or young person is in or beyond year 9,[125] the review meeting must also consider what provision is required to assist the child or young person in preparation for adulthood and independent living.[126]

2.66   Following the meeting, the headteacher or principal of the school must prepare a written report on the child or young person, setting out the headteacher or principal's recommendations on any amendments to be made to the EHC plan, and referring to any difference between those recommendations and the recommendations of others attending the meeting.[127] The report must be prepared within two weeks of the meeting and circulated to all of the invitees.[128]

2.67   The local authority must then decide whether to:

- continue to maintain the EHC plan in its current form;
- amend it; or
- cease to maintain it;

and must notify the child's parent or the young person, and the headteacher or principal of its decision within four weeks of the review meeting.[129]

Amending an EHC plan following a review[130]

2.68   Where the local authority is considering amending an EHC plan following a review, it must (in broad terms) undertake the same process as when it initially determined the content of the EHC plan (see paras 2.41–2.49 above).[131] Thus the local authority must:[132]

123 SEND Regs reg 20(4).

124 SEND Regs reg 20(5).

125 SEND Regs reg 2 defines 'year 9' as 'the year of compulsory schooling in which the majority of pupils in the class attain the age of 14'.

126 SEND Regs reg 20(6).

127 SEND Regs reg 20(7). This only applies to the types of schools specified in reg 20(12). If a child does not attend one of the listed types of schools, the local authority must write the report, see SEND Regs reg 20(8).

128 SEND Regs reg 20(9).

129 SEND Regs reg 20(10). Further, the local authority must notify the child's parent or the young person of their rights of appeal, see SEND Regs reg 20(11).

130 See Code, paras 9.193–9.198.

131 SEND Regs reg 22(1); and see SEND Regs regs 11 and 12, and CFA 2014 ss33, 39 and 40.

132 SEND Regs reg 22(2).

- send the child's parent or the young person a copy of the EHC plan, together with a notice specifying the proposed amendments, together with copies of the evidence that supports the proposed amendments;
- provide the child's parent or the young person with notice of their right to request that a particular school or other institution is named in the EHC plan under CFA 2014 s38(2)(b)(ii);
- give the child's parent or the young person at least 15 days, beginning with the day on which the draft plan was served, in which to make representations about the content of the draft plan, request that a particular school or other institution be named in the draft plan, or request a meeting with an officer of the local authority if they wish to make representations orally;
- advise the child's parent or the young person where they can find information about the schools and colleges that are available for the child or young person to attend.

2.69 Where a local authority decides to amend an EHC plan following representations from the child's parent or young person, it must send the finalised EHC plan to the child's parent or young person, to the governing body (or proprietor or principal) of the school named in section I, and to the responsible commissioning body as soon as practicable but in any event within eight weeks of originally sending the EHC plan with the proposed amendments to the parent or young person.[133]

2.70 Conversely, where the local authority decides not to amend the EHC plan, it must notify the child's parent or the young person of its decision as soon as practicable, but in any event within eight weeks of originally sending the EHC plan with the proposed amendments to the parent or young person.[134]

2.71 In either case, the local authority must notify the child's parent or the young person of their rights of appeal to the FTT.[135]

---

133 SEND Regs reg 22(3).

134 SEND Regs reg 22(4).

135 SEND Regs reg 22(5). The notification must also include the following information: (a) the time limits for an appeal; (b) the information concerning mediation; (c) the availability of information, advice and support and disagreement resolution services; and (d) the FTT's power to make social care recommendations under a pilot scheme (on which, see paras 4.25–4.29 below).

Reassessments

When are reassessments required?[136]

2.72   A local authority must secure a reassessment of a child or young person's EHC plan where it receives a request to do so from the responsible commissioning body for that child or young person.[137]

2.73   Further, a local authority must secure a reassessment of the educational, health and social care needs of a child or young person for whom it maintains an EHC plan if a request is made to it by the child's parent or the young person, or the governing body (or proprietor or principal) of the school of institution which the child or young person attends unless:

- it has carried out an assessment or reassessment within the period of six months prior to that request; or
- it is not necessary for the authority to make a further assessment.[138]

2.74   A local authority may also secure a reassessment at any other time if it thinks it necessary.[139]

The process[140]

2.75   The local authority must notify the child's parent or the young person whether or not it is necessary to reassess within 15 days of receiving the request to reassess.[141] Where the local authority determines that it is not necessary to reassess the child or young person it must notify the child's parent or the young person of their right to appeal to the FTT.[142]

2.76   If it is necessary to reassess, the process follows that for statutory assessment (see paras 2.21–2.27 above).[143]

Amending or replacing an EHC plan following a reassessment[144]

2.77   Where the local authority decides to amend or replace an EHC plan following a reassessment it must comply with the same process that

---

136 Code, paras 9.186–9.192.
137 SEND Regs reg 23.
138 See CFA 2014 s44(2) and (3); and SEND Regs reg 24.
139 CFA 2014 s44(3).
140 See Code, paras 9.191–9.192.
141 SEND Regs reg 25(1).
142 SEND Regs reg 25(2).
143 SEND Regs reg 26: thus the process must follow SEND Regs regs 6–9.
144 See Code, paras 9.193–9.198.

applies to the issue of a draft EHC plan in the first instance (see paras 2.41–2.49 above).[145] The local authority must complete the whole process (ie send a copy of the finalised EHC plan to the child's parent or the young person, the governing body or principal of the school and the relevant responsible commissioning body) as soon as practicable and in any event within 14 weeks of notifying the child's parent or the young person that it was necessary to reassess.[146]

2.78   After having carried out a reassessment, the local authority must review the EHC plan within 12 months of the date on which a finalised plan is sent to the child's parent or the young person, and in each subsequent period of 12 months starting with the date on which the EHC plan was last reviewed.[147]

Amendment without a review or reassessment

2.79   If at any time the local authority proposes to amend an EHC plan, it shall proceed as if the amendment were an amendment proposed after a review (and follow the processes there applicable).[148]

Transfers from statements of SEN and LDAs to EHC plans

Introduction

2.80   When the CFA 2014 was introduced, the government put in place transitional arrangements to facilitate the transfer of children and young people with SEN statements and LDAs to EHC plans. The transitional arrangements are set out in the Children and Families Act 2014 (Transitional and Saving Provisions) (No 2) Order 2014 SI No 2270 (TSP Order) and explained in the guidance published by the Department for Education, *Special educational needs and disability: managing the September 2014 changes to the system. Advice for local authorities and their partners* ('the transfer advice').[149] The transfer

---

145 SEND Regs reg 27(1).
146 SEND Regs reg 27(2). This time limit can be extended in the circumstances set out at para 2.93 above.
147 SEND Regs reg 27(4).
148 SEND Regs reg 28.
149 The transfer advice is currently in its 4th edition and applies from 1 October 2016. Decisions taken by local authorities before that date are covered by earlier editions of the advice.

advice is non-statutory, which means that it is not binding on local authorities, but they must be able to explain any departures from it.

2.81   The transitional arrangements run from 1 September 2014 until 1 April 2018, by which point local authorities must have completed all the transfers of statements of SEN. Any new request for a statement or LDA must be processed as a request for an EHC plan in accordance with the provisions of the CFA 2014.[150]

2.82   Young people in further education and training who had an LDA should have been transferred to an EHC plan by 1 September 2016; any LDAs that exist after this date do not have any legal effect.[151]

2.83   During the transition period, local authorities must continue to comply with the relevant elements of the EA 1996 and the Learning and Skills Act 2000 (LSA 2000) in relation to those children and young people who still have statements.[152] The local authority should follow the annual review and amendment processes and parents continue to have the same rights of appeal under the EA 1996.[153]

2.84   The transfer process should not, in itself, have any effect on whether or not a child or young person is entitled to an EHC plan because there is no material difference between the legal test under the CFA 2014 and the EA 1996.[154] It is therefore expected in the transition guidance that children with statements should be transferred to an EHC plan. Young people with an LDA, including those in youth custody, should have been transferred to an EHC plan if they remained in education or training on 1 September 2016.[155]

Transition plans

2.85   Local authorities must produce transition plans which set out the timetable and process for transferring children to EHC plans.[156] Transition plans should include the following information:

- the groups that were consulted in developing the plan;
- the number of children and young people with statements of SEN and the number of young people receiving support as a result of

---

150 Transfer advice, para 2.1.

151 TSP Order arts 28 and 29.

152 TSP Order art 11.

153 Transfer advice, para 3.11. Parents appealing under the EA 1996 will not need to consider mediation before bringing their appeal, unlike parents appealing against a decision under the CFA 2014.

154 See para 2.28 above.

155 Transfer advice, para 1.8.

156 Transfer advice, paras 4.5–4.8.

an LDA for which the local authority is responsible and plans to transfer (where appropriate) to the new system in each year of the transition period;

- the order in which children and young people with statements of SEN in the area will be transferred to the new system;
- how and when parents of children with SEN and young people with SEN, and their educational institution, will be made aware of the arrangements for the transfer of a child or young person;
- details of the transfer review (EHC needs assessment) process;
- sources of impartial SEN information and advice; and
- details of who parents and young people can contact if they have queries about transition to the new system or if their child or they have not been transferred to the new system in accordance with the local transition plan.[157]

2.86 The transfer advice states that local authorities 'should aim to transfer children and young people with statements of SEN to the new SEN and disability system at points in their education at which a significant review of the statement would otherwise have taken place'.[158] In practice, this means that children and young people changing educational phases ought to be transferred to an EHC plan before the change occurs. The TSP Order makes specific provisions to guide local authority's timing of the transfer process:

- Children leaving youth custody[159] and those transferring from school to a post-16 institution or an apprenticeship must have their statement reviewed at that point with a view to issuing an EHC plan.[160]
- Children with non-statutory EHC plans issued by pathfinder local authorities before the commencement of the CFA 2014[161] and those with direct payments under the SEN direct payments pilot scheme, should have been transferred by Local authorities in the academic year 2014/15.[162]
- Local authorities must consult the parents of children who are in year 6 during the academic years 2015/16 and 2016/17 on whether

---

157 Transfer advice, para 4.6.
158 Transfer advice, para 4.9.
159 TSP Order art 14A,
160 TSP Order art 12.
161 Transfer advice, paras 4.18–4.20.
162 Transfer advice, para 5.29.

to conduct an EHC needs assessment.[163] The local authority must then consider whether to carry out an assessment and, if they decide to do so, complete it by end of year 6.

- During 2016 and 2017, local authorities should transfer children who are changing educational phases, or who have entered year 9.[164] A change in educational phase is defined as a child moving from early years to infant school, infant to junior school, primary to middle school, primary to secondary school, middle to secondary school, or a change in school setting from mainstream to special school and vice versa.[165]

2.87   These provisions do not apply if there is an ongoing appeal to the FTT in relation to a statement or if there are exceptional personal circumstances affecting the child, the child's parent or a young person.[166]

Transfer reviews

2.88   In order to transfer a child to an EHC plan, local authorities must conduct a transfer review.[167] This will often replace the annual review of the statement in the year in which the local authority intends to transfer the child. Like the annual review, the transfer review must be completed within 12 months of the date the statement of SEN was issued or of the previous annual review of the child's statement.[168] If a transfer review is carried out within 12 months of a forthcoming transfer between phases of education, it must be completed before 31 March in the year of a child's transfer from secondary school to a post-16 institution and before 15 February in all other cases.[169]

2.89   Parents of children with a statement can request a reassessment of the child's needs during the transition period. They can make the request under the EA 1996 or make a request for an EHC needs assessment. Local authorities must inform the parents whether or not they are going to carry out an assessment within six weeks of receiving the request.[170] Local authorities can decide to conduct an

---

163 TSP Order art 13. This does not apply to children who transferred from middle to secondary school in year 6.

164 TSP Order art 14.

165 TSP Order art 14(6); transfer advice, paras 4.12–4.13. This reflects the definitions in the Code, para 9.179.

166 TSP Order art 16.

167 Transfer advice, para 5.1.

168 Transfer advice, para 4.15.

169 SEND Regs reg 18.

170 SEND Regs regs 4(1) and 5(1).

EHC needs assessment instead of a reassessment under the EA 1996, but must obtain the agreement of the child's parents in order to do so.[171] The transfer guidance encourages local authorities to conduct transfer reviews rather than reassessments under the EA 1996 in order to speed up the process of transition.[172]

2.90   The child's parents and the child's headteacher must be given at least two weeks' notice of the local authority's intention to carry out a transfer review and the local authority must invite the parents to a meeting to contribute to the review before the EHC plan is finalised.[173] Transfer reviews must consist of an EHC needs assessment conducted in accordance with the SEND Regs.[174] The process for EHC needs assessments is discussed in detail in paras 2.5–2.27 above.

2.91   SEND Regs reg 6(4) provides that the local authority must not seek professional advice required for an EHC needs assessment if that advice has been previously provided and the person providing that advice, the local authority and the child's parents or the young person are satisfied that it is sufficient for the purposes of an EHC needs assessment. The transfer advice suggests that, in deciding whether existing advice is sufficient, the local authority should consider how recently advice was provided, whether and how far the needs of the child or young person have changed since it was given and whether it is sufficiently focused on the outcomes sought for the child or young person.[175]

2.92   While a local authority may not need to obtain additional advice for the purposes of the transfer review, the resulting EHC plan should not be a simple rebranding of the statement; it is intended to be more holistic, person-centred and outcome-focused than the statement and changes should be made to reflect the new approach.[176]

2.93   If the local authority decides that an EHC plan is necessary (which it should be in the vast majority of cases), the plan should be completed within 18 weeks from the day on which the needs assessment began.[177] This deadline was originally 14 weeks but, after local authorities complained that was too short, it was extended from September

---

171 TSP Order art 23(5); transfer advice, para 3.9.
172 Transfer advice, para 3.9.
173 TSP Order arts 18(1) and 20(3).
174 TSP Order art 20.
175 Transfer advice, para 5.10.
176 Transfer advice, para 5.1.
177 TSP Order art 21(3).

2015.[178] Local authorities do not need to comply with the deadline if they can show that they have requested advice from a school a week or less before the school is closed for a continuous period of four weeks or more (ie the summer holidays), or if there are exceptional personal circumstances affecting the child or their parents, or if the child or parents are absent for a continuous period of four weeks or more from the local authority area.[179]

2.94   If the local authority decides not to prepare an EHC plan follow-ing the transfer review, the local authority must cease to maintain the statement.[180] A child's parent can bring an appeal against the local authority's decision under CFA 2014 s51 and the statement will remain in force while any appeal against the local authority's deci-sion is ongoing.[181]

2.95   If reviews cannot be carried out before the deadline of 1 April 2018, the CFA 2014 will apply to the child or young person from that date and SEN provision specified in the statement will be treated as if it were made in an EHC plan. The transfer must be concluded as soon as reasonably practicable thereafter.[182]

Transfer reviews for children and young people in youth custody

2.96   The TSP Order also provides for transfer reviews to be conducted for children and young people in youth custody.[183] The provisions are broadly similar to those for children who are not in detention, described above.

2.97   Local authorities must not cease to maintain a statement because the child has entered custody.[184] If it appears to the local authority that SEN provision in the statement is no longer appropriate, or if the child, the parents or the person in charge of the youth accom-modation requests it, the local authority should commence a transfer review.[185] The EHC needs assessment process for children in youth custody is discussed in detail in chapter 5.

178 Children and Families Act 2014 (Transitional and Saving Provisions) (Amendment) (No 2) Order 2015 SI No 1619.
179 Transfer advice, para 5.15.
180 TSP Order art 22(4).
181 TSP Order art 22(7).
182 TSP Order art 17.
183 TSP Order arts 14A, 30 and 31.
184 Transition advice, para 6.2.
185 Transition advice, para 6.2.

2.98   The local authority may decide that an EHC plan is required and follow the process for issuing a plan.[186] If the local authority decides that an EHC plan is not necessary, it must cease to maintain the statement.[187] However, the ability to cease to maintain a statement for children in youth custody is in contrast to the provisions of the Code relating to EHC plans, which state that local authorities cannot cease to maintain them while a child is in custody.[188] In the authors' view, it would only be in very exceptional circumstances than the local authority could lawfully decide not to transfer a statement to an EHC plan.

Ceasing to maintain an EHC plan and transfer to another local authority

Ceasing to maintain an EHC plan[189]

2.99   A local authority may cease to maintain an EHC plan for a child or young person in two circumstances:[190]

(a) the local authority is no longer responsible for the child or young person; or

(b) the local authority determines that it is no longer necessary for the plan to be maintained.

2.100   A parent or young person has a right of appeal against a decision to cease to maintain an EHC plan. The decision to cease to maintain the EHC plan may not take effect until the following dates:[191]

- if no appeal to the FTT is brought: after the end of the period of two months (being the time limit on bringing an appeal in the FTT);[192] or
- if an appeal to the FTT is brought, after the appeal has been finally determined.

---

186 TSP Order art 34; see paras 5.28 and following.
187 TSP Order art 35.
188 Code, para 10.122.
189 Code, paras 9.199–9.210.
190 CFA 2014 s45(1).
191 CFA 2014 s45(4).
192 FTT Rules r20(1)(c).

No longer responsible

2.101   The circumstances in which a local authority is no longer responsible for a child or young person include:

- The young person reaching his or her 25th birthday: The Code notes that support should generally cease at the end of the academic year to allow young people to complete their course of study.[193] Further, CFA 2014 s46 empowers a local authority to continue to maintain an EHC plan for a young person until the end of the academic year during which the young person attains the age of 25.[194]
- The young person aged 16 or over leaves education to take up paid employment (including employment with training but excluding apprenticeships).[195]
- The young person enters higher education.[196]
- A young person aged 18 or over leaves education and no longer wishes to engage in further learning.[197]
- The child or young person has moved to another local authority area (on which see paras 2.111–2.117 below).

2.102   A local authority does not cease to be responsible for a child or young person because he or she has been given a custodial sentence. The details of the local authority's duties in these circumstances are set out in chapter 5 below.

No longer necessary: children and young people under the age of 18

2.103   A local authority may not cease to maintain an EHC plan for a child or young person under the age of 18 unless it determines that it is no longer necessary for special educational provision to be made for the child or young person in accordance with an EHC plan.[198]

2.104   Where a child or young person is not in education or training, the local authority must not cease to maintain the EHC plan, unless it decides that it is no longer necessary for special educational provision to be made for the child or young person in accordance with an

---

193 Code, para 9.207.
194 An 'academic year' is defined in SEND Regs reg 46(1).
195 Code, para 9.201.
196 Code, para 9.201.
197 Code, para 9.201.
198 SEND Regs reg 29(1).

EHC plan.[199] The Code observes that the 'focus of support should be to re-engage the young person in education or training as soon as possible and the local authority must review the EHC plan and amend it as appropriate to ensure that the young person continues to receive education or training'.[200]

No longer necessary: young people over the age of 18

2.105   When deciding whether to cease to maintain an EHC plan, the same test applies to young people over the age of 18 as to children and young people under the age of 18: does the young person no longer require the special educational provision specified in the EHC plan?[201] A local authority considering whether to cease to maintain the EHC plan of a young person over the age of 18 must have regard to a further consideration, namely whether the educational or training outcomes specified in the plan have been achieved.[202]

2.106   Further, when a young person over the age of 18 ceases to attend the educational institution specified in his or her EHC plan, so he or she is no longer receiving education or training, the local authority may not cease to maintain the EHC plan unless it has conducted an annual review and either:

• ascertained that the young person does not wish to return to education or training (either at the institution specified in the EHC plan or otherwise); or

• determined that returning to education or training would not be appropriate for the young person.[203]

2.107   In *Buckinghamshire CC v SJ*, UT Judge Jacobs considered whether the FTT had erred in concluding that a young person over the age of 18 did require the special educational provision in the EHC plan.[204]

---

199 SEND Regs reg 29(2); Code, para 9.202.

200 Code, para 9.202.

201 CFA 2014 s45(2).

202 CFA 2014 s45(3). See also the non-statutory (ie non-binding) guidance issued by the Department for Education on 21 February 2017, *SEND: 19- to 25-year olds' entitlement to EHC plans.*

203 SEND Regs reg 30(1); and see Code, para 9.203.

204 [2016] UKUT 254, [2016] ELR 350 at para 30. See also *Gloucestershire County Council v SH* [2017] UKUT 85 (AAC) in which UT Judge Mitchell held that the absence of evidence from a young person about the educational programme she wished to pursue did not prevent the FTT from lawfully concluding that an EHC plan was necessary, see para 48(a). The judge rejected an argument by the local authority that it had no duty to educate young people over compulsory school age, see para 48(f).

He rejected the submission that 'the attainment of qualifications is an essential element of education'. He noted that for many of those to whom the CFA 2014 applied, attaining any qualifications at all was not an option. That did not mean that such young people did not require, or would not benefit from, special educational provision.

2.108   Where, following a review, the local authority ascertains that the young person wishes to return to education or training (either at the educational institution specified in the EHC plan or any other) and the local authority considers that it is appropriate for the young person to return to education or training, the local authority must amend the EHC plan as necessary (following the processes laid down in SEND Regs reg 22).[205]

Ceasing to maintain: the procedure

2.109   Where a local authority is considering ceasing to maintain a child or young person's EHC plan, it must:

- inform the child's parent or the young person that it is considering ceasing to maintain the child or young person's EHC plan;
- consult the child's parent or the young person;
- consult the headteacher, principal or equivalent person at the educational institution named in the EHC plan.[206]

2.110   Where, following that consultation, the local authority determines to cease to maintain the child or young person's EHC plan, it must notify the child's parent or the young person, the institution named in the child's EHC plan and the responsible commissioning body of that decision.[207] The local authority must also notify the child's parent or the young person of their right to appeal.[208]

Transfer of EHC plans between local authorities[209]

Generally

2.111   In broad terms, a local authority in England will be responsible for a child or young person (and hence for supporting his or her SEN) if he or she is in the authority's area and has been identified as someone who has or may have SEN, or has been brought to the local

---

205 SEND Regs reg 30(2).
206 SEND Regs reg 31(1).
207 SEND Regs reg 31(2).
208 SEND Regs reg 31(3).
209 See Code, paras 9.157–9.165.

authority's attention by any person as someone who has or may have special educational needs.[210]

2.112 SEND Regs reg 15 makes provision for when a child or young person in respect of whom an EHC plan is maintained moves from the area of the local authority which maintains the EHC plan ('the old authority') into the area of another local authority ('the new authority').[211] The old authority shall transfer the EHC plan to the new authority on the day of the move (or where it did not become aware of the move at least 15 working days prior to the move, within 15 working days beginning with the date on which it did become aware).[212]

2.113 From the date of transfer the EHC plan is to be treated as if it had been made by the new authority on the date on which it was made by the old authority and must be maintained by the new authority.[213]

2.114 Within six weeks of the date of the transfer, the new authority must inform the child's parent or the young person of the following:[214]

- that the EHC plan has been transferred;
- whether it proposes to make an EHC needs assessment; and
- when it proposes to review the EHC plan.

2.115 The new authority must carry out an 'annual' review of the EHC plan before whichever is the later of: the period of 12 months beginning with the date of the making of the EHC plan or the date of the last review; or the period of three months beginning with the date of the transfer.[215]

2.116 If the new authority decides to conduct an EHC needs assessment there is a limit on the further evidence that may be obtained where: (a) the old authority has supplied the new authority with advice obtained in pursuance of the previous assessment; and (b) the person providing that advice, the old authority and the child's parent or young person are satisfied that the advice obtained in pursuance of previous assessment is sufficient for the purpose of the new authority arriving at a satisfactory assessment. In these circumstances the new authority must not seek further advice.[216]

210 CFA 2014 s24. For the meaning of 'in the authority's area', see para 9.4 below.
211 SEND Regs reg 15(1).
212 SEND Regs reg 15(2).
213 SEND Regs reg 15(3).
214 SEND Regs reg 15(4).
215 SEND Regs reg 15(5).
216 SEND Regs reg 15(3)(b).

2.117   Finally, where by virtue of the transfer the new authority comes under a duty to arrange the chid or young person's attendance at a school or other institution specified in the EHC plan but in light of the child or young person's move that attendance is no longer practicable, the new authority must arrange for the child or young person's attendance at another school or institution appropriate for him or her until such time as it is possible to amend the EHC plan.[217]

Change of responsible commissioning body[218]

2.118   Where, by virtue of a child or young person's move, another commissioning body becomes the responsible commissioning body for that child or young person, the original responsible commissioning body must notify the new responsible commissioning body of the move on the day of the move (or where it did not become aware of the move at least 15 working days prior to the move, within 15 working days beginning with the date on which it did become aware).[219]

2.119   Where it is not practicable for the new responsible commissioning body to arrange the healthcare provision specified in the EHC plan, it must within 15 working days beginning with the date on which it first became aware of the move, request that the new local authority makes an EHC needs assessment or reviews the EHC plan. Where the new local authority receives such a request it must comply with it.[220]

Personal budgets (including direct payments)

Introduction

2.120   The Code defines a 'personal budget' as 'an amount of money identified by the local authority to deliver provision set out in an EHC plan where the parent or young person is involved in securing that provision'.[221] Personal budgets are optional, but if a local authority maintains an EHC plan, or is securing the preparation of an EHC plan for a child or young person, the local authority must prepare a

---

217 SEND Regs reg 15(6).
218 See Code, paras 9.163–9.165.
219 SEND Regs reg 15(7).
220 SEND Regs reg 15(8). See also SEND Regs reg 16 which covers the situation in which the identity of the responsible commissioning body changes, but the identity of the responsible local authority does not.
221 Code, para 9.95, and see CFA 2014 s49(2).

personal budget for him or her if asked to do so by the child's parent or the young person.[222]

2.121 The Code identifies four ways in which a personal budget can be delivered:[223]

(1) direct payments: where individuals receive the cash to contract, purchase and manage services themselves;

(2) an arrangement where the local authority, school or college holds the funds and commissions the support specified in the plan (sometimes known as notional budgets);

(3) third party arrangements, where direct payments are paid to and managed by an individual or organisation on behalf of the child's parent or the young person;

(4) a combination of each.

2.122 A direct payment is therefore only one way of delivering a personal budget. Consequentially, it is important to distinguish between a personal budget and a direct payment. There are important differences, namely:

• If a local authority maintains an EHC plan, or is securing the preparation of an EHC plan, there is a right to a personal budget.[224] There is no equivalent *right* to a direct payment: rather, a local authority must satisfy itself of certain matters prior to making a direct payment.

• A personal budget may include funding for special educational, health and social care provision.[225] A direct payment under the Special Educational Needs (Personal Budgets) Regulations 2014 SI No 1652 (SENPB Regs) must relate to special educational provision only (although separate direct payments for health[226]

---

222 CFA 2014 s49(1); Code, para 9.97.

223 Code, para 9.101.

224 CFA 2014 s49(1).

225 Code, para 9.99. The same paragraph adds that personal budgets should 'be focused to secure the provision agreed in the EHC plan and should be designed to secure the outcomes specified in the EHC plan'.

226 Code, paras 9.114–9.117, 9.124. Direct payments for health require the agreement of a care plan between the CCG and the recipient. This requirement can be fulfilled by sections G and J of the EHC plan, as long as it includes the information contained in the Code, para 9.124. If the healthcare provision specified in an EHC plan is secured by a direct payment, the commissioning body will be treated as having discharged its duty in CFA 2014 s42(3) to make the healthcare provision, see CFA 2014 s49(6)–(8). As to the relevant legislation and guidance governing direct payments for health provision, see National Health Service (Direct Payments) Regulations 2013 SI No 1617 and guidance produced by NHS England, *Guidance on direct payments for healthcare: understanding the regulations*, 20 March 2014.

and social care provision[227] may be made under other legislative provisions).

- Where special educational provision is made by a direct payment, the local authority will be deemed to have secured that provision for the purposes of CFA 2014 s42(2) (which places the statutory duty on a local authority to make the special educational provision in an EHC plan).[228] There is no equivalent provision in respect of personal budgets.

Information, advice and support

2.123   Where a local authority maintains an EHC plan or is securing the provision of an EHC plan for a child or young person, it must make arrangements for the provision to the child's parent or young person of the following information:[229]

- the provision for which a personal budget may be available;
- details of organisations that provide advice and assistance in connection with personal budgets; and
- the conditions which must be met before direct payments may be made.

2.124   The information should be provided as part of the Local Offer.[230] The Local Offer should include a policy on personal budgets that sets out a description of the services across education, health and social care that currently lend themselves to the use of personal budgets, how that funding will be made available, and clear and simple statements of eligibility criteria and the decision-making process.[231]

2.125   Further, local authorities must provide information about organisations that might be able to provide advice and assistance to parents and young people to make decisions about personal budgets.[232]

---

227   Code, paras 9.118, 9.123. For those aged 18 or under, see CA 1989 s17A; Community Care, Services for Carers and Children's Services (Direct Payment) (England) Regulations 2009 SI No 1887; and Department of Health, *Guidance on direct payments: for community care, services for carers and children's services*, 2009. For those aged 18 or over, see Care Act 2014 ss31–33; Care and Support (Direct Payments) Regulations 2014 SI No 2871; and Department of Health, *Care and support statutory guidance*, 2014, chapter 12.
228   CFA 2014 s49(5).
229   SENPB Regs reg 3.
230   See paras 1.39–1.44 above.
231   Code, para 9.96.
232   Code, para 9.97.

Right to a personal budget

2.126 If a local authority maintains an EHC plan, or is securing the preparation of an EHC plan for a child or young person, the local authority must prepare a personal budget for him or her if asked to do so by the child's parent or the young person.[233]

2.127 There is one exception to the right to a personal budget, namely where:[234]

- the provision is secured by the local authority by arrangements between the local authority and a third party under which the local authority pays an aggregate sum for special educational provision which includes the specified provision;
- the aggregate sum paid by the local authority under the arrangements includes a notional amount for the specified provision; and
- the notional amount cannot be disaggregated from the aggregate sum because the disaggregation: (a) would have an adverse impact on other services provided or arranged by the local authority for children or young people with an EHC plan, or (b) would not be an efficient use of the local authority's resources.

2.128 Where the exception applies, the local authority must inform the child's parent or the young person of the reasons it is unable to identify a sum of money and work with them to ensure that services are personalised through other means. Further, if there is demand from parents and young people for services that are disaggregated, this should inform future commissioning arrangements.[235]

When requests for a personal budget (including direct payments) can be made

2.129 A child's parent or a young person may make a request to a local authority for a personal budget, including a request for direct payments, at any time during the period in which the draft EHC plan is being prepared (in accordance with CFA 2014 s38), or the EHC plan is being reviewed or re-assessed (in accordance with CFA 2014 s44).[236]

233 CFA 2014 s49(1); Code, para 9.97.
234 SENPB Regs reg 4A; Code, para 9.106.
235 Code, para 9.106.
236 SENPB Regs reg 4(1); Code, para 9.98.

2.130 Where a request for direct payments has been made, a local authority must consider that request (although as noted below, it can only accede to the request where certain requirements are met).[237]

Settling and agreeing a personal budget

2.131 The Code provides that the child's parent or young person should be given an indication of the level of funding that is likely to be required to make the provision specified, or proposed to be specified in the EHC plan. An indicative figure can be identified through a resource allocation or banded funding system.[238]

2.132 The Code indicates that local authorities should agree the provision they propose to make in the EHC plan and help the child's parent or the young person to decide whether he or she wants to take up a personal budget.[239]

2.133 If the personal budget is implemented by way of a direct payment, the local authority must identify the 'agreed provision' which must be specified in the notice provided to the parent or young person under SENPB Regs reg 8(2)(b) (see para 2.142 below).[240]

2.134 Further, if the personal budget is implemented by way of a direct payment, the final amount of the direct payment specified by the local authority must be sufficient to secure the agreed provision.[241]

2.135 Where any special educational provision is to be secured by a direct payment, section J of the EHC plan must set out the special

---

237 SENPB Regs reg 4(2); Code, para 9.98.
238 There has been case-law in the community care context about the method of calculation of the indicative amount: see *R (JL) v Islington LBC* [2009] EWHC 458 (Admin), (2009) 12 CCLR 413 (per Black J at para 39); *R (Savva) v Kensington and Chelsea RLBC* [2010] EWCA Civ 1209, (2011) 14 CCLR 75 (per Maurice Kay LJ at para 7); and *R (KM) v Cambridgeshire CC* [2012] UKSC 23, (2012) 15 CCLR 374 (per Lord Wilson at para 28).
239 Code, para 9.102.
240 SENPB Regs reg 2 defines 'agreed provision' as 'the goods or services specified in the local authority's notice under regulation 8(2)(b)' of the SENPB Regs.
241 SENPB Regs reg 10(1); Code, para 9.102. The local authority can increase or reduce the amount of the direct payment provided that the local authority is satisfied that the new amount is sufficient to secure the agreed provision, see SENPB Regs reg 10(2). The local authority may reduce the amount of the direct payment where payments remain unused, and the local authority considers that it is reasonable to offset unused direct payments against the outstanding amount to be paid, see SENPB Regs reg 10(3).

educational needs to be secured by a direct payment, and the outcomes to be met by a direct payment.[242]

Persons to whom direct payments may be made

2.136   A local authority may make direct payments, as appropriate, to the child's parent, to the young person, or to a person nominated in writing by the child's parent or the young person to receive direct payments on their behalf ('a nominee').[243]

2.137   There are some limits on the persons to whom a direct payment may be made, namely:[244]

- the person must appear to the local authority to be capable of managing direct payments without assistance or with such assistance as may be available to him or her;
- the recipient must be over compulsory school age;
- the recipient must not lack capacity within the meaning of the Mental Capacity Act 2005 to consent to the making of direct payments to them or to secure the agreed provision with any direct payment; and
- the person must not be a person listed in the Schedule to the SENPB Regs (namely a person subject to specified orders imposed by the criminal courts).

Deciding whether to make direct payments (SEN)

2.138   A local authority may only make a direct payment where a request has been made, and where the local authority is satisfied that:[245]

- the recipient will use the direct payment to secure the agreed provision in an appropriate way;
- where the recipient is the child's parent or a nominee, that person will act in the best interests of the child or the young person when securing the proposed agreed provision;

242 SEND Regs reg 12(1)(j); Code, paras 9.102–9.103.
243 SENPB Regs reg 5(1). If the child's parent or young person notifies the local authority in writing that they wish to withdraw or change their nomination, the local authority must stop making direct payments to the nominee as soon as reasonably practicable and, where applicable, consider whether to make direct payments to the alternative nominee, see SENPB Regs reg 5(3). Further, SENPB Regs reg 16 makes provision for the situation in which either the child's parent or the young person lacks capacity.
244 SENPB Regs reg 5(2).
245 SENPB Regs reg 6(1); Code, para 9.123.

- the direct payments will not have an adverse impact on other services which the local authority provides or arranges for children and young people with an EHC plan which the local authority maintains; and
- securing the proposed agreed provision by direct payments is an efficient use of the local authority's resources.

2.139   Further, there are limits on the manner in which direct payments can be used:

- Direct payments can only be used to make the special educational provision specified in an EHC plan. A local authority may not make direct payments for the purpose of funding a place at a school or post-16 institution.[246]
- A local authority may not make direct payments in respect of any goods or services which are to be used or provided in a school or post-16 institution without the written consent of the head-teacher.[247] Local authorities should normally do this when they consult the institution about naming it on the child or young person's EHC plan. Further, the local authority should seek assurances from the child's parent, young person or nominee that any person employed by them, but working on school or college premises, will confirm to the policies and procedures of that institution and may write such an assurance into the conditions for receipt of the direct payment.[248]

2.140   Finally, a local authority may not make direct payments unless various conditions have been satisfied (see paras 2.141–2.143 below).

Direct payments: the conditions

2.141   Even if the local authority is satisfied: (a) the recipient is a person to whom direct payments can be made; (b) of the matters set out in para 2.138 above, the SENPB Regs set out a process by which the local

---

246 SENPB Regs reg 6(2).
247 SENPB Regs reg 9(1) (and the same applies in respect of premises at which early years education is provided, see SENPB Regs reg 9(2)).
248 Code, para 9.104; para. 9.105 makes clear that where the educational institution's agreement cannot be reached, the local authority must not go ahead with the direct payment, but that they should continue to explore other opportunities for personalisation of provision in the EHC plan (and in particular, the potential for arrangements under which the educational institution holds a notional budget with a view to involving the child's parent or young person in securing the provision).

authority must secure the agreement of the recipient to the making of direct payments, which includes agreement to any conditions imposed by the local authority.

2.142   First, the local authority must provide written notice to the recipient specifying:[249]

- the name of the child or young person in respect of whom the direct payments are to be made;
- the goods or services which are to be secured by direct payment;
- the proposed amount of the direct payments;
- any conditions on how direct payments may be spent;
- the dates for payment into the bank account approved by the local authority.

2.143   Upon receipt of this notice, the recipient[250] must notify the local authority in writing that they agree to:[251]

- receive the direct payments;
- use the direct payments only to secure the agreed provision;
- comply with any conditions on how direct payments made by spent imposed by the local authority;
- notify the local authority of any changes in circumstances which might affect the need for the agreed provision;
- use the bank account approved by the local authority solely for the purposes of direct payments;[252]
- ensure that the bank account approved by the local authority is only accessible by the recipient or any other person approved in writing by the local authority; and
- keep a record of money paid in and withdrawn from the bank account approved by the local authority and, on request, or at intervals specified by the local authority, provide the local authority

---

249 SENPB Regs reg 8(1).
250 Where the recipient is a nominee, the child's parent or the young person must provide written consent to the local authority to direct payments being used to secure the agreed provision, and the nominee must provide written confirmation to the local authority that he or she is responsible as a principal for all contractual arrangements entered into for the benefit of the child or young person and secured by means of direct payments, see SENPB Regs reg 8(4).
251 SENPB Regs reg 8(2).
252 Although this account can be for the use of direct payments for special educational provision under the SENPB Regs, and for direct payments for social care pursuant to the Community Care, Services for Carers and Children's Services (Direct Payments) (England) Regulations 2009 SI No 1887, and/or for direct payments for healthcare provision under the National Health Service (Direct Payments) Regulations 2013 SI No 1617.

with information or evidence relating to the account and the agreed provision.

Deciding not to make a direct payment

2.144   Where a local authority decides not to make a direct payment, it must inform the child's parent or the young person of its decision in writing, the reasons for its decision, and the right to request a review.[253] Where requested to do so, the local authority must review its decision. In carrying out the review, the local authority must consider any representations made by the child's parent or the young person.[254] Further, the local authority must inform the child's parent or young person of the outcome of the review in writing, and give reasons.[255]

Consequences of the local authority making a direct payment

2.145   Where a local authority makes a direct payment in respect of special educational provision, it is to be treated as having secured the special educational provision for the child or young person for the purposes of CFA 2014 s42(2).[256]

Monitor and review of direct payments

2.146   The local authority must monitor the use of direct payments by the recipient.[257] The local authority must review and monitor the making and use of direct payments at least once within the first three months of direct payments being made, and when conducting a review or re-assessment of an EHC plan (under CFA 2014 s44).[258]

---

253 SENPB Regs reg 7(a); Code para 9.107. If the CCG also decide not to make a direct payment when requested and/or social care also decide not to make a direct payment when requested, the Code suggests that the local authority and partners should consider sending a single letter setting out the reasons for the decisions: Code, para 9.109.

254 SENPB Regs reg 7(b); Code, para 9.107.

255 SENPB Regs reg 7(c); Code, para 9.107.

256 CFA 2014 s49(5).

257 SENPB Regs reg 11(1).

258 SENPB Regs reg 11(2).

2.147 Alternatively, a recipient may make a request for a local authority to review the making and use of direct payments and the local authority must then consider whether to carry out a review.[259]

2.148 When carrying out a review in either case, the local authority must consider whether:[260]

- it should continue to secure the agreed provision by means of direct payments;
- the direct payments have been used effectively;
- the amount of the direct payments continues to be sufficient to secure the agreed provision;
- it is still satisfied of the matters set out in SENPB Regs reg 6(1) (and set out at para 2.138 above); and
- the recipient has complied with the conditions set out in SENPB Regs reg 8(3).

2.149 The local authority has a number of powers after a review, namely it may:[261]

- substitute the person receiving the direct payments with a nominee, the child's parent or the young person, as appropriate (where the conditions in SENPB Regs reg 8(3) have been complied with in respect of that person);
- increase, maintain or reduce the amount of direct payments;
- require the recipient to comply with either or both of the following conditions: (a) the person must not secure a service from a particular person; (b) the person must provide such information as the local authority considers necessary;
- stop making direct payments.

2.150 Where the local authority decides to reduce the direct payment, or to stop making direct payments, SENPB Regs contain procedural requirement with which the local authority must comply.[262]

2.151 The recipient of a direct payment can require the local authority to stop making the direct payment at any time.[263]

259 SENPB Regs reg 11(4).
260 SENPB Regs reg 11(3) and (4)(b).
261 SENPB Regs reg 11(5).
262 See SENPB Regs regs 12 and 14 respectively. The local authority also has the power to require the recipient to repay all or part of the direct payments in the circumstances set out in SENPB Regs reg 13.
263 SENDPB Regs reg 14(1)(a).

Transition: when a child becomes a young person

2.152   Where a child in respect of whom direct payments are being made becomes a young person, the local authority must take reasonable steps to ascertain whether the young person consents to receive direct payments.[264]

2.153   The legislation contemplates three possibilities on transition:

(1) Where the young person has notified the local authority in writing that he or she wishes to receive direct payments, the local authority must make direct payments where the making of such payments is in accordance with SENPB Regs regs 5 and 6.[265]

(2) Where the young person consents in writing that the local authority continue to make direct payments to the young person's parent or nominee, the local authority must do so.[266]

(3) Where the young person notifies the local authority in writing that they do not consent to the making of direct payments, the local authority must stop direct payments as soon as reasonably practicable.[267]

Disputes

2.154   There is no right of appeal against a decision not to provide a direct payment or against the amount of a direct payment. A challenge to this decision must be brought by way of judicial review in the Administrative Court (or by a complaint under the local authority's complaints procedure).

---

264 SENPB Regs reg 15(1).
265 SENPB Regs reg 15(2).
266 SENPB Regs reg 15(3).
267 SENPB Regs reg 15(4).

Content of EHC plans

continued

Key points

Special educational needs and provision

- An education, health and care (EHC) plan must contain (among other things) a description of the child or young person's needs (section B) and the special educational provision required for the child or young person (sections F and I).
- The special educational provision for a child must be 'appropriate'.
- Special educational provision is provision that is additional to, or different from, that made generally for others of the same age in mainstream schools institutions. Special educational provision for a child under the age of two is educational provision of any kind.
- Some provision is unequivocally educational; some is unequivocally non-educational. Between these two categories is a grey area of provision which might, depending on the facts of the case, be either.
- The provision in section F must be detailed and specific so that there is no room for doubt as to what has been decided in any given case. The provision should usually be quantified (in terms of the type, hours, frequency of support and level of expertise).

Section I – the name of the school or institution and/or the name or type of school or institution to be attended by the child or young person

- Where a parent or young person requests one of the following types of school, the local authority will name it in section I of the EHC plan unless one of the exceptions applies: a maintained school; a maintained nursery school; an academy; a further education institution in England; a non-maintained special school; or an approved independent special school or post-16 institution is named in section I of the EHC plan.
- The relevant exceptions are: (a) the school or institution requested is unsuitable for the age, ability, aptitude or special educational needs (SEN) of the child or young person; (b) compliance with the preference would be incompatible with the provision of efficient education for others; and (c) compliance with the preference would be incompatible with the efficient use of resources.

continued

- The EHC plan must provide for the child or young person to be educated in a mainstream school unless that is incompatible with: (a) the wishes of the parent or the young person; or (b) the provision of efficient education for others. There is no exception where the local authority (or First-tier Tribunal (FTT)) forms the view that a mainstream school or post-16 institution cannot provide for the child's SEN.
- Special educational provision can be made otherwise than at a school, but only where the local authority (or the FTT) is satisfied that it would be inappropriate for the provision to be made in a school or post-16 institution.
- Where an EHC plan names a residential school, the local authority must pay any fees in respect of the education or training provided. The local authority must also pay any fees in respect of board and lodging if it is satisfied that the special educational provision cannot be provided at the school or institution unless the boarding and lodging are provided.
- Unless required to name a specific school by the exercise of parental preference, the local authority may name a type of school or institution in section I of the EHC plan.
- Where a child or young person already attends the school or institution for which the parent or young person has expressed a preference, the local authority or FTT must evaluate the difficulties for the child or young person in moving from that school or institution.
- The local authority may make provision for a child or young person for whom it maintains an EHC plan to attend a school or institution outside of England and Wales which specialises in providing for children or young people with SEN.
- In drafting an EHC plan the local authority and the FTT must have regard to the views of the child or young person. The weight to be attached to those views is a matter for the local authority (or the FTT on an appeal).

Health and social care needs and provision

- An EHC plan must include the child or young person's healthcare needs which relate to his or her SEN (section C) and his or her social care needs which relate to his or her SEN or to a disability (section D).

- The EHC plan must include any healthcare provision reasonably required by the learning difficulties and disabilities which result in the child or young person having SEN (section G) and any social care provision which must be provided under CSDPA 1970 s2 (or which is reasonably required as a result of the child or young person having SEN) (sections H1 and H2).
- The FTT has no jurisdiction to hear appeals against the description of healthcare or social care needs, or against the description of healthcare or social care provision in the EHC plan.

Aspirations and outcomes

- An EHC plan must contain the views, interests and aspirations of the child and his parents or the young person.
- An EHC plan must also specify the outcomes sought for a child or young person.

Special educational needs and provision

Introduction and overall approach

3.1 CFA 2014 s37(2) requires, among other things, an education, health and care (EHC) plan to contain a description of the child or young person's special educational needs (SEN) (section B) and the special educational provision required for the child or young person (sections F and I). These were previously included in part 2 (need), part 3 (provision) and part 4 (school or type of school) respectively of a statement of SEN.

3.2 The description of a child or young person's SEN (section B), and the identification of the special educational provision required (sections F and I), have been likened to a medical diagnosis and prescription.[1] In *Learning Trust v SENDIST and MP*, Andrew Nicol QC, sitting as a Deputy Judge of the High Court, stated:[2]

> It is important then to identify or diagnose the need before going on to prescribe the educational provision to which that need gives rise, and only once the necessary educational provision has been identified can one specify the institution or type of institution which is appropriate to provide it.

---

1 *R v Secretary of State for Education and Science ex p E* [1993] 2 FCR 752.
2 [2007] EWHC 1634, [2007] ELR 658 at para 42.

3.3   In *S v City of Swansea* Sullivan J stated that the mischief to be avoided was 'putting the cart before the horse', but accepted that once section B and section F had been settled, the 'prescription in [section F] may be 'informed' by what is actually available at a particular school'.[3]

3.4   Further, section F ought to mirror section B. Thus provision in section F must be specified for 'each and every need specified in Section B'.[4]

3.5   For these reasons, the starting point for the FTT on an appeal will always be to correctly identify the child or young person's special educational needs, before going on to identify the special educational provision required.

3.6   The local authority must make provision that is 'appropriate' to the needs of the child (that which is 'adequate' will not suffice).[5] It follows that a local authority is not obliged to make the 'best possible education. Parliament has imposed an obligation to meet the needs of the child and not more'.[6] 'Need' in this context means 'what is reasonably required'.[7]

Section B: special educational needs

3.7   A child or young person has SEN if he or she has a learning difficulty or disability[8] which calls for special educational provision to be

3   [2000] ELR 315 at 322H-323A. See also *A v Barnet LBC* [2003] EWHC 3368, [2004] ELR 293 per Lloyd Jones J at para 17; *Learning Trust v SENDIST and MP* [2007] EWHC 1634, [2007] ELR 658 per Andrew Nicol QC sitting as a Deputy Judge of the High Court at para 42.

4   See Department for Education and Department of Health, *Special educational needs and disability code of practice: 0 to 25 years. Statutory guidance for organisations which work with and support children and young people who have special educational needs or disabilities*, current version published 2015 ('the Code'), table at para 9.69 (in the row describing the content of section F). See also *R v Secretary of State for Education ex p E* [1992] 1 FLR 377.

5   *C v Buckinghamshire CC* [1999] ELR 179, per Thorpe LJ at 189; *NM v Lambeth LBC* [2011] UKUT 449 (AAC), [2012] ELR 224 per UT Judge Marks at para 15.

6   *S v Special Educational Needs Tribunal* [1995] 1 WLR 1627, per Latham J at 1638. See also *R v Surrey CC ex p H* (1984) 83 LGR 219 and *R v Cheshire CC ex p C* [1998] ELR 66.

7   *R (A) v Hertfordshire CC* [2006] EWHC 3248 (Admin), [2007] ELR 95 at para 25 per HHJ Gilbart QC sitting as a Deputy Judge of the High Court (and see the judge's comment that a child is 'not entitled to "Rolls Royce" provision', at para 25). See also *Devon CC v OH* [2016] UKUT 292 (AAC), [2016] ELR 377 per UT Judge Ward at paras 30–38.

8   CFA 2014 s83(3) provides that a child or young person has a disability for the purposes of CFA 2014 Part 3 if he or she has a disability for the purposes of the EA 2010 (see EA 2010 s6) and see para 6.38–6.74 below.

made for him or her. A child of compulsory school age[9] or a young person has a learning difficulty or disability if he or she has a significantly greater difficulty in learning than the majority of others of the same age, or has a disability which prevents or hinders him or her from making use of facilities of a kind generally provided for others of the same age in mainstream schools or mainstream post-16 institutions.[10]

3.8　　In *Bromley LBC v SENDIST* Sedley LJ stated that a learning difficulty is 'anything inherent in the child which makes learning significantly harder for him than for most others or which hinders him from making use of ordinary school facilities'.[11]

3.9　　Section B of a child or young person's EHC plan must specify all of the child or young person's identified SEN.[12] Further, SEN may include needs for health and social care provision that are treated as special educational provision because they educate or train the child or young person (see para 3.15 below).

3.10　　Children and young people's SEN often arise in the following broad areas of need:[13]

a) communication and interaction;
b) cognition and learning;
c) social, emotional and mental health; and
d) sensory and/or physical needs.

3.11　As the Code makes clear, however, these are just an overview of the range of needs that children and young people may have: 'individual children often have needs that cut across all these areas and their needs may change over time. For instance speech, language and communication needs can also be a feature of a number of other areas of SEN, and children with an autism spectrum disorder may have needs across all areas'.[14]

9　EA 1996 s8 contains the definition of 'compulsory school age'. Very broadly, a child will be of compulsory school age between the age of five and the end of the school year during which he or she turns 16.

10　CFA 2014 s20(2). A child who is not of compulsory school age has a learning difficulty or a disability if he or she is likely to be within subsection (2) when of compulsory school age (or would be likely, if no special educational provision were made); see CFA 2014 s20(3).

11　[1999] ELR 260 at 295. It does not matter if the behaviour said to give rise to a learning difficulty is learned, see *H v A London Borough* [2015] UKUT 316, [2015] ELR 503 per UT Judge Ward at paras 23–26.

12　Code, table at para 9.69 (in the row describing the content of section B).

13　Code, paras 5.32 and 6.28–6.35.

14　Code, paras 5.33 and 6.27.

3.12   A child or young person does not have a learning difficulty or disability solely because the language (or form of language) in which he or she will be taught is different to a language (or form of language) which is or has been spoken at home.[15]

Section F: the definition of special educational provision

Generally

3.13   CFA 2014 s21(1) defines 'special educational provision', in respect of a child aged two or more or a young person, as 'educational or training provision that is additional to, or different from, that made generally for others of the same age' in mainstream schools or post-16 institutions, and in maintained nursery schools.[16] CFA 2014 s21(2) defines 'special educational provision', for a child aged under two, as meaning educational provision of any kind.

3.14   The definition of special educational provision can be contrasted with that of 'health care provision': namely 'the provision of health care services as part of the comprehensive health service in England continued under section 1(1) of the National Health Service Act 2006'.[17] Further, it can be contrasted with the definition of 'social care provision': namely 'the provision made by a local authority in the exercise of its social services functions'.[18]

3.15   CFA 2014 s21(5) provides, however, that healthcare provision or social care provision which educates or trains a child or young person is to be treated (or deemed) as special educational provision (instead of as healthcare provision or social care provision).[19] The FTT must consider any social care or healthcare provision in sections D and G, and whether any parts of that provision educate or train. Any parts that have that effect must be moved to section F.[20]

3.16   There are two reasons why the distinction between special educational provision, and non-educational provision, is important under the CFA 2014. First, the local authority has a duty to secure the special

---

15 CFA 2014 s20(5).

16 In *Buckinghamshire CC v HW* [2013] UKUT 470 (AAC), [2013] ELR 519 UT Judge Jacobs stated that 'made generally' meant provision that is meant for all children regardless of any SEN (see para 13).

17 CFA 2014 s21(3).

18 CFA 2014 s21(4).

19 See Code, table at para 9.69 (in the row describing the content of section F) in which it is stated that where 'health or social care provision educates or trains a child or young person, it must appear in this section' (emphasis in original).

20 *East Sussex CC v TW* [2016] UKUT 528 (AAC) per UT Judge Jacobs at para 24.

educational provision contained in section F of an EHC plan.[21] Second, the FTT only has jurisdiction to hear an appeal against the contents of an EHC plan concerning special educational provision (it has no analogous jurisdiction in respect of either health or social care needs or provision).[22]

3.17 The Court of Appeal considered the definition of the phrase 'special educational provision' in *Bromley LBC v Special Educational Needs Tribunal and others.*[23] Sedley LJ held that some provision was 'unequivocally educational', some was 'unequivocally non-educational'. Between these two categories was a grey area which might, on the particular facts of any given case, be either. Whether provision in the grey area was educational provision was a question of fact for the local authority (and on appeal, the FTT).[24]

3.18 In *DC and DC v Hertfordshire CC* the UT considered the meaning of special educational provision.[25] UT Judge Lane stated:

16. If a form of provision relates to a matter within the curriculum, there will probably be little doubt that provision is educational. Education is clearly not confined to the acquisition of knowledge such as the principles of physics or French verbs ... and even provision requiring the adaptation of a school's physical environment may constitute educational provision. An example would be the provision of a low noise or low distraction environment for a pupil with a sensory disorder.

17. Education, although it may be very wide ranging in concept, is about instruction, schooling or training, so one or more of these factors is likely to be discernible in provision which is asserted to be educational. The provision should, of course, be directly related to the pupil's learning difficulty or disability ... The provision should relate to a specified educational objective and it should be possible to see what the provision is trying to instil, teach or train the pupil to do ...

18. A few examples may be contrasted. (i) A SSEN provides mindfulness training for a pupil with an anxiety disorder. The objective is to enable the pupil to remain calm, keep focussed in class and relate to other children at playtime. Mindfulness is based on principles and practice to secure what is learned. (ii) The same pupil is also provided with cognitive behavioural therapy to teach him how to deal with

---

21 CFA 2014 s42(2).
22 CFA 2014 s51(2)(c).
23 [1999] ELR 260, 295–296. See also *A v Hertfordshire CC* [2006] EWHC 3468, [2007] ELR 95 per HHJ Gilbart QC sitting as a Deputy Judge of the High Court at para 24.
24 In *H v A LBC* [2015] UKUT 316 (AAC), [2015] ELR 503 UT Judge Ward held that whether behaviour is learned is not relevant to the question of whether educational provision was directly related to a child's learning difficulties (see paras 23–24).
25 [2016] UKUT 379 (AAC), [2017] ELR 27 per UT Judge Lane at paras 16–18.

anxiety that pops up suddenly. (iii) The pupil also undergoes hypnosis regularly to help him stop self-harming. In the first two examples, the child is receiving systematic training and learning coping strategies to help him learn in the classroom and learn to get along with fellow pupils, as a member of the school community. Both appear to be educational. In the third examples the child is being practiced upon in order to change his behaviour. His behaviour is affected subliminally. It may be thought unlikely that this would be educational provision any more than taking an anti-biotic for a sore throat.

3.19   The case-law establishes that speech and language therapy is almost always special educational provision.[26]

3.20   The position is less clear for other provision in the 'grey area'. In the experience of the authors: (a) occupational therapy is almost always treated as being special educational provision;[27] (b) physiotherapy is usually (but not always) treated as being special educational provision; and (c) counselling is sometimes treated as special educational provision.

3.21   As for provision from nurses, doctors and other medical staff, older case-law stated that the provision of nursing care is unequivocally a non-educational need.[28] More recent case-law has concluded, however, that the question is not whether the provision is medical, but whether the learning difficulty called for that provision.[29] It follows that the support of a psychiatrist might amount to special educational provision.[30]

26 *R v Lancashire CC ex p M* [1989] 2 FLR 279. See also the Code, which notes that speech and language therapy can, in principle, be either educational or non-educational provision, but provides 'since communication is so fundamental in education, addressing speech and language impairment [sic] should normally be recorded as special educational provision unless there are exceptional reasons for not doing so': see Code, para 9.74.

27 Although the older case-law is more mixed on this point (compare, for example, *R v Harrow LBC ex p M* [1997] ELR 62 and *B v Isle of Wight* [1997] ELR 279), the FTT will almost always treat occupational therapy as being educational provision unless there is clear and persuasive evidence pointing to the contrary.

28 *Bradford MBC v A* [1997] ELR 417 per Brooke J.

29 See *H v A London Borough* [2015] UKUT 316 (AAC), [2015] ELR 503 per UT Judge Ward at para 28; *DC and DC v Hertfordshire CC* [2016] UKUT 379 (AAC), [2017] ELR 27 per UT Judge Lane at paras 11–14.

30 *DC and DC v Hertfordshire CC* [2016] UKUT 379 (AAC), [2017] ELR 27 per UT Judge Lane at para 11.

3.22   Home to school transport is not a form of special educational provision.[31]

What must section F contain?

3.23   Broadly, section F will need to specify any educational provision that differs from the provision ordinarily to be expected in a mainstream school. The Code requires an EHC plan to specify 'any appropriate facilities and equipment, staffing arrangements and curriculum'.[32]

3.24   When seeking amendments to a draft EHC plan, or on an appeal to the FTT, parents and young people should consider specifying the following matters in section F (and, pursuant to paras 3.26–3.28 below, ensuring that the relevant matters are quantified):

- any modification to the application of the national curriculum;
- the need for one-to-one support (by whom and how many hours per week);
- the need for specialist teaching (by whom and how frequently);
- the qualifications and experience of teaching staff or other professionals working with the child;
- class size;
- the need for input from other professionals (for example, a speech and language therapist), the nature of the support (for example, direct or indirect,[33] and if indirect, who is to carry it out and where), and its frequency;
- the need for any specific equipment (or IT);
- the need for a waking day curriculum (see paras 3.29–3.32 below).

3.25   Section F of an EHC plan must not:

- purport to place a duty on parents to make special educational provision (in either section F or section I);[34] or
- purport to impose obligations on other public authorities.[35]

---

31   *R v Havering LBC ex p K* [1998] ELR 402, 404-405; *MM and DM v Harrow LBC* [2010] UKUT 395 (AAC) per UT Judge Jacobs at paras 27, 29; *Staffordshire CC v JM* [2016] UKUT 246 (AAC), [2016] ELR 307 per UT Judge Lane at paras 24–27.

32   Code, table at para 9.69 (in the row describing the content of Section F).

33   Direct therapy refers to therapy that is provided by a professional therapist. Indirect therapy refers to a programme of therapy designed by a therapist, but implemented by someone other than the professional therapist (usually a therapy assistant, or a parent or a teaching assistant).

34   See *A v Cambridgeshire CC* [2002] EWHC 2391, [2003] ELR 464.

35   In *JD v South Tyneside Council* [2016] UKUT 9 (AAC), [2016] ELR 118 UT Judge Mitchell stated that the FTT had erred in law by including the following entry

The requirement for specificity

3.26   The provision in section F must be detailed and specific so that there should be no room for doubt as to what has been decided in any particular case.[36] Further, the local authority (or the FTT on appeal) should not delegate its duty to specify the provision to any other person (for example, a therapist or member of the teaching staff), however well qualified.[37]

3.27   The provision should normally be quantified (for example, in terms of the type, hours and frequency of support and level of expertise).[38] The courts have considered when, and the extent to which, this principle applies:

- The statutory duty to specify the special educational provision does not extend to requiring the FTT to specify every single detail of the special educational provision to be made.[39]
- In *E v Newham LBC* Schiemann LJ stated that flexibility will be appropriate in some cases, and the decision as to the degree of flexibility appropriate in any given case is a question for the FTT.[40] For example, specifying minimum hours with a provision for amendment as a result of review is likely to be lawful.[41]
- Quantification will not be required if it is not in the best interest of the child.[42] Conversely, however, in *S v City and Council of Swansea and Confrey* Sullivan J said '[w]hilst there may have been a need for some flexibility, this should not have been used as an

in part 3 of the statement of SEN: 'an Occupational Therapy programme will be devised and implemented by Children's Integrated Therapies, South Tyneside NHS Trust' as it constituted healthcare provision, and not special educational provision.

36   *L v Clarke and Somerset CC* [1998] ELR 129, 136 per Laws J; *E v Newham LBC* [2003] ELR 286 (CA); *JD v South Tyneside Council* [2016] UKUT 9 (AAC) per UT Judge Mitchell at paras 3–11. See also the Code, table at para 9.69 (in the row describing the content of section F).

37   *E v Newham LBC* [2003] ELR 286 (CA) per Schiemann LJ at para 64.

38   See Code, table at para 9.69 (in the row describing the content of section F). See also *L v Clarke and Somerset CC* [1998] ELR 129, 136 ('very often a specification of hours per week will no doubt be necessary and there will be a need for that to be done').

39   *E v Newham LBC* [2003] ELR 286 (CA) per Schiemann LJ at para 64.

40   [2003] ELR 286 (CA) per Schiemann LJ at para 64. On the facts of *Newham* the tribunal was entitled to determine that the individual education plan referred to in Part 3 of the statement of SEN be determined not by it, but by the special school in accordance with the therapists.

41   *E v Newham LBC* [2003] ELR 286 (CA) at para 64.

42   *R (IPSEA Ltd) v Secretary of State for Education and Schools* [2003] ELR 393 per Schiemann LJ at para 14.

excuse for lack of specificity where detail could reasonably have been provided'.[43]

- The FTT may be required to ensure greater specification in section F where the child is to be placed in a mainstream school.[44] Conversely, in the experience of the authors, the FTT is usually more willing to accept a degree of flexibility where the school named in section I is a special school. In *East Sussex CC v TW* UT Judge Jacobs declined to lay down as a general proposition that flexibility was permissible when provision was being made at a special school, although it was 'a factor to be taken into account that may in an appropriate case permit more flexibility than when a mainstream school is involved'.[45]

3.28   Section F of EHC plans can refer to arrangements as between the local authority and the school for funding the provision (but not as an alternative to specifying or quantifying it), but in doing so the local authority cannot alter its legal duty to secure, by payment for, the provision.[46]

Residential placement or waking day curriculum

3.29   A 'waking day' curriculum (or 24-hour curriculum) may be required where a child or young person's SEN mean that he or she is unlikely to generalise skills from the classroom to other contexts, such that he or she requires a consistent approach that extends beyond the normal school day.[47]

3.30   The FTT must ask whether the child or young person's 'need for a consistent programme was such that his education could not reasonably be provided unless he was accommodated on the site where he was educated'.[48]

---

43 [2000] ELR 315, per Sullivan J at 328.
44 *E v Newham LBC* [2003] ELR 286 (CA) at para 65.
45 [2016] UKUT 528 (AAC) at para 41.
46 In *R v Oxfordshire CC ex p P* [1996] ELR 153 Laws J held that it was lawful for the local authority to agree with the school that the school should make some of the provision from its own budget, but he indicated that if the school refused to apply its budget to the cost of making provision, the local authority would immediately have to meet the full cost (at 159). See also *R v Hillingdon LBC ex p Governing Body of Queensmead School* [1997] ELR 331 per Collins J at 347.
47 See *Hammersmith and Fulham LBC v JH* [2012] UKUT 328 (AAC) per UT Judge Lane at paras 18–19.
48 *Hampshire CC v JP* [2009] UKUT 239 (AAC), [2010] ELR 413 at para 29.

3.31   The FTT's focus must, however, be on whether the child or young person requires *educational* programmes that extend beyond the ordinary school day. A requirement of consistency of approach during and after school hours will not necessarily mean that a child or young person has an *educational* need for *educational* provision that continue after the ordinary school day.[49] The FTT must, therefore, make very careful findings of fact as to the educational need that requires a waking day curriculum, and the educational programmes that are required as a result.[50]

3.32   Further, the FTT must be careful to distinguish between an *educational* need on the one hand, and a *social care* need on the other. In *H v East Sussex CC* the Court of Appeal held that the provision of carers was not the provision of education.[51]

The time period for assessing 'appropriateness'

3.33   The local authority (and the FTT on appeal) must look to the immediate future and not simply address the issues at the stage when the EHC plan is drawn up (or at the time the appeal is lodged). The Code states that 'EHC plans should be forward looking – for example, anticipating, planning and commissioning for important transition points in a child or young person's life, including planning and preparation for their transition to adult life'.[52]

3.34   In *Wilkins v Goldthorpe and Coventry CC*[53] Kay J held that a tribunal had erred in law in only considering placement for the final term of primary education. He stated: 'if by the time of the hearing there is but a short time left of the primary education ... the tribunal is bound to reach a conclusion as to the mode beyond that very short period and look to the future needs of the child'.[54]

---

49 *Learning Trust v SENDIST and MP* [2007] EWHC 1634, [2007] ELR 658, per Andrew Nicol QC sitting as a Deputy Judge of the High Court at paras 40–44. See also *T v Hertfordshire CC* [2004] EWCA Civ 927, [2005] LGR 262.

50 See *Hammersmith and Fulham LBC v JH* [2012] UKUT 328 (AAC) at para 23 per UT Judge Lane.

51 [2009] EWCA Civ 249, [2009] ELR 161 at para 48. See also *Bedfordshire CC v Haslam* [2008] EWHC 1070 (Admin), [2008] ELR 333; *The Learning Trust v MP* [2007] EWHC 1634, [2007] ELR 658 per Andrew Nicol QC sitting as a Deputy Judge of the High Court at para 43.

52 Code, at para 9.61.

53 [1998] ELR 345.

54 [1998] ELR 345, 349. See also *OR v Ealing LBC* [2012] UKUT 211 (AAC), [2012] ELR 436 per UT Judge Williams at paras 31-34.

Section I – the name of the school or institution and/or the name or type of school or institution to be attended by the child or young person

Introduction: the basic principles

3.35   When determining which school or educational institution to name in section I of an EHC plan, the starting point is the preference of the parent or young person. The type of school for which a preference is expressed will, however, affect the weight which the local authority must give the preference.

3.36   If a parent or young person expresses a preference for a specific type of school (referred to below as a 'qualifying school'), CFA 2014 s39(3) contains a presumption that a local authority will name the school requested by the child's parent or a young person in section I unless certain exceptions apply.[55] The exceptions are as follows:

- the school or institution requested is unsuitable for the age, ability, aptitude or special educational needs of the child or young person concerned;
- compliance with the preference would be incompatible with the provision of efficient education for others; or
- compliance with the preference would be incompatible with the efficient use of resources.[56]

3.37   As explained below, even if one of the exceptions apply so as to defeat parental preference, the local authority (or the FTT on appeal) must still comply with EA 1996 s9, and have regard to the general principle that pupils are to be educated in accordance with the wishes of their parents.

3.38   If the parent or young person expresses a preference for a non-qualifying school (for example, an independent mainstream school) there is no statutory presumption that the school will be named. Rather, the local authority (or the FTT on appeal) must only comply with EA 1996 s9, and have regard to the general principle that pupils are to be educated in accordance with the wishes of their parents.

---

55   The 'qualifying schools' are those listed within CFA 2014 s38(3), ie a maintained school, a maintained nursery school, an academy, an institution within the further education sector in England, a non-maintained special school or an institution approved by the secretary of state under CFA 2014 s41 (independent special schools and special post-16 institutions).

56   CFA 2014 s39(4). This provision is in materially identical terms to EA 1996 Sch 27 para 3.

3.39   In all cases in which there is a dispute as to which school should be named, the FTT's starting point will be to ask whether each of the competing schools is appropriate to meet the child's needs. As with section F, there is no requirement for the 'optimum available provision'; all that is required is appropriate provision.[57]

3.40   Assessment of whether a school is appropriate ought to follow from the identification of the child or young person's special educational needs in section B, and the special educational provision required to meet those needs in section F. In *C v Buckinghamshire CC* Thorpe LJ stated that to 'determine if the school is appropriate, an assessment must be made both of what it offers and what the child needs. Unless what the school offers matches what the child needs, it is unlikely to be appropriate'.[58]

The approach of the FTT on an appeal

3.41   On appeal to the FTT, where the parent or young person has sought the naming of a qualifying school in section I of the EHC plan, the approach of the FTT should be as follows:

-   Is each school appropriate to meet the child's needs?
-   If the local authority school is inappropriate, the FTT will normally name the school proposed by the parent or young person.[59]
-   If the parental school is not appropriate, the first exception in CFA 2014 s39(4) applies to defeat parental preference (namely that the

---

57   See *R v Surrey CC Education Committee ex p H* (1984) 83 LGR 219; *R v Cheshire CC ex p C* (1997) 95 LGR 299, 313 per Sedley J (as he then was) ('there is nothing in the statutory scheme which calls upon the local education authority to specify the optimum available provision and much in its general duty of financial husbandry to entitle it to choose the least expensive of the appropriate options').

58   [1999] ELR 179, per Thorpe LJ at 189.

59   There is some case-law to suggest that the FTT should not in these circumstances name a school or provision that offered more than the child or young person requires by way of special educational provision, and that a FTT should offer the local authority an opportunity to identify a fall-back position (ie a less expensive school or placement than that requested by the parent or young person) see *Hereford and Worcester CC v Lane* [1988] ELR 319. In *Bromley v SENT* [1999] ELR 260, however, Sedley LJ rejected an argument by the local authority that it ought to have had an opportunity to identify a fall back placement. See also *Hammersmith and Fulham LBC v Pivcevic* [2006] ELR 594 per Stanley Burnton J at para 62 ('if a considerable amount of money turns on a decision of the Tribunal it is incumbent on the local authority to prepare for and conduct its case with greater care'); and *Rhondda Cyon Taff CC v SENT* [2001] EWHC 823 (Admin), [2002] ELR 290 per Newman J at paras 10–14.

school or institution requested is unsuitable for the age, ability, aptitude of SEN of the child or young person concerned).

- If both schools are appropriate, the FTT will need to consider whether acceding to the preference of the parent or young person would fall within either of the remaining exceptions in CFA 2014 s39(4) (incompatibility with the provision of efficient education for others, or incompatibility with the efficient use of resources). If neither exception applies, the FTT should name the school preferred by the parent or young person.
- Where any of the exceptions in CFA 2014 s39(4) apply to defeat parental preference, the FTT must consider the obligation in EA 1996 s9. The FTT must consider CFA 2014 s39(3) and EA 1996 s9 separately: the two distinct tests must not be collapsed.[60]

3.42 On appeal to the FTT, where the parent or young person has sought the naming of a non-qualifying school in section I of the EHC plan, the approach of the FTT should be as follows:

- Is each school appropriate to meet the child's needs?
- If the local authority school is inappropriate, the FTT will normally name the school proposed by the parent or young person. Conversely, if the school proposed by the parent or young person is inappropriate, the FTT will normally name the school proposed by the local authority.
- If both schools are appropriate, the FTT must consider the obligation in EA 1996 s9.

3.43 These basic tests are explained in more detail as are the various practical and legal issues that might arise in respect of section I.

EA 1996 s9

3.44 EA 1996 s9 (which was not repealed by the CFA 2014) provides:

> In exercising or performing all their respective powers and duties under the Education Acts, the Secretary of State and local authorities shall have regard to the general principle that pupils are to be educated in accordance with the wishes of their parents, so far as that is compatible with the provision of efficient instruction and training and the avoidance of unreasonable public expenditure.

3.45 EA 1996 s9 requires only that the local authority 'have regard' to the general principle that pupils are to be educated in accordance with the wishes of their parents subject amongst other things to unreasonable

60 See *Ealing LBC v SENDIST* [2008] ELR 183 per Plender J at paras 14–15.

public expenditure (as compared to CFA 2014 s39(3) which places a duty on the local authority to name a requested school or institution unless, for example, it would be incompatible with the efficient use of resources). It has been described as being 'not a strong provision'.[61]

3.46   The weakness of EA 1996 s9 is illustrated by the following. Even if the FTT concludes that the naming of the school requested by the parent or the young person would not be incompatible with the provision of efficient instruction, and would not constitute unreasonable public expenditure, the parental preference under EA 1996 s9 is not determinative. It is merely something to which regard is to be had. As Denning LJ stated in *Watt v Kesteven CC*,[62] section 9:

> ... does not say that pupils must in all cases be educated in accordance with the wishes of their parents. It only lays down a general principle to which the county council must have regard. This leaves it open to the county council to have regard to other things as well, and also to make exceptions to the general principle if it thinks fit to do so.

3.47   It follows that where there are two schools appropriate to meet the needs of a child or young person, but the FTT considers that one is markedly more suitable than the other for the child's needs, the FTT is not obliged by EA 1996 s9 to give effect to the parent's choice for what it regards as being the less suitable of the two schools.[63]

Provision of efficient education to others

3.48   A preference expressed by a child's parent or a young person for a particular school or institution pursuant to CFA 2014 s38(2) may be defeated where compliance with the preference would be incompatible with the provision of efficient education for others.

3.49   The CFA 2014 does not define 'efficient education'. In *NA v Barnet LBC*[64] UT Judge Mesher stated that an efficient education did not connote the very highest desirable standard or the very basic minimum, but something in between, and incompatibility with the provision of efficient education did not entail no meaningful education being provided at all. Similarly, the Code defines 'efficient education' as meaning 'providing for each child or young person a suitable,

---

61 *CM v Bexley LBC* [2011] UKUT 215 (AAC), [2011] ELR 413 per UT Judge Ward at para 47.

62 [1955] 1 QB 408, 424.

63 *C v Buckinghamshire CC* [1999] ELR 179, 331 per Sedley LJ and see also *CM v Bexley LBC* [2011] UKUT 215 (AAC), [2011] ELR 413 per UT Judge Ward at para 51.

64 [2010] UKUT 180 (AAC), [2010] ELR 617 at paras 33–34.

appropriate education in terms of their age, ability, aptitude and any special educational needs they may have'.[65]

3.50 The Code provides that the reference to 'others' in CFA 2014 s39(4)(b)(i) is 'intended to mean the children and young people with whom the child or young person with an EHC plan will directly come into contact with on a regular day-to-day basis'.[66]

3.51 As to when it would be 'incompatible' with the provision of efficient education, in *R (Hampshire CC) v SENDIST*[67] Stadlen J held that the legislative provisions required the FTT to do more than simply conclude that the admission of the child to the school would have an adverse impact on the children with whom he was to be educated. Rather, the FTT had to ask itself whether the effect of the child attending the school, and any adverse impact on the efficient education of other children with whom he would be educated, 'would be so great as to be incompatible with the provision of efficient education'.[68]

Efficient use of resources/unreasonable public expenditure

3.52 Where a local authority opposes the naming of a school preferred by the parent or young person on the grounds of the cost of the preferred place, the following principles apply (and each are dealt with in turn below):

- The starting point is to ask whether naming the parental school would be incompatible with the efficient use of resources pursuant to CFA 2014 s39(4).
- Even where the duty in CFA 2014 s39(3) is displaced as it would be incompatible with the efficient use of resources (or indeed any of the other factors in subsection 39(4)), the FTT must separately consider the obligation in EA 1996 s9.

Efficient use of resources

3.53 The starting point, CFA 2014 s39(4), itself requires the FTT to undertake a two-stage process:

---

65 Code, para 9.79.
66 Code, para 9.79.
67 [2009] EWHC 626, [2009] ELR 371.
68 *R (Hampshire CC) v SENDIST* [2009] EWHC 626, [2009] ELR 371 per Stadlen J at para 48 (citing the decision of Gibbs J in *Essex CC v SENDIST* [2006] EWHC 1105 (Admin), [2006] ELR 452 at paras 27–32).

1) First, the FTT will need to make findings of fact as to the cost to the local authority of each school (and as to how this exercise should be carried out, see below at paras 3.55–3.65).

2) Second, if necessary because the school requested by the parent or young person costs more than the school proposed by the local authority, the FTT will have to exercise a judgment on whether, on the costs identified, placement at that school will constitute the inefficient use or resources.[69] It does not follow that any increase in costs, even an increase which goes beyond the 'merely trivial' is incompatible with the efficient use of resources.[70] Rather, the FTT must balance the statutory weight given to the parental preference against the extra cost: specifically the FTT must make a 'judgment about whether ... any extra expense in fulfilling parental wishes is ... disproportionate'.[71]

EA 1996 s9

3.54   If the FTT concludes that the parental placement would be incompatible with the efficient use of resources, it must go on to consider EA 1996 s9. Again, this requires the FTT to have made findings of fact as to the respective costs of making provision at each placement, and as a result, to make a finding as to whether placement at the school would constitute unreasonable public expenditure. As noted below at paras 3.56–3.58, this exercise may require different matters to be taken into account than in a consideration of whether expense would be incompatible with the efficient use of resources. Finally the FTT must ask whether the benefits of the placement preferred by the parents outweigh the extra cost of it to the public purse.[72] In carrying out this balancing exercise, all benefits (including educational, social care and health benefits) must be taken into account.[73]

---

69 See *Hammersmith and Fulham LBC v L* [2015] UKUT 523 (AAC), [2015] ELR 528 per UT Judge Mitchell at para 39(d).

70 *Essex CC v SENDIST* [2006] ELR 452 per Gibbs J at para 28.

71 *Essex CC v SENDIST* [2006] ELR 452 per Gibbs J at paras 31 to 33. The required comparison is between the costs of the placement and the educational advantages it would confer, and so in *EC v North Lincolnshire Council* [2015] UKUT 648 (AAC), [2016] ELR 109 the UT rejected the argument that the FTT should have taken account of the savings made previously by the authority when the child was not attending school, and the high fees of the school attended before.

72 *Oxfordshire CC v GB* [2001] EWCA Civ 1358, [2002] ELR 8 per Sedley LJ at para 16.

73 *SK v Hillingdon LBC* [2011] UKUT 71 (AAC), [2011] ELR 165.

Calculating the cost of placements

3.55   As noted above, in order to determine whether the naming of a specific school or institution would be incompatible with the efficient use of resources (CFA 2014 s39(4)) or constitute unreasonable public expenditure (EA 1996 s9) the FTT must make findings of fact as to the cost of naming the school requested by the parent or young person, and the cost of naming the local authority school.

Whose resources or whose expenditure?

3.56   The first question is whose resources or whose expenditure? The answer differs according to whether the question is posed under CFA 2014 s39(4) or under EA 1996 s9.

3.57   Under CFA 2014 s39(4) the resources to be considered are those of the local authority maintaining the EHC plan.[74] The resources of any other local authority, or any other public authority, are not to be taken into account.

3.58   Under EA 1996 s9, however, 'public expenditure' has a far wider scope. It encompasses public expenditure by all public bodies (so, for example, the social care costs of the placing authority, other local authorities, any health body etc).[75]

---

74   *B v Harrow LBC* [2000] 1 WLR 223, [2000] ELR 109 (HL) per Lord Slynn at 228–229. At the time of the decision of the House of Lords in *Harrow*, EA 1996 Sch para 3 (the predecessor to CFA 2014 s39(4)) referred to the 'local *education* authority' (LEA) (emphasis added). The Local Education Authorities and Children's Services Authorities (Integration of Functions) Order 2010 SI No 1158 (made pursuant to Education and Inspections Act 2006 s162) substituted the term 'local authority' for 'local education authority' wherever it appeared in the EA 1996. Thus in *O v Lewisham* [2007] EWHC 2130, [2007] ELR 633 (decided prior to the 2010 Order) the parties accepted that it was Lewisham's costs incurred as a local education authority only that fell to be considered when determining whether a placement at the requested school would constitute an 'inefficient use of resources'. Any social care costs occasioned by either placement were not to be considered under EA 1996 Sch 27 para 3 as they were not *local education authority* costs. It is at least arguable now that all costs incurred by a local authority fall to be considered in the calculation of resources under CFA 2014 s39(4) and not just those costs incurred in the exercise of the local authority's functions under the CFA 2014 (or any other Education Act). Compare, however, *H v Warrington BC* [2014] EWCA Civ 398, [2014] ELR 212 in which Dyson MR stated that parliament did not intend to make any substantive change to the EA 1996 by the 2010 Order (at para 38).

75   See *H v Warrington BC* [2014] EWCA Civ 398, [2014] ELR 212 per Lord Dyson MR at paras 27–37; *CM v Bexley LBC* [2011] UKUT 215 (AAC), [2011] ELR 413 per UT Judge Ward at paras 61–62.

How to calculate the cost

3.59   The second question is how to calculate the cost of each proposed school or other institution. The Court of Appeal in *Oxfordshire CC v GB* held that the basic principle is that only marginal (or additional) costs are to be taken into account. To put it another way, the relevant costs are the 'additional burden it will place on the [local authority's] annual budget'.[76] In very general terms, therefore, the 'existing costs of providing [the school] and of staffing it' are not to be included in the calculation.[77]

3.60   The method of calculating the cost of the school place varies according to the type of school. The following broad principles apply:[78]

- **Maintained mainstream school:** The Age-Weighted Pupil Unit (AWPU) will, in most cases, reflect the cost of the child or young person attending the school.[79]
- **Maintained special school with a vacancy:** The funding that the place attracted will not be treated as a marginal cost. Any 'top-up' funding for the child or young person's placement will be a marginal cost to be taken into account.[80]
- **Maintained mainstream school with reserved places for children or young people with SEN (for example, in a unit):** The funding

---

76   See *Oxfordshire CC v GB* [2001] EWCA Civ 1358, [2002] ELR 8 per Sedley LJ at para 16. In *Oxfordshire* the Court of Appeal rejected the submission that for the purposes of EA 1996 s9 the cost of sending a child to a maintained school could be ascertained by fractionalising the entire county or borough education budget (see paras 12, 15). In the subsequent decision of the Court of Appeal in *Slough BC v SENDIST* [2010] EWCA Civ 668, [2010] ELR 687 parts of Sedley LJ's judgment appeared to contradict that conclusion (see, eg, para 13). The decision of the Court of Appeal in *EH v Kent CC* [2011] EWCA Civ 709, [2011] ELR 433 re-emphasised that fractionalising the whole education budget was not the right approach (per Sullivan LJ at para 27).

77   See *Oxfordshire CC v GB* [2001] EWCA Civ 1358, [2002] ELR 8 per Sedley LJ at para 16.

78   If the local authority has a financial scheme that differs from the norm in any way, or if its per pupil funding in a mainstream school is greater than the AWPU minimum, it must bring this to the FTT's attention and it may well be that the cost of placement will need to be calculated in a different manner: see *EH v Kent CC* [2011] EWCA Civ 709, [2011] ELR 433 (per Sullivan LJ at para 31); *Hammersmith and Fulham LBC v L* [2015] UKUT 523 (AAC), [2015] ELR 528 per UT Judge Mitchell at para 128.

79   See *EH v Kent CC* [2011] EWCA Civ 709, [2011] ELR 433 (per Sullivan LJ at para 30).

80   *Hammersmith and Fulham LBC v L* [2015] UKUT 523 (AAC), [2015] ELR 528 per UT Judge Mitchell at para 126.

that the place attracted will not be treated as a marginal cost. Any 'top-up' funding for the child or young person's placement will be a marginal cost to be taken into account.[81]

- **Independent school:** The fees charged to the local authority should the school be named in section I of the EHC plan will reflect the cost of the child or the young person attending the school.[82]

3.61 To the cost of the school place, the FTT must add any additional costs of placing the child or young person at the school. According to the principle in *Oxfordshire*, such additional costs must be added only where they are marginal costs. For example:

- the cost of a teaching assistant assigned to the child or young person (but not if a teaching assistant was employed by the school already who had capacity to provide the support required in section F of the EHC plan);[83]
- the cost of home to school transport (plus an escort if necessary) unless the child or young person will be joining an existing route for which there is no additional cost to the local authority;[84]
- the cost of any specialist teacher support for the child or young person (but not if a specialist teacher was employed by the school or the local authority already who had capacity to provide the support required in section F of the EHC plan);
- the cost of providing speech and language therapy, occupational therapy or physiotherapy (any cost to the local authority will need to be taken into account under CFA 2014 s39(4) and under EA 1996 s9; any cost to a health authority will need to be considered under EA 1996 s9);[85]

---

81 *Hammersmith and Fulham LBC v L* [2015] UKUT 523 (AAC), [2015] ELR 528 per UT Judge Mitchell at para 126.

82 *Oxfordshire CC v GB* [2001] EWCA Civ 1358, [2002] ELR 8 per Sedley LJ at para 16.

83 Parents and young people should ensure that any costs provided by the local authority include the administrative costs of employing a teaching assistant (often referred to as 'on costs').

84 Parents and young people should not assume that the provision of a taxi gives rise to no marginal cost. The FTT will need evidence on the number of children in the existing taxi (and that there is a space for the child or young person), the suitability of the other children as travel companions, and whether an escort is needed (and if so, at what cost). See *W v Hillingdon LBC* [2005] EWHC 1580.

85 Parents and young people should ensure that any costs provided by the local authority include any payment to the therapist for his or her travel time where appropriate.

- any additional social care costs occasioned by the placement (possibly under CFA 2014 s39(4), see paras 3.57–3.58 above; certainly under EA 1996 s9).

3.62   A local authority will often assert that there is no marginal cost for additional provision in a maintained mainstream school or in a maintained special school as the provision can be met from the school's delegated budget. Whether a cost is marginal or not is a question of fact for the FTT. If the FTT is satisfied on the evidence before it that the provision for the child or young person can be met by the school from within the budget delegated to it by the local authority, the cost of the provision will not constitute a marginal cost.[86] The more extensive the provision proposed, however, the more critically the FTT ought to look at any such submission to see whether in fact there will need to be additional expenditure by the local authority.[87]

3.63   In respect of maintained mainstream schools, School and Early Years Finance (England) Regulations 2015 SI No 2033 reg 11(3) provides (broadly) that the school will be expected to meet the first £6,000 of SEN-related costs for each child per annum. Thereafter, any additional costs will be met by the local authority.[88] The sum of £6,000 represents a notional amount: a local authority is not required to add this amount to a school's budget share. In *Hammersmith and Fulham LBC v L*[89] UT Judge Mitchell left open the question of whether all or any costs under the £6,000 threshold ought to be treated as an additional cost for EA 1996 s9 purposes.[90]

3.64   The local authority (and the FTT on appeal) must consider the costs over the entire placement period (so, for example, if the child is starting secondary school, the costs from year 7 until the end of year 11).[91]

---

86 See *EH v Kent CC* [2011] EWCA Civ 709, [2011] ELR 433 (per Sullivan LJ at paras 24–26).

87 See, for example, *P v Worcestershire CC* [2016] UKUT 120 (AAC), [2016] ELR 194 in which the FTT, having ordered the amendment of part 3 of the statement of SEN to require 25 hours per week of teaching assistant provision, failed to consider whether that provision could be met within the £6,000 notional SEN budget or whether additional costs would be incurred, see paras 37–40.

88 See also *P v Worcestershire CC* [2016] UKUT 120 (AAC), [2016] ELR 194 per UT Judge Mitchell at paras 34(f) and (g).

89 [2015] UKUT 523 (AAC), [2015] ELR 528.

90 *Hammersmith and Fulham LBC v L* [2015] UKUT 523 (AAC), [2015] ELR 528 per UT Judge Mitchell at para 142 (and see his overview of School and Early Years Finance (England) Regulations 2013 reg 11(3) at paras 51–56).

91 See *Southampton CC v TG* [2002] ELR 698 per Sullivan J at paras 14–20.

3.65   It is necessary, finally, to deal with transport costs, which have raised two discrete issues.

1) First, it is open to a local authority to name two schools in section I of the EHC plan, and to state that the parental school has been named only on condition of the parent paying the transport costs.[92]

2) Second, in *Dudley Metropolitan BC v Shurvinton*[93] the Court of Appeal considered the proper approach of the FTT where two maintained mainstream schools were both suitable, but the local authority maintained that acceding to the parental preference would be incompatible with the efficient use of resources due to the costs of transporting the child to the parental school. Davis LJ (with whom Neuberger MR and Richards LJ agreed) stated that the FTT should carry out the following process:[94]

a) The FTT must first determine the relative transport costs of the two schools, assuming that the local authority will need to provide transport to both.

b) If the FTT determines that the cost of transport to the parental school is not incompatible with the efficient use of resources, the FTT must name the parental school (and only the parental school, even if the local authority school is also suitable).

c) If the FTT concludes that the cost of transport to the parental school is incompatible with the efficient use of resources then it should normally name the local authority school.

d) Alternatively, the FTT may name the parental school as well as the local authority school on condition that the parents pay the costs of transporting the child to the parental school.

Breakdown in the relationship between the parent or young person and the school

3.66   That the relationship between the parent or young person and the school has broken down, or become strained, is a factor to which the local authority (or on appeal, the FTT) is entitled to consider when

---

92 See *R v Essex CC ex p C* [1994] ELR 54 (a decision under the Education Act 1981); *R (M) v Sutton LBC* [2007] EWCA Civ 1205, [2008] ELR 123 per Moore-Bick LJ (with whom Pill and Richards LJJ agreed) at para 20; *Dudley MBC v Shurvinton* [2012] EWCA Civ 346, [2012] ELR 206 per Davis LJ at para 27.

93 *Dudley MBC v Shurvinton* [2012] EWCA Civ 346, [2012] ELR 206.

94 *Dudley MBC v Shurvinton* [2012] EWCA Civ 346, [2012] ELR 206 per Davis LJ at paras 32–34.

determining whether the school is appropriate. The weight to give the factor is a question for the local authority or the FTT.[95]

Parental part-payment of school fees

3.67　On occasion a parent or young person may offer to pay part of the preferred independent school fees in order to equalise the cost with the cost of a school proposed by the local authority. It is unclear what effect such an offer has on the calculation of the true cost of the school to the local authority for the purposes of CFA 2014 s39(4) or EA 1996 s9. In particular, it is not at all clear whether such an agreement is lawful or enforceable.

3.68　CFA 2014 s63 provides that where a school or institution is named in section I of an EHC plan, the local authority must pay any fees payable for the costs of education and training (and must also pay, in respect of a residential placement, any fees payable for board and lodging if satisfied that special educational provision cannot be provided at the school or institution unless the board and lodging are also provided).[96] It is unclear whether the effect of section 63 can be avoided by words in section I of an EHC plan to the effect that the local authority considers School A to be suitable to meet the child or young person's needs, but that the local authority has agreed to name School B on the condition that the parent or the young person part-fund the school fees. If the parent or young person ceases to pay, must the local authority pay the whole amount, at least until the EHC plan is amended?[97]

95　*R (L) v Wandsworth LBC* [2006] ELR 376 per Jack J at para 25.

96　See CFA 2014 s63(1), (2) and (5). The wording of CFA 2014 s63 is broader than EA 1996 s328, and might be thought to permit the local authority more scope for part-payment of fees. CFA 2014 s63 refers to the local authority having to 'pay any fees payable', whereas EA 1996 s328 required the local authority to 'pay the whole of the fees payable in respect of the education provided for the child at the school'.

97　A similar scenario arose in *R v Kent CC ex p W* [1995] 2 FCR 342 in which the statement of SEN named two maintained mainstream schools as suitable, but stated that the parental school had been named subject to the parents part-funding it. By the time of the hearing before Turner J, however, the local authority accepted that neither of the two maintained mainstream schools were suitable. The only suitable school was therefore the parental school. Turner J held that the local authority were liable to pay all of the fees for the parental school.

3.69   The Court of Appeal considered but did not resolve the issue in *Slough BC v SENDIST*.[98] Sedley LJ (with whom Rimer LJ and Sir Paul Kennedy agreed) stated (at para 18):

> [The argument] that parents can secure the school of their choice for a child with special needs by paying enough of the fees to make the alternative uneconomical – may well subvert the purpose of [EA 1996] section 348 [see now CFA 2014 s63]. It would permit parents with means, by striking a private bargain, to compel a public authority to part-fund schooling which the parents would otherwise have had to fund in full. The counter-argument is that, while s.348(2) manifestly forbids an educational authority to require parents to pay fees at a non-maintained school, it does not prevent parents from voluntarily doing so, even if their purpose is to bring an otherwise uneconomic placement within the s.9 objective; nor therefore should it prevent a local education authority from advising parents that this can be done.

3.70   In the experience of the authors, some local authorities will countenance such arrangements as a sensible compromise, others will not (either as a matter of principle, or because they are concerned about the risk of discontinuance of the part-payment). In the absence of any case-law clarifying the lawfulness or enforceability of such arrangements, both parents (and young people) and local authorities should proceed with caution.

Mainstream or special?

3.71   CFA 2014 s33 provides that where a local authority is securing the preparation of an EHC plan for a child or young person, the local authority must secure that the EHC plan provides for the child or young person to be educated in a mainstream school or mainstream post-16 institution[99] unless that is incompatible with (a) the wishes of the child's parent or the young person, or (b) the provision of efficient education for others.[100] Notably, the CFA 2014 provides no exemption for the requirement to educate a child or young person in a mainstream school or post-16 institution where the local authority

---

98 [2010] EWCA Civ 668, [2010] ELR 687.

99 CFA 2014 s33(2) does not require a parent or young person to choose mainstream education: if a parent expressed no view, a local authority would have to name a mainstream school unless that would be incompatible with the provision of efficient education for other children, see *Bury MBC v SU* [2010] UKUT 406 (AAC), [2011] ELR 14 at para 19.

100 CFA 2014 s33(1) and (2). This provision was previously EA 1996 s316(3).

(or the FTT) forms a view that a mainstream school or post-16 institution cannot meet a child's SEN.[101]

3.72   The definition of a 'mainstream school' in the CFA 2014 encompasses a maintained school or an academy that is not a special school. It does not include an independent school (other than academies or free schools).[102]

3.73   The courts have considered in some detail how CFA 2014 s33 (or previously, EA 1996 s316) is to be applied.[103] The following principles can be derived from the case-law:

- As CFA 2014 s33 only applies to a 'child or young person who is to be educated in a school or post 16-institution', in some cases there may be a preliminary step in determining whether it is appropriate for the child or young person to be educated in school or post-16 institution (as opposed to, say, at home).[104]

- In all other cases, CFA 2014 s39 should be considered first and s33 only applies if the local authority does not accede to the parents' request under section 39. The questions to be asked under each section are separate: a school rejected under s39 may still be named under s33.[105]

---

101 In *Harrow Council v AM* [2013] UKUT 157 (AAC), [2013] ELR 351 UT Judge Mark stated 'the apparent incompatibility between the provision of suitable education and the requirement to name a mainstream school without express regard to the suitability of the school for the children only be reconciled on the basis that the local authority is under an absolute obligation to make a school suitable ... subject only to the qualification in section [33(2)(b)]' at para 27. See also *ME v Southwark LBC* [2017] UKUT 73 (AAC) per UT Judge Jacobs at paras 16–18.

102 CFA 2014 s83(2) defines a 'mainstream school' as '(a) a maintained school that is not a special school, or (b) an Academy school that is not a special school'. It defines 'mainstream post-16 institution' as 'a post-16 institution that is not a special post-16 institution'. Further, it defines a 'maintained school' as meaning '(a) a community, foundation or special school, or (b) a community or foundation special school not established in a hospital'.

103 See *R (MH) v SENDIST* [2004] EWCA Civ 770, [2004] ELR 424; *Bury MBC v SU* [2010] UKUT 406 (AAC), [2011] ELR 14; *CCC v Tower Hamlets LBC* [2011] UKUT 393; *Harrow LBC v AM* [2013] UKUT 157 (AAC), [2013] ELR 351; *KC v Hammersmith and Fulham LBC* [2015] UKUT 177 (AAC), [2015] ELR 317; and *ME v Southwark LBC* [2017] UKUT 73 (AAC).

104 See *TM v Hounslow LBC* [2009] EWCA Civ 859, [2011] ELR 137; *KC v Hammersmith and Fulham LBC* [2015] UKUT 177 (AAC), [2015] ELR 317 per UT Judge Ward at para 15.

105 *R (MH) v SENDIST* [2004] EWCA Civ 770, [2004] ELR 424 at paras 71, 79–80 and *ME v Southwark LBC* [2017] UKUT 73 (AAC) per UT Judge Jacobs at para 12.

- If CFA 2014 s39(3) (preference of parent and young person) applies and the preference is not defeated by one of the exemptions in CFA 2014 s39(4), the preferred school should be named. It is only if one of the exemptions in CFA 2014 s39(4) applies that the local authority or the FTT needs to consider CFA 2014 s33.[106]
- Alternatively, if CFA 2014 s39(3) does not apply, the local authority (or the FTT on appeal) must consider EA 1996 s9.[107]
- A parent or young person who expresses a preference for a specific maintained special school under CFA 2014 s38(2), and whose preference is defeated by the exemptions in CFA 2014 s39(4), may express a fall back preference for mainstream education.[108] The fall-back preference could be defeated by the exemption in CFA 2014 s33(2)(b) ('the provision of efficient education for others') but not by s33(2)(a) ('the wishes of the child's parent or young person'). Subject to the exemptions being met, however, a local authority must agree to mainstream provision.
- Where there are more than two schools that could meet the fall back preference for mainstream education, the local authority or the FTT must apply EA 1996 s9 to determine which of the two schools should be named.[109]

3.74 The circumstances in which placement at a school would be incompatible with the provision of efficient education for others are set out in paras 3.48–3.51 above (in the context of CFA 2014 s39(4)).

3.75 CFA 2014 s33 provides further, however, that the local authority cannot rely on the exemption that a maintained school would be incompatible with the provision of efficient education for others unless:

a) in respect of maintained schools or post-16 institutions in its area taken as whole it shows that there are no reasonable steps that it could take to prevent the incompatibility; or

106 *R (MH) v SENDIST* [2004] EWCA Civ 770, [2004] ELR 424; *KC v Hammersmith and Fulham LBC* [2015] UKUT 177 (AAC), [2015] ELR 317 per UT Judge Ward at para 16.

107 *KC v Hammersmith and Fulham LBC* [2015] UKUT 177 (AAC), [2015] ELR 317 per UT Judge Ward at para 17.

108 See *CCC v Tower Hamlets LBC* [2011] UKUT 393 per UT Judge Lane at para 28; *KC v Hammersmith and Fulham LBC* [2015] UKUT 177 (AAC), [2015] ELR 317 per UT Judge Ward at para 18.

109 *KC v Hammersmith and Fulham LBC* [2015] UKUT 177 (AAC), [2015] ELR 317 per UT Judge Ward at para 24.

b) in respect of a particular school or institution, it shows that there are no reasonable steps that the governing body, proprietor or principal could take to prevent the incompatibility.[110]

3.76   The Code provides that what constitutes reasonable steps will depend on the circumstances of the case, but suggests that the following factors may be taken into account:[111]

- whether taking the step would be effective in removing the incompatibility;
- the extent to which it is practical for the early years provider, school, college or local authority to take the step;
- the extent to which steps have already been taken in relation to a particular child or young person and their effectiveness;
- the financial and other resource implications of taking the step;[112]
- the extent of any disruption that taking the step would cause.

3.77   The UT has considered whether a specialist unit attached to a mainstream school is in fact a separate special school (and is therefore not a mainstream school for the purposes of CFA 2014 s33). EA 1996 s4 defines a 'school' as 'an educational institution which is outside the further education sector and the higher education sector and is an institution for providing (a) primary education; (b) secondary education; or (c) both primary and secondary education'.[113] In *TB v Essex CC*[114] UT Judge Lane stated 'unless the context otherwise requires, it is not justifiable to encrust the words 'educational institution in s.4 with the technicalities relating to the regulation, governance, financing and administration of schools'[115]. The judge continued, however, to say that these factors were not irrelevant:

---

110 CFA 2014 s33(3)–(5). This was previously EA 1996 s316A(5) and (6).
111 Code, at para 9.91. Paragraph 9.92 gives specific examples of the kinds of reasonable steps a local authority may be expected to take in different circumstances.
112 In *Bury MBC v SU* [2010] UKUT 406 (AAC), [2011] ELR 14 UT Judge Ward accepted that, while resources were not relevant to the question of whether an exemption applied in the first place, resources were relevant in determining whether reasonable steps could be taken to remove the incompatibility (at paras 22–23). He also accepted that it might not be reasonable to take steps to remove the incompatibility with the education of others if the effect of doing so would be a material adverse effect on the pupil with SEN to receive the provision that he requires (at para 23).
113 EA 1996 s2 defines primary, secondary and further education.
114 [2013] UKUT 534 (AAC), [2014] ELR 46.
115 [2013] UKUT 534 (AAC), [2014] ELR 46 at para 33.

... they are factors which are helpful in assessing whether an entity is an educational institution. This is not, however, a tick-box exercise. Depending on the circumstances, a greater or smaller number of factors may serve to answer the question.[116]

Education otherwise than at school

3.78 CFA 2014 s61(1) empowers a local authority in England to arrange for any special educational provision to be made otherwise than in a school or post-16 institution. It must only do so if satisfied that it would be inappropriate for the provision to be made in a school or post-16 institution.[117] Parents or young people seeking home tuition, or home tuition in combination with a placement at school, may rely on this provision.

3.79 In *TM v Hounslow LBC*[118] the Court of Appeal held it was not sufficient to ask simply 'can' the school make the special educational provision for the child or young person. Rather, pursuant to what was then EA 1996 s319, the local authority had to determine whether it was inappropriate for the child or young person to be educated at school. Aikens LJ (with whom Patten and Thomas LJJ agreed) stated that this process involved consideration of all the circumstances of the case including the child or young person's background and medical history, the child's particular educational needs, the facilities that could be provided in and out of school, the comparative costs of the various alternative provisions, the child or young person's reactions and the parents' wishes (or those of the young person where relevant).

3.80 There are two ways in which the legislative regime concerning home education differs from the provisions in the EA 1996. First, the language of EA 1996 s319 differs to CFA 2014 s61(1). EA 1996 s319 empowered a local authority to arrange for special education provision 'or any part of such provision' to be made otherwise than in a school. In *MS v Brent LBC*[119] UT Judge Levenson emphasised that EA 1996 s319 addressed two situations: (a) where it was inappropriate for any provision to be made in school, and (b) where it is

---

116 [2013] UKUT 534 (AAC), [2014] ELR 46 at para 34. See also on this point, *MA v Kensington and Chelsea RLBC* [2015] UKUT 186 (AAC), [2015] ELR 326 at paras 23–30.

117 CFA 2014 s61(2). Further, pursuant to CFA 2014 s61(3) before doing so, the local authority must consult the child's parent or the young person. Similar provisions were contained in EA 1996 s319.

118 [2009] EWCA Civ 859, [2011] ELR 137 at para 26.

119 [2011] UKUT 50 (AAC), [2011] ELR 301.

inappropriate for any part of such provision to be made in school. UT Judge Levenson held that the FTT had to consider both limbs.[120]

3.81   CFA 2014 s61 does not, however, contain a reference to 'or any part of such provision'. It is probable that it is implicit in CFA 2014 s61(1) (and in particular in its reference to 'any' special educational provision), but it is unfortunate that the drafters have not made the point express as in EA 1996 s319.

3.82   Second, EA 1996 s324(2)(c) required that the statement of SEN should 'specify any provision for the child for which they [the local authority] make arrangements under section 319 and which they considered should be specified in the statement'. Education (Special Educational Needs) (England) (Consolidation) Regulations 2001 SI No 3455 Sch 2 required this to go into part 4 of the statement of SEN. There is no equivalent in the CFA 2014.

3.83   Further, reg 12(1)(i) requires the name of the school or institution (or the type of institution) 'to be attended' by the child or young person to be inserted into section I of the EHC plan. In *East Sussex CC v TW* UT Judge Jacobs held that the home could not properly be inserted into section I as it did not fit with the language of reg 12(1)(i).[121]

3.84   It follows that in cases of education otherwise than at school, the special educational provision ought to be set out in section F, but it would not be appropriate to insert the home into section I (whether the special educational provision is made in whole or in part at home).

Residential school

3.85   Where section I of a child or young person's EHC plan names a residential school, the local authority must pay any fees payable in respect of education or training provided.[122] The local authority must also pay any fees in respect of board and lodging it if it satisfied that the special educational provision cannot be provided at the school or other institution unless the board and lodging are provided.[123]

3.86   In practice, a residential school will be named in section I in one of two situations:

120 [2011] UKUT 50 (AAC), [2011] ELR 301 at para 23.
121 [2016] UKUT 528 (AAC) at para 32.
122 CFA 2014 s63(1) and (2).
123 CFA 2014 s63(5). In *JC v Bromley LBC* [2016] UKUT 388 (AAC), [2016] ELR 515 UT Judge Ward held (in respect of EA 1996 s517(1) and (5) which is in materially similar terms to CFA 2014 s63(5)) that 'board and lodging ... at the school' did not include lodging at a children's home (see para 7).

1) The local authority (or the FTT) has found that the child or young person has a need for a waking day curriculum (see paras 3.29–3.32 above). Section F of the EHC plan will normally contain a statement that a child needs a waking day curriculum, and an indication of the educational provision that needs to extend beyond the ordinary school day.[124]

2) If the journey that a child or young person would have to undertake to or from the nearest school that is capable of meeting her SEN would be unreasonably long, then it is likely that a residential placement will be held to be required on educational grounds.[125]

3.87   A child placed in a residential school to meet the child's (and his or her parents') social needs, as well as the child's educational needs, may become a looked after child for the purposes of CA 1989 s20.[126]

Naming a type of school or naming more than one school

3.88   Unless required to name a school requested by the parents in section I,[127] the local authority may name a type of school or other institution which it thinks would be appropriate for the child or the young person.[128] In such circumstances, the courts have emphasised that there is no requirement to name a specific school.[129]

---

124 Often a residential school named in section I by a local authority (in contradistinction to the FTT) will be the subject of bipartite or tripartite funding (ie education and social care, or education and health, or all three).

125 See *C v Oxfordshire CC* (UT) (HS/1288/2015).

126 *R (O) v East Riding of Yorkshire Council* [2011] EWCA Civ 196, [2011] 3 All ER 137 per Rix LJ at paras 114–116, 119, 125–129.

127 See CFA 2014 s39(3).

128 See CFA 2014 ss39(5), 40(2).

129 See *Richardson v Solihull* [1998] ELR 319. In *MH v Hounslow LBC* [2004] EWCA Civ 770, [2004] ELR 424 the Court of Appeal stated that the local authority (or the FTT on appeal) 'having concluded that mainstream schooling is the appropriate *type* of schooling for the child, ought normally to exercise its power to name a particular mainstream school in part 4 of the statement', per Jonathan Parker LJ at para 76 (emphasis in original). Further, 'type' of school requires an indication as to whether the education provided is primary or secondary, see *R (M) v East Sussex CC* [2009] EWHC 1651 per Timothy Brennan QC sitting as a Deputy Judge of the High Court at paras 10–13.

3.89   In order to ensure that a local authority can make the appropriate provision to meet a child's SEN, it is possible to name more than one school in section I of the EHC plan where that is appropriate.[130]

Considerations where a child or young person already attends the preferred school

3.90   A local authority (and the FTT on appeal) may be asked to name an independent school in section I that the child already attends (the parent having funded it pending the issue of an EHC plan and/or the outcome of an appeal). Two issues have arisen: (a) how should the local authority (or the FTT) deal with the difficulties of a child having to move from the school she attends; and (b) whether the local authority is liable for the historic fees paid by the parent.

3.91   On the first issue, in *W v Gloucestershire CC*[131] the court stated that in determining whether a named school was 'appropriate for the child', it was necessary for the local authority (and on appeal, the FTT) to evaluate the difficulties for the child in moving from the school in which the child had been placed by his or her parents.

3.92   On the second issue, the Court of Appeal in *R v Barnet LBC ex p G*[132] considered whether the liability of a local authority to pay the fees of a school named in part 4 of a statement of SEN by a tribunal on appeal dates only from the date of amendment or relates back to the date on which the statement of SEN was issued. Hutchison LJ (with whom Sir John Balcombe and Kennedy LJ agreed) stated that an amendment ordered by the tribunal did not require the local authority to meet any costs incurred since the date of the issue of the statement of SEN. He stated:[133]

> ... nowhere in the statute is there anything to indicate that an amendment to a statement is to have effect in monetary terms, let alone any express indication that if, on appeal, it is shown that the [local authority] should have made provision they are liable to make recompense in those cases where the parents have themselves incurred relevant expense. If that had been the intention of Parliament I would expect to find some express provision to that effect in the Act. As it is ... I read the relevant statutory provisions as being directed to what is to happen in the future.

130 *TB v Essex CC* [2013] UKUT 534 (AAC), [2014] ELR 46 at paras 42–47, per UT Judge Lane.
131 [2001] EWHC 481 (Admin) per Scott Baker J at paras 19, 21, 25.
132 [1998] ELR 281.
133 [1998] ELR 281, at 289.

Provision or school place not yet available

3.93   That a school does not yet have all the required provision in section F does not preclude it being named in section I if the FTT is satisfied by assurances that the provision will be put in place by the time the child attends.[134]

3.94   Similarly, in *Hampshire CC v JP* the FTT did not err in law in naming a school in part 4 of the statement of SEN which might not have a place for nine months, and also stating in part 4 that the child could continue to attend the existing school in the interim.[135]

Special educational provision outside England and Wales

3.95   A local authority may make arrangements for a child or young person for whom it maintains an EHC plan to attend an institution outside England and Wales which specialises in providing for children or young people with SEN. The arrangements may include contributing to or paying the fees charged by the institution, the child or young person's travelling expenses, expenses reasonably incurred in maintaining the child or young person while at the institution or travelling to and from it, and expenses reasonably incurred by someone accompanying the child or young person while travelling to and from the institution or staying there.[136]

The views of the child or young person

3.96   In drafting an EHC plan a local authority is obliged to have regard to the views of the child or the young person.[137] The Code provides that 'local authorities must have regard to the views, wishes and feelings of the child, child's parent or young person, their aspirations, the outcomes they wish to seek and the support they need to achieve them'.[138]

3.97   The weight to attach to the views of a child or young person is a matter for the local authority (or the FTT on appeal). The views of the child will not act as a veto to all other considerations, but it

---

134 *N v Southwark LBC* [2005] EWHC 1210, [2006] ELR 20.

135 *Hampshire CC v JP* [2009] UKUT 239 (AAC); 2010] ELR 413 at para 21.

136 CFA 2014 s62.

137 See CFA 2014 ss38–39 (in respect of the young person) and Code, paras 9.21–9.26 (in respect of both children and young people).

138 See Code, para 9.21.

is for the local authority (or the FTT) to decide whether or not they should be regarded as determinative of the matter.[139] Further, as a general proposition, the older and more mature the child the greater the weight that ought to attach to their views.[140]

3.98   A number of cases have considered how to assess the appropriateness of a school where it is said that attendance at it causes a child or young person stress or distress and/or where the child refuses to attend at all.

3.99   In *MW v Halton BC* the child had various physical ailments leading to him not attending at school thought by his doctors to have, at least in part, a psychological element. Having observed that on the evidence it was not possible to make a definitive finding on whether the school was the source of the stress, UT Judge Ward stated:[141]

> ... even if a tribunal were merely to find that a pupil, while attending or being expected to attend a school, experienced symptoms (from whatever cause) consistent with stress sufficient to be of evident concern to his medical advisers, it would need to be able to form a conclusion that the school proposed was nonetheless 'appropriate'. This implies a need to consider the impact, if any, of attendance on the child and how, if at all, the condition can be managed in such an environment and (since the circumstances are unlikely to be entirely fixed, or necessarily clear-cut) monitored.

3.100   Similarly, in *R (B) v The Vale of Glamorgan County Borough Council*[142] a 16 year old suffering from mental health difficulties refused to attend the school named in Part 4 of his statement of SEN. The FTT was held to have erred in law by failing to address how, notwith-

---

139 See *CB v Merton LBC* [2002] EWHC 877 (Admin) per Sullivan J at para 29.
140 See *West Sussex CC v ND* [2010] UKUT 349 (AAC) per HHJ Pearl sitting as a Judge of the UT at paras 30–33.
141 [2010] UKUT 34 per UT Judge Ward at para 37. He went on to state (at para 38) that if 'remedial or supporting measures cannot be taken and the stressors are an unavoidable part of attending a given school, then that in my view would be highly relevant to determining whether a proposed school was "appropriate"'. Finally, he set out a non-exhaustive and non-prescriptive list of facts that ought to be considered and found: 'When and in what circumstances did B exhibit unusual behaviour patterns? When and in what circumstances did he exhibit physical symptoms? What else was going on at the time? What alternative explanations are there and what are the facts in relation to them? When did the unusual behaviour and'/or physical symptoms stop? Again, in what circumstances? How is he most of the time at school and at home? What are said by B and those in contact with him to be the stressors? What are the facts in relation to them? What, if anything, can be done in relation to the factors that may trigger stress? What is known about B's morale and self-esteem in the school context? What can be done to help with this?'
142 [2001] ELR 529.

standing her refusal to attend, it had concluded that the school could provide for her needs.

Health and social care needs and provision

Introduction and overview

3.101 SEND Regs reg 12(1) and the Code[143] require an EHC plan to include the child or young person's health care needs which relate to their SEN (section C) and the child or young person's social care needs which relate to their SEN or to a disability (section D).

3.102 CFA 2014 s37(2) (and SEND Regs reg 12(a) and the Code) require the EHC plan to include any healthcare provision reasonably required by the learning difficulties and disabilities which result in the child or young person having special educational needs (section G) and any social care provision which must be provided pursuant to CSDPA 1970 s2 (or which is reasonably required by the learning difficulties and disabilities which result in the child or young person having SEN) (sections H1 and H2).

3.103 As noted above, the FTT does not have jurisdiction to hear appeals against either the description of a child or young person's health or social care needs, or against health or social care provision.[144] The only remedy where a parent or young person disagrees with these parts of an EHC plan is an application for judicial review, or mediation, or a complaint under the local authority's complaints procedure.

Section C: health needs which relate to a child or young person's SEN

3.104 The EHC plan must specify any health needs identified through the EHC needs assessment which relate to the child or young person's SEN. The Code observes that some heath care needs, such as routine dental health needs, are unlikely to be related.[145]

3.105 The Code notes that the CCG may also choose to specify other healthcare needs which are not related to the child or young person's

---

143 Code, para 9.62.
144 But see the social care pilot scheme described at paras 4.25–4.29 below.
145 Code, table at para 9.69 (in the row describing the content of section C).

SEN (for example, a long-term condition which might need manage-ment in an educational setting).[146]

Section D: social care needs which relate to a child or young person's SEN

3.106   The EHC plan must specify any social care needs identified through the EHC needs assessment which relate to the child or young person's SEN or which require provision for a child or young person under 18 under CSDPA 1970 s2.[147]

3.107   The Code advises that the local authority may also choose to spe-cify other social care needs which are not linked to the child or young person's SEN or disability. This could include reference to any child in need or child protection plan which a child may have relating to other family issues such as neglect. The Code suggests that such an approach could help the child and their parents manage the different plans and bring greater co-ordination of services. The Code notes that inclusion must only be with the consent of the child and their parents.[148]

Section G: health provision[149]

3.108   The Code observes that healthcare provision contained in section G should be detailed and specific and should normally be quantified – for example, in terms of the type of support and who will provide it. It should be clear how the provision will support achievement of the outcomes, including the health needs to be met and any outcomes to be achieved through provision secured through a personal (health) budget.

3.109   The Code provides:

> Health care provision reasonably required may include special-ist support and therapies, such as medical treatments and delivery of medications, occupational therapy and physiotherapy, a range of nursing support, specialist equipment, wheelchairs and continence supplies. It could include highly specialist services needed by only a small number of children which are commissioned centrally by NHS England (for example therapeutic provision for young offenders in the secure estate).

---

146   Code, table at para 9.69 (in the row describing the content of section C).
147   Code, table at para 9.69 (in the row describing the content of section E).
148   Code, table at para 9.69 (in the row describing the content of section E).
149   Code, table at para 9.69 (in the row describing the content of section G).

3.110 The Code adds that the local authority and CCG may also choose to specify other healthcare provision reasonably required by the child or young person, which is not linked to his or her learning difficulties or disabilities, but which should sensibly be co-ordinated with other services in the plan.

Sections H1 and H2: social care provision

3.111 Section H1 should include any social care provision in respect of which the local authority is under a duty, imposed by CSDPA 1970 s2, to provide. Section H1 must include all services assessed as being necessary for the chid or young person. These may include:[150]

- practical assistance in the home;
- provision or assistance in obtaining recreational or educational facilities at home and outside home;
- assistance in travelling to facilities;
- adaptations to the home;
- facilitating the taking of holidays;
- provision of meals at home or elsewhere;
- provision or assurance in obtaining a telephone; and
- non-residential short breaks (or respite care).

3.112 If the child's parent is assessed as needing services under CA 1989 ss17ZD–17ZF (parent carers' needs assessment), these should be included in section H1.[151]

3.113 Like in section F, the provision in section H1 should be detailed and specific, and should normally be quantified.

3.114 Section H2 must contain any other social care provision reasonably required by the learning difficulties or disabilities which result in the child or young person having SEN. This must only list provision not required under CSDPA 1970 s2.[152]

Aspirations and outcomes

Introduction and overview

3.115 SEND Regs reg 12(1) requires an EHC plan to contain 'the views, interests and aspirations of the child and his parents or the young

---

150 Code, table at para 9.69 (in the row describing the content of section H1).
151 Code, table at para 9.69 (in the row describing the content of section H1).
152 Code, table at para 9.69 (in the row describing the content of section H2).

person' (in section A). CFA 2014 s37(2) requires an EHC plan to specify the outcomes sought for a child or young person (section E).[153]

Section A: the views, interests and aspirations of the child and his parents or the young person

3.116   The Code observes that the following matters should be included in section A:[154]

- Details about the child or young person's aspirations and goals for the future (but not details of outcomes to be achieved – see section above on outcomes for guidance). When agreeing the aspirations, consideration should be given to the child or young person's aspirations for paid employment, independent living and community participation
- Details about play, health, schooling, independence, friendships, further education and future plans including employment (where practical)
- A summary of how to communicate with the child or young person and engage them in decision-making
- The child or young person's history
- If written in the first person, the plan should make clear whether the child or young person is being quoted directly, or if the views of parents or professionals are being represented.

Section E: outcomes sought for the child or young person

3.117   In *Devon CC v OH* UT Judge Ward defined 'outcomes' as 'the intended consequences of the provision for the particular person receiving it'.[155] The Code provides detailed guidance on setting 'outcomes', to be included in section E of an EHC plan. In summary, the guidance provides:

- Outcomes in EHC plans should be specific, measurable, achievable, realistic and time-bound ('SMART').[156]
- EHC plans should be focused on education and training, health and care outcomes that will enable children and young people to progress in their learning and, as they get older, to be well prepared for adulthood. EHC plans can include wider outcomes

---

153   See also SEND Regs reg 12(1) and the Code, para 9.62.
154   Code, para 9.69.
155   [2016] UKUT 292 (AAC), [2016] ELR 377 at para 41.
156   Code, para 9.61.

such as positive social relationships and emotional resilience and stability.[157]

- The Code emphasises the difference between long-term aspirations on the one hand (to be recorded in section A, and for which the local authority cannot be held accountable), and outcomes on the other (which should be measurable).[158]

- Outcomes are meant to describe what the expected benefit to the individual of the (say) education or training will be. They are not a description of the service being provided, but of what the service provision is expected to achieve.[159]

- The EHC plan should identify the arrangements for the setting of shorter term targets by the child or young person's educational institution.[160]

3.118   The Code summarises the material to be included in section E as follows:[161]

- A range of outcomes over varying timescales, covering education, health and care as appropriate but recognising that it is the education and training outcomes only that will help determine when a plan is ceased for young people aged over 18. Therefore, for young people aged over 17, the EHC plan should identify clearly which outcomes are education and training outcomes.

- A clear distinction between outcomes and provision. The provision should help the child or young person meet an outcome. It is not an outcome in itself.

- Steps towards meeting the outcome.

- The arrangements for monitoring progress, including review and transition review arrangements and the arrangements for setting and monitoring shorter term targets by the early years provider, school, college or other education or training provider.

- Forward plans for key changes in a child or young person's life, such as changing schools, moving from children's to adult care and/or from paediatric services to adult health, or moving from further education to adulthood.

- For children and young people preparing for the transition to adulthood, the outcomes that will prepare them well for adulthood and are clearly linked to the achievement of the aspirations in Section A.

---

157 Code, para 9.64.
158 Code, para 9.65.
159 Code, para 9.66.
160 Code, para 9.69.
161 Code, para 9.69.

CHAPTER 4

Disagreement – appeals to the First-tier Tribunal, mediation and complaints

continued

Key points

Overview of appeals: rights of appeal and powers of the First-tier Tribunal

- A decision that disposes of proceedings made at, or following, a hearing, must be made by at least one judge and one or two specialist members (depending on the experience of the member and the complexity of the appeal).
- The FTT must give effect to the overriding objective, namely to deal with cases fairly and justly. The parties must help the FTT to further the overriding objective and 'co-operate with the Tribunal generally'.
- A child's parent or a young person has a right of appeal to the FTT.
- The CFA 2014 and SEND Regs make provision for the circumstance in which either the parent or the young person lacking capacity to bring an appeal.
- The FTT has the power to hear appeals against the matters set out in CFA 2014 s51(2).
- In respect of nearly all types of appeal to the FTT, the parent or young person must at least consider mediation with the local authority.
- The child or young person may also enter into mediation with the local authority or responsible commissioning body respectively in respect of disputes concerning social care and healthcare provision.
- The FTT has the powers on an appeal that are set out in SEND Regs reg 43.
- A pilot scheme is in operation that permits the FTT to make recommendations in respect of social care needs and provision, and healthcare provision.
- Where the FTT makes an order, the local authority must comply with the order within the period specified in SEND Regs reg 44.

Commencing an appeal

- To commence an appeal in the FTT, the parent or young person must send an application notice to the FTT within two months of the decision under challenge (or within one month of receiving a mediation certificate, if that date is later).

continued

- The local authority must respond within 30 days after receiving the application notice.
- Where a parent or young person has appealed to the FTT and the local authority notifies the FTT that it will not oppose the appeal before it submits a response, the appeal is treated as having been determined in favour of the appellant and the FTT does not need to make an order.
- Rule 12 of the Tribunal Procedure (First-tier Tribunal) (Health, Education and Social Care Chamber) Rules 2008 SI No 2699 (FTT Rules) sets out specific rules for calculating periods of time in SEN cases, specifically in respect of the Christmas period and August.
- The FTT has the power to extend time to comply with a rule or direction.
- The FTT has no power to make an order for interim relief; any such application must be made to the Administrative Court.

The preparatory stage of an appeal

- The FTT has the power to regulate its own procedure.
- When a SEN appeal is registered the FTT will usually issue standard directions.
- If a parent or young person wishes to apply for further directions or to vary those that have already been issued, he or she should use the 'Request for Changes' form (form SEND7).
- The FTT has powers to deal with a party who fails to comply with the FTT Rules or a direction; these include the striking out of a party's case.
- There is no limit on the number of written expert reports a party can provide, but the FTT limits witnesses to three per party. If a party wishes to bring four or more witnesses, an application will need to be made.
- The standard directions will make provision for the production and submission of a working document, which is a copy of the final education, health and care (EHC) plan, on which both parties have worked, showing the changes that have been agreed and the outstanding areas of dispute.
- The standard directions will make provision for an attendance form to be lodged, which set out who will attend the hearing on behalf of each party.
- A parent or young person may withdraw the appeal but will need the FTT's consent to do so. The FTT also has the power to make a consent order.

Mediation

- There are two routes into mediation under the CFA 2014: (a) in respect of matters that can be appealed to the FTT, and (b) in respect of the health and social care elements of the EHC plan.
- A parent or young person has a right to mediation in respect of the matters that can be appealed to the FTT. However, mediation functions as a gateway to an appeal, so that a parent or young person must consider mediation (which consideration is demonstrated by obtaining a mediation certificate from a mediation adviser). If mediation is conducted, a mediation certificate will be issued at its conclusion.
- The mediation certificate permits a parent or young person to lodge his or her appeal, either within two months of the date of the original decision, or within one month of receiving the certificate (whichever is the later).
- A mediation certificate does not have to be obtained where the parent or young person seeks to appeal only in respect of section I of the EHC plan.
- A local authority must arrange mediation within 30 days of the parent or young person requesting it (a responsible commissioning body must arrange mediation within 30 days of being notified by the local authority that the parent or young person wishes to attend mediation).
- The local authority (or, where relevant, the responsible commissioning body) must participate in the mediation and ensure that it is attended by individuals who have the authority to resolve the mediation issues.
- Mediation meetings are confidential and without prejudice to the FTT process.
- Mediation is to be provided free of charge, and the local authority or responsible commissioning body must pay the reasonable expenses of the parent or young person attending the mediation.

Complaints

- The local authority has a duty to set up a complaints procedure to address disputes in respect of SEN between a parent or young person, and the local authority or a governing body of a school.

Overview of appeals: rights of appeal and powers of the First-tier Tribunal

Introduction

4.1   Tribunals, Courts and Enforcement Act (TCEA) 2007 s3(1) created the FTT. The FTT is organised into a number of chambers. [1] One such chamber is the Health, Education and Social Care Chamber.[2] The Health, Education and Social Care Chamber's functions include all functions relating to an appeal against a decision related to children with SEN, and a claim of disability discrimination in the education of a child.[3]

4.2   The First-tier Tribunal (Health, Education and Social Care Chamber) has tribunal procedure rules,[4] namely the Tribunal Procedure (First-tier Tribunal) (Health, Education and Social Care Chamber) Rules 2008 SI No 2699 (FTT Rules).

4.3   The Senior President of the FTT has issued practice directions which give practical advice to parties on the FTT Rules, for example, *Special educational needs or disability discrimination in schools cases* (October 2008) ('SEN Practice Direction').[5] There are also available on the FTT's website a number of pieces of guidance, such as SEND25, *How to appeal a special educational needs and disability (SEND) decision* (2014).

Composition of the FTT

4.4   A decision that disposes of proceedings made at, or following, a hearing must be made by one judge and:

- one specialist member where the member has substantial experience of SEN and/or disability and both have sat on at least 25 hearings within the jurisdiction; or
- in complex appeals, designated as such by a judge, two other members with substantial experience of SEN and/or disability,

---

1   TCEA 2007 s7(1) empowered the Lord Chancellor to, with the concurrence of the Senior President of Tribunals, by order make provision for the organisation of the FTT into a number of chambers.

2   See First-tier Tribunal and Upper Tribunal (Chambers) Order 2010 SI No 2655 reg 2.

3   See First-tier Tribunal and Upper Tribunal (Chambers) Order 2010 SI No 2655 reg 4.

4   Made under TCEA 2007 s27(1).

5   These can be issued to the FTT in general by the Senior President of Tribunals, see TCEA 2007 s23(1), or by a Chamber President, see TCEA 2007 s23(2).

and where the content of the appeal demands, specialism in health and/or social care.[6]

4.5 Where there is a clear disagreement (other than in respect of a matter of law) between a judge and a member sitting as a two person panel, then the judge must direct a hearing before a newly appointed three-person panel.[7]

4.6 The FTT must have the same, no more than three, person constitution throughout the appeal proceedings.[8]

The overriding objective

4.7 FTT Rules r2 sets out the overriding objective. Pursuant to rule 2(3), the FTT must seek to give effect to the overriding objective when it exercises any power under the FTT Rules, or interprets any rule or practice direction.

4.8 Rule 2(1) provides that the 'overriding objective of these Rules is to enable the FTT to deal with cases fairly and justly'. Rule 2(2) provides that dealing with a case fairly and justly includes:

(a) dealing with the case in ways which are proportionate to the importance of the case, the complexity of the issues, the anticipated costs and the resources of the parties;

(b) avoiding unnecessary formality and seeking flexibility in the proceedings;

(c) ensuring, so far as practicable, that the parties are able to participate fully in the proceedings;

(d) using any special expertise of the Tribunal effectively; and

(e) avoiding delay, so far as compatible with proper consideration of the issues.

4.9 Rule 2(4) requires the parties to help the FTT to further the overriding objective and 'co-operate with the Tribunal generally'.

---

6 See First-tier Tribunal and Upper Tribunal (Composition of Tribunal) Order 2008 SI No 2835, and Practice Statement, *Composition of Tribunals in relation to matters that fall to be decided by the Health, Education and Social Care Chamber on or after 16 December 2015.*

7 See Practice Statement, *Composition of Tribunals in relation to matters that fall to be decided by the Health, Education and Social Care Chamber on or after 16 December 2015.*

8 See *GO and HO v Barnsley MBC* [2015] UKUT 184 (AAC), [2015] ELR 421 per UT Judge Wright at paras 43–61, relying on *MB v SSWP* [2013] UKUT 111 (AAC), [2014] AACR 1.

Who has a right of appeal?

4.10   A child's parent or a young person has the right to appeal to the FTT.[9] A 'young person' means a person over compulsory school age,[10] but under 25.[11] In practice, therefore, a parent has a right of appeal until his or her child reaches compulsory school age.[12] Thereafter, the young person has a right of appeal.

4.11   The legislative scheme makes provision for appeals where either the child's parent, or the young person, lacks capacity to bring an appeal. Capacity is governed by the Mental Capacity Act (MCA) 2005.[13] Capacity depends on the matter in respect of which a decision has to be made.[14] A person may have capacity at one time but not at another. Further, a person may have capacity in respect of one matter but not another. The FTT will be concerned with whether the parent or the young person has capacity to bring an appeal. A person is presumed to have capacity unless the contrary is shown, and then only after all practical steps have been taken without success to help him or her to make a decision.[15] Whether a person has capacity is a question of fact for the FTT.

4.12   If a child's parent lacks capacity[16] at the relevant time,[17] then the rights conferred on parents within the legislative scheme are conferred on the representative of the parent ('representative' in this context has a different meaning to the sense in which it is usually

---

9   CFA 2014 s51(1); Code, para 11.44. In *SG v Denbighshire CC* [2016] UKUT 460 (AAC), [2017] ELR 99 the UT gave guidance on the approach to a disagreement between parents as to the school to be named in section I.

10   EA 1996 s8 defines 'compulsory school age' as (very broadly) between the first day of the term immediately after the term in which the child turns five, and the end of the academic year in which the child turns 16.

11   CFA 2014 s83(2).

12   CFA 2014 s58 makes provision for the secretary of state to, by order, make pilot schemes enabling children to appeal to the FTT under CFA 2014 s51 or to make a claim to the FTT under Equality Act 2010 Sch 17 that the responsible body in England has discriminated against the child because of his disability. No such order has been made.

13   See also Code, Annex 1.

14   MCA 2005 s2(1).

15   MCA 2005 s1(2) and (3).

16   The references in the CFA 2014 and the SEND Regs to 'lacking capacity' are to lacking capacity within the meaning of the MCA 2005, see CFA 2014 s80(5).

17   CFA 2014 s80(4) defines the 'relevant time' as the time at which, under the statutory provision in question, something is required or permitted to be done by or in relation to the parent or young person. In this context, it would mean at the time the appeal is required to be brought.

used, namely to denote a person who advocates or acts for the parent or the young person).[18]

4.13   If a young person lacks capacity to bring an appeal, an appeal may be brought on his or her behalf by an 'appropriate person'.[19] The result is:

> ... a statutory substitution of the alternative person for the young person. The appeal under section 51 is brought by the alternative person in that capacity but in the best interests of the young person.

> An alternative person may act on his or her own or use the services of a representative in the advocacy sense.[20]

4.14   If the young person's capacity is in doubt, the most efficient way to resolve it may be as a preliminary issue that the FTT will have to decide before it identifies the correct parties under FTT Rules r5(3)(e).[21] If a young person's capacity changes during the course of proceedings, the FTT may substitute another party as an appellant under FTT Rules r9.

---

18 SEND Regs reg 63, CFA 2014 s80(6) defines a 'representative' as: (a) a deputy appointed by the Court of Protection under MCA 2005 s16(2)(b) to make decisions on the parent's behalf in relation to a child's special educational needs; (b) the donee of a lasting power of attorney (within the meaning of MCA 2005 s9) appointed by the parent to make decisions on his or her behalf in relation to matters concerning a child's SEN; or (c) an attorney in whom an enduring power of attorney (within the meaning of MCA 2005 Sch 4) created by the parent or young person is vested, where the power of attorney is registered in accordance with MCA 2005 Sch 4 paras 4 and 13 or an application for registration of the power of attorney has been made.

19 SEND Regs reg 64 and Sch 3. An 'alternative person' is defined as: (a) a representative of the young person (where a 'representative' has the definition in CFA 2014 s80(6)), (b) the young person's parent, where the young person does not have a representative, or (c) a representative of the young person's parent, where the young person's parent also lacks capacity at the relevant time and the young person does not have a representative.

20 See *Hillingdon LBC v WW* [2016] UKUT 253 (AAC), [2016] ELR 431 per UT Judge Jacobs at paras. 13–14; *Buckinghamshire CC v SJ* [2016] UKUT 254 (AAC), [2016] ELR 350 per UT Judge Jacobs at paras 13–14.

21 *Hillingdon LBC v WW* [2016] UKUT 253 (AAC), [2016] ELR 431 per UT Judge Jacobs at para 18; *Buckinghamshire CC v SJ* [2016] UKUT 254 (AAC), [2016] ELR 350 per UT Judge Jacobs at para 18. In the experience of the authors, the FTT may require the parties to instruct a single joint expert in respect of the young person's capacity.

What decisions give rise to a right of appeal?

4.15   The following matters give rise to a right of appeal to the FTT (subject to the requirement to consider mediation in certain types of appeal, on which see paras 4.139, 4.146–4.147 below):[22]

- a decision of the local authority not to secure an education, health and care (EHC) needs assessment for the child or young person;[23]
- a decision of the local authority, following an EHC needs assessment, that it is not necessary for special educational provision to be made for the child or young person in accordance with an EHC plan;
- where an EHC plan is maintained for the child or young person, an appeal lies against: (a) the description of the SEN as specified in the plan; (b) the special educational provision specified in the plan; (c) the school or other institution named in the plan, or the type of school or other institution named in the plan; or (d) if no school or other institution is named in the plan, that fact.[24] This right of appeal arises only: (a) when an EHC plan is first finalised for the child or young person; and (b) following an amendment or replacement of the plan;
- a decision of the local authority not to secure a re-assessment of the needs of the child or young person under CFA 2014 s44 following a request to do so;
- a decision of the local authority not to secure the amendment or replacement of an EHC plan it maintains for the child or young person following a review or re-assessment under CFA 2014 s44;
- a decision of the local authority under CFA 2014 s45 to cease to maintain an EHC plan for the child or young person.

4.16   Most notably, no right of appeal to the FTT lies against the description in the EHC plan of the child or young person's health care needs or social care needs which relate to their SEN (sections C and D) or any health care provision or social care provision which is specified in the EHC plan (sections G and H).[25] Neither does a right of appeal

---

22 CFA 2014 s51(2).

23 Note that since 1 August 2016 the FTT is considering all such appeals on the papers (ie without an oral hearing). See paras 4.117–4.118 below.

24 This accords with sections B, F and I of the EHC plan.

25 Although the FTT must consider the social care and healthcare provision in sections D and H to see if the provision of any part of it constitutes special educational provision under CFA 2014 s21(5) (as it educates or trains a young

lie against 'aspirations' in section A or 'outcomes' in section E.[26] The only mechanism by which to challenge these matters in Court proceedings is by an application to the Administrative Court for judicial review (see para 4.32 below) (although note that mediation may be undertaken, see para 4.137 below).

Mediation: the gateway to an appeal to the FTT

4.17 Mediation is discussed in detail at paras 4.137–4.162 below. There are two relevant routes into mediation under the CFA 2014:

1) in respect of the matters that can be appealed to the FTT; and
2) in respect of the health and social care elements of EHC plans.

4.18 As to the matters which can be appealed to the FTT, a parent or young person has a right to mediation.[27] However, mediation also functions as a gateway to an appeal to the FTT. Therefore, parents and young people who wish to appeal to the FTT may do so only after they have obtained a certificate from a mediation adviser.[28] A parent or young person must contact the mediation adviser within two months after written notice of the local authority's decision was sent, and inform the mediation adviser that he or she wishes to appeal and inform the mediation adviser whether they wish to pursue the mediation.[29]

4.19 A mediation adviser must issue a certificate to a parent or young person where:

• the adviser has provided information and advice about pursuing mediation, and the parent or young person has informed the adviser that he or she does not wish to pursue mediation;[30] or

person), and if so, move the provision to section F, see *East Sussex CC v TW* [2016] UKUT 528 (AAC) per UT Judge Jacobs at para 25.
26 In *S v Worcestershire County Council* [2017] UKUT 92 (AAC), however, UT Judge Mitchell stated that it was open to the FTT, having allowed an appeal and recast the specified special educational needs and provision, to alter outcomes that no longer related to the needs or provision determined by the FTT, see para. 85. He relied on reg 43(2)(f) SEND Regs which empowers the FTT to make 'any other consequential amendments' to the EHC plan as it thinks fit.
27 CFA 2014 s52(1).
28 CFA 2014 ss51(1), 55(1) and (3). A 'mediation adviser' is defined as an independent person who can provide advice and information about pursuing mediation, see CFA 2014 s56(2). The Code deals with mediation advice that must be given by a mediation adviser prior to mediation, see paras 11.21–11.23.
29 SEND Regs reg 33.
30 CFA 2014 s55(4). Where a parent or young person who is required to obtain a mediation certificate informs the mediation adviser that he does he does not wish to pursue mediation, the mediation adviser must issue a

- the parent or young person has participated in the mediation.[31]

4.20   A mediation certificate does not have to be obtained where the parent or young person seeks to appeal only in respect only of the school or other institution named in the EHC plan, the type of school or other institution specified in an EHC plan or the fact that an EHC plan does not name a school or other institution.[32] The mediation arrangements do not apply to a disability discrimination claim.

4.21   A parent or young person may still bring an appeal in the FTT where he or she was required to obtain a mediation certificate, but has failed to do so and the time limit for doing so has passed. Such an appeal requires the permission of the FTT.[33]

4.22   As noted above, there is no right of appeal to the FTT in respect of the description of health and social care needs, and the provision to meet those needs in the EHC plan. There is, however, a right to mediation with the relevant commissioning body[34] and the local authority respectively.[35]

Powers of the FTT on appeal

4.23   Before determining any appeal, the FTT may, with the agreement of the parties, correct any deficiencies in the EHC plan which relate to the special education needs or the special educational provision for the child or the young person.[36]

4.24   The FTT has the following powers on an appeal.[37] Which is relevant will depend on the nature of the appeal brought:

- dismiss the appeal;
- where the appeal is brought against the local authority's decision not to secure an EHC assessment or against the local authority's

mediation certificate within 3 working days of being informed by the parent or young person, SEND Regs reg 34(1). The mediation adviser may not issue a mediation certificate if the parent or young person did not contact the mediation adviser within 2 months of the date of the notice issued by the local authority, SEND Regs reg 34(2).

31 CFA 2014 s55(5). The mediation adviser must issue a certificate to the parent or young person within three working days of the conclusion of the mediation, see SEND Regs reg 39(1).
32 CFA 2014 s55(2); Code, paras 11.24 and 11.25.
33 SEND Regs reg 34(3).
34 CFA 2014 s53.
35 CFA 2014 ss52(1) and 54.
36 SEND Regs reg 43(1).
37 SEND Regs reg 43(2).

decision not to secure a reassessment of the child or young person's SEN – order the local authority to arrange an assessment or a reassessment of the child or young person;

- where the appeal is brought against the local authority's decision, following an EHC assessment, that it is not necessary to make an EHC plan – (a) order the local authority to make and maintain an EHC plan; or (b) refer the case back to the local authority for them to reconsider whether, having regard to any observations made by the FTT, it is necessary for an EHC plan to be made and maintained;
- where the appeal is brought against the local authority's decision to cease to maintain the EHC plan – order the local authority to continue to maintain the EHC plan in its existing form;
- where the appeal is brought against the contents of the EHC plan, or a decision not to amend the EHC plan, or against the decision to cease to maintain the EHC plan – order the local authority to continue to maintain the EHC plan with the amendments ordered by the FTT (although such amendments can only relate to the SEN, or the special educational provision and the name or type of school or other institution named).[38]

4.25 A pilot scheme is presently in operation that enables the FTT to make recommendations in respect of social care needs and provision, and healthcare needs and provision (despite there being no right of appeal to the FTT against these matters). The Special Educational Needs and Disability (First-tier Tribunal Recommendation Power) (Pilot) Regulations 2015 SI No 358 (SEND (Pilot) Regs) came into force on 1 April 2015.[39] They apply to the pilot local authorities listed in the Schedule.[40] Where an appeal against a pilot local authority is to be determined in favour of the child's parent or the young person, the FTT has the power to recommend that health or social care needs which relate to the child or young person's SEN are specified in the

---

38 When the FTT has ordered amendments to the EHC plan it may also 'make any other consequential amendments' as it thinks fit, SEND Regs reg 43(2)(f).
39 Made under CFA 2014 s51(4) and (5).
40 The pilot local authorities are: London Borough of Barking and Dagenham, Bedford Borough Council, Blackpool Council, Cheshire West and Chester Council, London Borough of Ealing, East Riding of Yorkshire Council, London Borough of Hackney, Kent County Council, London Borough of Lambeth, Liverpool City Council, Sandwell Metropolitan Borough Council, Stockport Metropolitan Borough Council and Wokingham Borough Council.

EHC plan.[41] Further, the FTT has the power to recommend that health care or social care provision is specified in the EHC plan.[42]

4.26   When the FTT makes a recommendation in respect of health-care needs or healthcare provision, it must send a copy of the recommendation and a copy of its decision letter to the responsible commissioning body.[43] The responsible commissioning body must respond within five weeks (or within the time-period specified by the FTT) from the date of the recommendation to the child's parent or the young person and the local authority that maintains the EHC plan.[44] The response must:

- be in writing;
- state what steps if any the responsible commissioning body has decided to take following its consideration of the recommendation; and
- give reasons for any decision not to follow the recommendation (or any part of it).[45]

4.27   When the FTT makes a recommendation in respect of social care needs or social care provision, the pilot local authority must respond to the child's parent or the young person within five weeks from the date of the recommendation (or such time period directed by the FTT).[46] A response must:

- be in writing;
- state what steps if any the pilot local authority has decided to take following its consideration of the recommendation; and
- give reasons for any decision not to follow the recommendation (or any part of it).[47]

4.28   As to the procedure, the FTT has two appeal forms for use in pilot areas: form SEND29 (for use by the parent of a child seeking a recommendation); and form SEND29A (for use by a young person seeking a recommendation). The appeal form asks the parent or young person to set out the details of the issues in the appeal and provide as much detail as possible about the changes sought to the plan, and to specify the wording of the recommendation sought.

41 SEND (Pilot) Regs reg 3.
42 SEND (Pilot) Regs reg 4.
43 SEND (Pilot) Regs reg 5(1) and (2).
44 SEND (Pilot) Regs reg 5(3) and (4).
45 SEND (Pilot) Regs reg 5(5).
46 SEND (Pilot) Regs reg 6(1) and (2).
47 SEND (Pilot) Regs reg 6(3).

4.29 Depending on the nature of the recommendation sought, the local authority will send a copy of the notice of appeal to the health commissioner and/or social care team. The health or social care commissioner will not be made a party to the appeal, and so must rely on the local authority to present its response to the request in evidence to the FTT.

The obligation on the local authority to implement the FTT decision and the period for compliance

4.30 SEND Regs reg 44 sets out the period within which a local authority must comply with an FTT order. The prescribed period varies according to the type of order made:

- Where the FTT dismisses an appeal against a determination to cease an EHC plan – the local authority shall cease to maintain the EHC plan immediately.[48]
- Where the FTT requires the local authority to make an assessment or reassessment – the local authority shall within two weeks of the order being made, notify the child's parent or the young person that it shall make the assessment or reassessment and:
  - where following the assessment or reassessment the local authority decides not to make and maintain an EHC plan – it must notify the child's parent or young person of its decision, with reasons, as soon as practicable but in any event within ten weeks of the date of the FTT order; or
  - where following the assessment or reassessment the local authority decides to make an EHC plan – the local authority must send the finalised plan to the child's parent or young person as soon as practicable, but in any event within 14 weeks of the date of the FTT order.[49]
- Where the FTT requires the local authority to make and maintain an EHC plan – the local authority shall issue a draft EHC plan within five weeks of the FTT order, and shall send a copy of the

---

48 SEND Regs reg 44(2)(a).
49 SEND Regs reg 44(2)(b). Pursuant to SEND Regs reg 44(3) the local authority need not comply with the time limits specified if it is impractical to do so because: (a) exceptional personal circumstances affect the child or child's parent, or the young person, during that period of time; (b) the child or child's parent or the young person is absent from the area of the local authority for a continuous period of two weeks or more during that period of time; or (c) any of the reasons in SEND Regs reg 13(3) apply.

finalised plan to the child's parent or the young person within 11 weeks of the FTT order.[50]

- Where the FTT refers the case back to the local authority for it to reconsider – the local authority shall do so within two weeks of the FTT order, and shall either send a copy of the draft EHC plan or shall give notice of a decision not to maintain a EHC plan pursuant to SEND Regs reg 5.[51]

- Where the FTT requires the local authority to amend the special educational provision specified in an EHC plan – the local authority shall issue the amended EHC plan within five weeks of the order being made.[52]

- Where the FTT requires the local authority to amend the name of the school or other institution (or the type of school or institution) – the local authority shall issue the amended EHC plan within two weeks of the order being made.[53]

- Where the FTT requires the local authority to continue to maintain an EHC plan in its existing form – the local authority shall continue to maintain the EHC plan.[54]

- Finally, where the FTT orders the local authority to continue and amend an EHC plan – the local authority shall continue to maintain the EHC plan and amend it within five weeks of the order being made.[55]

4.31   In *G v Barnet LBC*[56] the Court of Appeal held that the local authority's liability to pay the fees of an independent school ordered to be substituted into part 4 of the statement of SEN dated only from the date of the amendment of the statement, and not from the date on which the statement was made.

---

50 SEND Regs reg 44(2)(c). Again, the time limit may be extended in the circumstances set out in SEND Regs reg 44(3).
51 SEND Regs reg 44(2)(d).
52 SEND Regs reg 44(2)(e).
53 SEND Regs reg 44(2)(f).
54 SEND Regs reg 44(2)(g).
55 SEND Regs reg 44(2)(h).
56 [1998] ELR 281 at 289, see para 3.92 above.

Enforcement by an application for judicial review

4.32 There are a number of other problems that commonly arise in SEN cases that can only be enforced by an application to the Administrative Court for permission to apply for judicial review. Some non-exhaustive examples are provided below:

- As noted above at para 4.16, the FTT has no jurisdiction to hear an appeal against the description in the EHC plan of the child or young person's healthcare needs or social care needs which relate to his or her SEN (sections C and D) or any healthcare provision or social care provision which is specified in the EHC plan (sections G and H). The only mechanism by which to challenge these matters is by an application for judicial review (or mediation, as explained at paras 4.137–4.162 above).

- CFA 2014 s42(2) requires a local authority to secure the specified special educational provision in an EHC plan for the child or young person. A failure to do so can only be enforced by judicial review.[57]

- Similarly, a breach of the duty on the responsible commissioning body to deliver the healthcare provision specified in an EHC plan (contrary to CFA 2014 s42(3) and (4)) can only be enforced by an application for judicial review.

- The FTT has no jurisdiction to hear disputes arising in respect of the provision of home to school transport under the Education Act 1996.[58] Such disputes must be determined by the Administrative Court on an application for judicial review.

- The FTT has no power to grant interim relief (see paras 4.60–4.70 below). An application for interim relief must be brought by an application for judicial review.

57 *R v Harrow LBC ex p M* [1997] ELR 62, and *R (N) v North Tyneside BC* [2010] EWCA Civ 135, [2010] ELR 130 at para 11 (per Elias LJ).

58 *Staffordshire CC v JM* [2016] UKUT 246, [2016] ELR 307 per UT Judge Lane at para 41.

Commencing an appeal

The application notice

Submission of the application notice

4.33   The child's parent or a young person starts proceedings before the FTT by sending an application notice to the FTT so that it is received either:[59]

- within two months after written notice of the decision being challenged was sent to the child's parent or the young person; or
- within one month of the date of issue of the mediation certificate, if that date is later.[60]

4.34   The FTT must send a copy of the application notice and the accompanying documents to the local authority.[61]

General matters to be included in an application notice

4.35   The FTT Rules[62] and the SEN Practice Direction collectively require the following matters to be included in an application notice (although in practice, the prescribed form on the FTT's website directs an answer to each of the points):

- the name and address of the appellant;
- the name and address of the appellant's representative (if any);
- an address where documents for the appellant may be sent or delivered;
- the name and date of birth of the child or young person;
- if possible, the names and addresses of all persons or bodies who have or share parental responsibility for the child or have care of the child;
- the name of the local authority and the date upon which the appellant was notified of the decision in relation to which the application is made;
- the details of the decision to which the proceedings relate;
- the result the appellant is seeking;

---

59   The forms are available at: http://hmctsformfinder.justice.gov.uk/HMCTS/ GetForms.do?court_forms_category=Special%20Educational%20Needs%20 and%20Disability%20Tribunal. The relevant form will depend on the precise appeal being made.

60   FTT Rules r20(1).

61   FTT Rules r20(6).

62   FTT Rules r20.

- the grounds on which the appellant relies;
- if the appellant seeks an order that a child or young person's EHC plan or statement of SEN shall be amended, details as to which part or parts of the EHC plan or statement the application relates as well as details of the changes sought;
- if the appellant seeks an order that a different school from that already named in the EHC plan or statement of SEN be named in it either: the name and address of the preferred school, or a sufficient description of the type and nature of the school which the appellant considers would constituted an appropriate placement for the child or young person;
- if the school is an independent or non-maintained school: written confirmation that there is a place available for the child or young person; or (if not an independent or non-maintained school) written confirmation that the appellant has informed the school that they propose to request that it be named in the EHC plan or statement of SEN in proceedings before the FTT;
- a copy of the EHC plan or statement of SEN and supporting documentation (or appendices) where available.

4.36 Further:

- the application notice has to be signed by the child's parent or the young person;
- the child's parent or the young person must also send a copy of the decision under appeal, any written reasons for it, and a copy of any mediation certificate obtained;[63] and
- the appellant should provide a list of documents included in or provided with the application notice.

4.37 It is often helpful to include a full chronology. This should set out the key dates such as:

- the date of the EHC assessment and/or of any EHC plan being issued;
- the date of any professional assessments carried out on the child or young person;
- the dates of any annual reviews; and
- the dates of any amendments to the EHC plan.

---

63 FTT Rules r20(3).

4.38   It is also sensible to:

- address any issues that might be raised concerning the FTT's jurisdiction, eg whether it is a type of appeal that the FTT has the power to determine; and
- deal with any preliminary points, such as whether the appeal has been made in time.

4.39   Application notices should be specific. If the appeal is against the contents of the EHC plan, the parent or young person should identify the ways in which he or she disagrees with the identification of the SEN and the special educational provision in the EHC plan (preferably in turn). Where possible, identify why the EHC plan is wrong or inaccurate, and identify what the child's parent or the young person would like the EHC plan to say instead (where possible by referring to expert evidence). If the appeal is against the school that has been named, identify the reasons why the school named cannot meet the child or young person's needs, and say why the preferred school can. The application notice must be sufficiently particularised to allow the local authority and the FTT to understand what is in dispute.

4.40   Parents and young people should ensure that they link the special educational provision proposed in section F with the school they wish to be named in section I. In particular, they should be careful to ensure that the school they want to be named can in fact make the special educational provision said to be required by the child or young person.

4.41   A checklist of the evidence that may need to be included is as follows (not all of the items in the list below will be appropriate in every appeal):

- the EHC plan and appendices;
- reports of any recent annual reviews of the EHC plan that have taken place;
- evidence about the child or young person's educational record[64] – for example:
  - national curriculum levels;
  - Individual Education Plans (and reviews);
  - any reports or advice from the local authority's professionals (such as specialist teachers or educational psychologists);
  - school reports;

---

64 Education (Pupil Information) (England) Regulations 2005 SI No 1437 reg 5 requires the governing body of a maintained school to make a child's educational record available for inspection free of charge within 15 days of receiving a request in writing from the parent.

- attendance record; and
- records of any exclusions or disciplinary record (if appropriate);
- any relevant NHS reports or advice – for example from:
  - speech and language therapists;
  - psychiatrists; or
  - paediatricians;
- independent expert reports obtained by the parent or young person;[65] where expert evidence is relied on, the FTT will normally place more weight on it where the evidence is up to date and the expert has met and assessed the child;
- where relevant, information from others involved with the child or family –for example a social worker.

4.42 Where the appeal is against the school named, the evidence will need to deal with SEN provision at the preferred school (and also identify why the local authority school is unable to provide the required SEN provision). Broadly, it may be helpful to consider the following in respect of each programme or activity:

a) a description;
b) how it is to be delivered (eg small group or whole class or one-to-one),
c) duration and frequency of the activity or programme;
d) the identity, qualifications and experience of the person delivering it;
e) the arrangements (if any) for supervision and monitoring of the delivery of the activity or programme (and the time allotted to the person for the supervision or monitoring);
f) arrangements for preparation, liaison, attendance at meetings and writing reports (and specify the time to be allotted); and
g) any necessary equipment to be provided.

Specific issues to be considered

4.43 Parents and young people may wish to consider the following more specific suggestions (not all will be relevant in every case).[66]

---

65 In *LM v Lewisham LBC* [2009] UKUT 204 (AAC) the UT held, in the context of letters of instruction to expert witnesses, that a FTT direction to disclose letters of instruction should not require disclosure of any material in breach of legal advice privilege.

66 See also the FTT guidance, *Information about schools* (SEND14), August 2014, available on the FTT's website.

4.44 About the preferred school:

- What type of school is it? Does the school specialise, or have experience, in teaching children with the SEN the child or young person has?
- How many pupils are there? How many have SEN, how many have an EHC plan or statement of SEN, and what are their primary diagnoses? How many pupils is the school able to accommodate in total? What is the age range of the pupils? Will the child or young person have a suitable peer group in the school?
- How many classes are there in each year? What size are they? How many members of staff are usually in each classroom?
- Does the school teach the full national curriculum? Where appropriate, what qualifications are achieved by pupils on leaving the school?
- Include the school's prospectus/brochure, Ofsted reports, SEN policies and behaviour policies.
- In some cases (for example, where the child or young person has a physical disability or a hearing impairment) it may be necessary to describe the physical environment of the school in some detail (for example, the extent to which it is wheelchair accessible or has been acoustically treated).
- Detail any specific facilities the school has which may assist in meeting a child or young person's SEN (for example, a sensory room or a hydrotherapy pool).

4.45 About the staffing of the school:

- What is the total number of teaching staff?
- What specific qualification and experience do the teaching staff have of SEN, or of the type of SEN that the child or young person has?
- What qualifications and experience does any learning support assistant have who will be in the classroom with the child or young person? Will the learning support assistant be full time with the child or young person, and if not, how many dedicated hours will he or she provide (and if none, how many other children are the learning support assistant supporting in the classroom and what are their needs)?
- Are there any other specific members of staff that the child or young person might come into contact with (eg a specialist teacher or a school counsellor)?
- What relevant training has been recently delivered to staff?

4.46 About the child or young person's peers:

- How many children will be in the child's class?
- What are the range and nature of the difficulties of the other pupils who would be in the child or young person's class? And in particular, their primary diagnosis, the range in their cognitive ability and curriculum levels?
- It may also be necessary to provide information specific to the particular appeal (for example, in the case of a hearing impaired child, how many of the children use British Sign Language, or are oral or use Sign Supported English).

4.47 About the proposed curriculum:

- How would the child or young person spend their time in the school? A timetable (even if in draft form) is often the easiest way of conveying this information.
- What strategies would be deployed by the school for working with the child (for example, visual timetables or individual work-stations for children with an autistic spectrum disorder)?
- Where appropriate, identify what subjects the child or young person will study, and what qualifications he or she would be expected to work towards achieving.
- What arrangements are in place for co-operation between the child or young person's home and the school?

4.48 About the therapeutic input at the school:

- Is there a speech and language therapist or occupational therapist or physiotherapist employed by the school? And if so, for how many hours per week; how many children do they see each week; and how many children are on their case load?
- If the school has a visiting speech and language therapist, or occupational therapist or physiotherapist from the NHS, the frequency and length of their visits to the school, and the number of pupils at the school on their case load.
- Details of whether, and if so how, therapy is delivered in the school – for example, is it by withdrawal only, or do the therapists work with the teaching staff, and are the learning support assistants trained and experienced in delivering therapeutic programmes?

4.49 Specific types of schools or provision:

- **Units in mainstream school:** Where the proposed school is a unit in a mainstream school, percentage of time (and which lessons) the child spends in the unit and the mainstream school and how the child will be supported in mainstream.

- **Education at home (or in some combination of home and school):** Why it would not be appropriate for the child or young person to be educated in a school. Whether the arrangement is proposed to be short or long term.
- **Residential school:** Why this is necessary for educational reasons.

4.50   While transport is not for the FTT to determine, the cost of the transport may affect the decision. The application notice should set out:

- what is proposed by way of transport;
- how long the journey will take;
- whether it will be by taxi, bus provided by the local authority or by public transport;
- whether an escort is required;
- the estimated cost; and
- whether there is an existing service (and therefore whether any travel costs are marginal costs, see paras 3.59–3.65 above).

4.51   The application notice should also deal with the cost of the preferred school. The parent or young person should identify (where necessary, with assistance from the local authority) the cost of:

- a place at the school;
- any additional support (eg a learning support assistant, therapies, or additional equipment or aids);
- boarding; and
- transport (including the cost of any escort required).[67]

Local authority's response

4.52   Having received an application notice, a respondent local authority must submit a response no later than 30 working days after it received the application notice.[68] The FTT Rules prescribe various matters that a response must contain, most notably:

- a statement as to whether the local authority opposes the appeal;
- and if so, the grounds for the opposition; and

---

67   If any of this information is not available at the time the application notice is lodged, it should be included with the further evidence.
68   FTT Rules r21(1).

- the views of the child about the issues raised by the proceedings (or the reasons why the local authority has not obtained the views of the child).[69]

4.53 The local authority must send or deliver a copy of the response and any accompanying documents to each other party at the same time as it provides the response to the FTT.[70]

Unopposed appeals

4.54 Where a child's parent or a young person has appealed to the FTT and the local authority notifies the FTT that it will not oppose the appeal before it submits a response, the appeal is to be treated as if it was determined in favour of the appellant and the FTT is not required to make an order.[71]

Time

Calculating time

4.55 FTT Rules r12 sets out specific rules for calculating time in SEN appeals. They are as follows:[72]

- if the time for starting proceedings by providing the application notice to the FTT ends on a day from 25 December to 1 January inclusive, or on any day in August – the application notice is provided in time if it is provided on the first working day after 1 January or 31 August as appropriate; and
- the days from 25 December to 1 January inclusive and any day in August must not be counted when calculating the time by which any other act must be done.

Extending time

4.56 The FTT has the power to extend tine for complying with a rule.[73] This commonly arises where a parent or young person submits an application notice, or where a local authority submits a response, after the time limit for doing so has expired.

---

69 FTT Rules r21(2), and see also the SEN Practice Direction.
70 FTT Rules r21(5).
71 SEND Regs reg 45(1) and (2). Regulations 45(3)–(7) set out the time periods in which the local authority must do specified acts in consequence of not opposing an appeal.
72 FTT Rules r12(3).
73 FTT Rules r5(3)(a).

4.57   If the child's parent or the young person provides an application notice to the FTT after the time for doing so has expired, the application notice must include an application to extend the time for lodging the appeal and the reason why the application was not lodged in time.[74] Unless the FTT extends time for the application notice, the FTT must not admit the application notice.[75] Similarly, if the local authority provides a response to the FTT after the time for doing so has expired, the response must include an application to extend the time for lodging the response and the reason why the response was not lodged in time.[76]

4.58   In *CM v Surrey CC*[77] UT Judge Ward reviewed authorities on the extension of time that had arisen in the Social Entitlement Chamber, namely *R (KS) v First-tier Tribunal and the Criminal Injuries Compensation Authority*[78] (*KS*), and *R (YT) v First-tier Tribunal (Social Entitlement Chamber)*[79] (*YT*). Summarising the relevant principles as follows, the judge:[80]

- Stated that the FTT's power in FTT Rules r5(3)(a) to extend time 'is unfettered. As such it has to be exercised judicially and in accordance with the overriding objective in rule 2'.[81]
- Approved the comments of UT Judge Wikeley in *Information Commissioner v PS*[82] that 'it is not appropriate to import or create any specific guidance on the issue of extending the time limit to appeal; each case should be considered on its own facts with reference to the relevant rules governing the Tribunal'.
- Referred to the decision of the Court of Appeal in *Norwich and Peterborough Building Society v Steed*[83] in which McCowan LJ identified the following factors as being the principles that the FTT should apply when considering an application to extend time: 'first, the length of the delay; secondly, the reasons for the delay;

---

74 FTT Rules r20(4)(a).
75 FTT Rules r20(4)(b).
76 FTT Rules r21(4). FTT Rules r21 does not contain an equivalent provision to that in r20(4)(b) concerning late application notices (ie that if the FTT does not extend time it must not admit the application notice).
77 [2014] UKUT 4 (AAC), [2014] ELR 91.
78 [2010] UKUT 181 (AAC).
79 [2013] UKUT 201 (AAC).
80 [2014] UKUT 4 (AAC), [2014] ELR 91 at para 17.
81 See also *KS* [2010] UKUT 181 (AAC) at para 11; and *YT* [2013] UKUT 201 (AAC), appendix at para 2.5.
82 [2011] UKUT 94.
83 [1991] 1 WLR 449.

thirdly, the chances of the appeal succeeding if the application is granted; and fourthly the degree of prejudice to the respondent is the application is granted.'[84] The judge noted that the *Norwich and Peterborough Building Society* case was not strictly binding on the FTT, and that the FTT is not required to refer to the list it contains in a 'formulaic fashion'. However, as UT Judge Wikeley observed in *YT*, 'that case conveniently and compendiously refers to a range of considerations which are likely, and very often highly likely, to be relevant in the exercise of the rule 5(3)(a) discretion'.[85] The judge observed that it may be that other factors, such as impact on other users of the tribunal system, also need to be taken into account under the overriding objective.[86]

- Cited *YT* as to the relevance of merits:

  3.15. ... Dealing with cases 'fairly and justly' may well involve some consideration of the merits of the underlying appeal. If the delay is short and readily excusable, it may well be that the merits of the case may have little, if any, significance (see e.g. Lord Donaldson MR's observations on *Palata Investments Ltd v Burt & Sinfield Ltd* [1985] 1 WLR 942 in *Norwich and Peterborough Building Society v Steed* [1991] 1 WLR 449 at 455).

  3.16. In other cases, however, the merits (or rather the lack of merits) may assume greater importance. In particular, there may be a 'trade-off' between the period of the delay and the strength of the underlying appeal. Thus the longer the delay, the stronger the underlying case may need to be to justify extending time. So, as ever, the significance of any consideration of the merits will depend on the circumstances of the case. In any event, however, given that the decision on whether or not to extend time is a procedural or interlocutory decision, a detailed examination of the merits is not to be expected.

- Finally, cited *YT* in observing that the adequacy of the explanation for the late application:

  ... is certainly an important consideration under rule 5(3)(a), and indeed the starting point, but it is only the beginning of the enquiry. The watchwords of rule 2 are those of 'fairness' and

---

84 Other cases have confirmed that the merits of an appeal are relevant even if, as in SEN cases, the appeal lies as of right and without permission; see *R (Birmingham City Council) v Crown Court at Birmingham* [2009] EWHC 3329 (Admin), [2010] 1 WLR 1287 (per Beatson J at para 32).

85 See *YT* [2013] UKUT 201 (AAC), appendix at para 3.10.

86 See also *KS* [2010] UKUT 181 (AAC) at para 11.

'justice', which speak to a wider range of considerations than simply why the appeal was late.[87]

4.59   In *CM* UT Judge Ward identified two particular features of SEN appeals that may be relevant in deciding whether to extend time. First, the FTT operates on tight timescales to ensure that 'avoidable delay to a child's education is minimised'.[88] This was particularly so in cases dealing with 'important times of change in a child's school life, such as the transfer to secondary education'.[89] Second, over the course of a child's education, there may be numerous opportunities to appeal SEN-related matters (eg an appeal against the content of a statement when issued, and subsequent opportunities to appeal against a refusal to amend following annual review). It follows that 'the outcome of a particular piece of litigation will not be necessarily be determinative once and for all in the same way as, for instance, a decision on a compensation claim'.[90]

Interim relief

4.60   If a local authority amends an EHC plan, the amendment takes effect immediately.[91] It follows that the amendment of an EHC plan (to, for example, reduce or remove the hours of support provided by a learning support assistant, or to reduce or remove provision by a speech and language therapist, or even to amend the name of the school named) takes effect immediately. The local authority amendment is not stayed pending the outcome of an appeal against it.

4.61   Further, the FTT has no jurisdiction to grant interim relief (say, to maintain the status quo of provision pending a hearing).

4.62   The Administrative Court,[92] on an application for judicial review, does have the power to grant interim relief pending the decision of the FTT on an appeal. The court has proved reluctant to exercise this

---

87 See *YT* [2013] UKUT 201 (AAC), appendix at para 4.17.
88 See *CM* [2014] UKUT 4 (AAC), [2014] ELR 91 at para 20.
89 See *CM* [2014] UKUT 4 (AAC), [2014] ELR 91 at para 20.
90 See *CM* [2014] UKUT 4 (AAC), [2014] ELR 91 at para 21.
91 The one exception is where a local authority determines to cease to maintain an EHC plan for a child or young person: a local authority may not cease to maintain an EHC plan until the end of the period for an appeal (where no appeal is brought before the end of the period for an appeal) or after an appeal (brought in time) has finally been determined, see CFA 2014 s45(4).
92 Or, in the circumstances set out in TCEA 2007 s15, the UT.

power and will do so only in 'exceptional circumstances'[93] for the following two reasons:[94] First, the statutory structure clearly envisages that amendments to EHC plans will take effect forthwith despite any appeal. This can be distinguished from decisions to cease to maintain an EHC plan, which are suspended pending an appeal. Second, parliament must be taken as understanding that this may well lead to a period of time elapsing between the lodging of the appeal and the hearing of the appeal.

4.63   Where interim relief has been granted, it has been to maintain the status quo, in terms of both school placement and the funding of that placement. Thus a stay of the decision to amend the statement of SEN was granted in *R (G) v Barnet LBC*[95] and in *R (S) v Norfolk CC*[96] where the result of the amendment would have been to terminate a place at a residential school previously funded by the local authority.

4.64   Applications for interim relief that would require the local authority to provide disputed provision (ie that provision sought by the parents as part of their appeal to the FTT) have tended to fail. For example:

- In *R v Worcestershire CC ex p S*[97] the parents sought interim relief to require the local authority to fund the provision of the Lovaas programme pending the issue of an assessment of SEN, and a statement of SEN. The parents had been funding the programme, but could not afford to continue. Popplewell J refused to grant the relief, stating that maintaining the status quo 'with a totally different paymaster' was not in fact maintaining the status quo.

- In *R (JW) v The Learning Trust*[98] the parent sought interim relief to require the local authority to fund the school she wished the child to attend (and which was the subject of the appeal to the FTT) or the funding of home tuition. The UT (exercising its judicial review jurisdiction) declined the relief sought.

---

93 See *R (G) v Barnet LBC* [2005] EWHC 1946 (Admin), [2006] ELR 4 per Ouseley J (considering the decision of the Court of Appeal in *Re M (a minor)* [1996] ELR 135); and *R (JW) v The Learning Trust* [2009] UKUT 1997 (AAC), [2010] ELR 15 at para 29.

94 *R (JW) v The Learning Trust* [2009] UKUT 1997 (AAC), [2010] ELR 15 at paras 27–29.

95 *R (G) v Barnet LBC* [2005] EWHC 1946 (Admin), [2006] ELR 4.

96 [2005] EWHC 1946 (Admin), [2006] ELR 4.

97 [1999] ELR 46.

98 [2009] UKUT 1997 (AAC), [2010] ELR 115 (at paras 31–37).

4.65   The UT in *R (JW) v The Learning Trust*[99] identified the following factors as relevant in its decision to decline relief:

- the time period until the FTT hearing was relatively short;
- there was no evidence that any provision was being considered for JW at the parent's school in respect of which he would lose an opportunity if he could not start it immediately (indeed the evidence was that the programme at the parent's school was individualised and so capable of being delivered from a later start date);
- the parent had allowed an entire school term to elapse after lodging an appeal before seeking judicial review; and
- the parent had failed to apply to the FTT for expedition of her appeal.

4.66   There may be an alternative route by which interim educational provision will be ordered by the Administrative Court (or the UT on an application for judicial review) pending the determination of an appeal by the UT. EA 1996 s19 obliges a local authority to make arrangements for the provision of suitable education[100] at school or otherwise for child who, by reason of illness, exclusion or otherwise, may not receive suitable education unless such arrangements are made for them.

4.67   In *R (G) v Westminster City Council*[101] Lord Phillips MR, giving the judgment of the Court of Appeal, held that if there was no suitable education available that is reasonably practicable for the child to attend, the local authority will be in breach of EA 1996 s19. If suitable education has been made available which is reasonably practicable, but for one reason or another the child is not taking advantage of it, the local authority will not be in breach of section 19.

4.68   What constitutes 'suitable education' and what is 'reasonably practicable' is for the local authority to determine, which judgment is only open to challenge on public law principles.[102] The test of 'reasonable

---

99 [2009] UKUT 1997 (AAC), [2010] ELR 115 (at paras 31–37).
100 EA 1996 s19(6) defines 'suitable education' as being 'efficient education suitable to his age, ability and aptitude and to any special educational needs he may have'.
101 [2004] EWCA Civ 45, [2004] 1 WLR 1113 (at paras 42–48).
102 See *C v Brent LBC* [2006] EWCA Civ 728, [2006] ELR 435 (at paras 45 (per Smith LJ) and 52 (per Laws LJ)); *R (R) v Kent CC* [2006] EWHC 2135, [2007] ELR 648 at paras 21–22 per Blake J; *R (B) v Barnet LBC* [2009] EWHC 2842 (Admin) in which HHJ McKenna sitting as a Deputy Judge of the High Court held that it was not reasonably practicable for a child to attend a school which the headteacher had described as not being a suitable placement (see para 39); *R (HR) v Medway Council* [2010] EWHC 731 (Admin) (at paras 44–45,

practicability' was described by Blake J in *R (R) v Kent CC*[103] as being 'strict ... verging upon but not quite the same as impossibility'.

4.69   In *R (Y) v Croydon LBC*[104] Leggatt J considered a case in which there had been a dispute between a parent and the local authority as to the school to be named in part 4 of the child's statement of SEN. The FTT had dismissed the parent's appeal, and she had an extant appeal in the UT. By the date of the hearing (in May 2015) the child had refused to attend the school named in his statement of SEN since January 2015. The local authority had advanced a plan in February 2015 to try to get the child back into school, but it had not succeeded. No further plan had been proposed. Leggatt J held that the local authority's view that it was reasonably practicable for the child to take advantage of the education offered at the school named in the statement of SEN was irrational.[105]

4.70   Leggatt J declined, however, to order the local authority to provide home tuition and the therapies set out in the statement of SEN at home (as requested by the parent), as it was for the local authority, and not for the court, to determine what steps were needed in order to fulfil the obligation under EA 1996 s19.[106]

The preparatory stage of an appeal

FTT's case management powers: an overview

4.71   In general, the FTT has the power to regulate its own procedure.[107] In particular, the FTT may:[108]

---

per Geraldine Andrews QC sitting as a deputy judge of the High Court); and *R (KS) v Croydon LBC* [2010] EWHC 339 (Admin), [2011] ELR 109 in which Lindblom J held that a language college was not suitable for a looked after child, see paras 35–38). Without any reasoning on the point, the Court of Appeal in *R (G) v Westminster City Council* [2004] EWCA Civ 45, [2004] 1 WLR 1113 determined for itself whether it was reasonably practicable for the child to attend the local authority school (see paras 42–48), but in the light of subsequent case law this can no longer be regarded as the correct approach.

103 [2006] EWHC 2135, [2007] ELR 648 at para 25.
104 [2015] EWHC 3033 (Admin), [2016] ELR 138.
105 [2015] EWHC 3033 (Admin), [2016] ELR 138 at paras 18–19.
106 [2015] EWHC 3033 (Admin), [2016] ELR 138 at paras 23–24. Rather, he made a direction that an assessment of the child's needs take place by a specified date.
107 FTT Rules r5(1).
108 FTT Rules r5(3).

- extend or shorten the time for complying with any rule, practice direction or direction (unless such extension or shortening would conflict with a provision of another enactment containing a time limit);
- consolidate or hear together two or more sets of proceedings or parts of proceedings raising common issues, or treat a case as a lead case;
- permit or require a party to amend a document;
- permit or require a party or another person to provide documents, information or submissions to the FTT or a party;
- deal with an issue in the proceedings as a preliminary issue;
- hold a hearing to consider a matter, including a case management issue;
- decide the form of any hearing;
- adjourn or postpone a hearing;
- require a party to produce a bundle for a hearing;
- stay proceedings;
- transfer proceedings to another court or tribunal if that other court or tribunal had jurisdiction in relation to the proceedings; or
- suspend the effect of its own decision pending the determination by the FTT or the UT of an application for permission to appeal against, and any appeal or review of, that decision.

Directions

4.72   The FTT may give a direction on the application of one or more of the parties, or on its own initiative.[109]

4.73   When a SEN appeal is registered, the FTT will usually issue standard directions. The content of the standard directions varies according to the type of appeal. In appeals against the content of the EHC plan, the standard directions will:

- require the local authority to send its response and the child's views on the issues in question by a specified date;
- require both parties to send any final evidence or information by a specified date, and an order that any further evidence after that date will require the permission of the FTT;
- require the EHC plan and its full appendices to be provided (if not already);

---

109 FTT Rules r6(1). Directions are instructions to the parties on how they are to prepare the case.

- require the parties to liaise on a working document (on which see paras 4.101–4.106 below) and for a final version of the working document to be sent to the FTT so that it is received at least ten working days prior to the hearing;
- where there is a dispute about the school or institution to be named in section I, require the parties to provide specified information;
- require the local authority to prepare a hearing bundle by a specified date[110] (and state that failure to do so will result in the local authority being automatically barred from taking part in the proceedings pursuant to FTT Rules r8(2));
- require the parties to complete an attendance form (see para 4.107 below) by a specified date;
- note that in a specified week the parties may receive an active case management call from an FTT registrar (see paras 4.108–4.109 below);
- identify the date on which the hearing will take place.

4.74   If a parent or young person wishes to apply for further directions (or to vary those already issued) – for example, for a hearing or an adjournment to a hearing or for a further witness – he or she should use the 'Request for Changes' form (form SEND7) on the FTT's website.[111] The parent or the young person should send the Request for Changes form to the local authority at the same time as sending it to the FTT.

4.75   The FTT must send written notice of any direction made to each party (unless it considers that there is good reason not to).[112] If a parent or young person wishes to challenge a direction given by the FTT (either on its own initiative or on request by the local authority), he or she may do so by applying for another direction which amends, suspends or sets aside the first direction.[113]

Failure to comply with the FTT Rules or a direction

4.76   If a party fails to comply with the FTT Rules or a direction, the FTT may take such action as it considers just. This may include:

- waiving the requirement;
- requiring the failure to be remedied;
- exercising its power under FTT Rules r8 to strike out a party's case;

---

110   See the guidance produced by the FTT, *Guidance for the local authority producing the hearing bundle*, April 2016.

111   See also FTT Rules r6(2) and (3).

112   FTT Rules r6(4).

113   FTT Rules r6(5).

- referring the matter to the UT;[114] or
- restricting a party's participation in the proceedings.[115]

Striking out a party's case

4.77   The FTT Rules distinguish between three situations in which a strike out may occur:

1) **Automatic strike out:** The proceedings, or the appropriate part of them, will be automatically struck out if the applicant has failed to comply with a direction that stated that failure by the applicant to comply with the direction would lead to the striking out of the proceedings or that part of them.[116]

2) **Mandatory strike out:** The FTT must strike out the whole or a part of the proceedings if the FTT does not have jurisdiction in relation to the proceedings or part of them, and does not exercise its power under FTT Rules r5(3)(k)(i) to transfer the proceedings to another court or tribunal.[117]

3) **Discretionary strike out:** The FTT may strike out the whole or a part of the proceedings if:

   a) the applicant has failed to comply with a direction which stated that failure by the applicant to comply with the direction could lead to the striking out of the proceedings or part of them;

   b) the applicant has failed to comply with the FTT to such an extent that the FTT cannot deal with the proceedings fairly and justly; or

   c) the FTT considers there is no reasonable prospect of the applicant's case, or part of it, succeeding.[118]

4.78   In a mandatory or discretionary strike out, the FTT may not strike out the whole or a part of the proceedings without first giving the applicant an opportunity to make representations in relation to the

---

114 This power arises under FTT Rules r7(3). It allows the FTT to refer the matter to the UT for the UT to exercise its power under TCEA 2007 s25 in relation to a failure to comply with a requirement imposed by the FTT: (a) to attend at any place for the purposes of giving evidence; (b) otherwise to make themselves available to give evidence; (c) to swear an oath in connection with the giving of evidence; (d) to give evidence as a witness; (e) to produce a document; or (f) to facilitate the inspection of a document or any other thing (including any premises).

115 See FTT Rules r7(2).

116 FTT Rules r8(2).

117 FTT Rules r8(3).

118 FTT Rules r8(4).

proposed striking out.[119] In the case of an automatic strike out, or a strike out where the applicant has failed to comply with a direction which stated that failure by the applicant to comply with the direction could lead to the striking out of the proceedings or part of them, the applicant may apply for the proceedings, or part of them, to be reinstated.[120]

4.79 The striking out rules apply to a local authority, but instead of striking a claim out the FTT may bar the local authority from taking further part in the proceedings (and the reference to proceedings being reinstated should be read as a reference to lifting of the bar on the local authority from taking further part in the proceedings).[121] If a local authority has been barred from taking further part in proceedings, the FTT need not consider any response or other submission made by that local authority (and may summarily determine any or all issues against the local authority).[122]

4.80 The UT has considered the application of the striking out provisions to the local authority:[123]

- In *Camden LBC v FG*[124] the UT rejected an argument that a decision barring a local authority would be proportionate only if there had been wilful and repeated disobedience. Further, the UT stated that the local authority ought to have sought to appeal the FTT's decision refusing to lift the bar on taking part, rather than waiting until after the final hearing to appeal.

---

119 FTT Rules r8(5).
120 FTT Rules r8(6). Such an application must be made in writing, and must be received by the FTT within 28 days of the date on which the FTT sent notification of the striking out to that party: FTT Rules r8(7).
121 FTT Rules r8(8).
122 FTT Rules r8(9).
123 In *Revenue and Customs Commissions v BPP Holdings Ltd* [2016] EWCA Civ 121, [2016] STC 84 the Court of Appeal considered the correct approach under the Tribunal Procedure (First-tier Tribunal) (Tax Chamber) Rules 2009 (which are, in this respect, in materially identical terms to those in the FTT Rules) to the imposition of a sanction for breach of a rule or a direction, and to applications for relief from a sanction. The Court of Appeal held (see paras 15–18) that the tribunal should apply a strict approach, as taken in respect to the Civil Procedure Rules 1998 in *Mitchell v News Group Newspapers Ltd* [2013] EWCA Civ 1537, [2014] 1 WLR 795 and *Denton v TH White Ltd* [2014] EWCA Civ 906, [2014] 1 WLR 3926. The Court of Appeal rejected the argument that a less strict approach was more appropriate in the tribunals system. The Supreme Court is hearing the appeal in June 2017.
124 [2010] UKUT 249 (AAC) at paras 46–51, 54 per HHJ Pearl sitting as a Judge of the UT.

- In *FC v Suffolk CC*[125] the UT held (in respect of the equivalent provision in the UT Rules) that the rule was 'a draconian provision' which should be used 'only in the most blatant cases of disregard on the part of a party to the proceedings'.

4.81   The FTT may strike out a claim without holding a hearing.[126]

Substitution and addition of parties

4.82   The FTT may give a direction substituting a party if the wrong person has been named as a party, or if the substitution has become necessary because of a change in circumstances since the start of proceedings.[127] The FTT may also give a direction adding a person to the proceedings as a respondent.[128] In either case, the FTT may give such consequential directions as it considers appropriate.[129]

Disclosure and orders to answer questions

4.83   The FTT has a general case management power to permit or require a party to provide documents, information, evidence or submissions to the FTT or a party.[130] The FTT has a further power, on the application of a party or on its own initiative, to order any person to answer any questions or produce any documents in that person's possession or control which relate to any issue in the proceedings.[131]

4.84   An order under FTT Rules r16 must:

1) state that the person on whom the requirement is imposed may apply to the FTT to vary or set aside the order, if the person has not had an opportunity to object to it; and
2) state the consequences of failure to comply with the order.[132]

---

125 [2010] UKUT 368 (AAC), [2011] ELR 45 at para 13 per HHJ Pearl sitting as a Judge of the UT.
126 FTT Rules r23(3).
127 FTT Rules r9(1). This is common in claims under the EA 2010 in which the school has, since the claim was issued, become an academy school. The governing body ceases to exist, and the appropriate defendant is the local authority, see *ML v Tonbridge Grammar School* [2012] UKUT 283 (AAC), [2012] ELR 508 at paras 9–12 per UT Judge Rowland.
128 FTT Rules r9(2).
129 FTT Rules r9(3).
130 FTT Rules r5(3)(d).
131 FTT Rules r16(1)(b).
132 FTT Rules r16(4).

Order requiring a child to be made available for examination or assessment

4.85 In a SEN case the FTT may require the parents of the child (or any other person with care of the child or parental responsibility for the child) to make the child available for examination or assessment by a suitably qualified professional, or the person responsible for a school or educational setting to allow a suitably qualified professional person to have access to the school or educational setting for the purpose of assessing the child or provision made, or to be made, for the child.[133]

4.86 If such an order is made, the FTT may consider a failure by a party to comply with it, in the absence of good reason for the failure, as a failure to co-operate with the FTT, which could lead to a result adverse to that party's case.[134]

Restrictions on the use of documents and information

4.87 The FTT may make an order prohibiting the disclosure or publication of specified documents or information relating to the proceedings, or any matter likely to lead members of the public to identify any person whom the FTT considers should not be identified.[135]

4.88 The FTT may give a direction prohibiting the disclosure of a document or information to a person if:

1) the FTT is satisfied that such disclosure would be likely to cause that person or some other person serious harm; and
2) the FTT is satisfied, having regard to the interests of justice, that it is proportionate to give such a direction.[136]

4.89 If it makes such an order, the FTT must conduct proceedings 'as appropriate in order to give effect to [such] a direction'.[137]

---

133 FTT Rules r16(4).
134 FTT Rules r16(5).
135 FTT Rules r14(1).
136 FTT Rules r14(2). The procedure for obtaining such an order is set out in rule 14(3). If the party has a representative, the FTT may (in the circumstances set out in rule 14(5)) make disclosure to the representative. Such documents or information disclosed to a representative must not be disclosed either directly or indirectly to any other person without the FTT's consent: see FTT Rules r14(5) and (6).
137 FTT Rules r14(4).

Evidence, submissions and witnesses

4.90   The FTT Rules give the FTT wide powers to make directions in respect of evidence, submissions and witnesses.[138] There is no limit on the number of reports or witness statements that can be provided. As for witnesses at the hearing, parties do not have to bring any witnesses at all, but if they do the FTT has a practice of limiting the number of witnesses to no more than three (not including the parent or young person). If a party wishes to bring more than three witnesses, an application (on a Request for Changes form (form SEND7)) will need to be made. The application will need to explain why the evidence cannot be provided on paper in the form of a report or witness statement, and why it is necessary for the witness to attend in person.

4.91   The FTT has a power to require the parties to instruct a single joint expert to provide expert evidence.[139] In 'non-standard evidence cases' (ie cases which involve expert evidence other than from an educational psychologist, a speech and language therapist or an occupational therapist) the FTT ought to give consideration to directing the parties to instruct a single joint expert.[140] Further, in the experience of the authors, the FTT has sometimes required the instruction of a single joint expert to determine whether the young person has capacity.

4.92   As a broad rule of thumb, it is usually only necessary to bring expert witnesses (eg an educational psychologist, speech and language therapist or occupational therapist) where a part of the working document on which the expert can give direct evidence remains in dispute. If, for example, the speech and language need and provision is agreed, it is unlikely to be necessary for the speech and language therapist to attend the hearing (unless, for example, he or she can also give direct and relevant evidence as to the school or institution required by the child or young person).

---

138 FTT Rules r15(1) provides that the FTT may give directions on: (a) issues on which it requires evidence or submissions; (b) the nature of the evidence or submissions it requires; (c) whether the parties are permitted or required to provide expert evidence, and if so whether the parties must appoint a single expert to provide such evidence; (d) any limit on the number of witnesses whose evidence a party may put forward (whether in relation to a particular issue or generally); (e) the manner in which evidence or submissions are to be given (ie orally, or by written submissions or witness statement); and (f) the time at which any evidence or submissions are to be provided.

139 FTT Rules 2008 r15(1)(c).

140 *Kensington and Chelsea RLBC v CD* [2015] UKUT 396, [2015] ELR 493 per UT Judge Rowley at paras 32–38 (the case concerned acoustic evidence).

4.93   Much of the evidence given at the FTT will be from expert witnesses. The FTT has produced guidance setting out its expectations of expert witnesses providing written and/or oral evidence in an appeal or claim: *Guidance for expert witnesses giving evidence in special educational needs appeals and disability discrimination claims hearings* (SEND10) (March 2013)[141] ('the Expert Witness Guidance'). The Expert Witness Guidance in its introductory text emphasises that:

> All witnesses are expected to assist the tribunal by giving full, frank and honest evidence in a fair, impartial and independent way, regardless of whether they are employed by, or paid by, one of the parties.

4.94   The Expert Witness Guidance continues by setting out the following 'key points':

- Opinion evidence will be accorded little weight unless provided by a witness who has expertise in the relevant area.
- Experts are witnesses with particular qualifications, knowledge and/or skills, which enable them to give an opinion within their area of expertise. They do not need to be medically or scientifically qualified but must have specialist knowledge acquired by education or experience. They should avoid expressing opinions on matters beyond their expertise.
- All witnesses should assist the tribunal in accordance with the overriding objective of enabling the tribunal to deal with appeals justly and fairly.

4.95   The Expert Witness Guidance sets out the following requirements of expert reports:[142]

- state the purpose for which they were originally written;
- set out the substance of all material instructions (whether written or oral) and facts supplied that are relevant to the conclusions and opinions expressed;
- give details of any documents, literature or other research material relied on;
- describe the assessment process and process of differential diagnosis, highlighting factual assumptions, deductions from those assumptions, and any unusual, contradictory or inconsistent features of the case;
- state whether other experts have been consulted, at what stage in the process, what information was shared and how did this inform the views expressed;
- include all relevant information whether this supports one party's case or not, including confidence in quoted test scores;

---

141 This is available on the FTT's website.
142 Expert Witness Guidance, at para 5. The requirements of a letter of instruction from a representative to an expert are set out in para 4.

- identify, narrow and agree any issues where possible;
- make it clear if there is not enough information on which to reach a conclusion on a particular issue or point;
- identify any relevant facts not requiring an expert explanation in order to understand or interpret the observation, comprehension and description given, as well as any such facts that do require an explanation e.g. properly conducted examinations or appropriate tests;
- explain relevant technical subjects, or the meaning and application of applicable technical terms where helpful;
- indicate whether an opinion is provisional or qualified, stating the qualification and the reason for it, and identifying what further information is required to give an opinion without qualification;
- summarise opinions expressed with sound reasons for them;
- explain any delay between assessment and finalising the report;
- give a clear summary of the recommendations made; and
- be clearly dated and signed by the author.

4.96   Expert witness reports should also contain the following statements of truth:[143]

'I understand that my overriding duty is to assist the tribunal in matters within my expertise, and that this duty overrides any obligation to those instructing me or their clients. I confirm that I have complied with that duty and will continue to do so'

'I confirm that I have made clear which facts and matters referred to in this report are within my own knowledge and which are not. Those that are within my own knowledge I confirm to be true. The opinions I have expressed represent my true and complete opinions on the matters to which they refer'

Summoning of witnesses

4.97   The FTT also has a power, on the application of a party or on its own initiative, by summons to require any person to attend as a witness at a hearing at the time and place specified in the summons.[144]

4.98   The FTT may not compel a person to give evidence or produce any document that the person could not be compelled to give or produce on a trial of an action in a court of law.[145]

---

143 Expert Witness Guidance, para 5.
144 FTT Rules r16(1)(a). A summons must give the person required to attend 14 days' notice of the hearing (or such shorter period as the FTT may direct) and, where the person is not a party, make provision for the person's necessary expenses of attendance to be paid, and state who is to pay them; see FTT Rules r16(2).
145 FTT Rules r16(3).

Late evidence

4.99 If a party wishes to introduce evidence after the last date in the directions for doing so, permission will be required. The party will need to make an application to adduce late evidence in the Request for Changes form (form SEND7). The application will need to explain:

1) why the evidence is relevant;
2) why it was not adduced before; and
3) whether it is in the possession of the other party, and if not, when it was sent to the other party.

4.100 If the application is made very late, it is likely the FTT will determine the application at the outset of the hearing.

Working document

4.101 A working document is a copy of the final EHC plan, on which both parties have worked, that shows the changes to the wording that they want or can agree, as well as the outstanding issues in dispute on which the FTT must decide at the hearing.

4.102 The local authority should send an electronic version of the final EHC plan to the parent or the young person with its response. The parent or young person must amend it following the key below, and then send it to the local authority for its input. The final version of the EHC plan should be sent to the FTT (in electronic and hard version) before the hearing by the date specified in the directions (usually ten days prior to the hearing). It is common, however, for negotiation to continue right up to the date of the hearing and for a yet further amended version to be provided to the FTT on the morning of the hearing.

4.103 The FTT recommends a standard key to the working document which will show each party's position, as follows. The key should be included in the working document.[146]

Normal type	Original statement
Underlined type/~~strikethrough~~	Amendments/deletions agreed by both parties
Bold type	Parent or young person's proposed amendments

---

146 See the FTT's *Working document guidance* (SEND23) (available on the FTT's website).

Bold ~~strikethrough~~	Parent or young person's proposed deletions
Italic type	local authority's proposed amendments
~~Italic strikethrough~~	local authority's proposed deletions

4.104   If specific wording is derived from written evidence contained in the tribunal bundle, include a reference to the page or pages, but avoid footnotes.

4.105   There is no need to send every version of the working document prepared during the course of negotiations. The FTT needs only the last version.

4.106   The FTT ought not to accept or adopt agreed wording in the working document without checking it.[147]

Attendance forms

4.107   The standard directions make provision for the parties to complete and lodge attendance forms. These require the parties to identify:

- their witnesses;
- any representative;[148] and
- (in respect of the parent or young person) any supporter[149] or observer

that it is proposed will attend.[150]

Telephone case management calls and active case management calls

4.108   Although the FTT deals with many applications on the papers, on occasion it will be necessary to hold a telephone case management

---

147   *East Sussex CC v TW* [2016] UKUT 528 (AAC) at para 38.

148   This does not have to be a legal representative, see FTT Rules r11(1).

149   The guidance, *How to appeal a special educational needs and disability (SEND) decision* (SEND25) states that parent or young person will be limited to one supporter only, and that he or she will not be permitted to participate in the hearing. A parent or young person who wishes to have more than one supporter attend an application will need to make an application.

150   Observers are usually either local authority officers with conduct of the case who are not acting as a witness or a representative, or individuals training to participate in hearings. Observers are not allowed to participate in hearings (and some judges will require an observer not to take notes).

hearing to deal with a particular issue that has arisen. The hearing is conducted on the telephone, but with all parties (and/or their representatives) present. During the hearing the judge will invite each party to give their views on the issue, and will usually make a decision (although on occasion, the judge may reserve the decision to be provided in writing after the end of the hearing). In either case, a copy of the decision and any further directions will be sent after the hearing.

4.109   In some appeals, a week or so prior to the hearing, a FTT registrar will telephone each party to check that they are ready to proceed at the hearing, and to check whether they require the assistance of a judge to ensure that the hearing is effective (an active case management call). If necessary, the registrar can issue further directions, or arrange a telephone management hearing with a judge.

Consent orders and withdrawal

4.110   A party may withdraw the appeal, but will need the FTT's consent to do so. A withdrawal can be applied for orally at a hearing, or by a notice in writing sent to the FTT.[151]

4.111   If an application to withdraw is made in writing, it will need to set out the reasons for the application.

4.112   SEND25, *How to appeal a special educational needs and disability (SEND) decision* (2014) deals with late requests to withdraw. It explains that if the application to withdraw is made within five working days of the final hearing, then the party may be directed to attend before a FTT judge with the other party to explain the sequence of events that has led to the late withdrawal.[152]

4.113   Where the FTT agrees to the withdrawal, it must notify each party in writing that the withdrawal has taken effect.[153]

4.114   Further, the FTT has the power to make a consent order, which may be appropriate where (for example) the parties have agreed some or all of the amendment of the EHC plan such that there remains no dispute between them. The FTT must provide its agreement to a consent order, and must do so only where 'it considers it

---

151 FTT Rules r17(1) and (2). By rule 17(4) a party which has withdrawn its case may apply to the FTT for reinstatement.
152 This warning is also reflected in the standard directions.
153 FTT Rules r17(6).

appropriate'.[154] The FTT can make a consent order[155] with or without a hearing.[156]

Appeal hearings, decisions and costs

Hearings

Introduction[157]

4.115   In general the FTT will hold a hearing prior to determining an appeal.[158] Each party is entitled to attend the hearing.[159] The child may attend a hearing, and the FTT may permit the child to give evidence and to address the FTT.[160] The FTT will give the parties at least 14 days' notice of the time and place of the hearing.[161]

Hearings in private

4.116   Hearings in SEN and disability cases must be heard in private.[162] The FTT can determine who is permitted to attend the hearing or any part of it (so, for example, if a young child attends to give evidence, the FTT will sometimes direct that the child is not to be present for the remainder of the hearing).[163]

---

154   FTT Rules r29(1).
155   A consent order is a 'decision', and can be reviewed by the FTT under FTT Rules Part 5, see *R (LR, by his litigation friend, ER) v First-tier Tribunal (HESC)* [2012] UKUT 213 (AAC), [2012] ELR 456 per UT Judge Ward at para 31.
156   FTT Rules r29(2).
157   A film explaining what happens at a hearing is available on YouTube (search for 'special educational needs tribunal hearing' in the search box). Further, the FTT have produced a DVD which explains what happens at a hearing. A copy of the DVD can be requested from the FTT.
158   The FTT must hold a hearing before making a decision which disposes of proceedings unless (a) each party has consented to the matter being decided without a hearing; and (b) the FTT considered that it is able to decide the matter without the hearing, see FTT Rules r23(1). Although see paras 4.117–4.118 below in respect of failure to assess hearings.
159   FTT Rules r24(a).
160   FTT Rules r24(b).
161   FTT Rules r25.
162   FTT Rules r26(2). The FTT has the power to hold a hearing in public if the FTT considers that it is in the interests of justice.
163   FTT Rules r26(4) and (5).

Appeals against a refusal to secure an EHC needs assessment

4.117 Since 1 August 2016 the FTT has been determining all appeals against a refusal to secure an EHC needs assessment on the papers (ie without an oral hearing). The notice sent to local authorities announcing this change of approach provided that if a party requires an oral hearing, a request can be made in writing which would be 'considered' by a registrar or a judge.

4.118 It is difficult to see how this approach complies with FTT Rules r23 by which the FTT can dispose of an oral hearing only where each party has consented, and where the FTT considers it is able to decide the matter without a hearing.

What happens at the hearing?

4.119 The procedure to be adopted will depend on each judge (and on the type of appeal being heard).

4.120 In respect of appeals against the contents of EHC plans, the judge will often start by asking the parent to explain to the panel a little about the child, or by asking the young person about himself or herself. If the child or the young person is not present, the FTT will often ask to see a photograph.

4.121 As to the disputed issues, some judges will approach the appeal by dealing with the disputed issues in each section in turn (eg section B, then section F and finally section I). Other judges will approach the appeal by dealing with issues (eg speech and language, both need and provision). In either case:

- Each party will take it in turns to give evidence. The judge will often require the parties and their witnesses to confine the evidence on each issue to the matters in dispute, and will usually ask each witness not to repeat the information provided in any written report.
- Each party will be permitted to ask questions of each other's witnesses.
- The FTT will often have questions for each witness.
- When all of the evidence has been given, each party will have an opportunity to sum up (with the parent or the young person going last).

Failure of a party to attend a hearing

4.122 If a party fails to attend a hearing, the FTT may proceed with the hearing if satisfied that the party has been notified of the hearing (or that reasonable steps have been taken to notify the party of the hearing), and considers that it is in the interests of justice to proceed with the hearing.[164]

The appeal decision

4.123   When it has reached a decision that disposes of an appeal, the FTT must provide to the parties 'as soon as reasonably practicable':

1) a decision notice stating the FTT's decision;
2) written reasons for the decision; and
3) notification of any rights of review or appeal against the decision and the time within which, and the manner in which, such rights of review or appeal may be exercised.[165]

4.124   The FTT ordinarily sends the decision within ten working days.

Costs

The principles

4.125   The usual rule in the FTT is that both parties are responsible for their legal costs. The FTT has a power to make an order in respect of costs in two circumstances only:

1) in respect of wasted costs; and
2) where the FTT considers that a party or its representative has acted unreasonably in bringing, defending or conducting the proceedings.[166]

4.126   The power to award costs where a party or its representative has acted unreasonably was considered in *HJ v Brent LBC*,[167] a case in which the local authority conceded the father's appeal at the door of the tribunal.

4.127   UT Judge Jacobs held that the discussion of the Court of Appeal in *Ridehalgh v Horsefield*[168] as to the meaning of 'unreasonable' applied to FTT Rules r10(1)(b).[169] In *Ridehalgh* the Court of Appeal stated:[170]

---

164 FTT Rules r27.
165 FTT Rules r30(2). A decision may be given orally at a hearing (see FTT Rules r30(1)) but this is not the FTT's practice.
166 FTT Rules r10(1).
167 [2011] UKUT 191 (AAC), [2011] ELR 295.
168 [1994] Ch 205.
169 [2011] UKUT 191 (AAC), [2011] ELR 295 at para 7.
170 [1994] Ch 205 at 232.

'Unreasonable' also means what it has been understood to mean in this context for at least half a century. The expression aptly describes conduct which is vexatious, designed to harass the other side rather than advance the resolution of the case, and it makes no difference that the conduct is the product of excessive zeal and not improper motive. But conduct cannot be described as unreasonable simply because it leads in the event to an unsuccessful result or because other more cautious legal representatives would have acted differently. The acid test is whether the conduct permits of a reasonable explanation. If so, the course adopted may be regarded as optimistic and as reflecting on a practitioner's judgment, but it is not unreasonable.

4.128　UT Judge Jacobs applied the comments made in the context of employment tribunal proceedings by Mummery LJ in *McPherson v BNP Paribas (London Branch)*:[171]

1) First, the proper issue was the conduct of proceedings and not the decision to withdraw.
2) Second, the costs that may be awarded are not limited to those that are attributable to the unreasonable conduct: the receiving party does not have to prove that specific unreasonable conduct by the paying party caused particular costs to be incurred.
3) Third, costs must not be punitive.
4) Fourth, the unreasonable conduct is relevant at three stages: it is a precondition to an order for costs, and it is also a relevant factor to take into account in deciding whether to make an award for costs and the form of the order.[172]

4.129　The judge also stated that two principles deriving from another decision of the Court of Appeal concerning employment law, *Kovacs v Queen Mary and Westfield College*[173] were relevant, namely that a party's ability to pay is not a relevant factor, and that an award should cover as a minimum the costs attributable to the unreasonable behaviour.[174]

4.130　The judge declined to make an award of costs in favour of the father. He stated that he could not make an award of costs simply because the father won his case.[175] Further, it was not proper to second guess a party's decisions in the course of litigation. He stated that 'merely because particular evidence in the end secured

171 [2004] ICR 1398 at paras. 30, 40 and 41.
172 [2011] UKUT 191 (AAC), [2011] ELR 295 at paras 8–12.
173 [2002] ICR 919.
174 [2011] UKUT 191 (AAC), [2011] ELR 295 at para 13.
175 [2011] UKUT 191 (AAC), [2011] ELR 295 at para 16.

a particular outcome, it does not follow that it was unreasonable to defend the case or that it was unreasonably conducted'.[176]

4.131   In *Buckinghamshire CC v ST*[177] UT Judge Jacobs considered how the costs regime should apply when a late compromise is achieved (in this case, following a provisional view expressed by the FTT as to the evidence). Setting aside the FTT's cost order against the local authority, the judge stated that the FTT should:

> ... make appropriate allowances when judging the reasonableness of a party's conduct for the fact that the proceedings were compromised with the result that arguments were left undeveloped and unexplored in the context of a full analysis of a child's needs. This does not mean that a party is entitled to pursue a hopeless argument for tactical advantage ...[178]

Making an application for costs

4.132   The FTT may make an order in respect of costs either on application by a party or on its own initiative.[179]

4.133   A person who applies for a costs order must:

1) send a written application to the FTT and to the person against whom it is proposed that the order be made; and
2) send a schedule of the costs claimed with the application.[180]

4.134   Such an application can be made at any time during the proceedings, but must not be made later than 14 days after the date on which the FTT sends:

1) a decision notice recording the decision which finally disposes of all issues in the proceedings; or
2) notice under FTT Rules r17(6) that a withdrawal that ends the proceedings has taken effect.[181]

4.135   The FTT may not make a costs order against a person ('the paying person') without first:

1) giving the paying person an opportunity to make representations; and

---

176 [2011] UKUT 191 (AAC), [2011] ELR 295 at para 17.
177 [2013] UKUT 468 (AAC), [2013] ELR 528.
178 [2013] UKUT 468 (AAC), [2013] ELR 528, at para 28.
179 FTT Rules r10(3).
180 FTT Rules r10(4).
181 FTT Rules r10(5). For the resolution of an apparent contradiction between rules 10(5) and 17(6) see *UA v Haringey LBC* [2016] UKUT 87 (AAC) per UT Judge Jacobs at para 13.

2) if the paying person is an individual, considering that person's financial means.[182]

4.136 The amount of costs payable may be ascertained by:

1) summary assessment by the FTT;
2) the agreement of a specified sum by the paying person and the person entitled to receive the costs ('the receiving person'); or
3) assessment of the whole or a specified part of the costs, including the costs of the assessment, incurred by the receiving person, if not agreed.[183]

Mediation

Introduction

4.137 There are two relevant routes into mediation under the CFA 2014:

1) in respect of the matters that can be appealed to the FTT; and
2) in respect of the health and social care elements of the EHC plan.

The former requires mediation advice to be obtained prior to attending mediation, the latter does not.[184]

4.138 Despite the two routes into mediation, the Code notes that mediation about the education, health and social care elements of an EHC plan provide an opportunity for disagreements to be dealt with at one venue and holistically. Where there are disagreements about more than one area of the plan, the local authority should ensure that one mediation is arranged to cover all areas.[185]

---

182 FTT Rules r10(6).
183 FTT Rules r10(7). If the FTT makes an order for assessment under rule 10(7)(c), the paying person or the receiving person may apply to a county court for a detailed assessment of costs in accordance with the Civil Procedure Rules 1998 on the standard basis or, if specified in the order, on the indemnity basis (see FTT Rules r10(8)). Further, the FTT has the power upon making an order for the assessment of costs, to order an amount to be paid on account before the costs or expenses are assessed (see FTT Rules r10(9)).
184 Code, para 11.31.
185 Code, para 11.37.

Matters that can be appealed to the FTT: mediation advice

4.139   As to the matters which can be appealed to the FTT, a parent or young person has a right to mediation.[186] However, mediation also functions as a gateway to an appeal to the FTT. Therefore, parents and young people who wish to appeal to the FTT may do so only after they have contacted a mediation adviser, discussed whether mediation might be a suitable way of resolving the dispute, and obtained a certificate from the mediation adviser (a mediation certificate).[187] A mediation certificate can be provided either after a parent or young person decides not to proceed to mediation, or after they have completed mediation.

4.140   When a local authority sends a notice of a decision (for example, that it will not conduct an EHC needs assessment, or that it will not issue an EHC plan) which is required to include information about mediation, the notice must provide the following information:[188]

- the right of the child's parent or the young person to request mediation;
- the requirement to obtain a mediation certificate before any appeal can be made to the FTT;
- contact details for the mediation adviser that the child's parent or young person should contact to obtain the certificate;
- the timescales for requesting mediation;
- the requirement to inform the local authority if the child or young person wishes to pursue mediation, the mediation issues and (if the mediation concerns healthcare provision) the healthcare provision that the child's parent or young person wishes to be specified in the EHC plan;
- contact details for any person acting on behalf of the local authority whom the child's parent or young person should contact if they wish to pursue mediation.

4.141   A parent or young person must contact the mediation adviser within two months after written notice of the local authority's decision was sent, and inform the mediation adviser that he or she wishes to appeal.[189]

---

186   CFA 2014 s52(1).
187   CFA 2014 ss51(1), 55(1) and (3); Code, para 11.18. A 'mediation adviser' is defined as an independent person who can provide advice and information about pursuing mediation: see CFA 2014 s56(2).
188   SEND Regs reg 32; Code, para 11.19.
189   SEND Regs reg 33.

4.142   The mediation adviser will provide information on mediation, and answer any questions which the parent or the young person may have. More detail of the information to be provided is set out in the Code at paras 11.21 and 11.22. The information will normally be provided on the telephone, although information can be provided in written form, through face-to-face meetings or through other means if the parent or young person prefers.[190]

4.143   Once the information has been provided, the parent or the young person must decide whether he or she wishes to attend mediation before any appeal to the FTT, and must inform the mediation adviser of his or her decision.[191]

4.144   A mediation adviser must issue a certificate to a parent or young person where:

- the adviser has provided information and advice about pursuing mediation, and the parent or young person has informed the adviser that he or she does not wish to pursue mediation;[192] or
- the parent or young person has participated in the mediation.[193]

4.145   The certificate enables the parent or the young person to lodge an appeal, either within two months of the date of the original decision by the local authority, or within one month of receiving the certificate, whichever is the later.[194]

Exceptions to the requirement to contact a mediation adviser

4.146   A mediation certificate does not have to be obtained where the parent or young person seeks to appeal only in respect of the school or other institution named in the EHC plan, the type of school or other

---

190 Code, para 11.20.

191 SEND Regs reg 33; Code, para 11.23.

192 CFA 2014 s55(4). Where a parent or a young person who is required to obtain a mediation certificate informs the mediation adviser that he or she does not wish to pursue mediation, the mediation adviser must issue a mediation certificate within three working days of being informed by the parent or young person: SEND Regs reg 34(1). The mediation adviser may not issue a mediation certificate if the parent or young person did not contact the mediation adviser within two months date of the notice issued by the local authority: SEND Regs reg 34(2). See Code, para 11.23.

193 CFA 2014 s55(5). The mediation adviser must issue a certificate to the parent or young child within three working days of the conclusion of the mediation: see SEND Regs reg 39(1). See Code, para 11.23.

194 FTT Rules 2008 reg 20(1(c); Code, para 11.23.

institution specified in an EHC plan or the fact that an EHC plan does not name a school or other institution.[195] The mediation advice arrangements do not apply to a disability discrimination claim.

4.147   A parent or young person may still bring an appeal in the FTT where he or she was required to obtain a mediation certificate, but has failed to do so and the time limit for doing so has passed. Such an appeal requires the permission of the FTT.[196]

Arranging mediation

Where no healthcare issues arise

4.148   Where a parent or a young person informs the local authority that he or she wishes to pursue mediation, and the mediation issues do not relate to healthcare provision (ie they concern SEN and/or social care only), the local authority must arrange for mediation between it and the parent or young person within 30 days of the date on which it was informed that he or she wished to pursue mediation.[197]

Where healthcare issues arise

4.149   A parent or young person may inform the local authority that he or she wishes to pursue mediation, and the mediation issues relate solely or in part to the healthcare provision specified in the EHC plan, or the fact that no healthcare or no healthcare of a particular kind is specified in the EHC plan.[198] The local authority must, within three working days of the date of being informed that the parent or the young person wishes to pursue such mediation notify each relevant commissioning body of:

- the mediation issues; and
- the healthcare provision that the parent or young person wishes to be specified in the EHC plan.[199]

4.150   Where the mediation issues relate *solely* to healthcare provision, the responsible commissioning body (or if more than one, bodies acting jointly) must arrange for mediation between it (or them) and the

---

195 CFA 2014 s55(2); Code, paras 11.24 and 11.25.
196 SEND Regs reg 34(3),
197 SEND Regs reg 36; Code, para 11.26.
198 SEND Regs reg 35(1); Code, para 11.32.
199 SEND Regs reg 35(2); Code, para 11.33.

child's parent or the young person within 30 days from the date on which they received notification from the local authority.[200]

4.151 Where the mediation issues do not just include healthcare provision (but also include SEN and/or social care), the local authority must arrange for mediation between it and each responsible commissioning body and the parent or the young person within 30 days from the date on which it was informed by the parent or young person that he or she wished to pursue mediation.[201]

The mediation[202]

4.152 If the parent or the young person wishes to attend mediation, the local authority must take part and attend the mediation.[203] Similarly, where the mediation issues concern health care provision, the responsible commissioning body must take part in the mediation.[204]

4.153 Further, the local authority (or the responsible commissioning body) must ensure that the mediation is attended by representatives who have authority to resolve the mediation issues.[205] That body must inform the child's parent or the young person of the date and place of mediation at least five working days prior to the mediation, unless the child's parent or the young person consents to this period of time being reduced.[206]

4.154 The legislation limits attendance at the mediation to the following:

1) the parties to the mediation;
2) any advocate or supporter the child's parent or young person wishes to attend the mediation;
3) where the child's parent is a party to the mediation, the child (with the agreement of the parent and the mediator);
4) where the young person's alternative person[207] is a party to the mediation, the young person (with the agreement of the alternative person or the mediator); and

---

200 SEND Regs reg 35(3); Code, para 11.35.
201 SEND Regs reg 35(4); Code, para 11.34.
202 The Code sets out the elements of an effective mediation at para 11.38.
203 Code, paras 11.26–11.27.
204 Code, para 11.34.
205 SEND Regs reg 37(1).
206 SEND Regs reg 37(2).
207 Where a young person does not have capacity, see SEND Regs reg 64(2).

5) any other person, with the consent of all of the parties to the mediation, or where there is no such agreement, with the consent of the mediator.[208]

4.155   The mediator must have sufficient knowledge of the legislation relating to SEN, health and social care to be able to conduct the mediation.[209] The mediator must have received accredited mediation training.[210] Further, the mediator must be independent of the local authority and/or the relevant health commissioners.[211]

4.156   Mediation meetings are confidential, and are conducted without prejudice to the to the FTT process.[212]

4.157   Where the child's parent is a party to the mediation, the mediator must take reasonable steps to ascertain the views of the child about the mediation issues.[213] Where the young person's alternative person is a party to the mediation, the mediator must take reasonable steps to ascertain the views of the young person about the mediation issues.[214]

4.158   Parents and young people do not have to pay any of the costs of the mediation.[215] Further, the SEND Regs make provision for the payment of the expenses of the child's parent or the young person attending mediation by the local authority.[216] The Code provides that where the responsible commissioning body arranges the mediation, they must pay the reasonable expenses of the parent or young person.[217]

Mediation certificate

4.159   Where mediation is pursued before making an appeal to the FTT, the mediation adviser must issue a certificate under CFA 2014 s55(5) to

208 SEND Regs reg 38(1).
209 SEND Regs reg 40.
210 Code, para 11.15.
211 Code, para 11.15. No one who is directly employed by a local authority in England can be a mediation adviser, and no one who is directly employed by a local authority in England or a relevant health commissioner can act as a mediator.
212 Code, para 11.29.
213 SEND Regs reg 38(2).
214 SEND Regs reg 38(3).
215 Code, para 11.26.
216 SEND Regs reg 41.
217 Code, para 11.34.

the parent or young person within 3 working days of the conclusion of the mediation.[218]

4.160 The mediation adviser must also issue a mediation certificate if the local authority is unable to arrange for mediation within 30 days (whether or not the parent or young person later participates in mediation).[219]

Steps to be taken by the local authority after mediation

4.161 Where a mediation has taken place, and the parties to the mediation reach an agreement to be recorded in writing (the mediation agreement), the local authority must take the following steps.[220]

1) First, where the mediation issues in the mediation agreement are those on which the child or young person has a right of appeal to the FTT, the local authority shall comply with the time limits applicable after the FTT has made an order.[221]

2) Second, where the mediation agreement requires the local authority or the responsible commissioning body to do something in respect of which there is no right of appeal to the FTT, that step must be taken within two weeks of the date of the mediation agreement.[222]

3) Third, where the local authority was not party to the mediation agreement, the responsible commissioning body must notify the local authority of the mediation agreement within one week of the date of the mediation agreement.[223]

4.162 The mediation agreement can make provision for different timescales if agreed by the parties.[224]

---

218 SEND Regs reg 39(1); Code, para 11.28.
219 SEND Regs reg 39(2) and (3). This should be done within three days of the mediation adviser being notified, see Code, para 11.27.
220 Code, para 11.30.
221 SEND Regs reg 42(2), referring to the time limits in reg 44 (and set out above at para 4.30).
222 SEND Regs reg 42(3).
223 SEND Regs reg 42(4).
224 SEND Regs reg 42(5).

Complaints

4.163   The local authority has a statutory duty to set up a complaints procedure to address disputes in respect of SEN between the local authority
or a relevant body,[225] and the parents or children or young people in
the local authority's area.[226] The complaints procedure must provide
for the appointment of independent persons.[227] The Code provides
a more detailed account of what the complaints procedure must
contain.[228]

225 Defined in CFA 2014 s57(10) as the governing body of a maintained school,
maintained nursery school or institution within the further education sector
or the proprietor of an academy.
226 CFA 2014 s57.
227 CFA 2014 s57(6).
228 Code, paras. 11.1–11.12.

CHAPTER 5

Children and young people with SEN in detention

continued

Key points

- All children and young people entering youth detention are given an educational assessment.
- Local authorities must not cease to maintain an education, health and care (EHC) plan when a child or young person with special educational needs (SEN) enters custody. They must keep the plan while the detained person is detained, and they must maintain it and review it when the detained person is released.
- If the detained person has an EHC plan prior to being detained (or one is completed while the detained person is in the relevant youth accommodation), the local authority must arrange special educational provision for the detained person while he or she is detained.
- If the EHC plan for a detained person specifies healthcare provision, the health services commissioner for the relevant youth accommodation must arrange appropriate healthcare provision for the detained person.
- If a young person is in detention within a year of the last review of the EHC plan, the home authority should conduct a monitoring meeting (and continue to do so at a minimum every 12 months).
- The home authority may assess the education, health and care needs of a detained child or young person.
- If the home authority undertakes a detained person's EHC needs assessment, it must obtain advice and information from specified professionals, as well as the child's parent or the young person.
- Having carried out a detained person's EHC needs assessment, the home authority must determine whether or not to issue an EHC plan.
- If the home authority determines that in the light of the detained person's EHC needs assessment it is necessary for special educational provision to be made for the detained person on release from detention, the home authority must prepare an EHC plan.
- On release, the home authority must maintain the EHC plan and review it as soon as reasonably practicable after the release date.
- The parent of a detained child, or a detained young person, has more limited rights of appeal than those which apply to the general regime.

Introduction

5.1   As noted in the Code, there are large numbers of detained children and young people with special educational needs (SEN): approximately 18 per cent of children and young people in custody have a statement of SEN, and over 60 per cent have speech, language and communication needs.[1]

5.2   Special provision is made in respect of 'detained persons' in:

- CFA 2014 ss48 and 70–75;
- the Special Educational Needs and Disability (Detained Persons) Regulation 2015 SI No 62 (SENDDP Regs); and
- the Code.[2]

5.3   A 'detained person' is a child or young person who is: (a) 18 or under; (b) subject to a detention order;[3] and (c) detained in relevant youth accommodation.[4] A 'detained person' includes, in respect of provisions applying on a person's release, a person who, immediately before release, was a detained person.[5] In general, therefore, the provisions of the CFA 2014 do not apply to a detained person.[6]

5.4   The following terms appear in the legislation:

- **Appropriate person:** Means, in relation to a detained person, the detained person's parent, or where the detained person is a young person, the detained person.[7] As with the general regime, if the appropriate person lacks capacity, then the definition is modified.[8]
- **Home authority:** Means the local authority in whose area the child or young person is ordinarily resident; or, in the case of a

---

1   Code, para 2.

2   Code, paras 10.60–10.150. Note that the local authorities, youth offending teams, health commissioners and those in charge of the relevant youth accommodation must have regard to the relevant provisions of the Code: see CFA 2014 s77(1); and Code, para 10.63.

3   A 'detention order' is defined in Education Act (EA) 1996 s562(1A)(a) as meaning a person detained in pursuance of an order made by a court, or an order of recall made by the secretary of state.

4   CFA 2014 s70(5).

5   CFA 2014 s70(5).

6   CFA 2014 s70(1). The following provisions do apply to detained children or young people (see CFA 2014 s70(2)): s28 (local authority duty to co-operate with local partners); s31 (duty of local authority to co-operate in specific cases); s77 (the applicability of the Code of Practice); s80 (parents and young people lacking capacity); and s83 (interpretation of CFA 2014 Part 3).

7   CFA 2014 s70(5).

8   SENDDP Regs regs 31–32 and Schedule; Code, annex 1.

child or young person who immediately before the beginning of the detention was, or at any time since then has been, a looked after child, means the local authority who are looking after or have most recently been looking after the child or young person.[9] The Code, however, refers throughout to 'local authority' and not to 'home authority'.

- **Relevant youth accommodation:** Means accommodation which is: (a) youth detention accommodation (within the meaning given by Powers of Criminal Courts (Sentencing) Act 2000 s107(1)); and (b) is not in a young offender institution, or part of such an institution, that is used wholly or mainly for the detention of persons aged 18 and over, but does not include relevant youth accommodation outside of England.[10]
- **Person in charge of the relevant youth accommodation:** In practice this means the governor, director or principal in charge of the accommodation.[11]

All children or young people entering detention

5.5   The youth offending team (YOT) must notify the local authority when a child or young person aged 18 or under is detained.[12] If the detained person has an education, health and care (EHC) plan the local authority must send it to the YOT, the person in charge of the relevant youth accommodation and the detained person's health commissioner[13] within five working days of becoming aware of the detention.[14]

---

9 CFA 2014 s70(6); and EA 1996 s562J(1). The Code gives further guidance in respect of looked after children at paras 10.142–10.145.

10   CFA 2014 s70(5); and EA 1996 s562J(1A)(b). In practice, relevant youth accommodation will be Youth Offender Institutions, Secure Training Centres, Secure Children's Homes and Secure Colleges, but not Young Offender Institutions for 18–21 year olds. The provisions do not apply to those serving their sentences in the community, or those detained in the adult prison estate.

11   Code, para 10.63.

12   Crime and Disorder Act 1989 s39A(1)(a), (2).

13   Defined in CFA 2014 s74(8) in relation to a detained person, as the body that is under a duty under the National Health Service Act 2006 to arrange for the provision of services or facilities in respect of the detained person during his or her detention.

14   SENDDP Regs reg 17(1); Code, paras 10.72, 10.76. The EHC plan will feed into the assessment undertaken by YOTs of all detained persons entering the youth justice system (Code, para 10.71), and into the educational assessment undertaken of all detained persons (Code, para 10.76).

5.6   If a detained child or young person has SEN but no EHC plan, the local authority should provide all available details to the YOT, including details of any assessments undertaken and the needs identified.[15]

5.7   All children and young people entering youth detention are assessed by the YOT using the approved Youth Justice Board (YJB) assessment process.[16] This includes an educational assessment.[17] Local authorities should respond to requests from the YOT for information as soon as possible.[18] Information from the local authority will feed into the YOT assessment.[19]

5.8   The results of the assessments should enable the education provider to develop an individual learning plan for the delivery of education for each detained person.[20] The Code requires special educational provision to be put in place 'as soon as possible'. Further, it advises that providers in relevant youth accommodation should:

- meet the educational needs of all detained persons, including those with SEN, whether they have an EHC plan or not;
- ensure SEN provision, identification and support of SEN follows the model for schools and colleges set out in chapter 6 of the Code;
- have staff who are suitably qualified to support this (such as SEN co-ordinators (SENCOs)) and make referrals to other specialist support where appropriate;
- liaise and co-operate with the local authority where a detained person has an EHC plan.

5.9   In respect of healthcare provision, all children and young people entering detention will be screened and assessed using the Comprehensive Health Assessment Tool (CHAT), which includes a screening for speech, language and communication needs. If a detained person has an EHC plan when he or she enters detention, the information in the EHC plan, as well as from the local authority provided by the YOT, should inform or supplement this assessment. This should lead to an individual healthcare plan for each detained person.[21]

15 Code, para 10.72.
16 Code, para 10.71.
17 Code, para 10.76.
18 Code, para 10.71.
19 Code, para 10.72.
20 Code, para 10.76.
21 Code, para 10.80.

Children or young people who enter detention with an EHC plan (or acquire one while detained)

5.10   If a detained person has an EHC plan immediately before the beginning of his or her detention, or has had an EHC plan secured while in detention, the home authority must keep the EHC plan while the person is detained in the relevant youth accommodation.[22]

5.11   The home authority must arrange appropriate special educational provision for the detained person while he or she is detained in relevant youth accommodation.[23] A modified definition of 'special educational provision' applies, namely:

(a) the special educational provision specified in the EHC plan, or

(b) if it appears to the home authority that it is not practicable for that special educational provision to be provided, educational provision corresponding as closely as possible to that special educational provision, or

(c) if it appears to the home authority that the special educational provision specified in the plan is no longer appropriate for the person, such special educational provision as reasonably appears to the home authority to be appropriate.[24]

5.12   Before deciding that the educational provision in the EHC plan is no longer appropriate, local authorities should seek appropriate professional advice and work with the custodial case manager, the YOT, the person in charge of the relevant youth accommodation (as well as the education provider) and the appropriate person to review the detained person's needs taking into account the information in the EHC plan, the literacy and numeracy assessment and any other assessment of the detained person's needs. On release, the local authority must review the EHC plan and the special educational provision and if the special educational provision specified in the plan is no longer appropriate this should trigger a reassessment of the child or young person's needs.[25]

5.13   Similarly, if the EHC plan specifies healthcare, the detained person's health services commissioner must arrange appropriate healthcare provision for the detained person while he or she is detained in relevant youth accommodation.[26] As with special educational

---

22 CFA 2014 s74(1), (2); Code, paras 10.109, 10.121.

23 CFA 2014 s74(4).

24 CFA 2014 s74(6); Code, paras 10.123–10.125.

25 Code, para 10.125.

26 CFA 2014 s74(5); Code, paras 10.78-10.80, 10.128-10.131.

provision, a modified definition of 'healthcare provision' applies, namely:[27]

    (a) the health care provision specified in the EHC plan, or

    (b) if it appears to the detained person's health services commissioner that it is not practicable for that health care provision to be provided, health care provision corresponding as closely as possible to that health care provision, or

    (c) if it appears to the detained person's health service commissioner that the health care provision specified in the plan is no longer appropriate for the person, such health care provision as reasonably appears to the detained person's health services commissioner to be appropriate.

5.14   As for social care provision, the Code provides that the home authority should consider whether any social care needs identified in the EHC plan will remain while the detained person is in detention and provide appropriate provision if necessary.[28]

5.15   Importantly, while the detained person is in custody, the home authority must not amend the EHC plan, carry out a reassessment or cease to maintain the EHC plan.[29]

Monitoring an EHC plan while in detention

5.16   The Code provides that a home authority must promote the fulfilment of the detained person's learning potential while the person is in custody and on his or her release. The home authority should use the EHC plan to actively monitor progress towards these and other long-term outcomes.[30]

5.17   Further, when a detained person is in detention within a year of the last review of the EHC plan, the home authority should conduct a monitoring meeting and continue to do so as a minimum every 12 months. The monitoring meeting should consider the special educational and health provision arranged for the detained person in custody and the appropriateness of the provision in the light of the detained person's progress or changed circumstances. If the

---

27 CFA 2014 s74(7).

28 Code, para 10.67. The Code gives the example of a detained child who is looked after, whose existing relationship with his or her social worker should continue and the detained child should continue to access specific services and support where needed.

29 Code, para, 10.122.

30 Code, para 10.132.

provision in the EHC plan appears inappropriate, the home authority should follow the guidance in the Code, para 10.125. The local
authority can request that the person in charge of the relevant youth
accommodation or the YOT convenes the monitoring meeting.[31]

Deciding whether to assess the education, health and care needs of detained persons[32]

5.18   CFA 2014 s71 makes provision for the assessment of the EHC
needs of detained persons for whom (a) the home authority is a local
authority in England; and (b) no EHC plan is being kept by a local
authority.[33]

5.19   Consideration of whether a 'detained person's EHC needs assessment'[34] is required may come about in one of two ways:[35]

1) a request to the home authority to secure a detained person's EHC
needs assessment may be made by the appropriate person, or the
person in charge of the relevant youth accommodation where the
detained person is being detained;[36] or
2) the detained person has been brought to the home authority's
attention by any person by someone who has or may have SEN, or
the detained person has otherwise come to the home authority's
attention as someone who has or may have SEN.[37]

5.20   In either case, as with CFA 2014 s36 (assessment of EHC needs),
CFA 2014 s71 mandates a two-stage process for assessing the EHC
needs of detained persons.

---

31 Code, para 10.133.
32 Code, paras 10.84-10.88.
33 CFA 2014 s71(1).
34 Defined in CFA 2014 s70(5) as 'an assessment of what the education, health
care and social care needs of a detained person will be on his or her release
from custody'.
35 CFA 2014 s71(4).
36 CFA 2014 s71(2).
37 CFA 2014 s71(4). The Code emphasises that anyone can bring the detained
person to the attention of their home authority if they are concerned that he or
she may have SEN. In particular, YOTs should consider bringing a detained
person to the attention of the home authority if the approved YJB assessment
tool raises concerns about a detained person who might have SEN. This should
be done with the knowledge, and preferably with the consent of, the child or
young person in question: Code, para 10.82.

5.21   The home authority must first determine whether it *may* be necessary for special educational provision to be made for the detained person in accordance with an EHC plan on release from detention (in effect, this is a screening decision).[38] In making such a determination, the home authority must consult the appropriate person and the person in charge of the relevant youth accommodation where the detained person is detained.[39]

5.22   Where the home authority determines that it will not be necessary for special educational provision to be made for the detained person in accordance with an EHC plan on release from detention, it must notify the appropriate person and the person in charge of the relevant youth accommodation where the detained person is detained of the decision, and of the reasons for that decision.[40]

5.23   The second stage of the process applies if the home authority determines that it may be necessary for special educational provision to be made for the detained person in accordance with the EHC plan on release from detention, and if the detained person has not had an EHC needs assessment within the previous six months.[41] The home authority must notify the appropriate person and the person in charge of the relevant youth accommodation where the detained person is detained:

- that it is considering securing a detained person's EHC needs assessment for the detained person; and
- that the appropriate person and the person in charge of the relevant youth accommodation where the detained person is detained each have the right to express views to the authority (orally or in writing) and submit evidence to the authority.[42]

---

38   CFA 2014 s71(3).
39   CFA 2014 s71(5).
40   CFA 2014 s71(6). This must be done as soon as practicable, but in any event within six weeks of receiving a request for a detained person's EHC needs assessment or the detained person coming to the local authority's attention: see SENDDP Regs reg 4(a).
41   Either under CFA 2014 s36 or s71.
42   CFA 2014 s71(7) and (8). The local authority must also notify: (a) the home commissioning body; (b) the detained person's health commissioner; (c) the officers of the home authority who exercise the home authority's social services functions for children or young people with SEN; (d) the YOT responsible for the detained person; and (e) if the detained person is a registered pupil at a school, or a student at a post-16 institution, the headteacher or principal respectively: see SENDDP Regs reg 4(2).

5.24   In deciding whether to carry out a detained person's EHC needs assessment, the issue for the home authority is if, after having regard to any views expressed and evidence submitted under CFA 2014 s71(8), it is of the opinion that the detained person has or may have SEN, and it may be necessary for special educational provision to be made for the detained person in accordance with an EHC plan on release from detention.[43]

5.25   In reaching this decision, the Code advises that a local authority should pay particular attention to the matters listed in the Code at para 10.87. Further, the Code provides that the local authority may develop criteria to guide them in deciding whether it is necessary to carry out an assessment of post-detention EHC needs and following this whether to issue an EHC plan. Local authorities must not apply a blanket policy of, for example, refusing to assess where the detained person has a long sentence or where the person has not been engaged in education for a number of years. Each case must be considered individually.[44]

5.26   The home authority must notify the appropriate person and the person in charge of the relevant youth accommodation of its decision whether or not it is necessary to secure a detained person's EHC needs assessment.[45] It must also notify the appropriate person of:

- his or her right to appeal the decision;
- the time limits for doing so;
- the relevant information on mediation;[46]
- the availability of information and advice in connection with a detained person's EHC needs assessment.

5.27   The time limit for determining whether to conduct a detained person's needs assessment is, as with the general regime, six weeks from the date on which the request was made or from the date on which the detained person came to the local authority's attention.[47] Time may be extended in specified circumstances.[48]

---

43 CFA 2014 s71(9).
44 Code, para 10.88.
45 SENDDP Regs reg 5(1), and it must notify the persons consulted who are listed in SENDDP Regs reg 4(2).
46 See SENDDP Regs reg 18.
47 SENDDP Regs regs 4(1) and 5(1).
48 SENDDP Regs reg 5(4): where the school is closed, or where exceptional personal circumstances affect the detained person (or if he or she is a child) his or her parent, or where (if the detained person is a child) the child's parent is absent from the area of the authority for a continuous period of four weeks during the relevant time period.

Carrying out a detained person's needs assessment

5.28   The process is broadly similar to that under the general regime. In particular, the Code notes the requirement that the assessment should be 'based on a co-ordinated assessment and planning process which puts the detained person, and the child's parent, at the centre'.[49]

5.29   The home authority must seek the prescribed advice,[50] namely:

- advice from the appropriate person;
- educational advice or information;[51]
- medical advice or information from a healthcare professional identified by the home commissioning body;
- psychological advice and information from an educational psychologist;
- advice and information in relation to social care;
- advice and information from the person in charge of the relevant youth accommodation where the detained person is detained;
- advice and information from the YOT responsible for the detained person;
- advice and information from any other person the home authority thinks is appropriate;
- where the detained person would have been in or beyond year 9 (if not for his or her detention), advice and information in relation to provision to assist the detained person in preparation for adulthood and independent living; and
- advice and information from any person the appropriate person reasonably requests that the home authority seek advice from.

---

49   Code, para 10.89.

50   SENDDP Regs reg 6(1); Code, para 10.91. In seeking the advice, the home authority must provide each person with copies of any representations made by the appropriate person, and any evidence submitted by or at the request of the appropriate person (and may, with their consent, provide the representations and evidence made by the person in charge of the relevant youth accommodation where the detained person is detained), see SENDDP Regs reg 6(3); and Code, para 10.92.

51   SENDDP Regs reg 6(1)(b): from the headteacher or principal of the school or post-16 institution that the detained person was attending immediately prior to their detention, or where not available, from a person who the home authority is satisfied has experience of teaching children or young people with SEN, or if any parent of the detained person is a serving member of the Armed Forces, from the Secretary of State for Defence.

5.30   There are particular obligations to seek advice from specialist teachers where the detained person is either hearing impaired or visually impaired.[52]

5.31   The bodies required to co-operate in the production of a detained person's EHC needs assessment must comply with the request within six weeks, unless one of the specified exceptions applies.[53]

5.32   The SENDDP Regs place specific duties on a home authority when securing a detained person's EHC needs assessment, namely to:[54]

- consult the detained person and, where the detained person is a child, the child's parent; and take into account his or her views, wishes and feelings;
- consider any information provided to the home authority by, or at the request of, the detained person and, where the detained person is a child, the child's parent;
- consider the information and advice obtained from the bodies specified in SENDDP Regs reg 6 and set out in para 5.29 above;
- engage the detained person, and where the detained person is a child, the child's parent, and ensure that he or she is able to participate in decisions;[55]
- have regard to the need to support the detained person in order to facilitate his or her development, and help the detained person to achieve his or her best educational and other outcomes; and
- minimise disruption for the detained person and his or her family.

Outcome of the detained person's needs assessment: deciding whether to issue an EHC plan

5.33   Having carried out a detained person's EHC needs assessment the home authority must decide whether to issue an EHC plan. The statutory test is whether in the light of the detained person's EHC

---

52 SENDDP Regs reg 6(2).
53 SENDDP Regs reg 8.
54 SENDDP Regs reg 7.
55 SENDDP Regs reg 9; Code, paras 10.90, 10.106–107: there is a further obligation to consider whether advice, information or support is necessary to enable the detained person or their parent (where the detained person is a child) to take part effectively in the assessment, and if so, to provide it.

needs assessment it is necessary for special educational provision to be made for the detained person on release from detention.[56]

5.34   The home authority will need to determine whether the special educational provision required to meet the needs of the detained person can reasonably be provided from within the resources normally available to schools and post-16 institutions, or whether an EHC plan may be needed to ensure that support is provided and co-ordinated effectively for the person on release from custody.[57]

Notification of the EHC plan decision

5.35   After a detained person's needs assessment has been carried out, the local authority must notify the appropriate person and the person in charge of the relevant youth accommodation where the detained person is detained of:

1) the outcome of the assessment;
2) whether it proposes to secure that an EHC plan is prepared for the detained person; and
3) the reasons for the decision.[58]

5.36   If the decision is *not* to issue an EHC plan, the notification should be made as soon as practicable, but in any event within 16 weeks of the date of the request for a detained person's EHC needs assessment or the date on which the detained person came to the local authority's attention.[59] This time limit is subject to limited exemptions.[60] If the exemptions apply, the appropriate person should be informed so that he or she is aware of, and understands, the reasons for the delay.[61]

5.37   Further, if the decision is not to issue an EHC plan, the home authority must also notify the appropriate person of his or her right to appeal the decision, the time limits for doing so, the information

---

56   CFA 2014 s72(1).
57   Code, para 10.99, and see paras 2.28–2.34 above in respect of the case-law under CFA 2014 s37.
58   CFA 2014 s71(10).
59   SENDDP Regs reg 10(1). Where the decision is negative, the home authority must also notify the home commissioning body, the detained person's health services commissioner, the YOT responsible for the detained person and the headteacher of the school or principal of a school or post-16 institution at which the child or young person is a registered pupil or student.
60   SENDDP Regs reg 10(4); Code, para 10.97.
61   Code, para 10.98.

regarding mediation[62] and the availability of information and advice relating to the SEN of children and young people.[63]

EHC plans

Form

5.38 The form of the EHC plan is the same as under the usual CFA 2014 provisions (see paras 2.39–2.40 above), save that it refers to the provision that will be required on release from detention.[64] The healthcare provision specified in the EHC plan must be agreed by the home commissioning body.[65] Where the detained person would have been in or beyond year 9 (if not for his or her detention) the EHC plan must include within the special educational provision, healthcare provision and social care provision specified, provision to assist the detained person in preparation for adulthood and independent living on release from detention.[66] The advice and information obtained in accordance with SENDDP Regs reg 6(1) (and listed in para 5.29 above) must be set out in appendices to the EHC plan.[67]

Preparation

5.39 When preparing a detained person's EHC plan, a home authority must take into account the evidence received when securing the detained person's EHC needs assessment, and consider how best to achieve the outcomes to be sought for the detained person on release from detention.[68]

5.40 The following provisions of the general regime apply when a home authority is securing an EHC plan for detained persons (with the language amended to reflect its application to detained persons as appropriate):[69]

- CFA 2014 s33(2)–(7): the presumption of mainstream institution (see paras 3.71–3.77 above);

---

62 SENDDP Regs reg 18.
63 SENDDP Regs reg 10(3); Code, para 10.95.
64 SENDDP Regs reg 12(1); Code, para 10.103.
65 SENDDP Regs reg 12(2).
66 SENDDP Regs reg 12(3).
67 SENDDP Regs reg 12(4).
68 SENDDP Regs reg 11.
69 CFA 2014 s72(2) and (3).

- CFA 2014 s37(2)–(5): the definition and content of an EHC plan (see chapter 3 above);
- CFA 2014 s38: the preparation of draft EHC plans (see paras 2.41–2.43 above);
- CFA 2014 s39: finalising EHC plans, request for particular school or other institution (see paras 2.44–2.45 above);
- CFA 2014 s40: finalising EHC plans, no request for particular school or other institution (see para 2.46 above).

5.41   In respect of draft plans, when a home authority sends a draft plan to the appropriate person it must:[70]

- give the person at least 15 days, beginning on the day on which the draft plan was served, in which to (a) make representations about the content of the draft plan and to request that a particular school or other institution be named in the plan, and (b) require the home authority to arrange a meeting between the person and an officer of the home authority at which the draft plan can be discussed; and
- advise the person where he or she can find information about the schools and colleges that are available for the detained person to attend on release from detention.

5.42   The final plan must be in the form of the draft plan, or in a form modified in the light of representations made by the appropriate person.[71]

5.43   The home authority must send the finalised EHC plan to:

- the appropriate person;
- the person in charge of the relevant youth accommodation where the detained person is detained;
- the YOT responsible for the detained person;
- the governing body, proprietor or principal of any school or other institution named in the EHC plan;
- the home commissioning body; and
- the detained person's health services commissioner.[72]

This should be done as soon as practicable, but in any event within 20 weeks of the date of the request for a detained person's EHC needs

---

70 SENDDP Regs reg 13(1).
71 SENDDP Regs reg 14(1).
72 SENDDP Regs reg 13(2); Code, para 108.

assessment or of the detained person coming to the attention of the home authority.[73]

5.44 When sending the final EHC plan to the appropriate person, the home authority must notify the person of:

- his or her right to appeal matters within the EHC plan;
- the time limits for doing so;
- the information concerning mediation;[74] and
- the availability of information and advice relating to the SEN of children and young people.[75]

Incomplete needs assessment on entering or leaving detention

5.45 As many children and young people will be serving short sentences, it may be that a detained person is part of the way through an assessment of EHC needs on release from detention. The timeframes for the EHC assessment, and issuing an EHC plan, do not start again just because the young person has left custody. Thus the home authority must ensure:

- any EHC plan is finalised within 20 weeks;
- any decision not to secure an EHC plan is finalised within 16 weeks;
- a decision whether or not to secure an EHC needs assessment is made within six weeks;

from the date on which the detained person has been brought or comes to the attention of the home authority.[76]

---

73 SENDDP Regs reg 13(3); Code, para 10.93. There are exceptions to this time limit, see SENDDP Regs reg 13(4).

74 SENDDP Regs reg 18.

75 SENDDP Regs reg 14(2).

76 SENDDP Regs reg 15(1); Code, para 10.113. This does not apply where the local authority carrying out the EHC needs assessment post-detention is different to the home authority which started the detained person's EHC needs assessment: see SENDDP Regs reg 15(3). If the detained person is released to a new local authority before the EHC needs assessment process has been completed, the new local authority needs to consider whether it needs to carry out an EHC needs assessment. The new local authority should take account of the fact that the old authority decided to carry out an EHC needs assessment (and should seek information concerning the assessment from the old local authority) when making its decision: Code, para 10.141.

5.46   In order for these timescales to be maintained, the SENDDP Regs permit a local authority to treat anything done in respect of a detained person's needs assessment as discharging any comparable requirement in relation to an EHC needs assessment.[77]

5.47   Conversely, children or young people who enter detention may be part of the way through the process of an EHC needs assessment which commenced prior to them entering detention. Again, the fact of the detention does not alter the applicable time periods.[78] Further, in such circumstances a home authority may treat anything done in relation to an EHC needs assessment as discharging any comparable requirement in relation to a detained person's EHC needs assessment.[79]

Transfer between places of relevant youth accommodation

5.48   The YOT must inform the home authority of any transfer of a detained person from one place of relevant youth accommodation to another.[80] If a home authority is informed that a detained person has moved, or will move, to new relevant youth accommodation, it must send a copy of the EHC plan to the person in charge of that relevant youth accommodation within five working days of the date on which it was informed.[81]

5.49   If the detained person is part-way through an assessment or the development of an EHC plan when he or she transfers from one place of relevant youth accommodation to another, the local authority and appropriate CCG must continue and complete the process following the guidance in the Code, para. 10.116. Specifically:

1) any EHC plan must be finalised within 20 weeks; and
2) anything already completed in relation to an EHC needs assessment by the person in charge of the relevant youth accommodation, including information and advice received, may be treated as having been completed in relation to the new relevant youth accommodation.[82]

---

77   SENDDP Regs reg 15(2); Code, para 10.114.
78   SENDDP Regs reg 15(4); Code, para 10.113.
79   SENDDP Regs reg 15(5); Code, para 10.114.
80   Crime and Disorder Act 1989 s39A(1)(b) and (2).
81   SENDDP Regs reg 17(2); Code, para 10.115.
82   Code, para 10.116.

Transfer from relevant youth accommodation to a custodial establishment for adults

5.50 When a detained person is transferred to an adult custodial establishment, the person in charge of the relevant youth accommodation should ensure that all relevant SEN information, including the EHC plan, is passed to the receiving establishment prior to transfer taking place, so that any additional support needs can be taken into account by the receiving establishment.[83] The SEN duties in the CFA 2014 no longer apply once a young person is transferred to the adult secure estate.

Cross-border provision between England and Wales

5.51 Local authorities in England should support detained persons with EHC plans whose home authority is in England but who are detained in Wales in the same way that they support detained persons whose home authority is in England and who are placed in England.[84]

5.52 Host local authorities in England must use their best endeavours to secure that appropriate provision is made for detained persons with statements under EA 1996 s562C whose home authority is in Wales but who are detained in young offender institutions in England.[85]

Release

General

5.53 Where a child or young person is released from detention, the YOT must inform the home local authority and any other local authority in whose area the YOT expects the person to live on release.[86]

---

83 Code, para 10.146.
84 Code, para, 10.149.
85 Code, para 10.150.
86 Crime and Disorder Act 1989 s39A(3) and (4); Code, paras 10.134–10.135.

Detained person with EHC plan

Released to home authority

5.54   When the detained person is released, the home authority must maintain the EHC plan and review it as soon as reasonably practicable after the release date.[87] If the EHC plan was issued while the detained person was in custody, the review should consider sections I and J of the EHC plan.[88]

Released to a local authority which is not the home authority

5.55   Where on the release date a detained person in respect of whom an EHC plan is kept becomes (or is to become) the responsibility of a local authority which is not the home authority ('the new authority'), the home authority must disclose the EHC plan to the new authority within five working days of being informed of the release of the detained person to the new authority.[89] The new authority will become responsible for maintaining the EHC plan and for securing the special educational provision specified in it.[90]

5.56   The new authority must disclose the EHC plan to the responsible commissioning body within five working days following the date it either became responsible for the child or young person, or if later, the date on which it received a copy of the EHC plan.[91] Where it is not practicable for the responsible commissioning body to arrange the healthcare provision specified in the EHC plan, it must within 15 working days following the date on which it received a copy of the EHC plan, request that the new authority makes an EHC needs assessment or reviews the EHC plan, and where the new authority receives such a request, it must comply with it.[92]

Education on release for those in a custodial establishment for adults

5.57   If a detained person in an adult custodial establishment had an EHC plan immediately before custody, or if the person was issued with a plan while in relevant youth accommodation, and if the person is

---

87   CFA 2014 s48; Code, paras 10.110, 10.136–10.137.
88   Code, para 10.136. The process in the Code, chapter 9 must be followed.
89   SENDDP Regs reg 16(1) and (2).
90   Code, para 10.140.
91   SENDDP Regs reg 16(3); Code, para 10.140.
92   SENDDP Regs reg 16(4); Code, para 10.140.

still under the age of 25 when he or she is released from custody, the local authority must maintain and review the EHC plan if the young person plans to stay in education.[93] If the young person plans to continue his or her education on release, the Offenders' Learning and Skills Service provider and the National Careers Service provider should liaise to ensure the responsible local authority can review the EHC plan as soon as possible.[94]

Rights of appeal

5.58   The rights of appeal of detained persons are more limited than those which apply in the general regime. An appropriate person in relation to a detained person may only appeal to the First-tier Tribunal (FTT) against the following matters:[95]

- a decision of the home authority not to secure a detained person's EHC needs assessment for the detained person;
- a decision of the home authority, following a detained person's EHC needs assessment that it is not necessary for special educational provision to be made for the detained person in accordance with an EHC plan on release from detention;
- where an EHC plan is secured for the detained person, (a) the school or other institution named in the plan or the type of school or other institution named in the plan; or (b) if no school or other institution is named in the plan, that fact.

5.59   It follows that an appropriate person has no right of appeal against the description of SEN or the special educational provision in an EHC plan.[96]

5.60   Before registering an appeal with the FTT, the appropriate person must consider mediation unless an exemption applies – see paras 4.139–4.147 below.[97]

---

93 Code, para 10.147. When reviewing the EHC plan, the local authority must follow the processes set out in chapter 9 of the Code, in particular those on 19–25 year olds.

94 Code, para 10.148.

95 CFA 2014 s73(1) and (2).

96 Although note if an otherwise valid appeal has been brought, the FTT can (with the agreement of the parties) correct any deficiencies in the EHC plan which relate to the SEN or the special educational provision for the detained person.

97 CFA 2014 s73(7) and (8); SENDDP Regs regs 18–27; and Code, paras 10.118–10.119.

5.61   If an appeal takes place, the person in charge should ensure that arrangements are made for the detained person to attend the FTT hearing. If there are security considerations involved, a FTT hearing could take place via a video link but only where this is accessible to the child or young person.[98]

5.62   The powers of the FTT on an appeal are materially the same as under the general regime,[99] as are the time limits for complying with FTT orders[100] and the power to deal with unopposed appeals.[101]

98 Code, para 10.120.
99 SENDDP Regs reg 28(2).
100 SENDDP Regs reg 29.
101 SENDDP Regs reg 30.

Disability discrimination

continued

Key points

Introduction and overview

- The Equality Act (EqA) 2010 prohibits discrimination on the basis of 'protected characteristics', including disability, in a range of circumstances including education.
- 'Discrimination' can includes not just less favourable treatment because of a person's protected characteristic, but also a number of other forms of treatment including (in the case of disability) a failure to make reasonable adjustments to accommodate that disability.
- The EqA 2010 prohibits harassment and victimisation, including the victimisation of a pupil by reason of his or her parents.
- The EqA 2010 imposes positive duties on all public authorities to pay 'due regard' to a number of equality-related needs.
- The EqA 2010 applies to discrimination in relation to every aspect of schooling, from admission to exclusion, but it does not apply to the content of the curriculum.
- Statutory guidance has been issued which tribunals and courts must take into account where relevant to the question of disability.
- The Equality and Human Rights Commission (EHRC) has not been permitted to issue statutory guidance on education, but has issued a number of technical codes which perform a similar function.

Disability

- The EqA 2010 defines disability by reference to a physical or mental impairment having a substantial and long-term adverse effect on a person's ability to carry out normal day-to-day activities.
- Statutory guidance has been issued which tribunals and courts must take into account where relevant to this issue.
- References to disability include references to *past* disability.
- An impact will be 'substantial' if it is as 'more than minor or trivial'.
- A 'normal' day-to-day activity is anything 'which is not abnormal or unusual', rather than anything which the majority of people do.
- The effect of an impairment will be regarded as 'long-term' if it has lasted for at least 12 months, is likely to last for at least 12

continued

months, or is likely to last for the rest of the life of the person affected.

- A number of conditions amount to disability regardless of whether a person's functioning is impaired.
- Other conditions are statutorily defined as not amounting to impairments for the purposes of the EqA 2010.
- Whether an impairment which is being treated or corrected is to be regarded as having a substantial adverse effect must be assessed as if the treatment or correction measures were not being taken.
- The only exception to the rule that the effect of treatment or correction measures must be left out of account is that impaired vision must be assessed taking into account any correction affected by glasses or contact lenses.

Discrimination and other forms of regulated conduct

- Discrimination may be direct, or indirect, or may (in the case of disability) be discrimination arising from disability or a failure to make a reasonable adjustment.
- Harassment and victimisation are also prohibited in the context of education, the former only in relation to the protected characteristics of disability, gender reassignment, race and sex (including pregnancy).
- In the case of disability (alone of the protected characteristics), the EqA 2010 only protects those who *are* disabled from discrimination relating to disability. In other words, it does not regulate disability discrimination against persons who are *not* disabled.
- Direct discrimination occurs (so far as relevant here) when, because of a pupil's protected characteristic, he or she is treated less favourably.
- It is a narrow concept, particularly when applied to disability, as it does not cover less favourable treatment resulting from a difference in ability, as distinct from the mere fact that the pupil is disabled.

Bringing a disability discrimination claim in the First-tier Tribunal

- A claim for disability discrimination against a school may be made by the person's parent, or if the person is over compulsory school age, his or her parent.

- The defendant to the claim will be the responsible body of the school. The responsible body for the school will depend on the type of school, and may depend on the act of discrimination alleged.
- A claim for disability discrimination against the responsible body of a school must be brought in the First-tier Tribunal (FTT).
- There is a time limit of six months for bringing the claim from the date on which the conduct complained of occurred. The time for bringing the claim may be extended by the FTT.
- A claim of disability discrimination in the FTT is governed by the Tribunal Procedure (First-tier Tribunal) (Health, Education And Social Care Chamber) Rules 2008 SI No 2699 (FTT Rules).
- The FTT applies a faster timetable for hearing a claim where the act complained of is the permanent exclusion of a child or young person and where the child or young person is seeking reinstatement to the school.
- If a claim for disability discrimination is upheld by the FTT, it may make such order as it thinks fit. The FTT does not, however, have the power to order a payment of compensation.

Introduction and overview

Equality Act 2010

6.1   The Equality Act 2010 (EqA 2010) , like its predecessor provisions (most relevantly, the Disability Discrimination Act (DDA) 1995, as successively amended) operates by:

1) establishing protected characteristics (previously protected 'grounds');
2) defining a variety of types of discrimination and other regulated conduct (harassment and victimisation);
3) prohibiting discrimination because of the protected characteristic in specific circumstances.

6.2   The characteristics protected by the EqA 2010 in relation to discrimination are age, disability, gender reassignment, marriage and civil partnership, race, religion or belief, sex (including pregnancy) and sexual orientation. As regards its application to schools *as educators*, however (as distinct from employers), the Act does not protect against discrimination on grounds of age or marriage/civil partnership.[1] Nor, in this context, does it regulate harassment related to religion or belief, or to sexual orientation (see further paras 6.135–6.138 below).

6.3   In addition to prohibiting various types of discrimination and related conduct, the EqA 2010 imposes positive duties on all public authorities (including the governing bodies/proprietors of publicly funded schools and institutions)[2] to pay 'due regard' to a number of equality-related needs. This positive duty (now generally referred to as the 'public sector equality duty') has evolved over time and is now to be found in EqA 2010 s149.

Application of the Equality Act 2010 in schools

Overview

6.4   The EqA 2010 provides, so far as relevant here, that the 'responsible bodies' of schools (see para 6.8 below) may not discriminate against, or victimise, pupils or prospective pupils:

- in the arrangements made for determining admission;
- in the terms of admission;
- by refusing to admit a pupil;
- in the way in which education is provided to a pupil;
- by not providing education to a pupil;
- in the way in which a pupil is afforded access to a benefit, facility or service;
- by not providing access to a benefit, facility or service to a pupil;
- by excluding the pupil from the school; or
- by subjecting the pupil to any other detriment.[3]

1   EqA 2010 s84.
2   EqA 2010 s150(1) provides that a public authority is one specified in Schedule 19. By Part 1 of Schedule 19 the following are listed as public authorities for the purposes of section 149(1): the governing body of a maintained school (as defined in Education and Inspections Act 2006 s162); a local authority with respect of pupil referral units; the proprietor of a city technology college, a city college for technology or an academy; the governing body of an institution within the further education sector (within the meaning of Further and Higher Education Act 1992 s91(3)); and the governing body of an institution in England within the higher education sector (within the meaning of Further and Higher Education Act 1992 s91(5)).
3   EqA 2010 s85(1), (2) (discrimination), (4) and (5) (victimisation).

6.5   Responsible bodies may also not harass pupils or prospective pupils[4] and are under a duty to make reasonable adjustments (see para 6.137 below).[5] Failure to make such adjustments is defined as a form of discrimination. Harassment and the duty to make reasonable adjustment are discussed at paras 6.135–6.138 and 6.104–6.127 below.

6.6   The meaning of victimisation is considered below (para 6.139). It should be emphasised that pupils are protected by EqA 2010 s86 from victimisation (essentially, unfavourable treatment connected with actual or suspected complaints of discrimination) where the person who has complained (or is suspected of having complained or intending to complain) is the parent or sibling of the pupil.

6.7   In England and Wales, the 'schools' covered by the EqA 2010 are (section 85(7)):

- those maintained by local authorities;
- independent educational institutions other than special schools;
- alternative provision Academies that are not independent educational institutions;
- special schools not maintained by local authorities.

6.8   The 'responsible body' for each such school is (section 85(9)):

- a school maintained by a local authority: the local authority or governing body;[6]
- otherwise, the proprietor.

6.9   The Equality and Human Rights Commission (EHRC) has issued non-statutory guidance, *What equality law means for you as an education provider: schools* (2014). It states that:

> ... the responsible body of a school ... is liable for ... the actions of its employees and agents of the school unless it can show that it took 'all reasonable steps' to prevent the discrimination, harassment or victimisation from taking place. The responsibility does not extend to cover the actions of pupils beyond the responsibility a school already has for the action of its pupils ...[7]

---

4   EqA 2010 s85(3).
5   EqA 2010 s85(6).
6   Which of these is the responsible body in relation to a particular claim will depend on the function in question; for example, if the local authority is the admission authority it will be responsible for any discrimination in admissions, whereas the school itself is likely to be the responsible body if the alleged discrimination concerned the delivery of education.
7   *What equality law means for you as an education provider: schools*, para 1.4.

Activities where discrimination and victimisation are prohibited

Arrangements made for determining admission

6.10   Taking the activities in para 6.4 above in turn, the 'arrangements made for determining admission' include all activities relating to admission arrangements including:

- information about the school and application process;
- admissions criteria;
- entrance exams and interviews.[8]

6.11   The EHRC's *Technical guidance for schools in England* (2014) states[9] that 'arrangements' include:

- admissions policies;
- drawing up of admissions criteria;
- application of admissions criteria;
- information about the school, including marketing material;
- open events and schools visits;
- application forms;
- decision-making processes;
- interviews (where permitted);
- tests (where permitted).

6.12   In *AB v Duke of York's Royal Military School*[10] the UT ruled that a claim could not be brought under the EqA 2010 against a school which advised the Claimants that it was not suitable for their child, who was physically disabled and had a statement of special educational needs (SEN). The parents' local authority had declined to name the school in their child's statement because of the school's conclusion that it was not suitable for him, but because they had never actually made an application to the school in respect of him they could not complain of discrimination by reason of the school's refusal to admit him. Nor could they complain about discrimination in the school's arrangements for determining admission, the UT dismissing as 'not arguable' any suggestion that the way that the school had formed the view that it was unsuitable for the child 'was in any way connected with arrangements made for deciding who was to be offered admission as a pupil because the respondent was not by then contemplating making any admissions decision in respect of [him] as a result of the appellants not having made the appropriate application'.

8   See *What equality law means for you as an education provider: schools*, para 3.3.
9   *Technical guidance for schools in England*, para 2.16.
10   [2014] UKUT 403 (AAC), [2014] ELR 443.

6.13   The EHRC's non-statutory guidance *What equality law means for you as an education provider: schools* (see further para 6.36 below), advises that schools' admissions information 'should not discriminate by suggesting that applications from people with certain protected characteristics would not be welcome' and 'must not result in a person with a relevant protected characteristic being treated worse than those not sharing the protected characteristic, unless the policy can be objectively justified' (see further paras 6.95–6.97). Further, that 'the information and application process [must be] accessible to disabled people' and that schools must 'make reasonable adjustments as necessary'. Admissions criteria must not discriminate directly or indirectly, and schools are advised to review admissions criteria regularly 'to ensure that they do not inadvertently exclude people with a particular characteristic'.[11]

6.14   Among the examples of discriminatory admissions criteria the EHRC's technical guidance lists are the requirement that prospective pupils played sport for their primary school, which 'is likely to be indirect discrimination against applicants with a physical disability who are less likely to have played competitive sport, unless the school can show that this is a proportionate means of achieving a legitimate aim.'[12] Selective schools must ensure that their requirements for, and assessments of, relevant ability are not such as to disproportionately exclude pupils of particular ethnic or other groups, unless such disproportionate exclusion is objectively justifiable. Selection criteria must also be applied so as not to discriminate directly against disabled pupils (the technical guidance provides an example of a pupil with cerebral palsy who is rejected after an interview on the assumption that her unclear speech indicates learning difficulties); and also so as to make reasonable adjustments for disabled pupils, for example by the provision of test papers in adapted forma, allowing a scribe or additional time as appropriate.[13] Provided there is no direct discrimination and the duty to make reasonable adjustments is complied with, the application of permitted academic selection criteria is not unlawful even though if they result in the non-selection of pupils for reasons which are the direct consequence of disability.[14]

---

11 *What equality law means for you as an education provider: schools*, para 3.4.
12 Technical guidance para 2.28.
13 *What equality law means for you as an education provider: schools*, para 3.4.
14 Technical guidance para 2.32.

Terms of admission

6.15   Discriminatory 'terms of admission' would include allowing 'a disabled pupil to attend school only on a part-time basis because the school does not have the resources to provide the pupil with the support he requires on a full-time basis', unless this could be justified.[15]

Refusal of admission

6.16   A discriminatory refusal of admission would be one which was based on the belief that a pupil would (by reason of her disability-related behavioural difficulties) be disruptive.[16]

Provision (or non-provision) of education or access to a benefit, facility or service

6.17   A school might discriminate in the provision (and/or non-provision) of (a) education or (b) access to benefits, facilities or services, by, for example:

- refusing to allow a pupil to progress;[17]
- failing to make reasonable adjustments for disabled pupils in relation to eg homework clubs or geography field trips; or
- failing to make adequate provision for the inclusion of disabled pupils within extra-curricular sporting or drama activities hosted at the school.

It may also discriminate in the arrangements it makes for pupils' work experience or work placement (where, for example, it failed to make the same level of effort to find suitable placements for disabled pupils as it did for others).

6.18   Additional steps may, of course, also be required in the case of disabled pupils. In *R (D) v Governing Body of Plymouth High School for Girls* Collins J ruled that a school should have taken steps in advance to ensure that a visually impaired pupil was not placed at a disadvantage by comparison with other pupils when it came to work placements; given that all year 10 pupils were required to undertake placements, and that any employer would have wished to be informed about a prospective pupil's disability, the school's failure to obtain and pass on relevant information to facilitate the organisation of the pupil's work placement was an act of unlawful discrimination.[18]

---

15 Technical guidance para 2.25.
16 *What equality law means for you as an education provider: schools*, para 3.6.
17 *M v SW School and SENDIST* [2004] EWHC 2586 (Admin), [2005] ELR 285.
18 [2004] EWHC (Admin), [2004] ELR 591.

6.19   The EqA 2010 does not apply to the content of the curriculum so schools are not constrained from teaching controversial or difficult subjects by the Act, unless the method of delivery was such that it included or amounted to harassment of or discrimination against pupils. *What equality law means for you as an education provider: schools* provides, as examples of discrimination in the provision of education, a school's refusal to permit an HIV-positive student to take part in PE lessons.[19] Where, however, a proper risk assessment concluded that the risk of infection resulting from a particular activity (rugby, for example) was significant, the exclusion of an HIV-positive student from that particular activity would likely be justified, though the school would remain under the duty to make reasonable adjustments (for example, by making alternative arrangements for that pupil) and to manage the situation so as to avoid making the pupil a 'pariah'.

Exclusions

6.20   Turning to exclusions, all schools are covered by the EqA 2010, though independent schools other than academies are not bound by the Department for Education's guidance *Exclusion from maintained schools, academies and pupil referral units in England* (2012).[20] The guidance provides that schools may only exclude pupils as a last resort and only on grounds of the pupil's behaviour. Independent schools other than academies may set their own exclusion criteria though these must be consistent with the EqA 2010.

6.21   Among the examples of discriminatory exclusion provided by *What equality law means for you as an education provider: schools* are:

- exclusion by reason of a pupil's diagnosis with autism; and
- exclusion of a pupil with attention deficit and hyperactivity disorder (ADHD) for behaviour 'including refusing to sit at his desk, distracting other pupils by talking and running around during classes', where the school has warned the pupil previously but has not engaged in any other efforts to help him manage his behaviour.

---

19 *What equality law means for you as an education provider: schools*, para 4.5.
20 *A guide for those with legal responsibilities in relation to exclusion*. And see also EA 2002 s51, and the School Discipline (Pupil Exclusions and Reviews) (England) Regulations 2012 SI No 1033 (although the application of the Guidance, the 2002 Act and the 2012 Regulations to academy schools arises as a result of the terms of their funding agreement and not from the legislation).

6.22   The non-statutory guidance advises that schools 'have a duty to disabled pupils to make reasonable adjustments to your procedures if needed'. This might include:

- disregarding behaviour which is a direct consequence of the pupil's disability;
- making reasonable adjustments to manage such behaviour;
- considering alternative, more appropriate punishments; and
- ensuring that a disabled pupil is able to present their case fully where the pupil's disability might hinder this.

6.23   The non-statutory guidance suggests that schools ought to disregard the involuntary calling-out and occasional swearing of a pupil with Tourette syndrome and to put in place inclusion strategies for pupils with ADHD which might include:

> ... providing a support worker, implementing specific behaviour management techniques, and using positive discipline and reward methods. When any behaviour that is related to the pupil's disability does occur, the teacher does not punish him but rather uses one of the agreed strategies to manage it effectively. These reasonable adjustments assist the pupil in managing his behaviour and improve his educational outcomes.

6.24   The EHRC's technical guidance provides an example of a discriminatory exclusion as follows:[21]

> A pupil with autism is excluded for flapping his arms at a supply teacher. The supply teacher was alarmed by what she perceived to be threatening behaviour. The reason why the pupil flapped his arms was that the supply teacher had told him that he could not sit in his normal seat, because it was not appropriate for the activity that they were doing. This upset the pupil and caused him to flap his arms in an agitated fashion. The pupil always sat in the same seat in the classroom and this was recognised as a reasonable adjustment for his autism by his class teacher. Since the pupil's reaction of flapping his arms was connected to his disability, the exclusion would be discrimination arising from disability. Because the school had not advised the supply teacher of the reasonable adjustment, the school would be unlikely to be able to justify the discrimination and therefore it would be unlawful.

Any other detriment

6.25   Finally, subjection to other 'detriment' may include being disciplined for failure to comply with policies of the school. This might amount

---

21 Technical guidance, para 4.11.

to discrimination where, for example, the uniform which pupils are required to wear exacerbates a pupil's eczema or psoriasis.

6.26   Schools are prohibited from discriminating against former pupils under the EqA 2010 where the discrimination (harassment or victimisation) arises out of, and is closely connected with, the person's previous relationship with the school and would have been unlawful if he or she were still a pupil. Examples provided by the technical guidance of potentially unlawful discrimination relate to the supply (or refusal) of references, and the provision of a school newsletter (where this is sent to former pupils the same obligation to make reasonable adjustments in respect of visually impaired former pupils will apply as in relation to current pupils).[22]

6.27   Schools are regulated by Part 6 of the EqA 2010 in relation to their educational and related functions. They are also regulated under Part 3 as service providers relation to persons other than pupils (for example to parents) and to pupils when they are using the school's services as members of the public rather than as pupils. The EHRC's *Technical guidance for schools in England* provides the following examples:

- A school with a swimming pool opens the pool to members of the public on a Saturday morning. A pupil of the school uses the pool with his parents on a Saturday morning. In this context, he would be covered by the services provisions of Part 3 of the Act rather than by the schools provisions of Part 6 of the Act. His parents would also be covered by Part 3 of the Act.

- A deaf parent who communicates through British Sign Language (BSL) attends a parent's evening. The school is under a duty (under Part 3 of the Act) to make reasonable adjustments to enable the parent to communicate with school staff and therefore to benefit from the parent's evening. This might include the school arranging and paying for a BSL interpreter.[23]

6.28   In *Lawrence and others v Cambridge CC* the High Court considered a disability discrimination claim brought by the mother of a disabled toddler to a 'no pushchairs' policy operated by the school at which her older child was a pupil.[24] The claim failed because the High Court ruled that the need for the use of a pushchair in relation to the toddler was not materially different from that in relation to any other child of his age. Had he been of an age at which his need for

---

22   Technical guidance, para 5.85.
23   Technical guidance, para 1.34.
24   [2005] EWHC 3189 (QB), [2006] ELR 343.

a pushchair resulted from his disability rather than his age the outcome may have been different, though this is not obvious in view of the decision in *Hainsworth v Ministry of Defence*,[25] in which the Employment Appeal Tribunal (EAT) ruled that the claimant, who was employed in Germany, was not entitled to demand a transfer to the UK by way of a reasonable adjustment in respect of the disability of her daughter.[26]

Codes of practice and guidance

6.29   The EqA 2010 defines disability by reference (section 6(1)) to a physical or mental impairment having a substantial and long-term adverse effect on a person's ability to carry out normal day-to-day activities. By section 6(5) the Act provides that 'A Minister of the Crown may issue guidance about matters to be taken into account in deciding any question for the purposes of subsection (1)'. Schedule 1 to the EqA 2010 then provides (para 12) that a court or tribunal or other body determining a claim of disability discrimination must '[i]n determining whether a person is a disabled person ... take account of such guidance as it thinks is relevant'. Guidance to the Act, *Guidance on matters to be taken into account in determining questions relating to the definition of disability*, issued by the Office for Disability Issues (2011), is discussed in paras 6.39 and following.

6.30   The Equality Act 2006, under which the EHRC was established, also provides (section 14) that the EHRC may issue codes of practice 'in connection with any matter addressed by the [EqA 2010] ... (to ensure or facilitate compliance with the [EqA 2010] or an enactment made under that Act, or (b) to promote equality of opportunity'. Draft codes must be laid by the EHRC before the secretary of state who has the power to approve or disapprove the draft. If the draft is approved, it is then laid before parliament where it can be blocked by resolution of either House.

6.31   Where a code of practice is issued, EqA 2006 s15 provides that a failure to comply with one of its provisions:

> ... shall not of itself make a person liable to criminal or civil proceedings; but a code –
>
> (a) shall be admissible in evidence in criminal or civil proceedings, and

---

25 [2014] EWCA Civ 763, [2014] IRLR 728.
26 [2014] EWCA Civ 763, [2014] IRLR 728.

(b) shall be taken into account by a court or tribunal in any case in which it appears to the court or tribunal to be relevant.

6.32 In *Clark v TDG Ltd t/a Novacold*,[27] an early decision under the DDA 1995, the Court of Appeal ruled that a tribunal had erred in deciding that any less favourable treatment of the appellant was justified because, in so doing, the tribunal had failed to have regard to the relevant provisions of the applicable code of practice.

6.33 A party who wishes to rely on any provision of a code should adduce it in evidence before the tribunal or court, or take the risk that the adjudicating body might fail to turn its attention to the relevant provision.[28]

6.34 The EHRC has issued codes of practice on employment, on equal pay and on 'services, public functions and associations'. However, after the issue in January 2011 of a draft code of practice for schools, and consultation on this and other draft codes, the EHRC announced in March 2012 that it could not proceed with the planned codes on education or the public sector equality duty (PSED) because (according to the EHRC's website): 'The Government is keen to reduce bureaucracy around the Equality Act 2010, and feels that further statutory guidance may place too much of a burden on public bodies'. The EHRC was obliged, accordingly, to proceed by way of non-statutory technical guidance which does not have the 'bite' of the statutory guidance (see paras 6.30–6.32 above) and codes of practice.

6.35 There is currently in existence:

- *Schools technical guidance – England – reasonable adjustments for disabled pupils – auxiliary aids technical guidance.*

In addition (so far as relevant for the purposes of this book) the EHRC has published:

- *Technical guidance on the public sector equality duty England* (2014);
- *Technical guidance on the public sector equality duty Scotland* (2014); and
- *Technical Guidance on the Public Sector Equality Duty England Wales* (2014).

Their provisions will be considered at various points below. Such guidance, being non-statutory, is not binding and need not (though it may) be taken into account by courts or tribunals.

---

27 [1999] EWCA Civ 1091, [1999] ICR 951.
28 See the comments of Lord Johnston in the employment case of *Arnold v Pointon York Ltd* EAT/0649/00, [2001] All ER (D) 267 (Nov).

6.36   Reference has been made in the text above to the EHRC's non-statutory guidance, *What equality law means for you as an education provider: schools* which, together with all of the guidance and codes of practice mentioned above, is available on the EHRC's website.[29]

6.37   The EHRC's *Technical guidance for schools in England* advises that schools are liable as service providers (as distinct from educational providers) to persons other than pupils (for example, to parents) and to pupils when they are using the school's services as members of the public rather than as pupils.

Disability

Definition

6.38   The EqA 2010 provides (section 6) that:

> (1) A person (P) has a disability if–
>   (a) P has a physical or mental impairment, and
>   (b) the impairment has a substantial and long-term adverse effect on P's ability to carry out normal day-to-day activities.

6.39   EqA 2010 s6(3) provides that a minister may issue guidance about matters to be taken into account in deciding any question for the purposes of subsection. The Office for Disability Issues *Guidance on matters to be taken into account in determining questions relating to the definition of disability* (2011) ('the Disability Guidance'), which was issued under EqA 2010 s6, states that 'In the vast majority of cases there is unlikely to be any doubt whether or not a person has or has had a disability', although 'this guidance should prove helpful in cases where the matter is not entirely clear'. The definition of disability is, however, fairly complex, and it is important to recognise that disability may be (and much disability is) hidden; as Morison J said in one of the early cases under the DDA 1995:

> ... a relatively small proportion of the disabled community are what one might describe as visibly disabled, that is people in wheelchairs or carrying white sticks or other aids. It is important, therefore, that when [employment tribunals[30]] are approaching the question as to whether someone suffers from a disability, they should not have in

---

29 See http://www.equalityhumanrights.com/legal-and-policy/legislation/ equality-act-2010/equality-act-guidance-codes-practice-and-technical-guidance#cop.

30 The case was an employment one. The principles apply also to education and other cases.

their minds a stereotypical image of a person in a wheelchair or moving around with considerable difficulty. Such persons may well have a physical impairment within the meaning of the Act and are thus to be treated as disabled, but it of course does not follow that other persons who are not in such a condition are inherently less likely to have a physical or mental impairment of a sort which satisfies the terms of the legislation.[31]

6.40 References to disability include references to *past* disability.[32] The Disability Guidance gives an example of a person who had experienced long-term debilitating mental illness in the past, from which she has fully recovered; such a person will continue to be protected from discrimination because of that (past) illness.

Impairment

6.41 'Physical or mental impairment' is not defined by the EqA 2010. The Disability Guidance states that the term 'should be given its ordinary meaning' and that it is 'not necessary for the cause of the impairment to be established, nor does the impairment have to be the result of an illness'.[33] Having suggested that the question of impairment (as distinct from whether it is substantial) is unlikely to be dispute in most cases, it goes on to point out that 'disability can arise from a wide range of impairments' including:

- sensory impairments, such as those affecting sight or hearing;
- impairments with fluctuating or recurring effects such as rheumatoid arthritis, myalgic encephalitis (ME), chronic fatigue syndrome (CFS), fibromyalgia, depression and epilepsy;
- progressive, such as motor neurone disease, muscular dystrophy, and forms of dementia;
- auto-immune conditions such as systemic lupus erythematosis (SLE);
- organ specific, including respiratory conditions, such as asthma, and cardiovascular diseases, including thrombosis, stroke and heart disease;
- developmental, such as autistic spectrum disorders (ASD), dyslexia and dyspraxia;
- learning disabilities;
- mental health conditions with symptoms such as anxiety, low mood, panic attacks, phobias, or unshared perceptions; eating disorders; bipolar affective disorders; obsessive compulsive disorders;

---

31 *Vicary v British Telecommunications plc* [1999] IRLR 680, EAT, at 682.
32 EqA 2010 s6(4), subject to exceptions which are not relevant here.
33 Disability Guidance, A3.

personality disorders; post traumatic stress disorder, and some self-harming behaviour;

- mental illnesses, such as depression and schizophrenia;
- produced by injury to the body, including to the brain.[34]

'Substantial impact'

6.42   'Substantial' is defined as 'more than minor or trivial'.[35] The Disability Guidance states that the 'time taken by a person with an impairment to carry out a normal day-to-day activity should be considered when assessing whether the effect of that impairment is substantial',[36] as should how the person has to carry out relevant activities (as in the example of a person with OCD who 'checks and rechecks that electrical appliances are switched off and that the doors are locked when leaving home'.[37] The Disability Guidance also points out that multiple minor impacts may become cumulative, as where minor breathing difficulties impact on a person's ability to wash and dress, walk and use public transport to (combined) significant effect, or impaired physical co-ordination is exacerbated by a mobility-limiting injury.[38]

6.43   The degree of impact of an impairment on a person's normal day-to-day activities must be assessed by considering how that person might operate absent the impairment, rather than by comparing that person to others. In *PP and SP v Trustees of Leicester Grammar School*,[39] for example, the UT ruled that the FTT had erred in finding that a pupil with dyslexia was not disabled because, her class and examination performance being good and average amongst her high achieving classmates, the condition could not be said to have had a substantial impact on her functioning.

6.44   The Disability Guidance goes on to suggest that: 'Account should be taken of how far a person can *reasonably* be expected to modify his or her behaviour, for example by use of a coping or avoidance strategy, to prevent or reduce the effects of an impairment on normal day-to-day activities'.[40] Whether a modification is reasonable will depend on the circumstances and the Disability Guidance suggests

---

34 Disability Guidance, A5.
35 s212 EqA 2010.
36 Disability Guidance, B2.
37 Disability Guidance, B3.
38 Disability Guidance, B5, B6.
39 [2014] UKUT 520 (AAC) [2015] ELR 86. See also *Paterson v Commissioner of Police of the Metropolis* [2007] ICR 1522, [2007] IRLR 763, EAT.
40 Disability Guidance, B7; emphasis in original.

that the avoidance of an allergen may result in a substantial impact on the activity of eating. And while 'it would be reasonable to expect a person who has chronic back pain to avoid extreme activities such as skiing', or someone with a phobia about heights to avoid climbing the Eiffel Tower, the Disability Guidance suggests that it would not be reasonable to expect those person to avoid, respectively, shopping or using public transport, and visiting any multi-storey buildings.[41]

6.45 In assessing the impact of an impairment the Disability Guidance suggests that account must be taken of what a person avoids (such as travelling in rush hour), or can do only with difficulty.[42] It points out, in addition, that the possibility of coping mechanisms breaking down in cases where (for example) a person is placed under additional stress 'must be taken into account when assessing the effects of the impairment'.[43]

6.46 Finally, the Disability Guidance points out that the environment may impact on an impairment such that its effects may fluctuate (severe asthma would be an example, as is rheumatoid arthritis). In such cases: 'It is necessary to consider the overall impact of the [impairment], and the extent to which it has a substantial adverse effect on [the person's] ability to carry out day-to-day activities'.[44]

'Normal day-to-day activities'

6.47 'Normal day-to-day activities' are not defined by the EqA 2010. The predecessor legislation (the DDA 1995) provided a (closed) list of capabilities on which an impairment had to impact in order to amount to a disability,[45] but this was abandoned by the EqA 2010. The Disability Guidance contains has an appendix which sets out an 'illustrative and non-exhaustive list of factors which, if they are experienced by a person, *it would be reasonable* to regard as having a substantial adverse effect on normal day-to-day activities' (emphasis in original). Among the examples it includes difficulties:

- getting dressed;
- preparing or eating a meal;

---

41 Disability Guidance, B7.
42 Disability Guidance, B9.
43 Disability Guidance, B10.
44 Disability Guidance, B11.
45 Mobility; manual dexterity; physical co-ordination; continence; the ability to lift, carry or otherwise move everyday objects; speech, hearing or eyesight; memory or ability to concentrate, learn or understand; perception of the risk of physical danger.

- toileting;
- using a computer or telephone or reading;
- going outside unaccompanied;
- walking;
- using transport or steps;
- waiting or queueing;
- crossing a road safely;
- moving around buildings; or
- picking up or holding objects of moderate weight.

These difficulties may be the result of mental rather than physical impairments. Other examples include:

- inability to converse;
- difficulties understanding instructions;
- difficulties 'entering or staying in environments that the person perceives as strange or frightening';
- manifesting challenging behaviour or experiencing persistent low motivation;
- frequent confusion or intrusive thoughts or delusions;
- compulsive behaviour;
- difficulties with concentration or recognition;
- significant social difficulties; and
- intermittent loss of consciousness.

6.49   An impairment experienced by a child under six will be regarded as having a substantial (and long-term) adverse effect on the ability of that child to carry out normal day-to-day activities, even if it does not in fact, where it would normally have such an effect on the ability of a person aged six years or over to carry out normal day-to-day activities.[46] The example given by the Disability Guidance is of a baby who is not yet old enough to crawl and who has no movement in her legs. This impairment does not have any apparent impact on her ability to move around but it is to be treated as having such, as it would have a substantial impact on a person aged six or more.

6.50   Leaving aside young children, the EAT ruled in *Ekpe v Metropolitan Police Commissioner*[47] that 'normal' is anything 'which is not abnormal or unusual', rather than anything which the majority of people do. The employment tribunal had ruled that the claimant, who could not carry heavy shopping, scrub pans, peel, grate, sew or put rollers in her hair, and who difficulty applying makeup, was not disabled

---

46 Equality Act 2010 (Disability) Regulations 2010 SI No 2128 reg 6.
47 [2001] IRLR 605.

because putting rollers in hair or applying make-up was not 'normal', being done for the most part only by women. The EAT disagreed, ruling that activities normally done by women could nevertheless be 'normal day-to-day activities', further that the effect of impairments had to be taken in the round (ie including the appellant's difficulties carrying shopping, scrubbing pans, peeling, grating and sewing).

6.51   In *Paterson v Comr of Police of the Metropolis* the EAT ruled (applying *Chacón Navas*[48]) that the appellant, a police officer, was disabled by dyslexia which, although it did not impact on his ability to carry out many of his job-related functions, did mean that he required additional to complete promotion examinations.[49] And in *Sobhi v Commissioner of Police of the Metropolis* the EAT ruled, relying on the decision of the Court of Justice of the European Union (CJEU) in *Ring* (para 6.53 below), that the claimant could be regarded as disabled because impairment affected the one-off activity of applying for the post of police constable.[50] There the claimant, a Police Community Support Officer, argued that she had failed to mention a conviction of theft in her application to become a police officer because of her dissociative amnesia which meant that she had not been able to remember her conviction. The medical evidence was that the 'relatively small gap' in Ms Sobhi's 'past remote memory' which arose from the traumatic events of that time did not affect her memory's day-to-day functioning or have any effect on her ability to perform as a PCSO/ or constable. The employment tribunal found that she was not disabled but the EAT disagreed, ruling that although her 'loss of memory was limited to just one aspect of her past, [it] had an adverse and long term effect on any activity of hers which required her to recall whether she had any previous convictions', and that this activity impacted on her effective participation in her professional life.[51]

6.52   In *Aderemi v London and South Eastern Railway Ltd* Langstaff J emphasised that what had to be considered:

> ... is an adverse effect ... not upon [the Claimant's] carrying out normal day-to-day activities but upon his ability to do so. Because the effect is adverse, the focus ... must necessarily be upon that which a Claimant maintains he cannot do as a result of his physical or mental

48   Case C-13/05 *Chacón Navas v Eurest Colectividades SA* [2006] IRLR 706, [2007] ICR 1.

49   [2007] IRLR 763, [2007] ICR 1522.

50   [2013] EqLR 785.

51   Compare *Bryan v British Telecommunications plc* [2014] EqLR 632 in which an employment tribunal ruled that an inability, by reason of tinnitus, to wear a headset did not impact on the claimant's 'normal day to day' activities.

impairment. Once he has established that there is an [adverse] effect ... upon his ability ... to carry out normal day-to-day activities, a Tribunal has then to assess whether that is or is not substantial. Here, however, it has to bear in mind the definition of substantial [as] ... more than minor or trivial. In other words, the Act itself does not create a spectrum running smoothly from those matters which are clearly of substantial effect to those matters which are clearly trivial but provides for a bifurcation: unless a matter can be classified as within the heading 'trivial' or 'insubstantial', it must be treated as substantial. There is therefore little room for any form of sliding scale between one and the other.[52]

6.53　Also relevant is the decision in *HK Danmark, acting on behalf of Ring v Dansk almennyttigt Boligselskab* in which the CJEU, taking into account the UN Convention on the Rights of Persons with Disabilities (UNCRPD), together with previous jurisprudence of the CJEU, ruled that:

> ... the concept of disability must be understood as referring to a limitation which results in particular from physical, mental or psychological impairments which in interaction with various barriers may hinder the full and effective participation of the persons concerned in professional life on an equal basis with other workers.[53]

6.54　Both *Aderemi* and *HK Danmark* were concerned with employment. Applied in the context of education, this suggests that the tribunals and courts should not (despite the wording of EqA 2010 s6(1)) concentrate only on the impact of an impairment on 'normal day to day activities', as distinct from a pupil's access to education.

'Long-term' and recurrent conditions

6.55　EqA 2010 s6 must be read with Schedule 1 which provides a statutory basis for regulations further defining disability. Para 2 provides that the effect of an impairment is to be regarded as 'long-term' for the purposes of section 6(1) if:

- it has lasted for at least 12 months,
- it is likely to last for at least 12 months, or
- it is likely to last for the rest of the life of the person affected.

6.56　Determining whether a condition is 'long-term' will generally require a diagnosis, if any hearing takes place before it has in fact lasted 12

---

52 [2013] ICR 591 para 14.
53 C-355/11, [2013] IRLR 571, referring to *Chacón Navas v Eurest Colectividades* SA C-13/05 [2006] IRLR 706, [2007] All ER (EC) 59.

months.[54] The question, as set out by the House of Lords in *SCA Packaging Ltd v Boyle*, is not whether the condition is more likely than not to persist for 12 months, rather whether 'it could well happen'.[55] It is worth bearing in mind that the length of effect likely to result from an impairment can include not only the effect of the impairment itself, but also that of any secondary impairment which results (or is likely to result) from it.[56]

6.57   In *DR v Croydon LBC*[57] the UT ruled that FTT had erred in deciding that a pupil with selective mutism was not disabled. The claim was brought against the LA in respect of its handling of the pupil (C) who had attended a special school until April 2008 and then been homed schooled until September 2009, when she commenced attendance at a second special school (L). In reaching its conclusions on disability, the FTT, which heard the claim in December 2009, had directed its focus exclusively (or almost exclusively) to the evidence from the period three months prior to the hearing, when C had been attending L school satisfactorily and had displayed no difficulties with speech. The UT found that the FTT should have started its analysis by considering C's functioning in the 12 months prior to the first incident of discrimination complained of (which was in October 2008), during which period there was a draft Statement of SEN with a diagnosis of selective mutism and other difficulties. The case was remitted to a newly constituted FTT to decide whether, on the basis of the relevant evidence, C was to be regarded as having been disabled at the material time.

6.58   Special provision is made for recurrent conditions, which will be treated as continuing to have a 'substantial adverse effect on a person's ability to carry out normal day-to-day activities' if they have had such an effect, and 'if that effect is likely to recur'.[58] In addition, a person who has a progressive condition as a result of which his or her normal day-to-day activities have been or are impaired (but not substantially so), will be treated as having a disability if the condition is likely to result in him or her having such a substantial impairment.[59]

---

54 This point was made in *Patel v Metropolitan Borough Council* [2010] IRLR 280.
55 [2009] UKHL 37, [2009] IRLR 746, [2009] ICR 1056.
56 *Patel v Metropolitan Borough Council* [2010] IRLR 280.
57 [2010] UKUT 387 (AAC), [2011] ECR 37.
58 At para 2(2).
59 At para 8.

Conditions automatically amounting to disability

6.59   A number of conditions amount to disability regardless of whether a person's functioning is impaired. These conditions are cancer, HIV infection and multiple sclerosis.[60] In addition, a person who has been certified as blind, severely sight impaired, sight impaired or partially sighted by a consultant ophthalmologist is deemed to be disabled for the purposes of the EqA 2010.[61]

Conditions not amounting to disability

6.60   Other conditions are statutorily defined as *not* amounting to impairments for the purposes of the EqA 2010. These are:

- addition to alcohol, nicotine or any other substance unless the addition was 'originally the result of administration of medically prescribed drugs or other medical treatment'.[62]

Also 'to be treated as not amounting to impairments' are:

- 'seasonal allergic rhinitis' (hayfever), except 'where it aggravates the effect of any other condition';

and:

- a tendency to set fires;
- a tendency to steal;
- a tendency to physical or sexual abuse of other persons;
- exhibitionism; and
- voyeurism.[63]

6.61   It is important to note that, because there is no need to consider how an impairment has been caused, an impairment caused by an excluded condition may still amount to a disability. An example given in the Disability Guidance concerns liver disease resulting from alcohol dependency which 'would count as an impairment', although an addiction to alcohol itself is expressly excluded from the scope of the definition of disability in the EqA 2010.[64] Other examples in the Disability Guidance concern obesity which, though 'in itself ... not an impairment', may cause difficulties with breathing and mobility

---

60   At para 6.
61   Equality Act 2010 (Disability) Regulations 2010 reg 7.
62   Equality Act 2010 (Disability) Regulations 2010 reg 3.
63   Equality Act 2010 (Disability) Regulations 2010 reg 4.
64   Disability Guidance, A7.

which may amount to disabilities. This is in line with the decision of the CJEU in the *Karsten Kaltoft* case.[65]

6.62   The Disability Guidance goes on to state that the exclusions at para 6.60 above apply whether the excluded tendencies 'constitute an impairment in themselves' or 'arise as a consequence of, or a manifestation of, an impairment that constitutes a disability for the purposes of the Act',[66] providing an example of a young man with ADHD which manifests both in an inability to concentrate and a tendency to exhibitionism: the ADHD will amount to a disability and the young man will be protected by the EqA 2010 from discrimination arising in relation to his inability to concentrate, but not from his tendency to exhibitionism. There were conflicting decisions in employment cases as to whether the DDA 1995 protected individuals from discrimination by reason of physical or sexual abuse (or other excluded matters) where these resulted from another impairment (in one case, paranoid schizophrenia, in another, depression), as distinct from being 'free-standing'.[67] The question appears to have been settled, at least in the education context, by a number of cases involving pupils who have acted violently for reasons connected with conditions such as autism, ADHD etc. These cases, which have concluded that the protections of the EqA 2010 did not apply (thus the approach articulated in the Disability Guidance), are considered at para 6.70 below.

Impact of treatment

6.63   Importantly, whether an impairment which is being treated or corrected is to be regarded as having a substantial adverse effect must be assessed as if the treatment or correction measures were not being taken.[68] In other words 'the impairment should be treated as having the effect that it would have without the measures in question'.[69] Schedule 1 of the EqA 2010 makes specific reference to 'medical treatment and the use of a prosthesis or other aid',[70] the Disability

---

65   *Fag Og Arbejde v Kommunernes Landsforening* [2015] IRLR 146, [2015] ICR 322 and see *Walker v Sita Information Networking Computing Ltd* UKEAT/0097/12, [2013] EqLR 476 para 138.

66   Disability Guidance, A13.

67   See, respectively, *Murray v Newham Citizens Advice Bureau* [2003] IRLR 340, *Edmund Nuttall Ltd v Butterfield* [2005] IRLR 751, EAT.

68   Para 5(1).

69   Disability Guidance, B12.

70   Para 5(2).

Guidance pointing out that 'medical treatments would include treatments such as counselling, the need to follow a particular diet, and therapies, in addition to treatments with drugs'.[71] This provision applies even if the measures are such that the person presents as having no impairment as a result,[72] though where treatment has been completed (successful surgical intervention, for example, a course of medication or counselling) the impairment will fall to be judged as it presents at the material time.[73] Thus a person may be disabled notwithstanding the fact that his or her epilepsy is successfully controlled by medication, or diabetes by insulin.

6.64   The only exception to the rule that the effect of treatment or correction measures must be left out of account[74] is that impaired vision must be assessed taking into account any correction affected by glasses or contact lenses. In *PP and SP v Trustees of Leicester Grammar School*,[75] for example, the UT ruled that the FTT had been entitled to find that a pupil was not disabled by reason of Mears Irlen syndrome (visual stress) in a case in which the impact of that condition had been corrected by tinted spectacles.

6.65   More difficult is the question whether a person is to be regarded as disabled when the 'medical treatment' relied upon consists of a particular diet. Notwithstanding the statement in the Guidance, mentioned above, that 'medical treatments would include treatments such as ... the need to follow a particular diet', in *Metroline Travel Ltd v Stoute* the EAT ruled that the avoidance by a claimant with Type 2 diabetes of sugary drinks could not amount to 'treatment' whose effects must be disregarded for the purposes of determining the extent of his impairment.[76] HHJ Serota QC, who disclosed that he himself had diabetes, made reference to para B7 of the Disability Guidance, which provides that:

> Account should be taken of how far a person can *reasonably* be expected to modify his or her behaviour, for example by use of a coping or avoidance strategy, to prevent or reduce the effects of an impairment on normal day-to-day activities. In some instances, a coping or

---

71   Disability Guidance, B12; and see (counselling) *Kapadia v Lambeth LBC* [2000] IRLR 699.

72   In such a case, medical evidence would have to be provided of the likely effect of ceasing treatment: *Woodrup v Southwark LBC* [2002] EWCA Civ 1716, [2003] IRLR 111.

73   *Abadeh v British Telecommunications plc* [2001] IRLR 23.

74   Though more may be provided by regulation.

75   [2014] UKUT 520 (AAC), [2015] ELR 86.

76   [2015] IRLR 465.

avoidance strategy might alter the effects of the impairment to the extent that they are no longer substantial and the person would no longer meet the definition of disability. In other instances, even with the coping or avoidance strategy, there is still an adverse effect on the carrying out of normal day-to-day activities.

For example, a person who needs to avoid certain substances because of allergies may find the day-to-day activity of eating substantially affected. Account should be taken of the degree to which a person can reasonably be expected to behave in such a way that the impairment ceases to have a substantial adverse effect on his or her ability to carry out normal day-to-day activities.

6.66 HHJ Serota took the view that the avoidance of sugary drinks was a strategy to alter the effects of the claimant's impairment, so that they were no longer substantial, and that 'abstention from Coca-Cola and fruit juice' was not properly to be regarded as 'any substantial interference with normal day-to-day activities'. He did accept that 'a particular diet may be regarded as something which is to be ignored when considering the adverse effects of a disability' (that is, as medical treatment), but 'd[id] not consider that abstaining from sugary drinks is sufficient to amount to a particular diet which therefore does not amount to treatment or correction'.

Perceived disability

6.67 In *Coleman v Attridge Law*, the European Court of Justice (ECJ – now the CJEU) ruled that the less favourable treatment of one person by reason of the disability of another person (in that case, a worker's son) breached the prohibition on disability discrimination in the Employment Equality Directive.[77] The CJEU (and, in particular, the Advocate General) took a broad approach to the concept of disability discrimination and harassment, the court ruling that they extended to the less favourable treatment or harassment of (there) a worker based on her son's disability.

6.68 The effect of the CJEU's decision, and the strong obligation placed on national courts to interpret domestic law so as to give effect to related EU law, was that the EAT subsequently ruled that it was possible to interpret the DDA 1995, which did not on its face apply to 'associative' discrimination, to extend to such discrimination without acting incompatibly with the scheme or underlying thrust of

---

77 C-303/06 [2008] ECR I-5603, [2008] ICR 1128.

the legislation or with its general principles.[78] What was significant about this case was that it involved reading such discrimination into a prohibition on discrimination which was defined in the DDA 1995 as less favourable treatment 'on the ground of the disabled person's disability'.[79] The prohibitions on race, religion and sexual orientation discrimination made reference to less favourable treatment 'on racial grounds', 'on grounds of sexual orientation' etc. It was clear as early as 1984 that the former applied to discrimination against one person by reason of another person's race,[80] and it was generally assumed that it and the formulation 'on grounds of' would apply to discrimination by reason of a person's *perceived* characteristic of sexual orientation or religion etc, though not to disability.

6.69   The EqA 2010 then prohibited discrimination 'because of' disability or other protected characteristics, and it was clear from the parliamentary debates and the explanatory memoranda to the bill and the Act that this formulation was understood by legislators to extend to associative discrimination and to discrimination by reason of a person's *perceived* protected characteristic (including disability). No reported case has been won on the basis that the claimant was *perceived to be*, rather than *was*, disabled,[81] though the cases in which this has been discussed (though not pleaded) arose under the DDA 1995. One difficulty which may arise in connection with perceived disability discrimination is the tension which exists between protecting from discrimination a person who is perceived to be (but is not) disabled (which appears to be required by the broad *Coleman* approach to discrimination[82]), and the principle that the prohibition on disability discrimination (by contrast with those on most other forms of discrimination) applies *asymmetrically*, that is, only to discrimination *against*, but not *in favour of*, disabled people. The asymmetric nature of the protection has resulted in a 'threshold' approach

---

78 [2010] ICR 242, [2010] IRLR 10.

79 See, similarly, the Employment Equality (Age) Regulations 2006 SI No 2408 reg 3.

80 *Showboat Entertainment Centre Ltd v Owens* [1984] ICR 65, [1984] IRLR 7 and see *Weathersfield v Sergent*, [1999] ICR 425, [1999] IRLR 94.

81 See *Redbridge LBC v Baynes* UKEAT/0293/09 (17 May 2010, unreported), *J v DLA Piper UK LLP* [2010] IRLR 936, [2010] ICR 1052: these cases, which were brought under the DDA 1995 rather than the EqA 2010, did not involve pleaded cases of discrimination by reason of perceived disability as distinct from cases which could have been so pleaded (the courts in the latter refusing permission to amend to allow this argument to be run in the EAT).

82 Though note that the CJEU did not address *perceived*, as distinct from *associative*, discrimination in terms.

within domestic legislation: a person does not (except where associative discrimination of victimisation is at issue) gain the benefit of
the prohibition on disability discrimination unless he or she passes
the threshold of disability. In *Hainsworth v Ministry of Defence* the
EAT ruled that the claimant, who was employed in Germany, was
not entitled to demand a transfer to the UK by way of a reasonable
adjustment in respect of the disability of her daughter.[83] That decision having been reached taking into account the requirements of
the Employment Equality Directive (which may confer additional
protections in the employment context), it is inconceivable that a different approach would be taken in a case in which the person seeking
an adjustment because of someone else's disability was a pupil.

Education-related case-law

6.70 Much of the case-law in the area of disability has arisen in the employment context, but the principles established are equally applicable in
the education context.

6.71 Of particular importance in the context of education has been
the question of excluded conditions, which has arisen in a number
of education-related cases. In *Governing Body of X Endowed Primary
School v Special Educational Needs and Disability Tribunal and others,*[84]
the High Court ruled that a primary school pupil with ADHD who
was excluded from school after a physical assault on a member of
staff could rely, in challenging that exclusion, on his ADHD, though
he could not rely on his tendency to physical abuse. Where, as here,
the exclusion was due to the physical assault, the claimant could not
rely on the prohibition on disability discrimination to challenge it. He
could, however, complain of the school's alleged failures to make reasonable adjustments in relation to his ADHD which, it was argued,
could have prevented the escalation which led to his exclusion.

6.72 In *P v Governing body of a primary school,*[85] the UT found that a
pupil who had Asperger's Syndrome and ADHD was permanently
excluded from school because of his violent behaviour which, the UT
was satisfied, showed 'a tendency to physical abuse'. The UT went on
to rule, however, that the FTT had erred in law in failing to recognise
that the pupil had also been excluded by reason of the governing
body's view that 'all recommended strategies to include and support'

---

83 [2014] EWCA Civ 763, [2014] IRLR 728.
84 [2009] EWHC 1842 (Admin), [2009] IRLR 1007.
85 [2013] UKUT 154 (AAC), [2013] EqLR 666.

him had been exhausted. That being the case, the FTT had failed to consider whether the decision to exclude had breached the school's duty to make reasonable adjustments.

6.73   Subsequently, in *X v Governing body of a school*,[86] the UT confirmed that (contrary to the argument put for the child) the exclusion from the definition of disability of a tendency to physical abuse applied to children as to adults. It went on to rule that the FTT had been correct to reject a challenge under EqA 2010 ss15 and 20 to the exclusion from school of a six-year-old child whose severe behavioural difficulties resulted from her autism.

6.74   Notwithstanding the fact that the excluded condition (a tendency towards physical abuse) was connected with autism (a non-excluded condition), the UT applied *Governing body of X Endowed Primary School v Special Educational Needs and Disability Tribunal and others*[87] in ruling that the exclusion applied. A similar approach was taken in *C v Governing Body of I School*[88] in which the UT rejected the argument put for the claimant that, in excluding him by reason of his tendency to physical abuse, the school had breached its duty to make reasonable adjustments in respect of his (non-excluded) ASD.

Discrimination and other forms of regulated conduct

Introduction

6.75   The EqA 2010 regulates a variety of types of conduct in the context of education, among them different forms of discrimination, harassment and victimisation. These forms of conduct are the subject matter of this chapter.

6.76   Discrimination may take the form of one or more of the following, so far as relevant here:[89]

1) direct discrimination;
2) indirect discrimination;
3) discrimination arising from disability;
4) failure to make a reasonable adjustment.

---

86 [2015] UKUT 7 (AAC), [2015] ELR 133.
87 [2009] EWHC 1842 (Admin), [2009] IRLR 1007.
88 [2015] UKUT 0217 (AAC).
89 This being a book about disability, pregnancy-related discrimination will not be considered.

6.77 Types (1) and (2) apply in relation to all of the protected characteristics – which, as we saw in para 6.2, are, in the context of education:[90] disability, gender reassignment, race, religion or belief, sex (including pregnancy) and sexual orientation. Types (3) and (4) apply only to the protected characteristic of disability, and it is disability with which this book is concerned though, because the case-law relating to types (1) and (2) arises in relation to all of the protected characteristics, some of the cases here discussed will concern other protected characteristics.

6.78 Harassment and victimisation are also prohibited in the context of education, the former only in relation to the protected characteristics of: disability, gender reassignment, race and sex (including pregnancy). Again, because case-law relating to harassment and victimisation arises in relation to protected characteristics other than disability, some of the cases here discussed will involve other protected characteristics.

6.79 In addition to the forms of prohibited conduct here discussed, the EqA 2010 provides that it is unlawful to instruct someone else to discriminate against a third party, or to cause, induce or assist a third party so to do.[91]

Direct discrimination

6.80 Turning to consider the various different types of discrimination, direct discrimination occurs (so far as relevant here) when, *because of a pupil's protected characteristic*, he or she is treated less favourably.[92] One example given in the *Technical guidance for schools in England* would be if a school were to refuse 'to admit a child to a school as a pupil because of his or her race, for example because he or she is Roma'.[93] Another might be where a child is not allowed to go on a school trip because she is pregnant. Direct discrimination (like other forms of discrimination or other prohibited conduct) will be unlawful where it takes place in relation to any of the matters set out in EqA 2010 s85, that is (see also para 6.4):

- in the arrangements made for determining admission;
- in the terms of admission;
- by refusing to admit a pupil;

90 Other than further and higher education
91 EqA 2010 ss111, 112.
92 EqA 2010 s13.
93 Technical guidance, para 5.3.

- in the way in which education is provided to a pupil;
- by not providing education to a pupil;
- in the way in which a pupil is afforded access to a benefit, facility or service;
- by not providing access to a benefit, facility or service to a pupil;
- by excluding the pupil from the school; or
- by subjecting the pupil to any other detriment.[94]

6.81   The EqA 2010 provides that, where a comparison is required for the purposes of establishing *less* favourable treatment (as will always be the case for direct discrimination),[95] the comparison must be such that there is 'no material difference' between the relevant circumstances of the claimant and those of his or her comparator(s). In the case of disability, the EqA 2010 further provides that the 'circumstances relating to a case include a person's abilities'.[96]

6.82   Comparators may be hypothetical as well as real (ie it is possible simply to claim that a person would have been treated more favourably had she been a boy instead of a girl, white instead of Asian or non-disabled instead of disabled).

6.83   One example of direct disability discrimination is provided in the EHRC's technical guidance. Having pointed out that direct discrimination is unlawful 'irrespective of the school's motive or intention and regardless of whether the less favourable treatment of the pupil is conscious or unconscious',[97] stating that staff 'may have prejudices that they do not even admit to themselves or may act out of good intentions – or may simply be unaware that they are treating the pupil differently because of a protected characteristic',[98] the guidance provides the following examples:[99]

> - A teacher decides to deny a pupil with a facial disfigurement a place on the school debating team, because he believes that other pupils taking part in the debates will make fun of the pupil and cause him distress. Although the teacher may think that he has good intentions, denying the pupil a chance to be on the team is likely to be direct disability discrimination.

---

94 EqA 2010 s85(1) and (2) (discrimination), (4) and (5) (victimisation).
95 EqA 2010 s23(1).
96 EqA 2010 s23(2).
97 Technical guidance, para 5.7. See *R (E) v Governing Body of JFS* [2009] UKSC 15, [2010] 2 AC 728.
98 Technical guidance, para 5.7.
99 Technical guidance, para 5.7.

- A school organises a trip to the theatre to see a Shakespeare play. The school decides that a pupil with a hearing impairment would receive greater benefit from watching a subtitled film version of the play, so it arranges for her to stay behind at school to watch the film in the audiovisual suite. The pupil, however, would prefer to attend the theatre to see the play with her peers. Although the school may consider its intentions to be good, preventing the pupil from seeing the play at the theatre is likely to be direct disability discrimination.

6.84 Another instance of direct discrimination might occur if a school were to advertise that it did not wish to have applications from – or would not admit – pupils with disabilities generally, or those with specific disabilities or categories of disability ('pupils with ASD need not apply').

6.85 Notwithstanding these examples, the requirement for comparators means that direct disability discrimination is a relatively narrow concept. A grammar school's refusal to admit a child with a disability whose cognitive ability (by reason of the disability) is less than that generally demanded by the school, would not amount to direct disability discrimination (because the relative abilities of the children can be taken into account). A refusal by a school to admit a child whose physical disability had the effect that the child was not safe in the school, and/or who presented a danger to others, would equally not be direct discrimination (assuming that the school would also refuse to admit a child who would pose a similar level of danger for other reasons). And (subject to the same proviso) an exclusion by a school of a child whose autistic spectrum disorder resulted in behaviour outside the school's behaviour code would not amount to direct discrimination,[100] though such an exclusion may be unlawful for other reasons. In each of these cases, however, the action might amount to another form of discrimination prohibited by the EqA 2010.

6.86 Where direct discrimination does occur, it is not possible to justify it. In other words, all direct discrimination that falls within the EqA 2010 is unlawful as such. This having been said, not all such discrimination in fact falls within the EqA 2010: single-sex schools are permitted, for example, and faith schools may discriminate on grounds of religion or belief in relation to admissions.[101]

---

100 Assuming it would have done the same to a non-disabled pupil.
101 EqA 2010 Sch 11 para 1.

6.87   It is important to be aware that only persons with disabilities are protected from any form of disability discrimination. The effect of this is that the EqA 2010 does not restrict the circumstances in which people can be treated *more* favourably because they have a disability (or a particular disability).[102]

Indirect discrimination

6.88   Indirect discrimination occurs (so far as relevant here) where a person (that is, a teacher, governor, school administrator or other member of staff, etc) applies to a disabled pupil (or prospective pupil) a *provision, criterion or practice* which:

- is also applied to pupils generally (or to a relevant category of them – choristers, for example, or footballers, or those in year 5 or in Ms X's class);
- puts, or would put, persons with the same disability as the disabled pupil at a particular disadvantage when compared with others;
- puts, or would put, the disabled pupil at that disadvantage; and
- cannot be shown by the person applying it to be a proportionate means of achieving a legitimate aim.[103]

6.89   The EqA 2010 does not define what is meant by a 'provision', 'criterion' or 'practice', but the concepts are intended to be broad and inclusive.[104] The EHRC's technical guidance suggests that they include:[105]

- arrangements (for example for deciding who to admit);
- the way in which education, or access to any benefit, service or facility is offered or provided;
- one-off decisions; and
- proposals or directions to do something in a particular way

It states further that PCPs (as they are commonly referred to):

> ... may be written out formally or they may simply have developed as the school worked out the best way of achieving its aims.

---

102 EqA 2010 s13(3). That being the case, there is no need to discuss the restrictions generally imposed by law on positive discrimination/ positive action (that is, discrimination in favour of those disadvantaged by sex, race, etc), or the circumstances under which such action may be lawful: EqA 2010 ss158, 159.

103 EqA 201 s190.

104 *British Airways plc v Starmer* [2005] IRLR 862 in which the concept was held to extend to a discretionary management decision applied only to the claimant.

105 Technical guidance, para 5.24.

6.90   PCPs are broad but they are not unboundaried. In *Nottingham City Transport Ltd v Harvey* (an employment case), the EAT ruled that:

> ... 'practice' has something of the element of repetition about it. It is, if it relates to a procedure, something that is applicable to others than the person suffering the disability. Indeed, if that were not the case, it would be difficult to see where the disadvantage comes in, because disadvantage has to be by reference to a comparator, and the comparator must be someone to whom either in reality or in theory the alleged practice would also apply.[106]

In that case the claimant, who had a history of mental ill-health, complained about his employer's refusal to consider exculpatory or (at least) mitigating evidence before dismissing him for a variety of disciplinary matters. An employment tribunal ruled that the application of the employer's disciplinary process had placed Mr Harvey at a substantial disadvantage because it had failed to address any of the issues that might have exonerated him and had failed to give sufficient credence to any mitigating factors, and that this had involved a failure to make reasonable adjustments. The employer successfully appealed on the basis that a one-off flawed application of a disciplinary process did not amount to or involve the application of a provision, criterion or practice. In allowing the appeal, the EAT ruled that 'not all unfair treatment involves a failure to adjust that which is a provision, criterion or practice.'

6.91   In another case in which a disabled employee complained that his payslip had been prepared incorrectly, the EAT ruled that 'the lack of competence in relation to a particular transaction cannot, as a matter of proper construction, in our view, amount to a 'practice' applied by an employer any more than it could amount to a 'provision' or 'criterion' applied by an employer'.[107]

6.92   Turning to the other requirements for establishing indirect discrimination, entrance criteria for an academically selective school may, for example, place pupils with Down syndrome at a particular disadvantage by comparison with others, because this disability is often associated with mild to moderate cognitive impairment. Also, a rule that only those pupils in the first basketball team may participate in a school trip for the purposes of playing in a competitive tournament in the Bahamas may place pupils with dyspraxia at a particular disadvantage by comparison with others, because the condition often impacts on ball skills. Strict 'no tolerance' behaviour policies may

---

106   *Nottingham City Transport Ltd v Harvey* (2012) UKEAT/0032/12, [2013] EqLR 4 para 17.
107   *Carphone Warehouse v Martin* UKEAT/0371/12 [2013] EqLR 481.

also impact disproportionately harshly on pupils with ADHD and/or ASD.

6.93   In each case, the question whether the rule is actionable as indirect discrimination will depend on (1) whether the particular pupil who is complaining about it (or on whose behalf complaint is made) is placed at a particular disadvantage by it; and (2) whether, if so, the rule is nevertheless justified. To take the first example, a pupil with Down syndrome who does not in fact have cognitive impairment, will not be able to complain of indirect discrimination if she failed the entrance examination because she was unwell with flu, or missed the bus and was late. Nor will a pupil with dyspraxia whose ball skills are such that he is on the first team for hockey but has, as a result, been unable to attend basketball practice.

6.94   Assuming that it can be shown that a pupil (or prospective pupil) has been or would be placed at a particular disadvantage by reason of his or her disability, the question will be whether the PCP is nevertheless justified. The EHRC's technical guidance suggests that the legitimate aims which a school might pursue would include:[108]

- ensuring that education, benefits, facilities and services are targeted at those who most need them;
- the fair exercise of powers;
- ensuring the health and safety of pupils and staff, provided that risks are clearly specified;
- maintaining academic and behaviour standards; and
- ensuring the wellbeing and dignity of pupils.

6.95   As the technical guidance goes on to point out, justification requires that any measures taken in pursuit of a legitimate aim are *proportionate*, which in turn requires that they are appropriate and *reasonably* necessary, though '"necessary" does not mean that the provision, criterion or practice is the only possible way of achieving the legitimate aim'.[109] In *G v St Gregory's Catholic Science College*[110] the High Court ruled that a school uniform policy which served the legitimate aim of discouraging gang culture nevertheless discriminated unlawfully on grounds of race. The policy, which prohibited boys from wearing their hair in cornrows, allowed no exceptions to accommodate genuine cultural or family practices, and was therefore found not to be 'proportionate'.

---

108 Technical guidance, para 5.34.
109 Technical guidance, para 5.35.
110 [2011] EWHC 1452 (Admin), [2011] EqLR 859, [2011] All ER (D) 113 (Jun).

6.96   Because the disparate impact in the *St Gregory's* case was on race rather than disability, the claimant had to succeed on an indirect discrimination claim if he was to win his case. Where disability is in issue, it is often easier to complain of a lack of reasonable accommodation, in which case there is no need to prove that the PCP complained of places the claimant *and others with his or her disability* at a particular disadvantage, as distinct from that it places the claimant himself or herself at a disadvantage for reasons connected with his or her disability.[111]

6.97   The more serious the impact of the PCP on the disabled pupil, the more is required by way of justification. Among the factors which can be taken into account is that of cost, though the EHRC warns that questions of cost alone cannot amount to a justification.[112] Finally: 'In a case involving disability, if a school has not complied with its duty to make relevant reasonable adjustments, it will be difficult for it to show that the treatment was proportionate'.[113]

Discrimination arising from disability

6.98   Discrimination arising from disability occurs (so far as relevant here) where a person (that is, a teacher, governor, school administrator or other member of staff, etc) treats a disabled pupil (or prospective pupil) unfavourably 'because of something arising in consequence of [the pupil's] disability', and 'cannot show that the treatment is a proportionate means of achieving a legitimate aim'.[114]

6.99   This form of discrimination will not be established if the person responsible for the unfavourable treatment 'did not know, and could not reasonably have been expected to know, that [the pupil] had the disability'. This is further discussed at paras 6.128–6.134 below.

---

111 Albeit this has to be a *substantial* disadvantage.

112 Whether the EHRC is correct is a difficult question. On the one hand (in the context of employment) the Court of Justice of the EU ruled in *O'Brien v Ministry of Justice* C-393/10 [2012] 2 CMLR 728, [2012] IRLR 421 that 'budgetary considerations cannot justify discrimination'. This was applied in the Supreme Court in *Ministry of Justice v O'Brien* [2013] UKSC 6, [2013] 1 WLR 522 but in *R (Unison) v Lord Chancellor* [2015] EWCA Civ 915, [2016] ICR 1 Underhill LJ suggested that the typical distinction between 'cost', 'which is said never to be an admissible justification, and "cost plus", in which the presence of some other factor appears magically to legitimate partial reliance on cost considerations' is a "crude dichotomy", and "respectfully agree[ing] with the Supreme Court in *O'Brien* that the issue is one of some subtlety'.

113 Technical guidance, para 5.38.

114 EqA 2010 s15.

6.100   It is important to note that this form of discrimination does not depend on any comparison between the treatment of the disabled pupil and that of others – the requirement is for *un*favourable, rather than *less* favourable, treatment.

6.101   The EHRC's technical guidance suggests that being treated *un*favourably means being placed at a disadvantage,[115] which might be something obvious such as being excluded from a school trip or something more subtle. For an actionable breach of the EqA 2010 there must be a causal link between the reason for the unfavourable treatment and the unfavourable treatment: a sixth former whose ADHD makes him prone to inattention and minor misbehaviour in class will not experience discrimination arising from disability if he is disciplined for persistent lateness arising out of a habit of leaving the school premises at lunchtime and playing football with his friends. If, by contrast, he is disciplined for persistent inattention in class, this form of discrimination may (subject to justification) be made out.

6.102   Behavioural issues are, of course, not the only discrimination-related reasons which may give rise to unfavourable treatment. A disability may give rise to physical restrictions, cognitive impairments, difficulties with toileting or eating and/or limitations on the ability to concentrate or communicate or cope with noise or other stimulation.

6.103   Discrimination arising from disability is capable of justification. The test for this is the same as that which applies in relation to indirect discrimination, and is set out at paras 6.95–6.97 above.

Failure to make reasonable adjustments

6.104   The EqA 2010 provides, so far as relevant, that schools have a duty to make reasonable adjustments in respect of disabled pupils and prospective pupils, and that a failure to comply with this duty amounts to unlawful discrimination. The duty to make reasonable adjustments comprises two requirements, as follows (EqA 2010 ss20 and 84 read with Sch 13):

1) a requirement, where a provision, criterion or practice applied by or on behalf of a school puts an actual or prospective pupil at a substantial disadvantage in relation to a relevant matter in comparison with persons who are not disabled, to take such steps as it is reasonable to have to take to avoid the disadvantage;

115 Technical guidance, para 5.44.

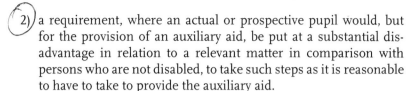 2) a requirement, where an actual or prospective pupil would, but for the provision of an auxiliary aid, be put at a substantial disadvantage in relation to a relevant matter in comparison with persons who are not disabled, to take such steps as it is reasonable to have to take to provide the auxiliary aid.

6.105 In order successfully to plead a failure to make reasonable adjustments it is necessary to identify the provision, criterion or practice etc in respect of which it is said that a reasonable adjustment could (and should) have been made. In *Environment Agency v Rowan*[116] the EAT allowed an appeal from a tribunal finding that there had been a failure to make a reasonable adjustment in circumstances in which the employee, a part-time clerk/typist who had injured her back in a work place accident, was not permitted to work from home. The EAT ruled that, in considering a reasonable adjustment claim, a tribunal must identify:

1) the provision, criterion or practice applied, or
2) the physical feature of premises,
3) the identity of non-disabled comparators (where appropriate), and
4) the nature and extent of the substantial disadvantage suffered.

6.106 A similar approach was taken by the EAT in *Royal Bank of Scotland v Ashton*,[117] allowing an appeal against a finding that the employer had failed to make reasonable adjustments in respect of the employee's severe migraines by issuing a disciplinary warning in respect of her attendance and suspending her sick pay for 12 months. The tribunal had accepted that the employer's sickness policy placed the claimant at a substantial disadvantage; that it would have been a reasonable adjustment for the employer to have exercised its discretion to defer the application of the disciplinary procedure; and that the enforcement of the policy constituted a failure to make a reasonable adjustment.

6.107 Those cases arose in the context of employment, but the principles discussed in them and in the other cases discussed in this chapter are of more general application.

6.108 The approach to PCP here is the same as that outlined at paras 6.88–6.91 above. The technical guidance suggests that a requirement to wear a specific school uniform is a PCP to which a duty of reasonable adjustment might apply (where, for example, it causes an allergic

116 [2008] ICR 218.
117 [2011] ICR 632.

reaction[118]). It further suggests that an 'auxiliary aid' may be a person as well as a thing,[119] as in the case of a support assistant provided to push a wheelchair user around the school.[120]

6.109   No duty is imposed by the EqA 2010 on schools to alter the physical features of premises in order to accommodate pupils with disabilities, but schools have a duty to plan improved access for disabled pupils generally, including in relation to their physical environment.

6.110   The EqA 2010 provides that, where the duty of reasonable adjustment imposes a requirement to provide information, that information should be provided in an accessible format. It also provides that the costs of complying with the duty of adjustment may not be passed onto a disabled pupil.[121] Interestingly, the EqA 2010 does not appear to prohibit the cost from being passed to a parent, though an insistence on so doing may mean that there is a failure to make reasonable adjustment where it would have been reasonable for the educational provider to bear that cost.

6.111   The duty to make adjustment only applies where a PCP or the lack of an auxiliary aid places the disabled pupil (or prospective pupil) at 'substantial disadvantage' by comparison with non-disabled pupils in relation to one of the matters set out at para 6.4 above (admission arrangements or decisions, educational arrangements, access to benefits, facilities or services, exclusions and other detriments). 'Substantial' means no more that 'not merely minor or trivial', however, so this is not a difficult test to satisfy.[122]

6.112   In *Royal Bank of Scotland v Ashton* (see above) the EAT ruled that a breach of the duty to make reasonable adjustments required a finding that a provision, criterion or practice had placed the disabled person, *not simply at some disadvantage viewed generally*, but at a disadvantage that was substantial viewed in comparison with persons who were not disabled.[123] Further (as regards adjustments), the focus had to be on the *practical result of the measures that could be taken.*

6.113   The technical guidance provides an example of a pupil with severe manual dexterity difficulties who is placed at a substantial disadvantage by a requirement to write large amounts of text by hand, and who would be placed at a substantial disadvantage in a lesson in

118 At para 6.17.
119 Such as a step to enable a pupil with restricted growth to reach the bench in a science lab.
120 At para 6.18.
121 Respectively EqA 2010 s20(6) and (7).
122 See, for example, *Greenwood v British Airways* [1999] ICR 969.
123 At para 14.

which large amounts of text have to be copied from the board, though not in a lesson in no handwriting is required.[124]

6.114   The duty imposed by the EqA 2010 is a duty to take 'reasonable steps ... to avoid the disadvantage' or to provide the auxiliary aid. 'Reasonable steps' are not defined. It is not possible to state in advance what steps will or will not be reasonable, this being a question which will vary from case to case. But it is possible to point to factors which are likely to influence that determination.

6.115   In *Project Management v Latif*[125] the EAT suggested that, although the claimant is not required to specify the nature of the adjustment required, there must be before the tribunal facts from which, absent any innocent explanation, it could be inferred that a particular adjustment could have been made. If this was not the case, the respondent would be placed in the 'impossible position' of having to prove a negative (ie that there was no reasonable adjustment that could have been made).[126] And in *Newcastle City Council v Spires* the EAT stated that tribunals must confine themselves to findings about proposed adjustments which had been identified as being in issue in the case.[127] It follows from this that it is important for claimants to specify what they say should have been done by way of adjustment.

6.116   It should be borne in mind that the purpose of taking steps to accommodate the needs of disabled pupils (or prospective pupils) is not as an exercise for its own sake: the point is to ensure that the disabled person is not placed at a substantial disadvantage by reason of his or her disability. This being the case, the duty will not require a school to take steps which are unlikely to alleviate that disadvantage (an example might be the installation of a hearing loop for a deaf child who does not use a hearing aid).

6.117   The technical guidance warns, however, that 'if an adjustment, when taken alone, is of marginal benefit but may be one of several adjustments that, if grouped together, would be effective in overcoming the disadvantage, in that case, it would be reasonable for the school to make the adjustment'.[128] The example provided is of a pupil with chronic fatigue syndrome who is exhausted by the demands of moving around a large three-floor secondary school despite adjustments to her timetable and location of classes to minimise her need to travel

124 Technical guidance, para 6.14.
125 [2007] IRLR 579.
126 [2007] IRLR 579.
127 UKEAT/0034/10, [2011] All ER (D) 60 (May).
128 Technical guidance, para 6.39.

around the school: if further adjustments of 'giving her a "buddy" to carry her books for her, using a dictaphone to record those lessons that she misses and establishing a policy that she will not be penalised for arriving at lessons late ... enable her to attend more lessons and to be less disadvantaged when she does miss lessons', the guidance suggests that failure to take these steps may amount to a breach of the duty to make reasonable adjustments in her case.

6.118   The starting point for determining which steps might be taken to alleviate the substantial disadvantage suffered by a pupil is likely to be consultation with the pupil and/or, as appropriate, his or her parents, and it is in the interests of pupils for parents to be open with schools about what their children need. It may also be wise for a school to seek expert advice. It is important to note, however, that there is no duty under the EqA 2010 to consult or to assess: the duty is to make any reasonable adjustment, and if that is done it does not matter what process was followed in achieving that.[129]

6.119   The technical guidance sets out the following factors which, it suggests are among those 'likely to be taken into account when considering what adjustments it is reasonable for a school to have to make':[130]

- The extent to which special educational provision will be provided to the disabled pupil under Part 3 of the Children and Families Act 2014.
- The resources of the school and the availability of financial or other assistance.
- The financial and other costs of making the adjustment.
- The extent to which taking any particular step would be effective in overcoming the substantial disadvantage suffered by a disabled pupil.
- The practicability of the adjustment.
- The effect of the disability on the individual.
- Health and safety requirements.
- The need to maintain academic, musical, sporting and other standards.
- The interests of other pupils and prospective pupils.

6.120   The technical guidance points out that there is a substantial overlap between the duties imposed by the EqA 2010 and those which apply under the SEN framework, and that: 'In some cases, the substantial disadvantage that [pupils] experience may be overcome by support received under the SEN framework and so there will be no obligation

---

129 *Tarbuck v Sainsbury Supermarkets Ltd* [2006] IRLR 664 para 71, *Royal Bank of Scotland v Ashton* para 24.
130 Technical guidance, para 6.26.

under the Act for the school or local authority to make reasonable adjustments'.[131] Whether this is in fact so will, of course, vary from case to case. Additional guidance is available in that document about all of the factors set out above.

6.121 Adjustments which might be made to accommodate the needs of pupils with disabilities might include the provision of coloured overlays and computer screens for pupils with dyslexia; specialist computer software for students with visual impairments and various specific learning disabilities; special chairs, gym equipment or toilet facilities for students with physical difficulties; additional supervision or one-to-one for children with ASD; the provision of assistance to children with asthma or diabetes to administer medication and (in the latter case) to monitor blood sugar levels.

6.122 Schools may have to adjust timetabling to ensure that pupils with disabilities can access lessons without substantial disadvantage, and may have to make adjustments in relation to school trips. They may also have to provide hands-on care. The EHRC's technical guidance gives the following examples:[132]

- A disabled pupil who attends a mainstream school has a tracheostomy, which needs monitoring, and he needs occasional intervention to clear his airways. The school carries out a risk assessment, and identifies that he needs to have a member of staff who is able to provide the necessary monitoring and intervention with him at all times. The school has several support staff who are trained and contractually obliged to administer medication to pupils. The school arranges for these staff and any others who volunteer to be trained in tracheostomy care, and then timetables the trained staff so that one is always able to monitor the pupil. All staff are trained in identifying when the pupil needs intervention and are provided with radio microphones, so that they can summon assistance from another member of staff if necessary. These are reasonable adjustments for the school to make in response to the risk assessment.

- A disabled pupil with epilepsy applies to be admitted to his local primary school. His parents speak to the head teacher and express their concern that someone at the school needs to be trained to provide the necessary medical support if the pupil has a seizure in school. The head teacher carries out a risk assessment, and seeks advice from the local authority and from another school in the area with a pupil with epilepsy. She identifies that the risks decrease the more members of staff are trained and able to assist

---

131 Technical guidance, para 6.28.
132 Technical guidance, para 6.46.

in the case of a seizure. The head teacher decides to provide training to all staff, teaching and non-teaching, as part of an Inset day;
then, after the training has been undertaken, she asks staff to volunteer to agree to support the pupil and to administer the necessary medication. The head teacher also puts in place an individual
healthcare plan for the pupil, which includes instructions on how
the medication is to be administered, and the need for a second
adult to witness the dosage and administration of the medication.
Although no individual member of staff is required to undertake
the training, by offering it to all staff it is possible to maximise the
number of people who can assist, to raise staff awareness generally and to minimise the health risk for the pupil. This could be a
reasonable adjustment for the school to make.

6.123   An important factor in assessing the reasonableness of any suggested
adjustment will be its impact on other pupils. The guidance gives
an example of a pupil whose skin condition is aggravated by cold
and whose parents ask the school to maintain room temperatures
at a very high level to the discomfort of other pupils. This is unlikely
to be a reasonable adjustment, though the school could 'take other
steps, such as raising the classroom temperature to a level that is
still comfortable for other pupils, placing the pupil in the hottest part
of the room, such as by a radiator, and relaxing the school uniform
policy to allow him to wear warmer and more comfortable cloth-
ing'.[133] The guidance goes on to state that compliance with the duty
to make reasonable adjustments may, however, require the imposition of 'some inconvenience to others' (this being a question of
proportionality). So:[134]

- A primary school plans a school trip to a local history museum in
  its town to undertake some activities. One of the pupils in the class
  is deaf and, because the museum does not have a hearing loop
  installed, she will be unable to participate in the trip. The school
  decides to change the trip and attend a museum in a neighbour-
  ing town, which has a hearing loop. Although this will cause some
  inconvenience to the other pupils because the travel time to and
  from school is longer, the school decides that this is a reasonable
  adjustment to make given the substantial disadvantage faced by
  the disabled pupil if she is unable to attend the trip.

- A secondary school takes its year 7 pupils on a week-long outdoor
  activity course every year. The school always goes to the same
  place, which offers a wide range of exciting activities in which the
  pupils can participate. This year, one of the year 7 disabled pupils

133 Technical guidance, para 6.48.
134 Technical guidance, para 6.49.

has to have kidney dialysis on a daily basis, so needs to be able to return home every day. In deciding on what adjustment to make for the disabled pupil, the school considers cancelling the trip and seeking an alternative, such as day trips closer to the school. The school weighs up whether denying pupils the opportunity to attend the week-long trip is reasonable and decides to stick with the planned trip to the outdoor activities centre so that pupils do not miss out on this valuable residential experience, and are not required to travel to and from activities each day. But, to minimise the disadvantage faced by the disabled pupil, the school arrange for transport from his home to attend the centre for day visits on three days of the week, so that the pupil has the benefit of being able to participate in the activities with his peers. If the school had not made this adjustment, he would not have been able to participate at all. This is likely to be a reasonable step for the school to have to take. It is unlikely to be reasonable for the school to have to alter its decision to undertake the week-long activities course.

 6.124 It is important to note that the duty to make reasonable adjustments is *prospective*. While a particular pupil may complain about a breach of that duty only once it has impacted on him or her, the fact that a school has not considered the possible application of the duty in advance, and made suitable arrangements, may mean that the duty is breached because the school is not in a position to make rapid adjustments when confronted by a particular need.

 6.125 If a disability is unusual or the adjustments which might be required to accommodate it very expensive, the fact that a school has not taken prospective action may not result in a breach of the duty. Where a disability is relatively commonplace and the adjustments which would accommodate it relatively low-cost and straightforward, a school may find itself in breach of the duty at a very early stage of a pupil's attendance (or because it cannot accommodate a pupil who would have been able to attend had the necessary adjustment(s) been made prospectively.

 6.126 Expense can be a reason why a particular accommodation may not be reasonable.[135] Whatever the reason which an educational provider may wish to rely on to resist an adjustment sought, it should be made clear at the time (and, when cost is an issue, should be carefully and transparently assessed).

6.127 A failure to comply with a duty of reasonable adjustment cannot be justified.

---

135 See *Cordell v Foreign and Commonwealth Office* [2012] ICR 280.

Knowledge of disability

6.128   Some forms of discrimination require that the alleged discriminator knows or should have known that the pupil (or prospective pupil) was disabled (or, more precisely, that the absence of such actual or constructive knowledge will provide a defence).[136] The knowledge at issue is not knowledge that the person would be categorised as disabled for the purposes of the EqA 2010, rather, knowledge (actual or constructive) of the facts which, as a matter of law, are sufficient to amount to disability.

6.129   A school will be regarded as having knowledge if anyone in a position of responsibility within the school is aware. By way of example, the EHRC's technical guidance suggests that, is a pupil has told the school's secretary that she has diabetes and that she needs to carry biscuits to eat if her blood sugar levels fall, the school is likely to be guilty of discrimination is a teacher who does not know about the pupil's diabetes refuses to allow her to bring the biscuits into his classroom and later disciplines her for eating them.[137]

6.130   Information held by a school secretary, a teacher or teaching assistant is likely to be attributable to the school, at least unless it has been provided in confidence. The fact that a fellow pupil is aware will not be attributable to the school, and knowledge that a teacher might have by reason of the fact that his child has reported something she has overheard or been told may or may not be so attributable.

6.131   The EHRC's technical guidance warns that:[138]

> A school must do all it that can reasonably be expected to do to find out whether a pupil has a disability. What is reasonable will depend on the circumstances. This is an objective assessment. When making enquiries about disability, schools should consider issues of dignity and privacy, and ensure that personal information is dealt with confidentially.

6.132   In the case of discrimination arising from a disability, the EqA 2010 provides that the prohibition does not apply if the discriminator 'shows that [s/he] did not know, and could not reasonably have been expected to know, that [the disabled person had the disability.'[139]

6.133   Prior to the replacement of the DDA 1995 by the EqA 2010, the DDA 1995 also provided that no duty to make reasonable adjustments applied if the employer did not know, and could not reasonably be

---

136   See EqA 2010 s15(2) (discrimination arising from a disability).
137   Technical guidance, para 5.51.
138   Technical guidance, para 5.52.
139   EqA 2010 s15(2).

expected to know, that that person has a disability *and* that s/he was likely to be 'place[d] ... at a substantial disadvantage in comparison with persons who are not disabled'.[140] Most recently, in *Newham Sixth Form College v Saunders* the Court of Appeal ruled that:[141]

> ... the nature and extent of the disadvantage, the employer's knowledge of it and the reasonableness of the proposed adjustment necessarily run together. An employer cannot ... make an objective assessment of the reasonableness of proposed adjustments unless he appreciates the nature and extent of the substantial disadvantage imposed upon the employee by the PCP.

6.134 That decision was made in the context of employment. The provision concerning knowledge had been preserved in EqA 2010 Sch 8 in relation to employers, but does not have an equivalent where education is concerned. This has the result that the duty to make reasonable adjustment applies whether or not the alleged discriminator knew or ought to have known not only about the disability, or about the impact of that disability in relation to the PCP or auxiliary aid at issue. This reflects the fact that the duty to make reasonable adjustments is anticipatory. On the other hand, it cannot be the case that a duty of reasonable adjustment could be breached in a case in which the nature of the adjustment required was specific to a particular disability which the educational provider did not and could not reasonably have known about; by way of example, a child whose undisclosed photosensitive epilepsy had the effect that she should use computers only with specific precautions.

Harassment

6.135 Harassment is defined by EqA 2010 s26 as occurring (so far as relevant here) where a person:

- engages in unwanted conduct related to a relevant protected characteristic, or of a sexual nature, which
- has the purpose or effect of–
  - violating another person's dignity; or
  - creating an intimidating, hostile, degrading, humiliating or offensive environment for the other person.

---

140 DDA 2010 s4A; and see *Department for Work and Pensions v Alam* [2010] IRLR 283, *Wilcox v Birmingham CAB Services Ltd* [2011] All ER (D) 73 (Aug).
141 [2014] EWCA Civ 734 para 14.

6.136   In deciding whether conduct has the *effect* of violating dignity or creating an intimidating, hostile, degrading, humiliating or offensive environment, a court or tribunal must take into account:[142]

- the perception of the person complaining of harassment,
- the other circumstances of the case, and
- whether it is reasonable for the conduct to have that effect.

6.137   Harassment related to sexual orientation or religion is not regulated as such in the educational context, and the prohibitions on discrimination and related conduct related to age do not apply in this context either. As far as sexual orientation and religion are concerned, however, harassment related to these protected characteristics could amount to discrimination (if the harasser would have treated a person with different religious characteristics or sexual orientation more favourably.

6.138   Perhaps the most significant limitation on the prohibition of harassment in the context of schools is that it will not apply to harassment by fellow students, as distinct from school staff. Harassment by fellow pupils is likely to be actionable under the EqA 2010 only if the school's failure to deal with it was found itself to have been influenced by the pupil's protected characteristic, in which case the failure ought to amount to direct discrimination.

Victimisation

6.139   Victimisation is defined in EqA 2010 s27 as occurring (so far as relevant here) where a person is treated unfavourably because he or she has:

- brought proceedings under the Act;
- given evidence or information in connection with proceedings under the Act;
- done any other thing for the purposes of or in connection with the Act;
- made an allegation (whether or not express) that someone has contravened the Act;

or where the person who subjects the other to unfavourable treatment believes that the other has done or may do one of these things (which are referred to as 'protected acts').

142 EqA 2010 s26(4).

6.140   The EqA 2010 provides that 'giving false evidence or information, or making a false allegation, is not a protected act if the evidence or information is given, or the allegation is made, in bad faith'.

6.141   Finally, of relevance here, is the fact that pupils are expressly protected from victimisation by reason of their parents' or siblings' conduct.[143] Where this type of victimisation is in issue, the EqA 2010 provides that the giving of evidence, making of a complaint etc will not be protected if *both* false evidence or false information is given, or a false allegation is made, and the *pupil* has acted in bad faith.

Bringing a disability discrimination claim in the First-tier Tribunal

Who can bring a claim?

6.142   A claim against a responsible body of a school in respect of disability discrimination may be made by the person's parent or, if the person is over compulsory school age,[144] the young person.[145]

Respondent to the claim

6.143   The respondent to the claim is the responsible body, as defined in EqA 2010 s85(9); see para 6.8 above.

6.144   If the school converts to an academy school after a claim has been issued but prior to its determination, the responsible body of the school has ceased to exist and the liability for the claim is transferred to the local authority.[146] In such circumstances, the FTT will order the local authority to be substituted for the responsible body of the school under FTT Rules r9(1)(b). Further, if it consents, the responsible body of the academy school should be added as a second respondent. This would not confer any power on the FTT to make orders against the academy school, but it would confer on the responsible body of the academy school the powers and rights of parties to

---

143 EqA 2010 s86.
144 Education Act 1996 s8 defines 'compulsory school age' as (very broadly) between the first day of the term immediately after the term in which the child turns 5, and the end of the academic year in which the child turns 16.
145 See EqA 2010 Sch 17 para 3(a).
146 *ML v Tonbridge Grammar School* [2012] UKUT 283, [2012] ELR 508 per UT Judge Rowland at paras 12–14.

the claim (including the power to participate in the hearing and to appeal).[147]

Jurisdiction to hear the claim

 6.145 A claim that the responsible body of a school has discriminated on the grounds of a person's disability (ie one that the responsible body has contravened EqA 2010 Part 6 ch 1) must be brought in the FTT.[148]

Time for bringing proceedings

6.146 Proceedings on a claim may not be brought after the end of the period of six months starting with the date when the conduct complained of occurred.[149] The EqA 2010 sets out certain rules for deciding when acts occurred, namely:

- conduct extending over a period is to be treated as occurring at the end of the period;[150]
- failure to do something is to be treated as occurring when the person in question decided on it;[151]
- in the absence of evidence to the contrary, a person (P) is to be taken to decide on failure to do something when P acts inconsistently

---

147 *ML v Tonbridge Grammar School* [2012] UKUT 283, [2012] ELR 508 per UT Judge Rowland at para 31.

148 See EqA 2010 ss113, 114, 116 and Sch 17 para 3(a). Note that a claim of disability discrimination against the responsible body of a further education institution under EqA 2010 Part 6 ch 2 must be brought in the County Court: see EqA 2010 ss114 and 116. Nothing in the EqA 2010 prevents a claim for judicial review: see EqA 2010 s113(3)(a).

149 EqA 2010 Sch 17 para 4(1).

150 EqA 2010 Sch 17 para 4(5)(b). This arises where there have been a series of events, said to be discriminatory, only some of which occurred within the six months prior to the issue of the claim. The FTT must determine whether this is a 'continuing act', so that all of the events are in time, or whether to treat each as a discrete event. See *Hendricks v Commissioner of Police for the Metropolis* [2002] EWCA Civ 1686, [2003] IRLR 96 at paras 29–31, 48 (per Mummery LJ). A relevant, although not conclusive factor, is whether the same or different individuals were involved in each incident, see *Aziz v FDA* [2010] EWCA Civ 304, at para 33. It will generally be an error of law for a tribunal to determine whether there is an act extending over a period of time on the basis of legal submissions alone: the tribunal will need to make findings of fact, see *Hendricks v Commissioner of Police for the Metropolis* [2002] EWCA Civ 1686, [2003] IRLR 96 at paras 33–35.

151 EqA 2010 Sch 17 para 4(5)(c). See *Matuszowicz v Kingston Upon Hull City Council* [2009] EWCA Civ 22, [2009] IRLR 288, at paras 22 (per Lloyd LJ) and 35 (per Sedley LJ).

with doing it, or if P does not act inconsistently, on the expiry of the period in which P might reasonably have been expected to do it.[152]

6.147 The FTT may consider a claim which is out of time.[153] A claimant who requires an extension of time ought to explain why the claim was not brought earlier in his or her claim form. There is no presumption that the FTT will extend time, and it will be for the claimant to persuade the FTT to exercise its discretion in his or her favour.

6.148 Factors that may be relevant to the exercise of the FTT's discretion to extend time are as follows:

- the length of the delay and the reasons for it;
- whether there is (or is not) prejudice to a respondent in allowing the claim out of time (and in particular, whether the cogency of the respondent's evidence will be affected by the delay in bringing the claim);
- the merits of the claim;
- the conduct of the parties since the act complained of; and
- whether any medical condition or disability of the claimant, or his or her child, affected his or her ability to bring the claim in time.

Commencing a claim[154]

6.149 The bringing of a claim for disability discrimination in the FTT is governed by the FTT Rules. For the most part, therefore, the discussion at paras 4.33–4.136 above will apply equally to discrimination claims. Only the features of the procedure that are different are dealt with below.

6.150 The claimant must start proceedings before the FTT by sending or delivering an application notice within the six-month time limit.[155] Pursuant to the Practice Direction: *First-tier Tribunal – Health Education and Social Care Chamber – Special educational needs or disability discrimination in schools cases* (October 2008) ('the SEN Practice Direction')[156] this will need to include:

---

152 EqA 2010 Sch 17 para 4(6).
153 EqA 2010 Sch 17 para 4(3); but the FTT may not consider a claim which is out of time if the FTT has previously decided under paragraph 4(3) not to consider a claim, see EqA 2010 Sch 17 para 4(4).
154 See SEND4A, *How to claim against disability discrimination in schools – a guide for parents*.
155 FTT Rules r20(1). The specific form to be used from the FTT's website will depend on the nature of the discrimination alleged.
156 Issued by the Senior President of Tribunals.

- a description of the child's disability, including evidence of a medical or other professional diagnosis, if available;
- details of the alleged discrimination, including the date or dates on which it is alleged to have taken place; and
- if there is a statement of SEN (or an education, health and care (EHC) plan) in relation to the child, a copy and a copy of the appendices (if available).[157]

6.151   The respondent responsible body must send a response to the FTT so that it is received within 30 working days after the respondent received the application notice.[158] The SEN Practice Direction requires this to include 'detailed grounds setting out what parts of the application are admitted, detailed grounds setting out what parts of the application are resisted, and details of any legal points that will be relied on at a final hearing'.[159]

6.152   The FTT will set directions (on occasion, prior to the response being due). The directions often make preliminary observations on the claim, and may direct the parties to make further submissions on specific points. The directions will make provision for a date on which final evidence must be sent to the FTT, the submission of an attendance form,[160] and list the claim for a hearing.

6.153   It is not presently the FTT's practice in most cases to list the claim for a case management hearing. In the experience of the authors that is regrettable, as many discrimination claims issued in the FTT would benefit from active case management, and in particular, identification of the issues to be determined at the hearing, early in the claim.

6.154   As in SEN cases, if a parent or young person wishes to apply for further directions or to vary those that have already been issued, he or she should use the 'Request for Changes' form (form SEND7).

6.155   While there is no requirement for witness statements to be prepared (and the FTT does not routinely order their preparation), a claimant might find it sensible to set out the evidence his or her witnesses propose to give in the form of a witness statement. This is for a number of reasons. First, the FTT will usually have read the papers prior to the hearing. Setting out the evidence in a witness statement means that the claimant's case will have been read in advance by the

---

157 SEN Practice Direction, para 6.
158 FTT Rules r21(1)(b).
159 SEN Practice Direction, para 11.
160 See para 4.107 above.

FTT. Second, the preparation of witness statements means that the hearing will proceed more efficiently.

6.156 The FTT will normally allow each party up to five witnesses (except in fast-track claims, on which see the next section).[161]

Fast-track procedure in permanent exclusion cases where the parent is seeking reinstatement

6.157 If a child or young person has been permanently excluded from school, the FTT recognises that any claim which might result in an order for reinstatement must be heard quickly. The FTT will apply an expedited timetable in such cases.[162]

6.158 The FTT will register any such claim on the same day as receiving it, or the next working day if received after midday.[163] The registration letter, sent to the parties, will contain directions (thus there will not be a separate case management order as in ordinary claims).

6.159 The respondent responsible body must submit a response within 15 working days of receiving the claim, and must submit an attendance form at the same time.[164] If the responsible body does not respond to an expedited claim, an order barring it from playing a further part in the proceedings will be made automatically (but the provisions for applying for reinstatement set out at para 4.78 above apply).[165]

6.160 Only two witnesses will be allowed for each party. The claimant should list his or her witnesses on the claim form.[166]

6.161 Expedited claims will be listed for half a day.[167] The hearing of a fast-tracked claim will normally take place five to six weeks after

---

161 See SEND4A, *How to claim against disability discrimination in schools – a guide for parents*, p16.

162 The FTT will not apply the expedited timetable if the claimant is awaiting a decision of the Independent Review Panel in respect of the exclusion. Instead the FTT will stay the disability discrimination claim until the claimant informs the FTT of the result of the review: see SEND4A, *How to claim against disability discrimination in schools – a guide for parents*, at pages 10-11.

163 SEND4A, *How to claim against disability discrimination in schools – a guide for parents*, p12.

164 SEND4A, *How to claim against disability discrimination in schools – a guide for parents*, p12.

165 SEND4A, *How to claim against disability discrimination in schools – a guide for parents*, p13.

166 SEND4A, *How to claim against disability discrimination in schools – a guide for parents*, p16.

167 SEND4A, *How to claim against disability discrimination in schools – a guide for parents*, p15.

the claim is received, with a decision on the day and written reasons either on the day or within five working days.[168]

Remedies

6.162   If the FTT concludes that the responsible body of the school has contravened the EqA 2010, the FTT may make such order as it thinks fit.[169] The power to make an order may, in particular, be exercised with a view to obviating or reducing the adverse effect on the person of any matter to which the claim relates.[170]

6.163   The FTT does not, however, have a power to order the payment of compensation.[171]

6.164   Some of the remedies that a claimant might ask the FTT to order are as follows:[172]

- training of school staff;
- drawing up new guidance for staff;
- changes to school policies;
- extra tuition, to make up for lost learning;
- changing the location of lessons or activities (but not changing physical premises);
- admission of the child or young person to an independent school if admission had previously been refused;
- a written apology to the child or young person;
- trips or other opportunities to make up for activities that the child or young person may have missed;
- meetings between the local authority, parents, the child or young person and the school to review what reasonable adjustments might be required; and
- in cases of permanent exclusion, an order reinstating the child or young person to the school.

6.165   The FTT will order the responsible body of a school to take the required steps within a specified period of time.

---

168 SEND4A, *How to claim against disability discrimination in schools – a guide for parents*, p11.

169 EqA 2010 Sch 17 para 5(1) and (2).

170 EqA 2010 Sch 17 para 5(3)(a).

171 EqA 2010 Sch 17 para 5(3)(b).

172 Taken from SEND4A, *How to claim against disability discrimination in schools – a guide for parents*, p17; and *ML v. Tonbridge Grammar School* [2012] UKUT 283, [2012] ELR 508 per UT Judge Rowland at para 18.

6.166   In *ML v Tonbridge Grammar School* UT Judge Rowland expressed
doubts about whether it would be appropriate to make orders other
than a declaration of disability discrimination or an apology against
a responsible body where the child had left the school. This was
because, in respect of orders requiring the school to, for example,
undertake training the claimant would not have sufficient interest to
enforce the order.[173] The judge also stated that where the school had
converted into an academy school since the claim had been issued,
it would be inappropriate to make an order other than a declaration
of disability discrimination against the new responsible body of the
school.[174]

6.167   In *Gayhurst Community School v ER* UT Judge Edwards stated
that the remedy ordered must be in proportion to what occurred.[175]
Further, he gave guidance on when it would be appropriate for the
FTT to order the responsible body of the school to apologise to the
child. The judge questioned the value of an apology contained under
compulsion, noting that an apology that was not sincerely meant
'merely creates resentment on one side and at best an illusion on the
other'.[176] It may be appropriate to order an apology where the responsible body, in the course of the hearing, shows a willingness to accept
what has happened, but the FTT should 'always satisfy itself, before
ordering an apology, that it will be of some true value'.[177]

173 [2012] UKUT 283, [2012] ELR 508 at para 21.

174 [2012] UKUT 283, [2012] ELR 508 at para 20.

175 [2013] UKUT 558 (AAC), [2014] ELR 103 at para 27. He noted that the order
    for monthly reports, following a fixed-term exclusion, was 'over-elaborate, out
    of proportion to what occurred and inappropriate given the short period of
    time that O would remain at the school'.

176 [2013] UKUT 558 (AAC), [2014] ELR 103 at para 25.

177 [2013] UKUT 558 (AAC), [2014] ELR 103 at para 26.

CHAPTER 7

Challenging the decision of the First-tier Tribunal

Key points

The First-tier Tribunal's power to amend or set aside its own decision

- The decision of the FTT can be amended or set aside by the FTT itself in certain limited circumstances.
- Accidental slips or omissions can be corrected by the FTT under rule 44 of the Tribunal Procedure (First-Tier Tribunal) (Health, Education And Social Care Chamber) Rules 2008 SI No 2699 (FTT Rules).
- The FTT may set aside a decision if there has been a procedural irregularity (under rule 45).
- The FTT can review its decision if there has been a change of circumstances (under rule 48).

Appeal to the Upper Tribunal

- Appeals can be brought against the decision of the FTT to the UT. Appeals can only be brought on the grounds that the FTT made an error of law and the parties cannot re-argue the merits of the case.
- Permission to appeal must first be sought from the FTT. If it is refused, permission can be sought from the UT itself.
- Certain FTT decisions are excluded from appeals to the UT and can only be challenged by judicial review.
- Once an application for permission to appeal has been made, the FTT must consider whether to review the decision for an error of law. If there has been an error of law, the FTT can amend its reasons, set aside the decision and re-decide it, or refer it to the UT.
- The decision of the FTT can be suspended pending an appeal if there are solid grounds for doing so.
- Common grounds for an appeal to the UT include illegality, procedural unfairness, failure to take account of relevant considerations, perversity and failure to give adequate reasons.
- If the UT grants the appeal, it can (a) set aside the decision and remit it to a new FTT panel or (b) re-decide the case itself.
- An appeal can be made from the UT to the Court of Appeal if it raises an important point of principle of practice or there is some other compelling reason to hear the appeal.

The First-tier Tribunal's power to amend or set aside its own decision

The slip rule

7.1 Tribunal Procedure (First-Tier Tribunal) (Health, Education And Social Care Chamber) Rules 2008 SI No 2699 (FTT Rules) r44 provides for correction of 'any clerical mistake or other accidental slip or omission in a decision, direction or any document'. The FTT must send notification of the amended decision, direction or document to all parties and make the necessary amendment.

7.2 If a party to an appeal believes that there has been a mistake in the decision, or other document, it should notify the FTT by letter or by using a 'Request for changes' form (SEND7).

Procedural irregularity

7.3 The FTT is also empowered to deal with procedural irregularities that preceded its decision. Under FTT Rules r45, the FTT has the power to set aside a decision and remake it if it is in the interests of justice to do so, and one or more of the following conditions is satisfied:

• a document relating to the proceedings was not sent to, or was not received at an appropriate time by, a party or a party's representative;

• a document relating to the proceedings was not sent to the FTT at an appropriate time;

• a party, or a party's representative, was not present at a hearing related to the proceedings; or

• there has been some other procedural irregularity in the proceedings.

7.4 An application to set aside a decision must be made in writing on the 'Application to set aside final decision' form (SEND 20C) within 28 days of the date on which the decision was sent.

7.5 The FTT should not deploy rule 45 to set aside decisions on substantive grounds. It is limited to correcting procedural irregularities.[1] If a party believes there has been an error of law, including failure to abide by standards of procedural fairness, they should make an application for permission to appeal.[2]

---

1 *Worcestershire CC v JJ (SEN)* [2014] UKUT 0406 (AAC), at para 16.
2 See paras 7.25–7.28 below.

Review where circumstances have changed

7.6   Under Tribunals Courts and Enforcement Act (TCEA) 2007 s9 and FTT Rules r48, parties can request a review of the decision by the FTT where circumstances have changed after the decision was made (this process is unique to special educational needs (SEN) cases).[3] An application for a review may be appropriate in cases where a specific factor which clearly affected the FTT's decision, such as the availability of a particular therapy or specialist equipment, has changed. The FTT will be wary of parties using the review power to challenge the merits of the decision.

7.7   The application must be received by the FTT within 28 days after the date on which the FTT sent its decision notice.[4] It should be made on the 'Application for review form' (SEND20B). If it is received outside the time limit, the application must include a request for an extension of time and explain the reason for the delay.[5] The FTT will consider whether to extend time under FTT Rules r5(3)(a). In cases where the change in circumstances was not known within 28 days, the FTT is likely to grant an extension.

7.8   The FTT must give all parties an opportunity to make representations about the review.[6] It must notify the parties of the outcome and any right of appeal.[7]

7.9   The powers of the FTT on review are set out in TCEA 2007 s9(4). The FTT may correct accidental errors in the decision or in a record of the decision, amend the reasons given for a decision, or set a decision aside. Where, as a result of a review, the FTT sets a decision aside, it must either re-decide the matter itself or refer it to the UT.[8]

---

3   Pursuant to FTT Rules r49(1) this is one of the two circumstances in which the FTT can review its own decision. The other arises under rule 47(1): on receiving an application for permission to appeal to the UT, the FTT must first decide whether to review the decision. This is dealt with at paras 7.18–7.24 below.

4   FTT Rules r48(3).

5   FTT Rules r48(4).

6   FTT Rules r49(4). See *GA v Southwark LBC (HB)* [2013] UKUT 170 (AAC) at para 16.

7   FTT Rules r49(3). Note that a decision not to review the decision is expressly excluded from appeal to the UT: see below para 7.12.

8   TCEA 2007 s9(5).

Appeal to the Upper Tribunal

The Upper Tribunal

7.10   The UT has the power to hear appeals against the decisions of the FTT.[9] Before November 2008, when the FTT and the UT were created, appeals against decisions of the FTT's predecessor, the Special Educational Needs and Disability Tribunal (SENDT), were brought to the High Court.[10]

7.11   UT appeals are heard by the Administrative Appeals Chamber (AAC). Decisions of the UT are binding on the FTT, and set precedents for future cases which the FTT must take into account.

Excluded decisions

7.12   There is no right of appeal to the UT against 'excluded decisions'.[11] These are set out in TCEA 2007 s11. The relevant FTT decisions which are excluded from the right to appeal are:

- a decision not to review an earlier decision of the FTT;
- a decision to set aside an earlier decision of the FTT; and
- a decision to refer or not to refer a matter to the UT.[12]

7.13   There *is* a right of appeal from an interlocutory decision of the FTT, such as a strike out decision.[13] In *LM v Lewisham LBC*[14] the UT held that there was a right of appeal against a refusal to review a case management direction, stating that 'the purpose of the exclusion in [TCEA 2007] s11(5)(d) is to prevent an appeal being brought against a review decision when it should be brought against the decision which it has been sought to have reviewed'.[15] The judgment suggests that the courts will permit an appeal against any decision of the FTT, including procedural decisions, or so long as it is not expressly excluded.

7.14   If a party wants to challenge an excluded decision, it must do so by judicial review. The UT has exclusive jurisdiction to hear such

---

9   TCEA 2007 s11.
10   TIA 1992 s11.
11   TCEA 2007 s11(1).
12   The excluded decisions relevant to SEN appeals are the general decisions described in TCEA 2007 s11(d).
13   *LS v Lambeth LBC* [2010] UKUT 461 (AAC) at paras 79–97.
14   [2009] UKUT 204 (AAC).
15   See also *P v Worcestershire CC (SEN)* [2016] UKUT 120 (AAC) at para 58.

applications for judicial review and they should not be brought in the High Court.[16] An application for judicial review of an excluded decision should be brought promptly and no later than three months after the FTT's decision.[17]

7.15   In *LW v Norfolk CC (SEN)*,[18] the UT declined to grant permission to judicially review a decision by the FTT reviewing and setting aside an earlier decision, on the basis that it was proportionate to deal with the case as an appeal against the substantive decisions of the FTT. This suggests that where there is an appealable decision of the FTT, it is preferable to bring an appeal rather than judicially review the FTT's review decision.

Requirement for permission to appeal

7.16   If a party considers that the FTT has made an error of law, they can make an application for permission to appeal. There is no automatic right of appeal to the UT and permission must be obtained from the FTT or the UT.[19]

7.17   An application for permission to appeal must be made first to the FTT.[20] FTT Rules r46(5) requires the application to identify the decision of the tribunal to which it relates, the alleged error of law in the decision and state the result the party making the application is seeking. The application should be made on the 'Application for permission to appeal' form (SEND20A). It must be sent or delivered to the FTT so that it is received no later than 28 days after the Tribunal sends the reasons for its decision.[21] If the application is sent out of time, the appellant must request an extension of time and give reasons for the delay. The FTT has the power to extend time and will take account of the overriding objective of the FTT Rules to deal with cases fairly and justly.[22]

---

16   *R (LR) v First-tier Tribunal and Hertfordshire CC* [2012] UKUT 213 (AAC), [2012] ELR 456.

17   TCEA 2007 s16; UT Rules r28.

18   [2015] UKUT 65 (AAC).

19   TCEA 2007 s11(3) and (4).

20   UT Rules r21(2). A party may only apply to the UT for permission to appeal to the UT against the decision of the FTT if they have made an application for permission to appeal to the FTT and the application has been refused, has not been admitted, or only granted on limited grounds.

21   FTT Rules r46(2).

22   FTT Rules rr5(3) and 46(4); and see para 4.8 above.

FTT's consideration of an application for permission to appeal

7.18   Before it considers whether to grant permission to appeal to the UT, the FTT is first obliged to consider whether to review the decision itself on the basis that it made an error of law.[23] It is important to distinguish this review process from those outlined in para 7.6 above. Review for an error of law can only be undertaken when there has been an application for permission to appeal, while review by the FTT after a change in circumstances can be requested without making an application for permission to appeal.[24]

7.19   The rules governing review of FTT decisions are complex and applications can sometimes be made under the wrong rule. The FTT has the power to treat an application to be corrected, set aside or reviewed, or for permission to appeal, as an application for any one of those things.[25] The FTT should therefore be able to treat mistaken applications as if they were made under the appropriate rule.

7.20   The UT has given guidance about the FTT's power to review its own decision. In *R (RB) v First-tier Tribunal*,[26] the UT held that the purpose of review is to enable action to be taken by the FTT to correct clear errors of law without delay.[27] It is not intended to be used to resolve contentious legal points. The UT has described the review power as 'a filter mechanism to help ensure that obvious errors based on oversight of a legislative provision or binding authority can be corrected'.[28]

7.21   On reviewing its own decision, the FTT has the power to correct accidental errors in the decision or in a record of the decision; amend reasons given for the decision; or set the decision aside, and then either re-decide the matter or refer it to the UT.[29] It does *not* have the power to set aside part of a decision or to amend an EHC plan.[30]

7.22   The UT has stated that the decision identifying an error of law and the decision how to address it (by amending reasons, re-deciding or

---

23 FTT Rules r47(1). The FTT's power to review its decision is contained in TCEA 2007 s9.

24 See paras 7.6–7.9 above.

25 FTT Rules r50.

26 [2010] UKUT 160 (AAC).

27 See also *B v Worcestershire CC* [2010] UKUT 292 (AAC) at para 8, in which the UT confirmed that the *RB* approach applied in SEN cases.

28 *AA (Upper Tribunal – review power)* [2015] UKUT 330 (IAC), at para 6.

29 TCEA 2007 s9(5).

30 *Harrow Council v AM* [2013] UKUT 0157 (AAC), [2013] ELR 351.

referring to the UT), are inter-dependent and should be taken together by the FTT.[31] If the FTT opts to re-decide the matter, it should usually hold an oral hearing unless the parties are content to make written submissions.[32]

7.23   If the FTT decides not to review the decision, or reviews the decision and decides to take no action in relation to the decision or part of it, the FTT must consider whether to give permission to appeal the decision, or part of it, to the UT.[33]

7.24   If the FTT refuses permission to appeal, it must send a record of its decision to the parties as soon as practicable.[34] The record of the decision must be accompanied by a statement of the reasons for refusal, notification of the right to make an application to the UT for permission to appeal together with the time limits for and the method for making the application to the UT.[35]

Application for permission to appeal in the UT

7.25   If a party's application for permission to appeal is refused by the FTT, the application can be renewed in the UT. The application should be made on the 'Application for Permission to Appeal' form (UT4) within one month of the date on which the FTT sent notice of its refusal of permission to appeal.[36] If there has been a delay in making the application, this should be explained in the application. The UT has a discretion to extend time which will be exercised in accordance with the overriding objective to deal with cases justly and fairly.[37]

7.26   If the FTT refused the application for permission to appeal because it was made out of time, the UT can grant the application only if it is in the interests of justice to do so.[38]

7.27   If the UT refuses permission without an oral hearing or grants permission on limited grounds only, the appellant may apply for the

31 *Essex CC v TB (SEN)* [2014] UKUT 0559 (AAC) at para 43.
32 *Essex CC v TB (SEN)* [2014] UKUT 0559 (AAC) at para 45.
33 FTT Rules r47(2).
34 FTT Rules r47(3).
35 FTT Rules r47(4). Rule 47(5) allows the FTT to give permission on limited grounds, but it must comply with rule 47(4) in relation to any grounds on which it has refused permission.
36 UT Rules r21(3)(b).
37 UT Rules r5(3)(b). The UT will take into account the list of considerations in rule 2(2) in determining an application to extend time.
38 UT Rules r21(7).

decision to be reconsidered at an oral hearing of the UT.[39] They must make the request with 14 days of the UT's decision.[40]

7.28 Notably, there is no requirement in either the FTT Rules or the UT Rules (Tribunal Procedure (Upper Tribunal) Rules 2008 SI No 2698) for the appellant or the tribunal to notify the respondent that an application for permission has been made.

Suspension of the FTT's decision

7.29 The FTT can suspend the effect of its decision pending the determination by the FTT or the UT of an application for permission to appeal against, and any appeal or review of, that decision.[41] The UT has the same power to suspend the effect of the FTT's decision.[42] If the appellant wants to suspend the decision pending an appeal, they should state this in the application form.

7.30 When the court considers whether to suspend its decision, it will ask whether the appellant has solid grounds for suspending the effect of FTT's decision and, if it has, whether on balance the effect of the decision should be suspended.[43] The court will explore the effect of suspension on the child. If the local authority appeals a decision to order a school to be named in an EHC plan and the child's parents can show, for example, that no appropriate provision is in place for the child while the decision is under appeal, the court will be less likely to suspend it.

Grounds of appeal

7.31 An appeal can only be made on the basis that the FTT has made an error of law in its decision. This means that the parties cannot seek to re-argue the merits of the decision in an appeal, but must identify a legal error on the part of the FTT. An error of law commonly constitutes one or more of the following issues:

- **Illegality:** The FTT has misunderstood or failed to apply the law. This can come about if the FTT relies on the wrong legislation, or the wrong part of a piece of legislation, or fails to cite, or misunderstands, relevant case-law. It is preferable for the FTT to set

---

39 UT Rules r22(3).
40 UT Rules r22(4).
41 FTT Rules r5(3)(l).
42 UT Rules r5(3)(m).
43 *Carmarthenshire CC v M and JW* [2010] UKUT 348 (AAC).

out the relevant legal provisions and passages from the Code[44] on which it relies, but failure to do so will not amount to an error law unless the omission is material to the FTT's analysis of the issue.[45]

- **Ultra vires:** The FTT has acted outside the scope of its legal powers (known as acting 'ultra vires'). The FTT can act ultra vires if it misinterprets the scope of the issues that fall within its jurisdiction.[46]

- **Procedural fairness:** There has been a procedural error on the part of the FTT that has caused unfairness towards one of the parties. For example, the FTT might unfairly refuse to admit evidence or fail to give one of the parties an opportunity to comment on the other party's evidence.[47]

- **Relevant considerations:** Failure by the FTT properly to analyse the evidence is a common ground for appeal. If it can be said that the FTT misunderstood the evidence, or failed to take account of relevant considerations, or took account of irrelevant ones, the UT may find that there has been an error of law.[48] The weight to be attached to any particular evidence is, however, a matter for the FTT (unless its approach can be said to be perverse or irrational).

---

44 Department for Education and Department of Health, *Special educational needs and disability code of practice: 0 to 25 years. Statutory guidance for organisations which work with and support children and young people who have special educational needs or disabilities*, current version published 2015 ('the Code').

45 *SG v Bromley LBC* [2013] UKUT 0619 (AAC) at para 27. Compare *Devon CC v OH* (SEN) [2016] UKUT 292 (AAC) para 52, in which the UT found that the FTT had failed to have adequate regard to the Code. The error of law could be categorised as failure to apply the right legal test or as a failure to provide adequate reasons.

46 See, for example, *AS v Buckinghamshire CC* [2010] UKUT 407 (AAC) in which the UT held that the FTT had no jurisdiction to consider whether the local authority's admission arrangements discriminated against the child on the grounds of his disability. See also *MH v Nottinghamshire CC* [2009] UKUT 178 (AAC), in which the FTT erroneously determined a school transport issue outside its jurisdiction.

47 See, for example, *Harrow LBC v AM* [2013] UKUT 0157 (AAC), [2013] ELR 351, in which the UT criticised the FTT for relying on its own knowledge and failing to give the parties a proper opportunity to comment on its views of appropriate local placements. It is, however, open to the FTT to use its own knowledge and expertise to assess the evidence put to it by the parties: see *MM and DM v Harrow LBC* [2010] UKUT 395 (AAC) at para 40.

48 See, for example, *MW v Halton BC* [2010] UKUT 34 (AAC). The UT held that evidence from psychiatrists can be relevant to the FTT's decision.

- **Perversity:** Parties can also argue that the FTT's decision was perverse and one that no reasonable tribunal could have reached. This is often a difficult argument to make, as the UT gives weight to the opinions of the FTT as a tribunal sitting with expert members.[49] The UT will be wary of perversity challenges that seek to re-argue the merits of the decision.

- **Reasons:** The FTT must provide written reasons for a final decision.[50] The reasons must be sufficient to explain to the informed reader why a party won or lost.[51] Many challenges to FTT decisions will include a reasons challenge. When the UT is critical of an FTT decision for inadequate reasons, it will usually also find an error of law on another ground.[52] There is no requirement for the FTT to give reasons for procedural decisions.[53]

Taking new points on appeal

7.32   The courts do not generally give appellants leave to raise new points in an appeal that were not raised in the court below. In the Court of Appeal's decision in *B v Harrow LBC*,[54] a more lenient approach was taken, permitting a point of statutory construction to be raised that had not been addressed in the tribunal, on the basis that the tribunal was informal and legal representation was discouraged. Subsequent cases have taken a different approach where appellants are represented and the points that they seek to raise in an appeal are not

---

49   *FC v Suffolk CC* [2010] UKUT 368 (AAC), at para 32; *MW v Halton BC* [2010] UKUT 34 (AAC) at para 43; *GC and JC v Tameside MBC* (SEN) [2011] UKUT 292 (AAC) at para 17. After some judicial debate about whether additional restraint was necessary for UT judges considering FTT decisions, the UT Judge Wikeley held in *GC* that an 'ordinary degree of caution is apt'.

50   FTT Rules r30(2).

51   *W v Leeds City Council and SENDIST* [2005] EWCA Civ. 988, [2005] ELR 617; *H v East Sussex CC* [2009] ELR 161; *Hampshire CC v JP* [2009] UKUT 239 (AAC); *DC v Ealing LBC* [2010] UKUT 10 (AAC).

52   See, for example, *Cambridgeshire CC v SF* (SEN) [2015] UKUT 231 (AAC) and *Devon CC v OH* (SEN) [2016] UKUT 292 (AAC). In both cases, the UT found that the errors in the FTT's decision could be characterised as a failure to give sufficient reasons and also as a misapplication of the law.

53   *KP v Hertfordshire CC* [2010] UKUT 233 (AAC), at paras 26–28.

54   [1998] ELR 351. The House of Lords reversed the Court of Appeal's decision on the substantive point in *B v Harrow* [2000] 1 WLR 223, but did not comment on this issue.

of general importance.[55] In *Hammersmith and Fulham LBC v JH*,[56] Judge Lane stated that it was not open to parents on an appeal to the UT to reserve their position on parts 2 and 3 of the statement for any remitted hearing, if they had not challenged parts 2 and 3 the first time round before the FTT.

Response to grant of permission

7.33   If the FTT or the UT grants permission to appeal to the UT, the respondent must send a response to be received by the UT no later than one month after the date on which the UT sent a notice of appeal to the respondent.[57] If the respondent provides the response to the UT later than the prescribed time, the response must include a request for the extension of time and the reason why the response was not provided in time.[58]

7.34   UT Rules r7(2)(d) gives the UT the power to restrict a party's participation in a hearing if it has failed to comply with a direction of the UT. In *FC v Suffolk CC*[59] the UT considered the failure by the respondent to file a defence and lodge a skeleton argument prior to the hearing in breach of a direction by the UT. The UT declined to exercise its power in rule 7(2)(d) and restricted it to 'blatant cases of disregard on the part of a party to the proceedings'.[60]

The UT's case management powers

7.35   The UT procedural powers are broadly similar to those of the FTT.[61] The UT Rules contain the same 'over-riding objective' as the FTT Rules to deal with cases 'fairly and justly'.[62] The UT has a general power to regulate its own procedure.[63] Certain specific case

---

55 *L v Hereford and Worcester CC and Hughes* [2000] ELR 375; *S v Hackney LBC* [2001] EWHC 572 (Admin), [2002] ELR 45; *T v SENT and Wiltshire CC* [2002] EWHC 1474 (Admin), [2002] ELR 704.
56 [2012] UKUT 328 (AAC).
57 UT Rules r24(2).
58 UT Rules r24(4).
59 [2010] UKUT 368 (AAC).
60 [2010] UKUT 368 (AAC) at para 13.
61 See para 4.71 above.
62 UT Rules r2. The principles set out in rule 2(2) replicate those in TCEA 2007 s22(4).
63 UT Rules r5(1).

management powers are set out in UT Rules r5(3).[64] These include the power to:

- extend or shorten time to comply with any rule or direction;
- permit or require a party to produce documents;
- deal with an issue as a preliminary issue;
- hold a hearing; and
- suspend the effect of the UT's decision.

7.36 The UT Rules give the UT a wide degree of discretion over the way in which it determines appeals. They may be decided with or without a hearing,[65] or disposed of by consent without a hearing.[66]

7.37 The UT will generally refuse to admit fresh evidence that was not considered by the FTT. In *Oxfordshire CC v GB and others* the Court of Appeal held that 'the one class of fresh information which the special nature of such appeals may call for is up-to-date evidence about the child's schooling and needs, but purely ... in order to enable relief to take a suitable form.'[67] This approach has been adopted in subsequent UT appeals.[68]

7.38 A typed transcript of FTT proceedings may be admissible before the UT on the basis that it is a record of proceedings.[69] The FTT judge's handwritten note of proceedings may also be admitted as an authoritative guide to the evidence before the FTT.[70] By contrast, a witness statement relating to what was said at the hearing will not generally be admissible unless there is dispute about oral evidence that was given by the witness and it is material to whether or not the FTT made an error of law.[71]

---

64 Further case management powers are contained in UT Rules rr6–9 and 14–16.
65 UT Rules r34. The UT must have regard to any view expressed by a party when determining whether to hold a hearing into any matter.
66 UT Rules r39.
67 [2001] EWCA Civ 1358, [2002] ELR 8 at para 9.
68 See *Renshaw v Sheffield City Council* [2002] EWHC 528 (Admin); *B v Worcestershire CC* [2010] UKUT 292 (AAC); *NC and DH v Leicestershire CC*[2012] UKUT 85 (AAC).
69 *Carmarthenshire CC v MW and JW* [2010] UKUT 348 (AAC), at paras 15–20. UT Judge Jacobs gave guidance on when a transcript might be useful and the process that parties should adopt before producing one. He noted that production of a transcript might be relevant in the assessment of costs.
70 *NC and DH v Leicestershire CC* [2012] UKUT 85 (AAC) at para 18.
71 *The Learning Trust v MP* [2007] EWHC 1634 (Admin), at paras 29–30; *C and S v SENDT and another* [2007] EWHC 1812 (Admin) at para 22. The witness statement must be confined to what was said at the hearing and not attempt to introduce new evidence: *R (TS) v Bowen (Chair of SENDIST)* [2009] EWHC 5 (Admin), [2009] ELR 148.

7.39   However, the UT has shown some flexibility about the evidence that it hears. In *Hammersmith & Fulham LBC v JH* the local authority's SEN case worker was allowed to 'provide input' on basic background facts at the UT hearing.[72]

Determination of the appeal by the UT

7.40   The remedial powers of the UT after the determination of the appeal are broad. If it concludes that the FTT made an error of law, the UT may (but need not) set aside the decision of the FTT. If the UT does set aside the decision of the FTT, the UT must either remit the case to the FTT with directions for its reconsideration or re-make the decision itself.[73] If the case is remitted, the UT can direct that a new FTT panel hears the case and give procedural directions to the FTT.[74] If the UT decides to re-make the decision itself, it may make any decision which the FTT could make it if were re-making the decision, and the UT may make such findings of fact as it considers appropriate.[75]

Costs

7.41   The UT may only make an award of costs to the extent that the FTT had the power to make an order in respect of costs.[76] It therefore applies the same principles and precedents that the FTT applies to costs decisions.[77] The UT may make an order for costs on an application or on its own initiative.[78]

7.42   An application for costs can be made at any time during proceedings and up to one month after the UT notifies the parties of its decision.[79] The application must be sent to both the UT and the other party with a schedule of costs sufficient to allow the UT to carry out a

---

72 [2012] UKUT 328 (AAC).
73 TCEA 2007 s12(2).
74 TCEA 2007 s12(3).
75 TCEA 2007 s12(4).
76 UT Rules r10(1)(b). It may make an award of costs in judicial review proceedings .In cases of judicial review of a FTT decision, the UT should exercise its discretion to award costs only in circumstances where costs could have been awarded in the FTT, see *R (LR) v FTT* [2013] UKUT 294 (AAC).
77 See paras 4.125–4.131 above.
78 UT Rules r10(4).
79 UT Rules r10(6).

summary assessment.[80] The UT must give the person against whom costs are sought an opportunity to make representations.[81]

Appeal to the Court of Appeal

7.43   The provisions governing an appeal from the UT to the Court of Appeal are very similar to those that apply to appeals from the FTT to the UT. Like the FTT, the UT has the power to correct accidental slips in a decision,[82] and to set aside a decision which disposes of proceedings where there has been a procedural irregularity,[83] but does not have the power to review the decision where there has been a change of circumstances. The UT also has the same power as the FTT to to review its own decision for an error of law when an application for permission to appeal has been made.[84] It may only set a decision aside for an error of law if it has overlooked a legislative provision or case which could have had a material effect on the decision, or if a higher court has made a decision since the UT decision which could materially affect the UT decision.[85]

7.44   There is no automatic right of appeal from the UT to the Court of Appeal and permission must be granted by the UT or the Court of Appeal.[86] An application for permission to appeal may only be made to the Court of Appeal if permission has been refused by the UT.[87] There is no right of appeal in respect of an 'excluded decision'.[88] These decisions can be challenged by way of judicial review, but only if the appeal raises an important point of principle or practice, or some other compelling reason.[89]

7.45   The test for granting permission to appeal is different for appeals from the UT to the Court of Appeal from that for appeals from the FTT. It is necessary for the appellant to show that the proposed appeal

80 UT Rules r10(5).

81 UT Rules r10(7).

82 UT Rules r42.

83 TCEA 2007 s10; UT Rules r43.

84 UT Rules r41.

85 UT Rules r45(1).

86 TCEA 2007 s13(3) and (4).

87 TCEA 2007 s13(5).

88 An excluded decision is defined in TCEA 2007 s13(8) as a decision of the UT on an application under s11(4)(b), an application for permission or leave to appeal, or a decision of the UT under s10 to review or not to review an earlier decision of the UT, or to take no action in the light of a review, or to set aside an earlier decision of the UT.

89 *R (Cart) v Upper Tribunal* [2011] UKSC 28, [2012] 1 AC 663.

(a) has a realistic prospect of success; and (b) that it would raise some important point of principle of practice or there is some other compelling reason for the relevant appellate court to hear the appeal.[90] UT Rules r44 sets out the procedure for making an application for permission to appeal. The Court of Appeal has the same powers as the UT to dispose of the appeal.[91]

---

90 Appeals from the Upper Tribunal to the Court of Appeal Order 2008 SI No 2834 reg 2; and CPR 52.7 (it being a second appeal).
91 TCEA 2007 s14.

School transport

Key points

- Local authorities are required by Education Act (EA) 1996 s508B to make travel arrangements free of charge to facilitate the attendance of 'eligible children' at school.
- Eligibility turns on the distance between the child's home and school (or other place at which the child is receiving education) and the child's SEN, disability and/ or mobility problems.
- Local authorities are not obliged to make travel arrangements if there is a closer suitable school in respect of which the local authority has made suitable arrangements for the child's attendance.
- The cost of travel arrangements may be taken into account by a local authority in determining whether naming a particular school in an education, health and care (EHC) plan would be incompatible with the efficient use of resources.
- The requirement applies in relation to transport to independent schools named in a child's EHC plan.
- Local authorities can rely on travel arrangements made other than by the local authority to discharge this duty, but can rely on such arrangements made by parents only if they are made voluntarily.
- Local authorities also have a power to make travel arrangements for other children.
- The obligation to make travel arrangements under EA 1996 s508B applies only in relation to children of compulsory school age, travel arrangements for older people falling to be determined in accordance with EA 1996 s408F.
- EA 1996 s508F places some obligations on local authorities to make travel arrangements free of charge for some adult in education, and some young adults with SEN in education or training.
- Consultation obligations are placed on local authorities in relation to the exercise of EA 1996 s508F and they are obliged to prepare annual transport policy statements.
- Local authorities are also required to prepare annual transport policy statements in relation to sixth form pupils by EA 1996 s509A.
- Challenges to local authority decision-making in relation to school transport may be made through the First-tier Tribunal system (if, for example, the decision relates to the naming of

The obligation to make transport arrangements

8.1   The obligations placed on local authorities in relation to pupil transport are found in Education Act (EA) 1996 s508B, which provides
that local authorities must make 'such travel arrangements as they
consider necessary' for 'eligible children' in their area who do not
otherwise benefit from suitable transport arrangements, free of
charge, to and from school, 'in order to secure that suitable home to
school travel arrangements, for the purpose of facilitating the child's
attendance at the relevant educational establishment in relation to
him'. Such arrangements must be free of charge.

8.2   The obligation to make transport arrangements applies in relation to 'eligible children'. An 'eligible child' is defined by EA 1996
Sch 35B, so far as relevant for the purposes of this book,[1] as a child
who is of compulsory school age and who is *either*:

- a registered pupil at a qualifying school (or other place at which
the child is receiving education), which is *not* within walking distance of his home (see para 8.7 below);[2] *or*
- who is a registered pupil at a qualifying school (or other place at
which the child is receiving education), which *is* within walking
distance of his home, but who by reason of his or her special educational needs (SEN), disability[3] and/ or mobility problems, cannot reasonably be expected to walk to that school or place.[4]

8.3   In either case the local authority will be required to make transport
arrangements under EA 1996 s508B if no suitable arrangements
have been made by the local authority to enable the pupil to become
a registered pupil at a qualifying school nearer to his or her home or,
in the case of children whose schools are more than walking distance

1 Children may also be eligible for transport because their routes to school,
though within normal walking distance, are unsuitable to walk.
2 EA 1996 Sch 35B paras 6 and 7.
3 As defined in Equality Act (EqA) 2010 s6.
4 EA 1996 Sch 35B paras 2 and 3.

from home, for boarding accommodation for the pupil at or near the school.

8.4   'Eligible schools' are defined to include community, foundation or voluntary schools or special schools, non-maintained special schools, pupil referral units, maintained nursery schools and city technology colleges, city colleges for the technology of the arts, academy schools and alternative provision academies. In addition, in the case of a child with SEN, an independent school, other than a college or academy will also be a 'qualifying school' if it is the only school named in the child's EHC plan or it is one of two or more schools named in that plan and is the nearer or nearest to the child's home.[5]

8.5   EA 1996 s508B(4) provides that

'Travel arrangements' ... are travel arrangements of any description and include –
(a) arrangements for the provision of transport, and
(b) ... only if ... made with the consent of a parent of the child –
   (i) arrangements for the provision of one or more persons to escort the child (whether alone or together with other children) when travelling to or from the relevant educational establishment in relation to the child;
   (ii) arrangements for the payment of the whole or any part of a person's reasonable travelling expenses;
   (iii) arrangements for the payment of allowances in respect of the use of particular modes of travel.

These arrangements may not result in any additional costs to the child's parents.

8.6   EA 1996 s508B(5) provides that local authorities may rely on arrangements made by *parents* to avoid the duty imposed by that section only where those arrangements are made *voluntarily*.

8.7   EA 1996 s508D(1) provides that the Secretary of State for Education must issue guidance in relation to the discharge by local authorities of their functions under, among other things, section 508B. EA 1996 s508D(3) provides that local authorities discharging their functions under, among other things, section 508B must have regard to such guidance. The *Home to school travel and transport guidance: statutory guidance for local authorities*[6] ('the Travel Guidance') was issued in July 2014. The Travel Guidance states, under the heading 'statutory walking distances eligibility', that:

---

5 EA 1996 Sch 35B para 15.
6 Department for Education, 2014.

... local authorities are required to ... provide free transport for all pupils of compulsory school age (5–16) if their nearest suitable school is:
- beyond 2 miles (if below the age of 8); or
- beyond 3 miles (if aged between 8 and 16)[7]

8.8 The Travel Guidance states that examples of arrangements made other than by the local authority under section 508B might include:

> ... a school or group of schools reaching an agreement with a local authority to provide transport in minibuses owned by the school; or a transport authority providing free passes for all children on public transport. For example, in London, Transport for London provides free bus passes for all children under the age of 16. In many circumstances, London Boroughs may therefore not need to make any additional travel arrangements for children living in their area, particularly when eligibility would be through statutory walking distances or extended rights.[8]

8.9 EA 1996 s508C(1) provides local authorities with a *power*, as distinct from a *duty*, to 'make such school travel arrangements as they consider necessary, in relation to any child in the authority's area to whom this section applies, for the purpose of facilitating the child's attendance at any relevant educational establishment in relation to the child'. This *power* applies in relation to children who are not *eligible* under section 508B.

8.10 The Travel Guidance provides in conformity with EA 1996 Sch 35B that, in the case of children with mobility problems or associated health and safety issues related to their SEN or disability, eligibility for transport should be 'assessed on an individual basis'.[9] It also states that:

> 17. In determining whether a child cannot reasonably be expected to walk for the purposes of 'special educational needs, a disability or mobility problems eligibility' or 'unsafe route eligibility', the local authority will need to consider whether the child could reasonably be expected to walk if accompanied and, if so, whether the child's parent can reasonably be expected to accompany the child. When considering whether a child's parent can reasonably be expected to accompany the child on the journey to school a range of factors may need to be taken into account, such as the age of the child and whether one would ordinarily expect a child of that age to be accompanied.

---

7 Travel Guidance, section 1.3 para 16.
8 Travel Guidance, para 31.
9 Travel Guidance, section 1.3 para 16.

18. The general expectation is that a child will be accompanied by a parent where necessary, unless there is a good reason why it is not reasonable to expect the parent to do so.

19. Local authorities should, however, promote and ensure equality of opportunity for disabled parents. For example, if a parent's disability prevents them from accompanying their child along a walking route that would otherwise be considered unsafe without adult supervision, a reasonable adjustment might be to provide free home to school transport for the child in question.

'Nearest suitable school'

8.11   A crucial question in determining a pupil's eligibility for transport arrangements under EA 1996 s508B concerns whether suitable arrangements have been made by the local authority to enable the pupil to become a registered pupil at a qualifying school nearer to his or her home.

8.12   The Travel Guidance suggests[10] that the 'nearest suitable school' will be 'the nearest qualifying school with places available *that provides education appropriate to the age, ability and aptitude of the child, and any SEN that the child may have*' (emphasis added). This is important, because at one stage the case-law suggested that a local authority could avoid responsibility under section 508B as long as its *arrangements* in respect of a closer school were suitable, rather than that *the school* was suitable. This had been the position adopted by the Court of Appeal in *Re S (minors)*, which had disapproved of the contrary position taken by the same Court two years previously.[11] Both cases had dealt with the legislation preceding the EA 1996 but the provisions were materially identical. Notwithstanding *Re S* and a subsequent Court of Appeal permission decision in the same vein,[12] a series of decisions of the Administrative Court, and one of the Court of Appeal, took the view that 'suitable arrangements' required a 'suitable school'.[13]

---

10   Travel Guidance, footnote 9, p10.

11   [1995] ELR 98 (CA), p104, the Court of Appeal ruling that Staughton LJ had been wrong in *R v Rochdale MBC ex p Schemet* [1993] LGR 10 p14 to state that 'suitable arrangements' required a suitable school.

12   *R v Bedfordshire ex p WE* [1996] EWCA Civ 912.

13   *R v Kent CC ex p C* [1998] ELR 108; *R (J) v Vale of Glamorgan CC* [2001] ELR 223 (Administrative Court) and [2001] ELR 758 (CA); *R (Jones) v Ceridigion CC* [2004] EWHC 1376 (Admin) and *R (R) v Leeds City Council* [2006] ELR 25.

8.13   This is not, however, to say (leaving aside cases in which a school is named in an EHC plan) that parents will be able to establish a right to free transport to a distant school on the basis of a preference (however strong or reasonable) for that school over a nearer one. Where the requirement of suitability has been applied to the *school*, as distinct from arrangements relating to it, the courts have ruled that the question of suitability is one for the local authority subject to challenge on the basis of irrationality alone.[14] In one case the court ruled that a Welsh speaking school was suitable for English speaking pupils despite up to 90 per cent of lessons being in Welsh.[15] In another, a non-selective school was regarded by the local authority as suitable for a child who had passed the 11+ test and was considered eligible by the relevant local authority for a place at a grammar school.[16] And in a third case, a non-Jewish school in Leeds was considered suitable in respect of Orthodox Jewish children who attended Orthodox Jewish schools in Manchester.[17]

8.14   Most recently, in *R (PA) v Lewisham LBC and Secretary of State for Education*[18] the High Court ruled both that the nearer school had to be suitable in order to relieve the local authority of its obligations under EA 1996 s508B, and also that suitability fell to be determined in accordance with EA 1996 s7 which imposes on parents a duty to secure for children of compulsory school age 'efficient full-time education' suitable:

- to the child's age, ability and aptitude; and
- to any SEN the child may have.

8.15   Sara Cockerill QC, sitting as a Deputy High Court Judge, ruled that 'the content of suitability is not an individually tailored one, to provide the best education for that child; rather it is one which effectively ensures that the broad baseline needs of the child are met'.[19] So 'if you had a child whose aptitudes were all in the mathematical and science departments and they were placed in a school which offered only the performing arts, then insufficient provision would be made for their

---

14 See *R v Kent CC ex p C* [1998] ELR 108, p.113, *R (J) v Vale of Glamorgan CC* [2001] ELR 758, CA at para 2; and *R (R) v Leeds City Council* [2006] ELR 25.

15 *Re S* before it was appealed to the CA which ruled that the school did not have to be suitable.

16 *R v Kent CC ex p C* [1998] ELR 108.

17 *R (R) v Leeds City Council* [2006] ELR 25.

18 [2016] EWHC 2328 (Admin).

19 At para 29.

aptitudes, because there was no provision for their aptitudes'.[20] This could not, however, be stretched to accommodate the parent's argument in that case that her son, who was very strongly interested in aviation engineering and so motivated to attend his chosen school, Heathrow Aviation Engineering University Technical College, that he got up at 5am to travel across London to it for an 8am start.

8.16   The judge went on to suggest that the local authority might exercise its power under EA 1996 s508C to make travel arrangements for the pupil, and that the survival of very specialist Free Schools such as the University Technical College he attended might require this to be done as they were likely to require children from a larger than normal catchment area to flourish. This, however, was not relevant to the obligations imposed by section 508B.

Transport for children with EHC Plans

8.17   As stated above, the position as regards local authority obligations to make transport provision in the case of children with disabilities and/or SEN and/or mobility problems differs from that in relation to other children. Not only may the geographical distance within which a local authority will be required to make transport arrangements vary according to the needs of the child, but transport arrangements will have to be made to a school named in an EHC plan which is too distant for the (individual) child to walk to, regardless of whether there is a suitable school closer to that child's home (unless that school is also named). Further, as stated above (para 8.4) local authorities will be required to make travel arrangements to independent schools in these circumstances.

8.18   The cost of transport arrangements will be one aspect of the costs of educational provision within an EHC plan, and so will be taken into account in determining whether naming a school would be incompatible with the efficient use of resources pursuant to CFA 2014 s39(4) (see chapter 3).

8.19   The Travel Guidance provides that:

> 34. As a general guide, transport arrangements should not require a child to make several changes on public transport resulting in an unreasonably long journey time. Best practice suggests that the maximum each way length of journey for a child of primary school age to be 45 minutes and for secondary school age 75 minutes, but these

20 At para 27.

should be regarded as the maximum. For children with SEN and/ or disabilities, journeys may be more complex and a shorter journey time, although desirable, may not always be possible.

35. Consideration should also be given to the walking distance required in order to access public transport. The maximum distances will depend on a range of circumstances, including the age of the child, their individual needs and the nature of the routes they are expected to walk to the pick up or set down points and should try to be combined with the transport time when considering the overall duration of a journey. With regards to pick up points, local authorities may at their discretion use appropriate pick up points when making travel arrangements. For arrangements to be suitable, they must also be safe and reasonably stress free, to enable the child to arrive at school ready for a day of study.

8.20 While it may be correct to say that children whose SEN and/or disabilities require particular schooling may need to travel for longer distances than other pupils in order to attend school, it is also the case that long journeys may be more problematic for some children with SEN and/or disabilities than for other children. Where this is the case, a journey which is shorter than that contemplated by the Travel Guidance may still be excessive and a school attendance at which would require such a journey may, accordingly, be inappropriate to their needs.

Transport for young people with EHC plans

8.21 EA 1996 s508B applies only in relation to 'eligible children', who must be of compulsory school age. Older people may have EHC plans which may well name schools or colleges at some distance from the young person's home. In *Staffordshire CC v JM*[21] the UT rejected an argument that such a young person could require that the local authority meet the cost of transport involved, ruling that the provision of transport did not amount to provision for SEN, and that the need for such transport could not be said to have arisen from the claimant's learning difficulties. The parents argued that their daughter (aged 21) required to be transported by taxi, accompanied, to the educational institution named in her EHC plan, for reasons which related to her particular vulnerabilities. The UT ruled that her transport-related needs, as a person of above compulsory school age, fell to be determined in accordance with EA 1996 s408F

---

21 [2016] UKUT 0246 (AAC), [2016] ELR 307.

which provides, so far as relevant, that local authorities in England must make 'such arrangements for the provision of transport and otherwise as they consider necessary, or as the secretary of state may direct, for the purposes of facilitating the attendance of':

- adults receiving education at institutions maintained or assisted by the authority and providing further or higher education (or both), or within the further education sector;
- relevant young adults receiving education or training at institutions outside both the further and higher education sectors where the local authority has secured for the adults in question:
  - the provision of education or training at the institution in question, and
  - the provision of boarding accommodation.[22]

A relevant young adult is a young adult for whom an EHC plan is maintained.

8.22   EA 1996 s508F provides that local authorities must have regard, in considering what travel arrangements it is necessary to make in relation to relevant young adults, to the obligation imposed on them by EA 1996 s15ZA to meet the reasonable needs of persons over the age of compulsory schooling but under 19, and those aged between 19 and 26 for whom EHC plans are maintained. It further states that such travel arrangements must be provided free of charge.

8.23   The FTT had accepted in the *Staffordshire* case that the local authority was entitled to have a policy under EA 1996 s508F for post-19 pupils which allowed the authority to seek information in respect of the travel needs of those it related to (as it had sought to do in this case). The FTT had concluded, nevertheless, that the local authority was required to provide the transport in this case as part of the provision for the young person's SEN (this was because building her independence required a programme at the college named in the EHC plan, which in turn required the provision of transport to enable her to access the college), and that the transport was itself a SEN. The UT disagreed, ruling that it was clear on the authorities that transport to and from a place of education named in an EHC plan is neither special educational provision nor a SEN.[23]

---

22   Under EA 1996 s514A.

23   Citing *R v Havering LBC ex p K* [1998] ELR 402; *Dudley MBC v JS* [2011] UKUT 67 (AAC), [2012] EWCA Civ 346, [2012] ELR 206 (CA); *MM and DM v Harrow LBC* [2010] UKUT 395 (AAC). See *R (S) v Education (Waltham Forest) and Waltham Forest LBC* [2006] EWHC 3144 (Admin) for a case in which EA 1996 ss509AA and 509AB, which are materially similar to section 508F, founded a successful application for judicial review.

8.24   EA 1996 s508G provides that local authorities making arrangements or proposing to pay travelling expenses, under section 508F in relation to relevant young adults must consult with a variety of bodies and with 'persons in the local authority's area who will be relevant young adults when the arrangements or payments have effect, and their parents' and must prepare for each academic year a transport policy statement which specifies:

- any transport or other arrangements, and any payment of travelling expenses, made or to be made in relation to the year under EA 1996 s508F in relation to relevant young adults;
- any travel concessions which are to be provided under any scheme established under Transport Act 1985 s93 to relevant young adults receiving education or training at an institution mentioned in para 8.21 above.

8.25   The publication of such a statement, which should take place by the end of May before the relevant academic year, does not prevent the local authority from making additional arrangements or payments under EA 1996 s508F or providing additional travel concessions in relation to the relevant academic year.

8.26   EA 1996 s509A makes similar provision in respect of transport policy statement to be made for the purpose of facilitating the attendance of persons of sixth form age receiving education or training, section 508B providing that such statements 'shall state to what extent arrangements specified ... include arrangements for facilitating the attendance at establishments such as are mentioned in that subsection of disabled persons and persons with learning difficulties or disabilities'. The arrangements specified for persons receiving full-time education or training at establishments other than schools maintained by the local authority must be no less favourable than those specified for pupils of the same age attending such schools, and those specified for persons with learning difficulties or disabilities receiving education or training at establishments other than schools maintained by the local authority which are no less favourable than the arrangements specified for pupils of the same age with learning difficulties or disabilities attending such schools.

The nature of the obligation to make transport arrangements under Education Act 1996 s508B

8.27   In *R (M and W) v Hounslow LBC*[24] Sales J considered a dispute as to whether the duty to make travel provision for children within section 508B required local authorities to make 'door to door' arrangements. The local authority wished to make arrangements for the children concerned, both of whom had SEN, to be collected by bus from a pick-up point some distance from their homes, which in practical terms would have required their parents to take them to and pick them up from the bus stop in the mornings and afternoons respectively. Sales J pointed out that EA 1996 s508B(3):

> ... does not say that the travel arrangements which constitute 'home to school travel arrangements' are travel arrangements which cover the whole journey from home to school; they only have to be travel arrangements 'relating to' travel in both directions between home and school.[25]

8.28   He concluded that the obligation on the local authority was to 'make travel arrangements relating to travel between home and school (ie travel arrangements which cover the whole *or part of* that journey)' which *the authority* was satisfied were:

> 'suitable' for the purpose of facilitating the child's attendance at their school ... the question of what travel arrangements are suitable for this purpose involves consideration of the circumstances of the particular case concerning both the abilities and disabilities of the child and the position of the parent, and what can reasonably be expected of them.[26]

8.29   In reaching this conclusion, Sales J took into account the fact that were the local authority would not have been under an obligation to make travel arrangements for either child if a 'suitable' free transport service had been provided by another body or person 'including one which involves a pick-up point at a reasonable distance from the child's home'.[27]

> The question would then arise whether ... it could be said that such a bus service does 'not provide suitable home to school travel arrangements' for that child. That would depend upon whether it was reasonable to expect the child to be able to walk between the bus stop and his

24 [2013] EWHC 579 (Admin), [2013] PTSR 942.
25 At para 16.
26 At para 17.
27 At para 18(i).

home, accompanied if need be by a parent. Since a local authority is under no duty under section 508B(1) to provide free home to school travel arrangements if there is, say, such a free public bus service which is suitable, it is difficult to infer that Parliament intended that the duty of the local authority under section 508B(1) should be more than to provide some equivalent substitute travel arrangements where no such public bus or other service is available ...

8.30   In *R (P) v East Sussex CC*[28] the claimant sought to argue that the local authority had failed to comply with EA 1996 s508B because the travel arrangements it had made in relation to her daughter's school attendance were not such that she was unable to attend after school clubs or to attend school on occasions when she had medical appointments (which was regularly). The pupil had disabilities and SEN and the school was 27 miles away from her home. The local authority had originally provided her with individual use of a taxi to her school, but had more recently arranged the shared use of that taxi which meant that the flexibility she had been used to was lost.

8.31   The High Court emphasised that the duty imposed on the local authority by EA 1996 s508B was a duty to provide 'such travel arrangements as *the authority* consider necessary' (emphasis in original) 'for the purpose of facilitating the child's attendance at her school'. It further ruled that the pupil was entitled by virtue of section 508B only to transport from home to school at the start of the school day (8am), and from school to home at the end of the school day (4pm), each week day.[29] The judge ruled that the local authority was entitled to take into account questions of cost and practicability, further that there was no duty on the authority to facilitate 'matters other than attendance at school' (that is, the pupil's medical appointments).[30]

School transport and disability discrimination

8.32   Disability discrimination has been considered in chapter 6 above. The argument was also made in *R (P) v East Sussex CC* that the local authority had indirectly discriminated against the pupil contrary to the EqA 2010, in that it had unjustifiably imposed a 'provision, criterion or practice' of providing transport services which were inflexible and that disabled students, being more likely to be dependent on

---

28 [2014] EWHC 4634 (Admin), [2015] ELR 178.
29 At paras 39, 41, 47–51.
30 At paras 58, 59.

such services (in part because they were more likely to be educated at a significant distance from home, also because they were less likely to be able to manage transport independently[31]). The court, having pointed out that no complaint was made as to the vehicle provided by the local authority, concluded that there was no disadvantage 'in the provision of transport' and that the 'real complaint is the inadequacy of local education provision, rather than the provision of transport'. This is not to say that a challenge could not successfully be brought under the EqA 2010 in another case.

Challenging school transport decisions

8.33   Challenges to local authority decision-making in relation to school transport may be made through the FTT system if, for example, the decision relates to the naming of school A rather than school B in an EHC plan for reasons associated with cost: see further chapter 3. Otherwise the remedy is by way of an application for judicial review where, for example, the challenge is to the nature of the travel arrangements made for a child or young person with SEN and an EHC, or those made for a child or young person with a disability, or to a refusal to make such travel arrangements.

8.34   The other route to challenge transport-related decisions made by local authorities is by way of a complaint to the Secretary of State for Education. EA 1996 s496 provides, so far as relevant, that if secretary of state decides, on a complaint by any person or otherwise, that a local authority has acted or is proposing to act unreasonably with respect to the exercise of any power conferred or the performance of any duty imposed by or under this Act, he or she may give such directions as to the exercise of the power or the performance of the duty as appear to him or her to be expedient. Section 497 provides an additional power allowing the secretary of state to declare (so far as relevant) a local authority to be in default of a duty imposed by the Act and giving such directions for the purpose of enforcing the performance of the duty as appear to him or her to be expedient. Directions made under section 497 are enforceable by the court.

---

31 There was some support for this approach in the decision of the Court of Appeal in *Bedfordshire CC v Dixon-Wilkinson* [2009] EWCA Civ 678, [2009] ELR 361 at paras 25, 27 (note that at the relevant time the predecessor to the EqA 2010 did not require the provision of auxiliary aids or services in this context; that is no longer the case).

8.35   Specific provision is made for the amendment by local authorities of transport policy statements made in respect of young adults subject to learning difficulty assessments and sixth-form pupils (see paras 8.21–8.26 above).[32] EA 1996 ss508I And 509AE provide that the secretary of state is not required to consider complaints made in relation to transport schemes unless the matter has been brought to the notice of the local authority concerned, which has had a reasonable opportunity to investigate the matter and respond.

32 See EA 1996 ss508I and 509AE.

Inter-authority disputes

Key points

- A local authority is responsible for identifying and assessing a child or young person's SEN if he or she is in the authority's area and has been identified by or brought to the authority's attention as someone who has or may have SEN.
- Financial responsibility for a child or young person's SEN provision (which may fall on a different local authority) arises if the child or young person 'belongs' to the local authority.
- Any dispute between two or more local authorities as to which of them is responsible for the provision of education to any pupil shall be determined by the secretary of state.

Inter-authority recoupment and disputes – introduction

9.1   In some circumstances a different local authority may be responsible for:

1) identifying and assessing the SEN of the child or young person and maintaining a child or young person's EHC plan; and
2) paying for SEN provision required for a child or young person with SEN.

9.2   As to (1), a local authority in England is responsible for a child or young person if he or she is in the local authority's area and has been identified by the local authority by someone who has or may have SEN, or has been brought to the local authority's attention by any person as someone who has or may have SEN.[1]

9.3   As to (2), financial responsibility for the SEN provision required by a child or young person arises if the child or young person 'belongs' to a local authority.[2] The Education (Areas to which Pupils and Students Belong) Regulations 1996 SI No 615 (EAPSB Regs) provide the mechanism for determining which local authority a person belongs. Having determined which local authority a person belongs to, the Inter-authority Recoupment (England) Regulations 2013 SI No 492 (IARE Regs)[3] make provision for determining when inter-local authority recoupment is either required or permitted.

---

1   CFA 2014 s24(1).
2   Education Act (EA) 1996 s579(4).
3   Made under Education Act 2002 s207.

Responsibility for assessing and identifying SEN, and maintaining the EHC plan

9.4   As noted above, a local authority will have responsibility for identifying and assessing SEN, and maintaining an EHC plan if a child or young person is 'in the authority's area'.[4] In *R (JG) v Kent CC*[5] Nicol J held that a child or young person will only be in the local authority's area where he or she lives there permanently. In deciding whether the child or young person resides in the local authority's area permanently it will be of assistance to determine whether the child or young person is ordinarily resident in the local authority, but the case-law on ordinary residence[6] can be no more than an indirect pointer in deciding the question (as the statutory provisions do not in fact refer to ordinary residence). The question of whether a child or young person is in the local authority's area is a question of fact for the local authority in the first instance, subject only to the ordinary principles of judicial review.[7]

Areas to which pupils and students belong

9.5   The EAPSB Regs do not apply for the purposes of determining which local authority's area a child is in for the purposes of CFA 2014 s24(1) (and thus do not apply for the purposes of determining which local authority has responsibility for identifying and assessing a child's SEN, and maintaining an EHC plan).[8]

---

4   CFA 2014 s24(1).
5   [2016] EWHC 1102 (Admin), [2016] ELR 396 at paras 133–134.
6   See *R v Brent LBC ex p Shah* [1983] 2 AC 309, 343–344 per Lord Scarman and *R (Cornwall Council) v Secretary of State for Health* [2015] UKSC 46, [2016] AC 137 at para 42. For the interpretation of 'habitual residence' in respect of children, see *A v A (children: habitual residence)* [2014] AC 1 at para 38 per Baroness Hale, and *In Re LC (Children)* [2014] AC 1038 at para 37.
7   In *R (JG) v Kent CC* [2016] EWHC 1102 (Admin), [2016] ELR 396 at paras 133–134 Nicol J rejected the submission that the question of whether a child or young person was in the local authority's area was one of precedent fact for determination by the court on an application for judicial review (see paras 135–145).
8   EAPSB Regs reg 2(4). The EAPSB Regs were amended to make this explicit following the judgment in *R (L) v Waltham Forest LBC* [2007] EWHC 2060, [2008] LGR 495 in which Rabinder Singh QC sitting as a Deputy Judge of the High Court held that the EAPSB Regs did apply for determining the local authority with responsibility for identifying and assessing SEN, and maintaining statements of SEN.

9.6   The general principle is that a person shall be treated as belong-
ing to the area of the local authority in which he is ordinarily resident
or, where he has no ordinary residence, the area of the local authority
in which he is for the time being resident.[9] The EAPSB Regs define
the place where a person is ordinarily resident as being

> ... the address where that person is habitually and normally resident
> apart from temporary or occasional absences, except that no school
> pupil[10] shall be treated as being ordinarily resident in the area of an
> education authority by reason only of his residing as a boarder at a
> school which is situated in the area of that authority.[11]

9.7   The EAPSB Regs set out specific rules as to which local authority a
pupil belongs in the following circumstances:

- pupils in a 52-week boarding school placement;[12]
- pupils with EHC plans registered as pupils in maintained special schools;[13]
- school pupils resident in hospital;[14] and
- children looked after by a local authority.[15]

Inter-authority recoupment

9.8   The IARE Regs apply where relevant educational provision is made
by a local authority (the providing authority) in respect of a person
who belongs to the area of another local authority (the home authority). The IARE Regs require or authorise the home authority to pay to
the providing authority such amount as the authorities may agree or,
failing agreement, such amount as may be determined by or under
the EAPSB Regs.[16]

---

9   EAPSB Regs reg 3.
10 Defined in EAPSB Regs reg 2(1) as 'a person in respect of whom provision for
    primary or secondary education is made and includes a person for whom such
    provision is made otherwise than at school'.
11 EAPSB Regs reg 2(2). As to the meaning of 'ordinary residence' more widely,
    see *R v Brent LBC ex p Shah* [1983] 2 AC 309; *R (Cornwall Council) v Secretary
    of State for Health* [2015] UKSC 46, [2016] AC 317 (although note that in the
    context of the meaning of 'habitual residence' the Supreme Court has held that
    the focus of where a child resides inevitably shifts to the purpose of the parent,
    see *A v A (children: habitual residence)* [2014] AC 1 per Baroness Hale at para 38).
12 EAPSB Regs reg 4.
13 EAPSB Regs reg 5.
14 EAPSB Regs reg 6.
15 EAPSB Regs reg 7.
16 See IARE Regs reg 10 as to how claims for recoupment are to be made.

9.9 As between English home and providing authorities, recoupment is required where (a) a looked after child[17] has an EHC plan, or attends a special school, and (b) a providing authority incurs cost by making educational provision for the child. In such circumstances, the home authority must pay to the providing authority such amount as they may agree.[18]

9.10 As between English home and providing authorities, recoupment is permitted where primary education, secondary education or part-time education (where the child has not attained the age of five years) is made by a providing authority in respect of a person who belongs to the area of a home authority in England. In such circumstances, the home authority may pay to the providing authority such amount as the authorities may agree.[19]

9.11 IARE Regs reg 10 sets out the procedure by which inter-local authority claim for recoupment must be made.

Dispute resolution

9.12 Any dispute between two or more local authorities as to which of them is responsible for the provision of education for any pupil shall be determined by the secretary of state.[20] This would apply, for example, to a dispute between two local authorities as to whether a child or young person was in the local authority's area.[21]

9.13 Similarly, any dispute between local authorities as to which local authority a child or young person 'belongs' shall be determined by the secretary of state.[22]

---

17 As defined in CA 1989 s22(1).

18 IARE Regs reg 5. Different rules apply where the providing authority is Welsh, see IARE Regs reg 4.

19 IARE Regs reg 8. See regulation 7 in respect of cases in which recoupment is permitted (English home authority, Welsh providing authority).

20 EA 1996 s495(3).

21 Although only in respect of disputes concerning a young person up to the age of 19 who is being educated in a school, see the definition of pupil in EA 1996 s3. In *R (JG) v Kent CC* [2016] EWHC 1102 (Admin), [2016] ELR 396 Nicol J gave 'pupil' a wide meaning, see para 145.

22 EA 1996 s579(4).

APPENDICES

Primary legislation: extracts[1]

---

1   © Crown Copyright. Legislation is reproduced, as amended, up to date to 1 February 2017.

CHILDREN AND FAMILIES ACT 2014

PART 3: CHILDREN AND YOUNG PEOPLE IN ENGLAND WITH SPECIAL EDUCATIONAL NEEDS OR DISABILITIES

Local authority functions: general principles

Local authority functions: supporting and involving children and young people

19 In exercising a function under this Part in the case of a child or young person, a local authority in England must have regard to the following matters in particular–

(a) the views, wishes and feelings of the child and his or her parent, or the young person;

(b) the importance of the child and his or her parent, or the young person, participating as fully as possible in decisions relating to the exercise of the function concerned;

(c) the importance of the child and his or her parent, or the young person, being provided with the information and support necessary to enable participation in those decisions;

(d) the need to support the child and his or her parent, or the young person, in order to facilitate the development of the child or young person and to help him or her achieve the best possible educational and other outcomes.

Special educational needs etc

When a child or young person has special educational needs

20 (1) A child or young person has special educational needs if he or she has a learning difficulty or disability which calls for special educational provision to be made for him or her.

(2) A child of compulsory school age or a young person has a learning difficulty or disability if he or she–

(a) has a significantly greater difficulty in learning than the majority of others of the same age, or

(b) has a disability which prevents or hinders him or her from making use of facilities of a kind generally provided for others of the same age in mainstream schools or mainstream post-16 institutions.

(3) A child under compulsory school age has a learning difficulty or disability if he or she is likely to be within subsection (2) when of compulsory school age (or would be likely, if no special educational provision were made).

(4) A child or young person does not have a learning difficulty or disability solely because the language (or form of language) in which he or she is or will be taught is different from a language (or form of language) which is or has been spoken at home.

(5) This section applies for the purposes of this Part.

Special educational provision, health care provision and social care provision

21 (1) 'Special educational provision', for a child aged two or more or a young person, means educational or training provision that is additional to, or different

from, that made generally for others of the same age in–
 (a) mainstream schools in England,
 (b) maintained nursery schools in England,
 (c) mainstream post-16 institutions in England, or
 (d) places in England at which relevant early years education is provided.
 (2) 'Special educational provision', for a child aged under two, means educational provision of any kind.
 (3) 'Health care provision' means the provision of health care services as part of the comprehensive health service in England continued under section 1(1) of the National Health Service Act 2006.
 (4) 'Social care provision' means the provision made by a local authority in the exercise of its social services functions.
 (5) Health care provision or social care provision which educates or trains a child or young person is to be treated as special educational provision (instead of health care provision or social care provision).
 (6) This section applies for the purposes of this Part.
   ...

Children and young people for whom a local authority is responsible

When a local authority is responsible for a child or young person

24 (1) A local authority in England is responsible for a child or young person if he or she is in the authority's area and has been–
 (a) identified by the authority as someone who has or may have special educational needs, or
 (b) brought to the authority's attention by any person as someone who has or may have special educational needs.
 (2) This section applies for the purposes of this Part.
   ...

Mainstream education

Children and young people with EHC plans

33 (1) This section applies where a local authority is securing the preparation of an EHC plan for a child or young person who is to be educated in a school or post-16 institution.
 (2) In a case within section 39(5) or 40(2), the local authority must secure that the plan provides for the child or young person to be educated in a maintained nursery school, mainstream school or mainstream post-16 institution, unless that is incompatible with–
 (a) the wishes of the child's parent or the young person, or
 (b) the provision of efficient education for others.
 (3) A local authority may rely on the exception in subsection (2)(b) in relation to maintained nursery schools, mainstream schools or mainstream post-16 institutions in its area taken as a whole only if it shows that there are no reasonable steps that it could take to prevent the incompatibility.
 (4) A local authority may rely on the exception in subsection (2)(b) in relation to a particular maintained nursery school, mainstream school or mainstream post-16 institution only if it shows that there are no reasonable steps that it or the governing body, proprietor or principal could take to prevent the incompatibility.

(5) The governing body, proprietor or principal of a maintained nursery school, mainstream school or mainstream post-16 institution may rely on the exception in subsection (2)(b) only if they show that there are no reasonable steps that they or the local authority could take to prevent the incompatibility.

(6) Subsection (2) does not prevent the child or young person from being educated in an independent school, a non-maintained special school or a special post-16 institution, if the cost is not to be met by a local authority or the Secretary of State.

(7) This section does not affect the operation of section 63 (fees payable by local authority for special educational provision at non-maintained schools and post-16 institutions).

...

Assessment

Assessment of education, health and care needs

36 (1) A request for a local authority in England to secure an EHC needs assessment for a child or young person may be made to the authority by the child's parent, the young person or a person acting on behalf of a school or post-16 institution.

(2) An 'EHC needs assessment' is an assessment of the educational, health care and social care needs of a child or young person.

(3) When a request is made to a local authority under subsection (1), or a local authority otherwise becomes responsible for a child or young person, the authority must determine whether it may be necessary for special educational provision to be made for the child or young person in accordance with an EHC plan.

(4) In making a determination under subsection (3), the local authority must consult the child's parent or the young person.

(5) Where the local authority determines that it is not necessary for special educational provision to be made for the child or young person in accordance with an EHC plan it must notify the child's parent or the young person–
   (a) of the reasons for that determination, and
   (b) that accordingly it has decided not to secure an EHC needs assessment for the child or young person.

(6) Subsection (7) applies where–
   (a) no EHC plan is maintained for the child or young person,
   (b) the child or young person has not been assessed under this section or section 71 during the previous six months, and
   (c) the local authority determines that it may be necessary for special educational provision to be made for the child or young person in accordance with an EHC plan.

(7) The authority must notify the child's parent or the young person–
   (a) that it is considering securing an EHC needs assessment for the child or young person, and
   (b) that the parent or young person has the right to–
      (i) express views to the authority (orally or in writing), and
      (ii) submit evidence to the authority.

(8) The local authority must secure an EHC needs assessment for the child or young person if, after having regard to any views expressed and evidence

submitted under subsection (7), the authority is of the opinion that–
  (a) the child or young person has or may have special educational needs, and
  (b) it may be necessary for special educational provision to be made for the child or young person in accordance with an EHC plan.
 (9) After an EHC needs assessment has been carried out, the local authority must notify the child's parent or the young person of–
  (a) the outcome of the assessment,
  (b) whether it proposes to secure that an EHC plan is prepared for the child or young person, and
  (c) the reasons for that decision.
(10) In making a determination or forming an opinion for the purposes of this section in relation to a young person aged over 18, a local authority must consider whether he or she requires additional time, in comparison to the majority of others of the same age who do not have special educational needs, to complete his or her education or training.
(11) Regulations may make provision about EHC needs assessments, in particular–
  (a) about requests under subsection (1);
  (b) imposing time limits in relation to consultation under subsection (4);
  (c) about giving notice;
  (d) about expressing views and submitting evidence under subsection (7);
  (e) about how assessments are to be conducted;
  (f) about advice to be obtained in connection with an assessment;
  (g) about combining an EHC needs assessment with other assessments;
  (h) about the use for the purposes of an EHC needs assessment of information obtained as a result of other assessments;
  (i) about the use of information obtained as a result of an EHC needs assessment, including the use of that information for the purposes of other assessments;
  (j) about the provision of information, advice and support in connection with an EHC needs assessment.

Education, health and care plans

Education, health and care plans
37 (1) Where, in the light of an EHC needs assessment, it is necessary for special educational provision to be made for a child or young person in accordance with an EHC plan–
  (a) the local authority must secure that an EHC plan is prepared for the child or young person, and
  (b) once an EHC plan has been prepared, it must maintain the plan.
 (2) For the purposes of this Part, an EHC plan is a plan specifying–
  (a) the child's or young person's special educational needs;
  (b) the outcomes sought for him or her;
  (c) the special educational provision required by him or her;
  (d) any health care provision reasonably required by the learning difficulties and disabilities which result in him or her having special educational needs;
  (e) in the case of a child or a young person aged under 18, any social care

provision which must be made for him or her by the local authority as a result of section 2 of the Chronically Sick and Disabled Persons Act 1970;

    (f) any social care provision reasonably required by the learning difficulties and disabilities which result in the child or young person having special educational needs, to the extent that the provision is not already specified in the plan under paragraph (e).

(3) An EHC plan may also specify other health care and social care provision reasonably required by the child or young person.

(4) Regulations may make provision about the preparation, content, maintenance, amendment and disclosure of EHC plans.

(5) Regulations under subsection (4) about amendments of EHC plans must include provision applying section 33 (mainstream education for children and young people with EHC plans) to a case where an EHC plan is to be amended under those regulations.

Preparation of EHC plans: draft plan

38 (1) Where a local authority is required to secure that an EHC plan is prepared for a child or young person, it must consult the child's parent or the young person about the content of the plan during the preparation of a draft of the plan.

(2) The local authority must then–

    (a) send the draft plan to the child's parent or the young person, and

    (b) give the parent or young person notice of his or her right to–

        (i) make representations about the content of the draft plan, and

        (ii) request the authority to secure that a particular school or other institution within subsection (3) is named in the plan.

(3) A school or other institution is within this subsection if it is–

    (a) a maintained school;

    (b) a maintained nursery school;

    (c) an Academy;

    (d) an institution within the further education sector in England;

    (e) a non-maintained special school;

    (f) an institution approved by the Secretary of State under section 41 (independent special schools and special post-16 institutions: approval).

(4) A notice under subsection (2)(b) must specify a period before the end of which any representations or requests must be made.

(5) The draft EHC plan sent to the child's parent or the young person must not–

    (a) name a school or other institution, or

    (b) specify a type of school or other institution.

Finalising EHC plans: request for particular school or other institution

39 (1) This section applies where, before the end of the period specified in a notice under section 38(2)(b), a request is made to a local authority to secure that a particular school or other institution is named in an EHC plan.

(2) The local authority must consult–

    (a) the governing body, proprietor or principal of the school or other institution,

(b) the governing body, proprietor or principal of any other school or other institution the authority is considering having named in the plan, and

(c) if a school or other institution is within paragraph (a) or (b) and is maintained by another local authority, that authority.

(3) The local authority must secure that the EHC plan names the school or other institution specified in the request, unless subsection (4) applies.

(4) This subsection applies where–

(a) the school or other institution requested is unsuitable for the age, ability, aptitude or special educational needs of the child or young person concerned, or

(b) the attendance of the child or young person at the requested school or other institution would be incompatible with–

(i) the provision of efficient education for others, or

(ii) the efficient use of resources.

(5) Where subsection (4) applies, the local authority must secure that the plan–

(a) names a school or other institution which the local authority thinks would be appropriate for the child or young person, or

(b) specifies the type of school or other institution which the local authority thinks would be appropriate for the child or young person.

(6) Before securing that the plan names a school or other institution under subsection (5)(a), the local authority must (if it has not already done so) consult–

(a) the governing body, proprietor or principal of any school or other institution the authority is considering having named in the plan, and

(b) if that school or other institution is maintained by another local authority, that authority.

(7) The local authority must, at the end of the period specified in the notice under section 38(2)(b), secure that any changes it thinks necessary are made to the draft EHC plan.

(8) The local authority must send a copy of the finalised EHC plan to–

(a) the child's parent or the young person, and

(b) the governing body, proprietor or principal of any school or other institution named in the plan.

Finalising EHC plans: no request for particular school or other institution

40 (1) This section applies where no request is made to a local authority before the end of the period specified in a notice under section 38(2)(b) to secure that a particular school or other institution is named in an EHC plan.

(2) The local authority must secure that the plan–

(a) names a school or other institution which the local authority thinks would be appropriate for the child or young person concerned, or

(b) specifies the type of school or other institution which the local authority thinks would be appropriate for the child or young person.

(3) Before securing that the plan names a school or other institution under subsection (2)(a), the local authority must consult–

(a) the governing body, proprietor or principal of any school or other institution the authority is considering having named in the plan, and

(b) if that school or other institution is maintained by another local authority, that authority.

(4) The local authority must also secure that any changes it thinks necessary are made to the draft EHC plan.

(5) The local authority must send a copy of the finalised EHC plan to–
   (a) the child's parent or the young person, and
   (b) the governing body, proprietor or principal of any school or other institution named in the plan.

   ...

Duty to secure special educational provision and health care provision in accordance with EHC Plan

42 (1) This section applies where a local authority maintains an EHC plan for a child or young person.

(2) The local authority must secure the specified special educational provision for the child or young person.

(3) If the plan specifies health care provision, the responsible commissioning body must arrange the specified health care provision for the child or young person.

(4) 'The responsible commissioning body', in relation to any specified health care provision, means the body (or each body) that is under a duty to arrange health care provision of that kind in respect of the child or young person.

(5) Subsections (2) and (3) do not apply if the child's parent or the young person has made suitable alternative arrangements.

(6) 'Specified', in relation to an EHC plan, means specified in the plan.

Schools and other institutions named in EHC plan: duty to admit

43 (1) Subsection (2) applies if one of the following is named in an EHC plan–
   (a) a maintained school;
   (b) a maintained nursery school;
   (c) an Academy;
   (d) an institution within the further education sector in England;
   (e) a non-maintained special school;
   (f) an institution approved by the Secretary of State under section 41.

(2) The governing body, proprietor or principal of the school or other institution must admit the child or young person for whom the plan is maintained.

(3) Subsection (2) has effect regardless of any duty imposed on the governing body of a school by section 1(6) of SSFA 1998.

(4) Subsection (2) does not affect any power to exclude a pupil or student from a school or other institution.

Reviews and re-assessments

44 (1) A local authority must review an EHC plan that it maintains–
   (a) in the period of 12 months starting with the date on which the plan was first made, and
   (b) in each subsequent period of 12 months starting with the date on which the plan was last reviewed under this section.

(2) A local authority must secure a re-assessment of the educational, health care and social care needs of a child or young person for whom it maintains an EHC plan if a request is made to it by–
   (a) the child's parent or the young person, or
   (b) the governing body, proprietor or principal of the school, post-16 institution or other institution which the child or young person attends.

(3) A local authority may also secure a re-assessment of those needs at any other time if it thinks it necessary.

(4) Subsections (1) and (2) are subject to any contrary provision in regulations made under subsection (7)(b).

(5) In reviewing an EHC plan maintained for a young person aged over 18, or deciding whether to secure a re-assessment of the needs of such a young person, a local authority must have regard to whether the educational or training outcomes specified in the plan have been achieved.

(6) During a review or re-assessment, a local authority must consult the parent of the child, or the young person, for whom it maintains the EHC plan.

(7) Regulations may make provision about reviews and re-assessments, in particular–

(a) about other circumstances in which a local authority must or may review an EHC plan or secure a re-assessment (including before the end of a specified phase of a child's or young person's education);

(b) about circumstances in which it is not necessary for a local authority to review an EHC plan or secure a re-assessment;

(c) about amending or replacing an EHC plan following a review or re-assessment.

(8) Regulations under subsection (7) about re-assessments may in particular apply provisions of or made under this Part that are applicable to EHC needs assessments, with or without modifications.

(9) Regulations under subsection (7)(c) must include provision applying section 33 (mainstream education for children and young people with EHC plans) to a case where an EHC plan is to be amended following a review.

Ceasing to maintain an EHC plan

45 (1) A local authority may cease to maintain an EHC plan for a child or young person only if–

(a) the authority is no longer responsible for the child or young person, or

(b) the authority determines that it is no longer necessary for the plan to be maintained.

(2) The circumstances in which it is no longer necessary for an EHC plan to be maintained for a child or young person include where the child or young person no longer requires the special educational provision specified in the plan.

(3) When determining whether a young person aged over 18 no longer requires the special educational provision specified in his or her EHC plan, a local authority must have regard to whether the educational or training outcomes specified in the plan have been achieved.

(4) A local authority may not cease to maintain an EHC plan for a child or young person until–

(a) after the end of the period allowed for bringing an appeal under section 51 against its decision to cease to maintain the plan, where no such appeal is brought before the end of that period;

(b) after the appeal has been finally determined, where such an appeal is brought before the end of that period.

(5) Regulations may make provision about ceasing to maintain an EHC plan, in particular about–

(a) other circumstances in which it is no longer necessary for an EHC plan to be maintained;

(b) circumstances in which a local authority may not determine that it is no longer necessary for an EHC plan to be maintained;

(c) the procedure to be followed by a local authority when determining whether to cease to maintain an EHC plan.

...

Personal budgets and direct payments

49 (1) A local authority that maintains an EHC plan, or is securing the preparation of an EHC plan, for a child or young person must prepare a personal budget for him or her if asked to do so by the child's parent or the young person.

(2) The authority prepares a 'personal budget' for the child or young person if it identifies an amount as available to secure particular provision that is specified, or proposed to be specified, in the EHC plan, with a view to the child's parent or the young person being involved in securing the provision.

(3) Regulations may make provision about personal budgets, in particular–

(a) about requests for personal budgets;

(b) about the amount of a personal budget;

(c) about the sources of the funds making up a personal budget;

(d) for payments ('direct payments') representing all or part of a personal budget to be made to a child's parent or a young person, or a person of a prescribed description in prescribed circumstances, in order to secure provision to which the budget relates;

(e) about the description of provision to which personal budgets and direct payments may (and may not) relate;

(f) for a personal budget or direct payment to cover the agreed cost of the provision to which the budget or payment relates;

(g) about when, how, to whom and on what conditions direct payments may (and may not) be made;

(h) about when direct payments may be required to be repaid and the recovery of unpaid sums;

(i) about conditions with which a person or body making direct payments must comply before, after or at the time of making a direct payment;

(j) about arrangements for providing information, advice or support in connection with personal budgets and direct payments.

(4) If the regulations include provision authorising direct payments, they must–

(a) require the consent of a child's parent or a young person, or a person of a prescribed description in prescribed circumstances, to be obtained before direct payments are made;

(b) require the authority to stop making direct payments where the required consent is withdrawn.

(5) Special educational provision acquired by means of a direct payment made by a local authority is to be treated as having been secured by the authority in pursuance of its duty under section 42(2), subject to any prescribed conditions or exceptions.

(6) Subsection (7) applies if–

(a) an EHC plan is maintained for a child or young person, and

(b) health care provision specified in the plan is acquired for him or her by means of a payment made by a commissioning body under section 12A(1) of the National Health Service Act 2006 (direct payments for health care).

(7) The health care provision is to be treated as having been arranged by the commissioning body in pursuance of its duty under section 42(3) of this Act, subject to any prescribed conditions or exceptions.

(8) 'Commissioning body', in relation to any specified health care provision, means a body that is under a duty to arrange health care provision of that kind in respect of the child or young person.

...

Appeals, mediation and dispute resolution

Appeals

51 (1) A child's parent or a young person may appeal to the First-tier Tribunal against the matters set out in subsection (2), subject to section 55 (mediation).

(2) The matters are–
   (a) a decision of a local authority not to secure an EHC needs assessment for the child or young person;
   (b) a decision of a local authority, following an EHC needs assessment, that it is not necessary for special educational provision to be made for the child or young person in accordance with an EHC plan;
   (c) where an EHC plan is maintained for the child or young person–
      (i) the child's or young person's special educational needs as specified in the plan;
      (ii) the special educational provision specified in the plan;
      (iii) the school or other institution named in the plan, or the type of school or other institution specified in the plan;
      (iv) if no school or other institution is named in the plan, that fact;
   (d) a decision of a local authority not to secure a re-assessment of the needs of the child or young person under section 44 following a request to do so;
   (e) a decision of a local authority not to secure the amendment or replacement of an EHC plan it maintains for the child or young person following a review or re-assessment under section 44;
   (f) a decision of a local authority under section 45 to cease to maintain an EHC plan for the child or young person.

(3) A child's parent or a young person may appeal to the First-tier Tribunal under subsection (2)(c)–
   (a) when an EHC plan is first finalised for the child or young person, and
   (b) following an amendment or replacement of the plan.

(4) Regulations may make provision about appeals to the First-tier Tribunal in respect of EHC needs assessments and EHC plans, in particular about–
   (a) other matters relating to EHC plans against which appeals may be brought;
   (b) making and determining appeals;
   (c) the powers of the First-tier Tribunal on determining an appeal;
   (d) unopposed appeals.

(5) Regulations under subsection (4)(c) may include provision conferring power

on the First-tier Tribunal, on determining an appeal against a matter, to make recommendations in respect of other matters (including matters against which no appeal may be brought).

(6) A person commits an offence if without reasonable excuse that person fails to comply with any requirement–

(a) in respect of the discovery or inspection of documents, or

(b) to attend to give evidence and produce documents,

where that requirement is imposed by Tribunal Procedure Rules in relation to an appeal under this section or regulations under subsection (4)(a).

(7) A person guilty of an offence under subsection (6) is liable on summary conviction to a fine not exceeding level 3 on the standard scale.

...

Special educational provision: functions of local authorities

Special educational provision otherwise than in schools, post-16 institutions etc

61 (1) A local authority in England may arrange for any special educational provision that it has decided is necessary for a child or young person for whom it is responsible to be made otherwise than in a school or post-16 institution or a place at which relevant early years education is provided.

(2) An authority may do so only if satisfied that it would be inappropriate for the provision to be made in a school or post-16 institution or at such a place.

(3) Before doing so, the authority must consult the child's parent or the young person.

...

Fees for special educational provision at non-maintained schools and post-16 institutions

63 (1) Subsection (2) applies where–

(a) a local authority maintains an EHC plan for a child or young person,

(b) special educational provision in respect of the child or young person is made at a school, post-16 institution or place at which relevant early years education is provided, and

(c) that school, institution or place is named in the EHC plan.

(2) The local authority must pay any fees payable in respect of education or training provided for the child or young person at that school, institution or place in accordance with the EHC plan.

(3) Subsection (4) applies where–

(a) a local authority is responsible for a child or young person for whom no EHC plan is maintained,

(b) special educational provision in respect of the child or young person is made at a school, post-16 institution or place at which relevant early years education is provided, and

(c) the local authority is satisfied that–

(i) the interests of the child or young person require special educational provision to be made, and

(ii) it is appropriate for education or training to be provided to the child or young person at the school, institution or place in question.

(4) The local authority must pay any fees payable in respect of the special

educational provision made at the school, institution or place in question which is required to meet the special educational needs of the child or young person.

(5) Where board and lodging are provided for the child or young person at the school, post-16 institution or place mentioned in subsection (2) or (4), the authority must also pay any fees in respect of the board and lodging, if satisfied that special educational provision cannot be provided at the school, post-16 institution or place unless the board and lodging are also provided.

...

Code of practice

Code of practice

77 (1) The Secretary of State must issue a code of practice giving guidance about the exercise of their functions under this Part to–

(a) local authorities in England;

(b) the governing bodies of schools;

(c) the governing bodies of institutions within the further education sector;

(d) the proprietors of Academies;

(e) the management committees of pupil referral units;

(f) the proprietors of institutions approved by the Secretary of State under section 41 (independent special schools and special post-16 institutions: approval);

(g) providers of relevant early years education;

(h) youth offending teams;

(i) persons in charge of relevant youth accommodation;

(j) the National Health Service Commissioning Board;

(k) clinical commissioning groups;

(l) NHS trusts;

(m) NHS foundation trusts;

(n) Local Health Boards.

(2) The Secretary of State may revise the code from time to time.

(3) The Secretary of State must publish the current version of the code.

(4) The persons listed in subsection (1) must have regard to the code in exercising their functions under this Part.

(5) Those who exercise functions for the purpose of the exercise by those persons of functions under this Part must also have regard to the code.

(6) The First-tier Tribunal must have regard to any provision of the code that appears to it to be relevant to a question arising on an appeal under this Part.

...

Supplementary

Parents and young people lacking capacity

80 (1) Regulations may apply any statutory provision with modifications, for the purpose of giving effect to this Part in a case where the parent of a child, or a young person, lacks capacity at the relevant time.

(2) Regulations under subsection (1) may in particular include provision for–

(a) references to a child's parent to be read as references to, or as including references to, a representative of the parent;

    (b) references to a young person to be read as references to, or as including references to, a representative of the young person, the young person's parent, or a representative of the young person's parent;

    (c) modifications to have effect in spite of section 27(1)(g) of the Mental Capacity Act 2005 (Act does not permit decisions on discharging parental responsibilities in matters not relating to a child's property to be made on a person's behalf).

(3) 'Statutory provision' means a provision made by or under this or any other Act, whenever passed or made.

(4) 'The relevant time' means the time at which, under the statutory provision in question, something is required or permitted to be done by or in relation to the parent or young person.

(5) The reference in subsection (1) to lacking capacity is to lacking capacity within the meaning of the Mental Capacity Act 2005.

(6) 'Representative', in relation to a parent or young person, means–

    (a) a deputy appointed by the Court of Protection under section 16(2)(b) of the Mental Capacity Act 2005 to make decisions on the parent's or young person's behalf in relation to matters within this Part;

    (b) the donee of a lasting power of attorney (within the meaning of section 9 of that Act) appointed by the parent or young person to make decisions on his or her behalf in relation to matters within this Part;

    (c) an attorney in whom an enduring power of attorney (within the meaning of Schedule 4 to that Act) created by the parent or young person is vested, where the power of attorney is registered in accordance with paragraphs 4 and 13 of that Schedule or an application for registration of the power of attorney has been made.

    ...

Interpretation of Part 3

83 (1) In this Part–

    'EA 1996' means the Education Act 1996;

    'ESA 2008' means the Education and Skills Act 2008;

    'SSFA 1998' means the School Standards and Framework Act 1998.

(2) In this Part–

    'appropriate person' has the meaning given by section 70(5);

    'beginning of the detention' has the meaning given by section 70(6);

    'detained person' has the meaning given by section 70(5);

    'detained person's EHC needs assessment' has the meaning given by section 70(5);

    'education, health and care provision' has the meaning given by section 26(2);

    'EHC needs assessment' has the meaning given by section 36(2);

    'EHC plan' means a plan within section 37(2);

    'health care provision' has the meaning given by section 21(3);

    'the home authority' has the meaning given by section 70(6) (subject to subsection (7) of that section);

    'mainstream post-16 institution' means a post-16 institution that is not a special post-16 institution;

    'mainstream school' means–

(a) a maintained school that is not a special school, or

(b) an Academy school that is not a special school;

'maintained school' means–

(a) a community, foundation or voluntary school, or

(b) a community or foundation special school not established in a hospital;

'post-16 institution' means an institution which–

(a) provides education or training for those over compulsory school age, but

(b) is not a school or other institution which is within the higher education sector or which provides only higher education;

'proprietor', in relation to an institution that is not a school, means the person or body of persons responsible for the management of the institution;

'relevant early years education' has the meaning given by section 123 of SSFA 1998;

'relevant youth accommodation' has the meaning given by section 70(5);

'social care provision' has the meaning given by section 21(4);

'social services functions' in relation to a local authority has the same meaning as in the Local Authority Social Services Act 1970;

'special educational needs' has the meaning given by section 20(1);

'special educational provision' has the meaning given by section 21(1) and (2);

'special post-16 institution' means a post-16 institution that is specially organised to make special educational provision for students with special educational needs;

'training' has the same meaning as in section 15ZA of EA 1996;

'young person' means a person over compulsory school age but under 25.

(3) A child or young person has a disability for the purposes of this Part if he or she has a disability for the purposes of the Equality Act 2010.

(4) A reference in this Part to 'education'–

(a) includes a reference to full-time and part-time education, but

(b) does not include a reference to higher education,

and 'educational' and 'educate' (and other related terms) are to be read accordingly.

(5) A reference in this Part to–

(a) a community, foundation or voluntary school, or

(b) a community or foundation special school,

is to such a school within the meaning of SSFA 1998.

(6) A reference in this Part to a child or young person who is 'in the area' of a local authority in England does not include a child or young person who is wholly or mainly resident in the area of a local authority in Wales.

(7) EA 1996 and the preceding provisions of this Part (except so far as they amend other Acts) are to be read as if those provisions were contained in EA 1996.

EQUALITY ACT 2010

PART 2: EQUALITY

...

Disability

6 (1) A person (P) has a disability if–

    (a) P has a physical or mental impairment, and

    (b) the impairment has a substantial and long-term adverse effect on P's ability to carry out normal day-to-day activities.

(2) A reference to a disabled person is a reference to a person who has a disability.

(3) In relation to the protected characteristic of disability–

    (a) a reference to a person who has a particular protected characteristic is a reference to a person who has a particular disability;

    (b) a reference to persons who share a protected characteristic is a reference to persons who have the same disability.

(4) This Act (except Part 12 and section 190) applies in relation to a person who has had a disability as it applies in relation to a person who has the disability; accordingly (except in that Part and that section)–

    (a) a reference (however expressed) to a person who has a disability includes a reference to a person who has had the disability, and

    (b) a reference (however expressed) to a person who does not have a disability includes a reference to a person who has not had the disability.

(5) A Minister of the Crown may issue guidance about matters to be taken into account in deciding any question for the purposes of subsection (1).

(6) Schedule 1 (disability: supplementary provision) has effect.

...

Chapter 2: Prohibited Conduct

Discrimination

Direct discrimination

13 (1) A person (A) discriminates against another (B) if, because of a protected characteristic, A treats B less favourably than A treats or would treat others.

(2) If the protected characteristic is age, A does not discriminate against B if A can show A's treatment of B to be a proportionate means of achieving a legitimate aim.

(3) If the protected characteristic is disability, and B is not a disabled person, A does not discriminate against B only because A treats or would treat disabled persons more favourably than A treats B.

(4) If the protected characteristic is marriage and civil partnership, this section applies to a contravention of Part 5 (work) only if the treatment is because it is B who is married or a civil partner.

(5) If the protected characteristic is race, less favourable treatment includes segregating B from others.

(6) If the protected characteristic is sex–

    (a) less favourable treatment of a woman includes less favourable treatment of her because she is breast-feeding;

(b) in a case where B is a man, no account is to be taken of special treatment afforded to a woman in connection with pregnancy or childbirth.

(7) Subsection (6)(a) does not apply for the purposes of Part 5 (work).

(8) This section is subject to sections 17(6) and 18(7).

...

Discrimination arising from disability

15 (1) A person (A) discriminates against a disabled person (B) if–

(a) A treats B unfavourably because of something arising in consequence of B's disability, and

(b) A cannot show that the treatment is a proportionate means of achieving a legitimate aim.

(2) Subsection (1) does not apply if A shows that A did not know, and could not reasonably have been expected to know, that B had the disability.

...

Indirect discrimination

19 (1) A person (A) discriminates against another (B) if A applies to B a provision, criterion or practice which is discriminatory in relation to a relevant protected characteristic of B's.

(2) For the purposes of subsection (1), a provision, criterion or practice is discriminatory in relation to a relevant protected characteristic of B's if–

(a) A applies, or would apply, it to persons with whom B does not share the characteristic,

(b) it puts, or would put, persons with whom B shares the characteristic at a particular disadvantage when compared with persons with whom B does not share it,

(c) it puts, or would put, B at that disadvantage, and

(d) A cannot show it to be a proportionate means of achieving a legitimate aim.

(3) The relevant protected characteristics are–

age;

disability;

gender reassignment;

marriage and civil partnership;

race;

religion or belief;

sex;

sexual orientation.

Adjustments for disabled persons

Duty to make adjustments

20 (1) Where this Act imposes a duty to make reasonable adjustments on a person, this section, sections 21 and 22 and the applicable Schedule apply; and for those purposes, a person on whom the duty is imposed is referred to as A.

(2) The duty comprises the following three requirements.

(3) The first requirement is a requirement, where a provision, criterion or practice of A's puts a disabled person at a substantial disadvantage in relation to a relevant matter in comparison with persons who are not disabled, to take such steps as it is reasonable to have to take to avoid the disadvantage.

(4) The second requirement is a requirement, where a physical feature puts a disabled person at a substantial disadvantage in relation to a relevant matter in comparison with persons who are not disabled, to take such steps as it is reasonable to have to take to avoid the disadvantage.

(5) The third requirement is a requirement, where a disabled person would, but for the provision of an auxiliary aid, be put at a substantial disadvantage in relation to a relevant matter in comparison with persons who are not disabled, to take such steps as it is reasonable to have to take to provide the auxiliary aid.

(6) Where the first or third requirement relates to the provision of information, the steps which it is reasonable for A to have to take include steps for ensuring that in the circumstances concerned the information is provided in an accessible format.

(7) A person (A) who is subject to a duty to make reasonable adjustments is not (subject to express provision to the contrary) entitled to require a disabled person, in relation to whom A is required to comply with the duty, to pay to any extent A's costs of complying with the duty.

(8) A reference in section 21 or 22 or an applicable Schedule to the first, second or third requirement is to be construed in accordance with this section.

(9) In relation to the second requirement, a reference in this section or an applicable Schedule to avoiding a substantial disadvantage includes a reference to–
(a) removing the physical feature in question,
(b) altering it, or
(c) providing a reasonable means of avoiding it.

(10) A reference in this section, section 21 or 22 or an applicable Schedule (apart from paragraphs 2 to 4 of Schedule 4) to a physical feature is a reference to–
(a) a feature arising from the design or construction of a building,
(b) a feature of an approach to, exit from or access to a building,
(c) a fixture or fitting, or furniture, furnishings, materials, equipment or other chattels, in or on premises, or
(d) any other physical element or quality.

(11) A reference in this section, section 21 or 22 or an applicable Schedule to an auxiliary aid includes a reference to an auxiliary service.

(12) A reference in this section or an applicable Schedule to chattels is to be read, in relation to Scotland, as a reference to moveable property.

(13) The applicable Schedule is, in relation to the Part of this Act specified in the first column of the Table, the Schedule specified in the second column.

Part of this Act	*Applicable Schedule*
Part 3 (services and public functions)	Schedule 2
Part 4 (premises)	Schedule 4
Part 5 (work)	Schedule 8
Part 6 (education)	Schedule 13
Part 7 (associations)	Schedule 15
Each of the Parts mentioned above	Schedule 21

Failure to comply with duty

21 (1) A failure to comply with the first, second or third requirement is a failure to comply with a duty to make reasonable adjustments.

(2) A discriminates against a disabled person if A fails to comply with that duty in relation to that person.

(3) A provision of an applicable Schedule which imposes a duty to comply with the first, second or third requirement applies only for the purpose of establishing whether A has contravened this Act by virtue of subsection (2); a failure to comply is, accordingly, not actionable by virtue of another provision of this Act or otherwise.

...

Other prohibited conduct

Harassment

26 (1) A person (A) harasses another (B) if–

(a) A engages in unwanted conduct related to a relevant protected characteristic, and

(b) the conduct has the purpose or effect of–

(i) violating B's dignity, or

(ii) creating an intimidating, hostile, degrading, humiliating or offensive environment for B.

(2) A also harasses B if–

(a) A engages in unwanted conduct of a sexual nature, and

(b) the conduct has the purpose or effect referred to in subsection (1)(b).

(3) A also harasses B if–

(a) A or another person engages in unwanted conduct of a sexual nature or that is related to gender reassignment or sex,

(b) the conduct has the purpose or effect referred to in subsection (1)(b), and

(c) because of B's rejection of or submission to the conduct, A treats B less favourably than A would treat B if B had not rejected or submitted to the conduct.

(4) In deciding whether conduct has the effect referred to in subsection (1)(b), each of the following must be taken into account–

(a) the perception of B;

(b) the other circumstances of the case;

(c) whether it is reasonable for the conduct to have that effect.

(5) The relevant protected characteristics are–

age;

disability;

gender reassignment;

race;

religion or belief;

sex;

sexual orientation.

Victimisation

27 (1) A person (A) victimises another person (B) if A subjects B to a detriment because–

(a) B does a protected act, or

  (b) A believes that B has done, or may do, a protected act.
(2) Each of the following is a protected act–
  (a) bringing proceedings under this Act;
  (b) giving evidence or information in connection with proceedings under this Act;
  (c) doing any other thing for the purposes of or in connection with this Act;
  (d) making an allegation (whether or not express) that A or another person has contravened this Act.
(3) Giving false evidence or information, or making a false allegation, is not a protected act if the evidence or information is given, or the allegation is made, in bad faith.
(4) This section applies only where the person subjected to a detriment is an individual.
(5) The reference to contravening this Act includes a reference to committing a breach of an equality clause or rule.
  ...

Pupils: admission and treatment, etc

85 (1) The responsible body of a school to which this section applies must not discriminate against a person–
  (a) in the arrangements it makes for deciding who is offered admission as a pupil;
  (b) as to the terms on which it offers to admit the person as a pupil;
  (c) by not admitting the person as a pupil.
(2) The responsible body of such a school must not discriminate against a pupil–
  (a) in the way it provides education for the pupil;
  (b) in the way it affords the pupil access to a benefit, facility or service;
  (c) by not providing education for the pupil;
  (d) by not affording the pupil access to a benefit, facility or service;
  (e) by excluding the pupil from the school;
  (f) by subjecting the pupil to any other detriment.
(3) The responsible body of such a school must not harass–
  (a) a pupil;
  (b) a person who has applied for admission as a pupil.
(4) The responsible body of such a school must not victimise a person–
  (a) in the arrangements it makes for deciding who is offered admission as a pupil;
  (b) as to the terms on which it offers to admit the person as a pupil;
  (c) by not admitting the person as a pupil.
(5) The responsible body of such a school must not victimise a pupil–
  (a) in the way it provides education for the pupil;
  (b) in the way it affords the pupil access to a benefit, facility or service;
  (c) by not providing education for the pupil;
  (d) by not affording the pupil access to a benefit, facility or service;
  (e) by excluding the pupil from the school;
  (f) by subjecting the pupil to any other detriment.
(6) A duty to make reasonable adjustments applies to the responsible body of such a school.

(7) In relation to England and Wales, this section applies to–
  (a) a school maintained by a local authority;
  (b) an independent educational institution (other than a special school);
  (ba) an alternative provision Academy that is not an independent educational institution;]
  (c) a special school (not maintained by a local authority).
(8) In relation to Scotland, this section applies to–
  (a) a school managed by an education authority;
  (b) an independent school;
  (c) a school in respect of which the managers are for the time being receiving grants under section 73(c) or (d) of the Education (Scotland) Act 1980.
(9) The responsible body of a school to which this section applies is–
  (a) if the school is within subsection (7)(a), the local authority or governing body;
  (b) if it is within subsection (7)(b), (ba)] or (c), the proprietor;
  (c) if it is within subsection (8)(a), the education authority;
  (d) if it is within subsection (8)(b), the proprietor;
  (e) if it is within subsection (8)(c), the managers.
(10) In the application of section 26 for the purposes of subsection (3), none of the following is a relevant protected characteristic–
  (a) gender reassignment;
  (b) religion or belief;
  (c) sexual orientation.

Victimisation of pupils, etc for conduct of parents, etc

86 (1) This section applies for the purposes of section 27 in its application to section 85(4) or (5).
(2) The references to B in paragraphs (a) and (b) of subsection (1) of section 27 include a reference to a parent or sibling of the child in question.
(3) Giving false evidence or information, or making a false allegation, in good faith is not a protected act in a case where–
  (a) the evidence or information is given, or the allegation is made, by a parent or sibling of the child, and
  (b) the child has acted in bad faith.
(4) Giving false evidence or information, or making a false allegation, in bad faith, is a protected act in a case where–
  (a) the evidence or information is given, or the allegation is made, by a parent or sibling of the child, and
  (b) the child has acted in good faith.
(5) In this section–
  'child' means a person who has not attained the age of 18;
  'sibling' means a brother or sister, a half-brother or half-sister, or a step-brother or stepsister.
  ...

Interpretation and exceptions

89 (1) This section applies for the purposes of this Chapter.
(2) Nothing in this Chapter applies to anything done in connection with the content of the curriculum.

(3) 'Pupil'–
  (a) in relation to England and Wales, has the meaning given in section 3(1) of the Education Act 1996;
  (b) in relation to Scotland, has the meaning given in section 135(1) of the Education (Scotland) Act 1980.
(4) 'Proprietor'–
  (a) in relation to a school in England and Wales, has the meaning given in section 579(1) of the Education Act 1996;
  (b) in relation to a school in Scotland, has the meaning given in section 135(1) of the Education (Scotland) Act 1980.
(5) 'School'–
  (a) in relation to England and Wales, has the meaning given in section 4 of the Education Act 1996;
  (b) in relation to Scotland, has the meaning given in section 135(1) of the Education (Scotland) Act 1980.
(6) A reference to a school includes a reference to an independent educational institution in England; and a reference to an independent educational institution in England is to be construed in accordance with Chapter 1 of Part 4 of the Education and Skills Act 2008.
(7) A reference to an independent educational institution is a reference to–
  (a) an independent educational institution in England, or
  (b) an independent school in Wales.
(8) 'Independent school'–
  (a) in relation to Wales, has the meaning given in section 463 of the Education Act 1996;
  (b) in relation to Scotland, has the meaning given in section 135(1) of the Education (Scotland) Act 1980.
(9) 'Special school' has the meaning given in section 337 of the Education Act 1996.
(10) 'Local authority' means–
  (a) in relation to England, an English local authority within the meaning of section 162 of the Education and Inspections Act 2006;
  (b) in relation to Wales, a Welsh local authority within the meaning of that section.
(11) 'Education authority', in relation to Scotland, has the meaning given in section 135(1) of the Education (Scotland) Act 1980.
(12) Schedule 11 (exceptions) has effect.

Chapter 4: Miscellaneous

Reasonable adjustments
98 Schedule 13 (reasonable adjustments) has effect.
  ...

PART 9: ENFORCEMENT

Chapter 1: Introductory

Proceedings

113 (1) Proceedings relating to a contravention of this Act must be brought in accordance with this Part.

(2) Subsection (1) does not apply to proceedings under Part 1 of the Equality Act 2006.

(3) Subsection (1) does not prevent–

(a) a claim for judicial review;

(b) proceedings under the Immigration Acts;

(c) proceedings under the Special Immigration Appeals Commission Act 1997;

(d) in Scotland, an application to the supervisory jurisdiction of the Court of Session.

(4) This section is subject to any express provision of this Act conferring jurisdiction on a court or tribunal.

(5) The reference to a contravention of this Act includes a reference to a breach of an equality clause or rule.

(6) Chapters 2 and 3 do not apply to proceedings relating to an equality clause or rule except in so far as Chapter 4 provides for that.

(7) This section does not apply to–

(a) proceedings for an offence under this Act;

(b) proceedings relating to a penalty under Part 12 (disabled persons: transport).

Chapter 2: Civil Courts

Jurisdiction

114 (1) The county court] or, in Scotland, the sheriff has jurisdiction to determine a claim relating to–

(a) a contravention of Part 3 (services and public functions);

(b) a contravention of Part 4 (premises);

(c) a contravention of Part 6 (education);

(d) a contravention of Part 7 (associations);

(e) a contravention of section 108, 111 or 112 that relates to Part 3, 4, 6 or 7.

(2) Subsection (1)(a) does not apply to a claim within section 115.

(3) Subsection (1)(c) does not apply to a claim within section 116.

(4) Subsection (1)(d) does not apply to a contravention of section 106.

(5) For the purposes of proceedings on a claim within subsection (1)(a)–

(a) a decision in proceedings on a claim mentioned in section 115(1) that an act is a contravention of Part 3 is binding;

(b) it does not matter whether the act occurs outside the United Kingdom.

(6) The county court or sheriff–

(a) must not grant an interim injunction or interdict unless satisfied that no criminal matter would be prejudiced by doing so;

(b) must grant an application to stay or sist proceedings under subsection (1) on grounds of prejudice to a criminal matter unless satisfied the matter will not be prejudiced.

(7) In proceedings in England and Wales on a claim within subsection (1), the power under section 63(1) of the County Courts Act 1984 (appointment of assessors) must be exercised unless the judge is satisfied that there are good reasons for not doing so.

(8) In proceedings in Scotland on a claim within subsection (1), the power under rule 44.3 of Schedule 1 to the Sheriff Court (Scotland) Act 1907 (appointment of assessors) must be exercised unless the sheriff is satisfied that there are good reasons for not doing so.

(9) The remuneration of an assessor appointed by virtue of subsection (8) is to be at a rate determined by the Lord President of the Court of Session.

...

Education cases

116 (1) A claim is within this section if it may be made to–
   (a) the First-tier Tribunal in accordance with Part 2 of Schedule 17,
   (b) the Special Educational Needs Tribunal for Wales in accordance with Part 2 of that Schedule, or
   (c) an Additional Support Needs Tribunal for Scotland in accordance with Part 3 of that Schedule.

(2) A claim is also within this section if it must be made in accordance with appeal arrangements within the meaning of Part 4 of that Schedule.

(3) Schedule 17 (disabled pupils: enforcement) has effect.

SCHEDULE 13: EDUCATION: REASONABLE ADJUSTMENTS

Section 98

Preliminary

1   This Schedule applies where a duty to make reasonable adjustments is imposed on A by this Part.

The duty for schools

2 (1) This paragraph applies where A is the responsible body of a school to which section 85 applies.

(2) A must comply with the first and third requirements.

(3) For the purposes of this paragraph–
   (a) the reference in section 20(3) to a provision, criterion or practice is a reference to a provision, criterion or practice applied by or on behalf of A;
   (b) the reference in section 20(3) or (5) to a disabled person is–
      (i) in relation to a relevant matter within sub-paragraph (4)(a), a reference to disabled persons generally;
      (ii) in relation to a relevant matter within sub-paragraph (4)(b), a reference to disabled pupils generally.

(4) In relation to each requirement, the relevant matters are–
   (a) deciding who is offered admission as a pupil;
   (b) provision of education or access to a benefit, facility or service.

...

SCHEDULE 17: DISABLED PUPILS: ENFORCEMENT

Section 116

PART 1: INTRODUCTORY
1   In this Schedule–
'the Tribunal' means–
(a) in relation to a school in England, the First-tier Tribunal;
(b) in relation to a school in Wales, the Special Educational Needs Tribunal for Wales;
(c) in relation to a school in Scotland, an Additional Support Needs Tribunal for Scotland;
'the English Tribunal' means the First-tier Tribunal;
'the Welsh Tribunal' means the Special Educational Needs Tribunal for Wales;
'the Scottish Tribunal' means an Additional Support Needs Tribunal for Scotland;
'responsible body' is to be construed in accordance with section 85.

PART 2: TRIBUNALS IN ENGLAND AND WALES
Introductory
2   This Part of this Schedule applies in relation to the English Tribunal and the Welsh Tribunal.

Jurisdiction – England and Wales
3   A claim that a responsible body has contravened Chapter 1 of Part 6 because of a person's disability may be made–
(a) to the English Tribunal by the person's parent or, if the person is over compulsory school age, the person;
(b) to the Welsh Tribunal by the person's parent.

...

Time for bringing proceedings
4 (1) Proceedings on a claim may not be brought after the end of the period of 6 months starting with the date when the conduct complained of occurred.
(2) [Repealed.]
(2A) If, in relation to proceedings or prospective proceedings on a claim under paragraph 3 or 3A, the dispute is referred for resolution in pursuance of arrangements under paragraph 6C ... before the end of the period of 6 months mentioned in sub-paragraph (1), that period is extended by 3 months.
(3) The Tribunal may consider a claim which is out of time.
(4) Sub-paragraph (3) does not apply if the Tribunal has previously decided under that sub-paragraph not to consider a claim.
(5) For the purposes of sub-paragraph (1)–
(a) if the contravention is attributable to a term in a contract, the conduct is to be treated as extending throughout the duration of the contract;
(b) conduct extending over a period is to be treated as occurring at the end of the period;
(c) failure to do something is to be treated as occurring when the person in question decided on it.

(6) In the absence of evidence to the contrary, a person (P) is to be taken to decide on failure to do something–

(a) when P acts inconsistently with doing it, or

(b) if P does not act inconsistently, on the expiry of the period in which P might reasonably have been expected to do it.

Powers

5 (1) This paragraph applies if the Tribunal finds that the contravention has occurred.

(2) The Tribunal may make such order as it thinks fit.

(3) The power under sub-paragraph (2)–

(a) may, in particular, be exercised with a view to obviating or reducing the adverse effect on the person of any matter to which the claim relates;

(b) does not include power to order the payment of compensation.

EDUCATION ACT 1996

PART I: GENERAL

Education in accordance with parental wishes

Pupils to be educated in accordance with parents' wishes

9 In exercising or performing all their respective powers and duties under the Education Acts, the Secretary of State and local authorities shall have regard to the general principle that pupils are to be educated in accordance with the wishes of their parents, so far as that is compatible with the provision of efficient instruction and training and the avoidance of unreasonable public expenditure.

Secondary legislation: extracts[1]

1   © Crown Copyright. Legislation is reproduced, as amended, up to date to 1 February 2017.

SPECIAL EDUCATIONAL NEEDS AND DISABILITY REGULATIONS 2014 SI NO 1530

PART 1: INTRODUCTION

Citation and commencement

1   These Regulations may be cited as the Special Educational Needs and Disability Regulations 2014 and come into force on 1st September 2014.

Interpretation

2 (1) In these Regulations–

'the Act' means the Children and Families Act 2014;

'the appropriate authority' means–

(a) in relation to a community, foundation or voluntary school or a maintained nursery school, the governing body of the school; and

(b) in relation to an Academy school, the proprietor;

'educational institution' means a school or post-16 institution;

'health care professional' means an individual who is a member of a profession regulated by a body mentioned in section 25(3) of the National Health Service Reform and Health Care Professions Act 2002;

'infant school' means a primary school for the purpose of providing education for children who are of compulsory school age but have not attained the age of eight, even though it may also provide education for children below compulsory school age;

'junior school' means a primary school for the purpose of providing education for children who are of compulsory school age who have attained the age of eight;

'relevant school' means a mainstream school or a maintained nursery school;

'responsible commissioning body' has the meaning given in section 42(4) of the Act;

'the SENCO', in relation to a relevant school, means the person who has been designated to be the special educational needs co-ordinator for the school by the appropriate authority in accordance with section 67 of the Act;

'transfer between phases of education' means a transfer from–

(a) relevant early years education to school;

(b) infant school to junior school;

(c) primary school to middle school;

(d) primary school to secondary school;

(e) middle school to secondary school; or

(f) secondary school to a post-16 institution;

'year 9' means the year of compulsory schooling in which the majority of pupils in the class attain the age of 14.

(2) Preparation for adulthood and independent living includes preparation relating to–

(a) finding employment;

(b) obtaining accommodation;

(c) participation in society.

PART 2: CHILDREN AND YOUNG PEOPLE WITH SPECIAL EDUCATIONAL NEEDS

Assessments

Consideration of request

3   A local authority must consult the child's parent or the young person as soon as practicable after–

(a) receiving a request for an EHC needs assessment under section 36(1) of the Act, or

(b) becoming responsible for the child or young person in accordance with section 24 of the Act,

before determining whether it may be necessary for special educational provision to be made in accordance with an EHC plan for the child or young person.

Determination whether or not special educational provision may be necessary

4 (1) Where a local authority determines that it is not necessary for special educational provision to be made in accordance with an EHC plan it must notify the child's parent or the young person in accordance with section 36(5) of the Act as soon as practicable, but in any event within 6 weeks of–

(a) receiving a request for an EHC needs assessment under section 36(1) of the Act, or

(b) becoming responsible for the child or young person in accordance with section 24 of the Act.

(2) Where the local authority is considering securing an EHC needs assessment it must also notify–

(a) the responsible commissioning body;

(b) the officers of the local authority who exercise the local authority's social services functions for children or young people with special educational needs;

(c) in relation to a child–

(i) if the child is a registered pupil at a school, the head teacher of that school (or the person holding the equivalent position), or

(ii) if the child receives education from a provider of relevant early years education, the person identified as having responsibility for special educational needs (if any) in relation to that provider; and

(d) in relation to a young person–

(i) if the young person is a registered pupil at a school, the head teacher of that school (or the person holding the equivalent position), or

(ii) if the young person is a student at a post-16 institution, to the principal of that institution (or the person holding the equivalent position).

Decision whether or not to conduct an EHC needs assessment

5 (1) The local authority must notify the child's parent or the young person as soon as practicable and in any event within 6 weeks of–

(a) receiving a request for an assessment under section 36(1) of the Act, or

(b) becoming responsible for the child or young person in accordance with section 24 of the Act of its decision whether or not it is necessary to secure an EHC needs assessment for the child or young person.

(2) The local authority must also notify the persons who were notified in accordance with regulation 4(2) of its decision.

(3) When notifying the child's parent or the young person of its decision that it is not necessary to secure an EHC needs assessment for the child or young person, it must also notify them of–

(a) their right to appeal that decision;

(b) the time limits for doing so;

(c) the information concerning mediation, set out in regulation 32; and

(d) the availability of–

(i) disagreement resolution services; and

(ii) information and advice about matters relating to the special educational needs of children and young people.

(4) The local authority need not comply with the time limit referred to in paragraph (1) if it is impractical to do so because–

(a) the local authority has requested advice from the head teacher or principal of a school or post-16 institution during a period beginning one week before any date on which that school or institution was closed for a continuous period of not less than 4 weeks from that date and ending one week before the date on which it re-opens;

(b) the authority has requested advice from the person identified as having responsibility for special educational needs (if any), in relation to, or other person responsible for, a child's education at a provider of relevant early years education during a period beginning one week before any date on which that provider was closed for a continuous period of not less than 4 weeks from that date and ending one week before the date on which it re-opens;

(c) exceptional personal circumstances affect the child, the child's parent, or the young person during the time period referred to in paragraph (1); or

(d) the child, the child's parent, or the young person, are absent from the area of the authority for a continuous period of not less than 4 weeks during the time period referred to in paragraph (1).

Information and advice to be obtained of EHC Needs Assessments

6 (1) Where the local authority secures an EHC needs assessment for a child or young person, it must seek the following advice and information, on the needs of the child or young person, and what provision may be required to meet such needs and the outcomes that are intended to be achieved by the child or young person receiving that provision–

(a) advice and information from the child's parent or the young person;

(b) educational advice and information–

(i) from the head teacher or principal of the school or post-16 or other institution that the child or young person is attending, or

(ii) where this is not available, from a person who the local authority is satisfied has experience of teaching children or young people with special educational needs, or knowledge of the differing provision which may be called for in different cases to meet those needs, or

(iii) if the child or young person is not currently attending a school or post-16 or other institution and advice cannot be obtained under sub-paragraph (ii), from a person responsible for educational provision for the child or young person, and

   (iv) if any parent of the child or young person is a serving member of Her Majesty's armed forces, also from the Secretary of State for Defence;

(c) medical advice and information from a health care professional identified by the responsible commissioning body;

(d) psychological advice and information from an educational psychologist;

(e) advice and information in relation to social care;

(f) advice and information from any other person the local authority thinks is appropriate;

(g) where the child or young person is in or beyond year 9, advice and information in relation to provision to assist the child or young person in preparation for adulthood and independent living; and

(h) advice and information from any person the child's parent or young person reasonably requests that the local authority seek advice from.

(2) Where it appears to the authority, in consequence of medical advice or otherwise, that the child or young person in question is either or both–

(a) hearing impaired;

(b) visually impaired,

and any person from whom advice and information is sought as provided in paragraph (1)(b) is not qualified to teach children or young people who are so impaired, then the advice sought shall be advice given after consultation with a person who is so qualified.

(3) When seeking advice in accordance with paragraph (1)(b) to (h), the local authority must provide the person from whom advice is being sought with copies of–

(a) any representations made by the child's parent or the young person, and

(b) any evidence submitted by or at the request of the child's parent or the young person.

(4) The local authority must not seek any of the advice referred to in paragraphs (1)(b) to (h) if such advice has previously been provided for any purpose and the person providing that advice, the local authority and the child's parent or the young person are satisfied that it is sufficient for the purposes of an EHC needs assessment.

Matters to be taken into account in securing an EHC needs assessment

7   When securing an EHC needs assessment a local authority must–

(a) consult the child and the child's parent, or the young person and take into account their views, wishes and feelings;

(b) consider any information provided to the local authority by or at the request of the child, the child's parent or the young person;

(c) consider the information and advice obtained in accordance with regulation 6(1);

(d) engage the child and the child's parent, or the young person and ensure they are able to participate in decisions; and

(e) minimise disruption for the child, the child's parent, the young person and their family.

Duty to co-operate in EHC needs assessments

8 (1) Where a local authority requests the co-operation of a body in securing an EHC needs assessment in accordance with section 31 of the Act, that body must comply with such a request within 6 weeks of the date on which they receive it.

(2) A body need not comply with the time limit referred to in paragraph (1) if it is impractical to do so because–

(a) exceptional circumstances affect the child, the child's parent or the young person during that 6 week period;

(b) the child, the child's parent or the young person are absent from the area of the authority for a continuous period of not less than 4 weeks during that 6 week period; or

(c) the child or young person fails to keep an appointment for an examination or a test made by the body during that 6 week period.

Provision of advice, information and support to parents and young people

9   When securing an EHC needs assessment the local authority must consider whether the child's parent or the young person requires any information, advice and support in order to enable them to take part effectively in the EHC needs assessment, and if it considers that such information, advice or support is necessary, it must provide it.

Decision not to secure an EHC plan

10 (1) Where, following an EHC needs assessment, a local authority decides that it is not necessary for special educational provision to be made for a child or young person in accordance with an EHC plan, the notification given in accordance with section 36(9) must be given as soon as practicable, and in any event within 16 weeks of the local authority receiving a request for an EHC needs assessment in accordance with section 36(1) of the Act, or of the local authority becoming responsible for the child or young person in accordance with section 24 of the Act.

(2) It must also notify the responsible commissioning body and the person notified in accordance with regulation 4(2)(c) or (d).

(3) When notifying a child's parent or young person in accordance with paragraph (1) the local authority must also notify them of–

(a) their right to appeal that decision;

(b) the time limits for doing so;

(c) the information concerning mediation, set out in regulation 32; and

(d) the availability of–

(i) disagreement resolution services; and

(ii) information and advice about matters relating to the special educational needs of children and young people; and

(e) the First-tier Tribunal's power to make recommendations under the Special Educational Needs and Disability (First-tier Tribunal Recommendation Power) (Pilot) Regulations 2015.

(4) The local authority need not comply with the time limit referred to in paragraph (1) if it is impractical to do so because–

(a) the authority has requested advice from the head teacher or principal of a school or post-16 institution during a period beginning one week before any date on which that school or institution was closed for a continuous period of not less than 4 weeks from that date and ending one week before the date on which it re-opens;

(b) the authority has requested advice from the person identified as having responsibility for special educational needs (if any) in relation to, or other person responsible for, a child's education at a provider of relevant early years education during a period beginning one week before any date on which that provider was closed for a continuous period of not less than 4 weeks from that date and ending one week before the date on which it re-opens;

(c) exceptional personal circumstances affect the child or the child's parent, or the young person during that time period ; or

(d) the child or the child's parent, or the young person, are absent from the area of the authority for a continuous period of not less than 4 weeks during that time period.

EHC Plans

Preparation of EHC plans

11 When preparing a child or young person's EHC Plan a local authority must–

(a) take into account the evidence received when securing the EHC needs assessment; and

(b) consider how best to achieve the outcomes to be sought for the child or young person.

Form of EHC plan

12 (1) When preparing an EHC plan a local authority must set out–

(a) the views, interests and aspirations of the child and his parents or the young person (section A);

(b) the child or young person's special educational needs (section B);

(c) the child or young person's health care needs which relate to their special educational needs (section C);

(d) the child or young person's social care needs which relate to their special educational needs or to a disability (section D);

(e) the outcomes sought for him or her (section E);

(f) the special educational provision required by the child or young person (section F);

(g) any health care provision reasonably required by the learning difficulties or disabilities which result in the child or young person having special educational needs (section G);

(h) (i) any social care provision which must be made for the child or young person as a result of section 2 of the Chronically Sick and Disabled Persons Act 1970 (section H1);

(ii) any other social care provision reasonably required by the learning difficulties or disabilities which result in the child or young person having special educational needs (section H2);

(i) the name of the school, maintained nursery school, post-16 institution or other institution to be attended by the child or young person and the type of that institution or, where the name of a school or other institution is not specified in the EHC plan, the type of school or other institution to be attended by the child or young person (section I); and

(j) where any special educational provision is to be secured by a direct payment, the special educational needs and outcomes to be met by the direct payment (section J),

and each section must be separately identified.

(2) The health care provision specified in the EHC Plan in accordance with paragraph (1)(g) must be agreed by the responsible commissioning body.

(3) Where the child or young person is in or beyond year 9, the EHC plan must include within the special educational provision, health care provision and social care provision specified, provision to assist the child or young person in preparation for adulthood and independent living.

(4) The advice and information obtained in accordance with regulation 6(1) must be set out in appendices to the EHC plan (section K).

Timescales for EHC plans

13 (1) When a local authority sends a draft plan to a child's parent or young person it must–

(a) give them at least 15 days, beginning with the day on which the draft plan was served, in which to–

(i) make representations about the content of the draft plan, and to request that a particular school or other institution be named in the plan; and

(ii) require the local authority to arrange a meeting between them and an officer of the local authority at which the draft plan can be discussed; and

(b) advise them where they can find information about the schools and colleges that are available for the child or young person to attend.

(2) A local authority must send the finalised EHC plan to–

(a) the child's parent or to the young person;

(b) the governing body, proprietor or principal of any school, other institution or provider of relevant early years education named in the EHC plan; and

(c) to the responsible commissioning body,

as soon as practicable, and in any event within 20 weeks of the local authority receiving a request for an EHC needs assessment in accordance with section 36(1) of the Act, or of the local authority becoming responsible for the child in accordance with section 24 of the Act.

(3) The local authority need not comply with the time limit referred to in paragraph (2) if it is impractical for any of the reasons set out in regulation 10(4)(a) to (d).

Sending the finalised EHC plan

14 (1) The finalised EHC plan must be in the form of the draft plan sent in accordance with regulation 13(1), or in a form modified in the light of the representations made in accordance with that regulation.

(2) When sending a copy of the finalised EHC plan to the child's parent or the young person in accordance with section 39(8)(a) or 40(5)(a) of the Act, the

local authority must notify them of–

(a) their right to appeal matters within the EHC plan in accordance with section 51(2)(c) of the Act;

(b) the time limits for doing so;

(c) the information concerning mediation, set out in regulation 32; and

(d) the availability of–

    (i) disagreement resolution services; and

    (ii) advice and information about matters relating to the special educational needs of children and young people; and

(e) the First-tier Tribunal's power to make recommendations under the Special Educational Needs and Disability (First-tier Tribunal Recommendation Power) (Pilot) Regulations 2015.

Transfer of EHC plans

15 (1) This regulation applies where a child or young person in respect of whom an EHC plan is maintained moves from the area of the local authority which maintains the EHC plan ('the old authority') into the area of another local authority ('the new authority').

(2) The old authority shall transfer the EHC plan to the new authority ('the transfer') on the day of the move or, where it has not become aware of the move at least 15 working days prior to that move, within 15 working days beginning with the day on which it did become aware.

(3) From the date of the transfer–

(a) the EHC plan is to be treated as if it had been made by the new authority on the date on which it was made by the old authority and must be maintained by the new authority; and

(b) where the new authority makes an EHC needs assessment and the old authority has supplied the new authority with advice obtained in pursuance of the previous assessment the new authority must not seek further advice where the person providing that advice, the old authority and the child's parent or the young person are satisfied that the advice obtained in pursuance of the previous assessment is sufficient for the purpose of the new authority arriving at a satisfactory assessment.

(4) The new authority must, within 6 weeks of the date of the transfer, inform the child's parent or the young person of the following–

(a) that the EHC plan has been transferred;

(b) whether it proposes to make an EHC needs assessment; and

(c) when it proposes to review the EHC plan in accordance with paragraph (5).

(5) The new authority must review the EHC plan in accordance with section 44 of the Act before the expiry of the later of–

(a) the period of 12 months beginning with the date of making of the EHC plan, or as the case may be, with the previous review, or

(b) the period of 3 months beginning with the date of the transfer.

(6) Where, by virtue of the transfer, the new authority comes under a duty to arrange the child or young person's attendance at a school or other institution specified in the EHC plan but in the light of the child or young person's move that attendance is no longer practicable, the new authority must arrange for the child or young person's attendance at another school or other institution

appropriate for him or her until such time as it is possible to amend the EHC plan.

(7) Where, by virtue of the child or young person's move, another commissioning body becomes the responsible commissioning body for that child or young person, the original responsible commissioning body must notify the new responsible commissioning body of the move on the day of the move or where it has not become aware of the move at least 15 working days prior to that move, within 15 working days beginning on the day on which it did become aware.

(8) Where it is not practicable for that new commissioning body to arrange the health care provision specified in the EHC plan, it must, within 15 working days beginning with the date on which it became aware of the move, request that the new local authority makes an EHC needs assessment or reviews the EHC Plan, and where the new local authority receives such a request it must comply with that request.

Change of responsible commissioning body

16 (1) This regulation applies where, in relation to a child or young person in respect of whom an EHC plan is maintained, another commissioning body becomes the responsible commissioning body for that child or young person, and the local authority which maintains the EHC plan remains the same.

(2) The original responsible commissioning body must notify the new responsible commissioning body of the change in responsible commissioning body within 15 working days beginning on the day on which it became aware of the change.

(3) Where it is not practicable for the new commissioning body to arrange the health care provision specified in the EHC plan, it must, within 15 working days beginning with the date on which it became aware that it is the new responsible commissioning body, request the local authority makes an EHC needs assessment or reviews the EHC Plan, and where the local authority receives such a request it must comply with that request.

Restriction on disclosure of EHC plans

17 (1) Subject to the provisions of the Act and of these Regulations, an EHC plan in respect of a child or young person shall not be disclosed by the local authority without the child or young person's consent except–

   (a) to persons to whom, in the opinion of the local authority concerned, it is necessary to disclose the whole or any part of the EHC plan in the interests of the child or young person;

   (b) for the purposes of any appeal under the Act;

   (c) for the purposes of educational research which, in the opinion of the local authority, may advance the education or training of children or young persons with special educational needs, if, but only if, the person engaged in that research undertakes not to publish anything contained in, or derived from, an EHC plan otherwise than in a form which does not identify any individual including, in particular, the child concerned and the child's parent or the young person;

   (d) on the order of any court or for the purposes of any criminal proceedings;

(e) for the purposes of any investigation under Part 3 of the Local Government Act 1974 (investigation of maladministration);

(f) to the Secretary of State when he requests such disclosure for the purposes of deciding whether to–
  (i) give directions, make determinations, or exercise any contractual rights under an Academy's funding agreement (for any purpose), or
  (ii) make an order under section 496, 497 or 497A of the Education Act 1996.

(g) for the purposes of an assessment of the needs of the child or young person with respect to the provision of any statutory services for him or her being carried out by officers of an authority by virtue of arrangements made under section 5(5) of the Disabled Persons (Services, Consultation and Representation) Act 1986;

(h) for the purposes of a local authority in the performance of its duties under sections 22(3)(a), 85(4)(a), 86(3)(a) and 87(3) of the Children Act 1989;

(i) to Her Majesty's Chief Inspector of Education, Children's Services and Skills, exercising the right to inspect and take copies of an EHC plan in accordance with section 10(1)(e) of the Education Act 2005 and section 140(2)(a) of the Education and Inspections Act 2006;

(j) to the person in charge of any relevant youth accommodation for the purposes of the provision of education or training for a detained person;

(k) to a youth offending team for the purposes of the provision of education or training for a detained person.

(2) A child may consent to the disclosure of an EHC plan for the purposes of this regulation if his or her age and understanding are sufficient to allow him or her to understand the nature of that consent.

(3) If a child does not have sufficient age or understanding to allow him or her to consent to such disclosure, the child's parent may consent on the child's behalf.

(4) The arrangements for keeping a child or young person's EHC plan must be such that they ensure, so far as is reasonably practicable, that unauthorised persons do not have access to it.

(5) In this regulation, any reference to an EHC plan includes a reference to any representations, evidence, advice or information obtained in relation to an EHC plan.

Reviews and re-assessments

Circumstances in which a local authority must review an EHC plan

18 (1) Except where paragraph (3) applies, where a child or young person is within 12 months of a transfer between phases of education, the local authority must review and amend, where necessary, the child or young person's EHC plan before–

(a) 31 March in the calendar year of the child or young person's transfer from secondary school to a post-16 institution; and

(b) 15 February in the calendar year of the child's transfer in any other case, and where necessary amend the EHC plan so that it names the school, post-16 or other institution, or type of school or institution, which the child or young person will attend following that transfer.

(2) Where it is proposed that a young person transfers from one post-16 institu-

tion to another post-16 institution at any other time, the local authority must review and amend, where necessary, the young person's EHC plan at least five months before that transfer takes place so that it names the post-16 institution that the young person will attend following the transfer.

(3) Where a child or young person is due to transfer from a secondary school to a post-16 institution on 1 September 2015 the local authority must amend and review the EHC plan under paragraph (1)(a) before 31 May 2015.

Conduct of reviews

19   When undertaking a review of an EHC plan, a local authority must–

(a) consult the child and the child's parent or the young person, and take account of their views, wishes and feelings;

(b) consider the child or young person's progress towards achieving the outcomes specified in the EHC plan and whether these outcomes remain appropriate for the child or young person;

(c) consult the school or other institution attended by the child or young person.

Review where the child or young person attends a school or other institution

20(ZA1) This regulation applies where a local authority carry out a review of an EHC plan and the child or young person concerned attends a school or other institution.

(1) As part of a review of a child or young person's EHC plan, the local authority must ensure that a meeting to review that EHC plan is held and in the case of a child or young person attending a school referred to in paragraph (12), can require the head teacher or principal of the school to arrange and hold that meeting.

(2) The following persons must be invited to attend the review meeting–

(a) the child's parent or the young person;

(b) the provider of the relevant early years education or the head teacher or principal of the school, post-16 or other institution attended by the child or young person;

(c) an officer of the authority who exercises the local authority's education functions in relation to children and young people with special educational needs;

(d) a health care professional identified by the responsible commissioning body to provide advice about health care provision in relation to the child or young person;

(e) an officer of the authority who exercises the local authority's social services functions in relation to children and young people with special educational needs.

(3) At least two weeks' notice of the date of the meeting must be given.

(4) The person arranging the review meeting must obtain advice and information about the child or young person from the persons referred to in paragraph (2) and must circulate it to those persons at least two weeks in advance of the review meeting.

(5) The child or young person's progress towards achieving the outcomes specified in the EHC plan must be considered at the meeting.

(6) When the child or young person is in or beyond year 9, the review meeting must consider what provision is required to assist the child or young person in preparation for adulthood and independent living.

(7) Where the child or young person attends a school referred to in paragraph (12), the local authority must ask the head teacher or principal of the school to prepare a written report on the child or young person, setting out that person's recommendations on any amendments to be made to the EHC plan, and referring to any difference between those recommendations and recommendations of others attending the meeting.

(8) Where the child or young person does not attend a school referred to in paragraph (12), the local authority must prepare a written report on the child or young person, setting out its recommendations on any amendments to be made to the EHC plan, and referring to any difference between those recommendations and recommendations of others attending the meeting.

(9) The written report must include advice and information about the child or young person obtained in accordance with paragraph (4) and must be prepared within two weeks of the review meeting, and sent to everyone referred to in paragraph (2).

(10) The local authority must then decide whether it proposes to–
  (a) continue to maintain the EHC plan in its current form;
  (b) amend it; or
  (c) cease to maintain it,
and must notify the child's parent or the young person and the person referred to in paragraph (2)(b) within four weeks of the review meeting.

(11) If the local authority proposes to continue or to cease to maintain the child or young person's EHC plan, it must also notify the child's parent or the young person of–
  (a) their right to appeal in accordance with section 51(2)(e) or (f) of the Act;
  (b) the time limits for doing so;
  (c) the information concerning mediation, set out in regulation 32; and
  (d) the availability of–
    (i) disagreement resolution services; and
    (ii) information and advice about matters relating to the special educational needs of children and young people; and
  (e) the First-tier Tribunal's power to make recommendations under the Special Educational Needs and Disability (First-tier Tribunal Recommendation Power) (Pilot) Regulations 2015.

(12) Schools referred to in this paragraph are–
  (a) maintained schools;
  (b) maintained nursery schools;
  (c) Academy schools;
  (d) alternative provision Academies;
  (e) pupil referral units;
  (f) non-maintained special schools;
  (g) independent educational institutions approved under section 41 of the Act.

Review of EHC plan where the child or young person does not attend a school or other institution

21 (1) This regulation applies where a local authority carry out a review of an EHC plan and the child or young person concerned does not attend a school or other institution.

(2) The local authority must invite the following persons to a meeting as part of the review of an EHC plan–

(a) the child's parent or the young person;

(b) an officer of the authority who exercises the local authority's education functions in relation to children and young people with special educational needs;

(c) a health care professional identified by the responsible commissioning body to provide advice about health care provision to the child or young person;

(d) an officer of the authority who exercises the local authority's social services functions in relation to children and young people with special educational needs;

(e) any other person whose attendance the local authority considers appropriate.

(3) At least two weeks' notice of the date of the meeting must be given.

(4) The local authority must obtain advice and information about the child or young person from the persons referred to in paragraph (2) and must circulate it to those persons at least two weeks in advance of the review meeting

(5) The meeting must consider the child or young person's progress towards achieving the outcomes specified in the EHC plan.

(6) When the child or young person is in or beyond year 9, the review meeting must consider what provision is required to assist the child or young person in preparation for adulthood and independent living.

(7) The local authority must prepare a report on the child or young person within two weeks of the review meeting setting out its recommendations on any amendments required to be made to the EHC plan, and should refer to any difference between those recommendations and recommendations of others attending the meeting.

(8) The written report must include advice and information about the child or young person obtained in accordance with paragraph (4) and must be prepared within two weeks of the review meeting, and sent to everyone referred to in paragraph (2).

(9) The local authority must decide whether it proposes to–

(a) continue to maintain the EHC plan in its current form;

(b) amend it; or

(c) cease to maintain it,

and must notify the child's parent or the young person within four weeks of the review meeting.

(10) If the local authority proposes to continue or to cease to maintain the child or young person's EHC plan, it must also notify the child's parent or the young person of–

(a) their right to appeal in accordance with section 51(2)(e) or (f) of the Act;

(b) the time limits for doing so;

(c) the information concerning mediation, set out in regulation 32; and

(d) the availability of–
   (i) disagreement resolution services; and
   (ii) advice and information about matters relating to the special educational needs of children and young people; and
(e) the First-tier Tribunal's power to make recommendations under the Special Educational Needs and Disability (First-tier Tribunal Recommendation Power) (Pilot) Regulations 2015.

Amending an EHC plan following a review

22 (1) Where the local authority is considering amending an EHC plan following a review it must comply with the requirements of regulations 11, and 12, and with sections 33 of the Act, and with sections 39 and 40 of the Act (as appropriate).

(2) Where the local authority is considering amending an EHC plan following a review it must–
   (a) send the child's parent or the young person a copy of the EHC plan together with a notice specifying the proposed amendments, together with copies of any evidence which supports those amendments;
   (b) provide the child's parent or the young person with notice of their right request the authority to secure that a particular school is or other institution is named in the plan under section 38(2)(b)(ii)
   (c) give them at least 15 days, beginning with the day on which the draft plan was served, in which to–
      (i) make representations about the content of the draft plan;
      (ii) request that a particular school or other institution be named in the plan;
      (iii) request a meeting with an officer of the local authority, if they wish to make representations orally.
   (d) advise them where they can find information about the schools and colleges that are available for the child or young person to attend.

(3) Where the local authority decides to amend the EHC plan following representations from the child's parent or the young person, it must send the finalised EHC plan to–
   (a) the child's parent or to the young person;
   (b) the governing body, proprietor or principal of any school or other institution named in the EHC plan; and
   (c) to the responsible commissioning body
as soon as practicable, and in any event within 8 weeks of the local authority sending a copy of the EHC plan in accordance with paragraph (2)(a).

(4) Where the local authority decides not to amend the EHC plan, it must notify the child's parent or the young person of its decision and its reasons for this as soon as practicable and in any event within 8 weeks of the local authority sending a copy of the EHC plan in accordance with paragraph (2)(a).

(5) When sending a the finalised EHC plan to the child's parent or the young person in accordance with paragraph (3), or notifying them in accordance with paragraph (4) the local authority must also notify them of–
   (a) their right to appeal matters within the EHC plan in accordance with section 51(2)(c) or 51(2)(e) of the Act (as appropriate);
   (b) the time limits for doing so;

(c) the information concerning mediation, set out in regulation 32; and

(d) the availability of–

    (i) disagreement resolution services; and

    (ii) advice and information about matters relating to the special educational needs of children and young people; and

(e) the First-tier Tribunal's power to make recommendations under the Special Educational Needs and Disability (First-tier Tribunal Recommendation Power) (Pilot) Regulations 2015.

Other circumstances in which a local authority must secure a re-assessment

23   A local authority must secure a re-assessment of a child or young person's EHC Plan where it receives a request to do so from the responsible commissioning body for that child or young person.

Circumstances in which it is not necessary to re-assess educational, health care and social care provision

24   Where a local authority receives a request to re-assess a child or young person in accordance with section 44(2) of the Act it does not need to do so where–

(a) it has carried out an assessment or re-assessment within the period of six months prior to that request, or

(b) it is not necessary for the authority to make a further assessment.

Notification of decision whether it is necessary to re-assess educational, health care and social care provision

25 (1) The local authority must notify the child's parent or the young person whether or not it is necessary to reassess the child or young person within 15 days of receiving the request to re-assess.

(2) Where the local authority does not need to re-assess the child or young person the notification under paragraph (1) must also notify them of–

(a) their right to appeal matters within the EHC plan in accordance with section 51(2)(d) of the Act;

(b) the time limits for doing so;

(c) the information concerning mediation, set out in regulation 32; and

(d) the availability of–

    (i) disagreement resolution services; and

    (ii) advice and information about matters relating to the special educational needs of children and young people; and

(e) the First-tier Tribunal's power to make recommendations under the Special Educational Needs and Disability (First-tier Tribunal Recommendation Power) (Pilot) Regulations 2015.

Securing a re-assessment of educational, health care and social care provision

26 (1) When securing a re-assessment of educational, health care and social care provision in a child or young person's EHC plan a local authority must comply with the requirements of regulations 6 and 7.

(2) Regulations 8 and 9 also apply to re-assessments.

Amending or replacing an EHC plan following a re-assessment

27 (1) Where the local authority decides to amend or replace an EHC plan following a reassessment it must comply with the requirements of regulations 11, 12, 13(1) and 14, and with sections 33 and 38 of the Act and with section 39 or 40 of the Act (as appropriate).

(2) The local authority must send a copy of the finalised EHC plan in accordance with section 39(8) or 40(5) of the Act (as appropriate) as soon as practicable, and in any event within 14 weeks of the notification under regulation 25(1)or of deciding it is necessary to reassess under section 44(3) to–
   (a) the child's parent or the young person;
   (b) the governing body, proprietor or principal of any school or other institution named in the plan; and
   (c) the relevant responsible commissioning body.

(3) The local authority need not comply with the time limit referred to in paragraph (2) if it is impractical to do so because–
   (a) the authority has requested advice from the head teacher or principal of a school or post-16 institution during a period beginning one week before any date on which that school or institution was closed for a continuous period of not less than 4 weeks from that date and ending one week before the date on which it re-opens;
   (b) the authority has requested advice from the person identified as having responsibility for special educational needs (if any) in relation to, or other person responsible for, a child's education at a provider of relevant early years education during a period beginning one week before any date on which that provider was closed for a continuous period of not less than 4 weeks from that date and ending one week before the date on which it re-opens;
   (c) exceptional personal circumstances affect the child or his parent, or the young person during that time period; or
   (d) the child or his parent, or the young person, are absent from the area of the authority for a continuous period of not less than 4 weeks, during that time period.

(4) (a) Where the local authority carries out a reassessment, it must review the EHC plan within 12 months of the date on which a copy of the finalised plan is sent to the child's parent or the young person in accordance with the requirements in Regulation 14; and
   (b) in each subsequent period of 12 months starting with the date on which the plan was last reviewed.

Amending an EHC plan without a review or reassessment

28 If, at any time, a local authority proposes to amend an EHC plan, it shall proceed as if the proposed amendment were an amendment proposed after a review.

Ceasing to maintain an EHC plan

Circumstances in which a local authority may not cease to maintain an EHC plan where the person is under the age of 18

29 (1) A local authority may not cease to maintain an EHC plan for a child or young person under the age of 18 unless it determines that it is no longer necessary

for special educational provision to be made for the child or young person in accordance with an EHC plan.

(2) Where a child or young person under the age of 18 is not receiving education or training, the local authority must review the EHC plan in accordance with regulations 18 and 19 and amend it in accordance with regulation 22 where appropriate, to ensure that the young person continues to receive education or training.

Circumstances in which a local authority may not cease to maintain an EHC plan where the person is aged 18 or over

30 (1) When a young person aged 18 or over ceases to attend the educational institution specified in his or her EHC plan, so is no longer receiving education or training, a local authority may not cease to maintain that EHC plan, unless it has reviewed that EHC plan in accordance with regulations 18 and 19 and ascertained that the young person does not wish to return to education or training, either at the educational institution specified in the EHC plan, or otherwise, or determined that returning to education or training would not be appropriate for the young person.

(2) Where following the review, the local authority ascertains that the young person wishes to return to education or training either at the educational institution specified in the EHC plan, or at another educational institution, and determines that it is appropriate for the young person to do so, it must amend the young person's EHC plan as it thinks necessary in accordance with regulation 22.

Procedure for determining whether to cease to maintain EHC plan

31 (1) Where a local authority is considering ceasing to maintain a child or young person's EHC plan it must–

    (a) inform the child's parent or the young person that it is considering ceasing to maintain the child or young person's EHC plan; and

    (b) consult the child's parent or the young person;

    (c) consult the head teacher, principal or equivalent person at the educational institution that is named in the EHC plan.

(2) Where, following that consultation the local authority determines to cease to maintain the child or young person's EHC plan, it must notify the child's parent or the young person, the institution named in the child or young person's EHC plan and the responsible commissioning body of that decision.

(3) When notifying the child's parent or the young person of its decision to cease to maintain the EHC plan, it must also notify them of–

    (a) their right to appeal that decision;

    (b) the time limits for doing so;

    (c) the information concerning mediation, set out in regulation 32; and

    (d) the availability of–

        (i) disagreement resolution services; and

        (ii) advice and information about matters relating to the special educational needs of children and young people; and

    (e) the First-tier Tribunal's power to make recommendations under the Special Educational Needs and Disability (First-tier Tribunal Recommendation Power) (Pilot) Regulations 2015.

...

Appeals

Powers of the First-tier Tribunal

43 (1) Before determining any appeal, the First-tier Tribunal may, with the agreement of the parties, correct any deficiencies in the EHC Plan which relate to the special educational needs or special educational provision for the child or the young person.

(2) When determining an appeal the powers of the First-tier Tribunal include the power to–

(a) dismiss the appeal;

(b) order the local authority to arrange an assessment of the child or young person under section 36 or a reassessment under section 44(2) where the local authority has refused to do so, where the appeal made under section 51(2)(a) or (d);

(c) order the local authority to make and maintain an EHC Plan where the local authority has refused to do so, where the appeal is made under section 51(2)(b);

(d) refer the case back to the local authority for them to reconsider whether, having regard to any observations made by the First-tier Tribunal, it is necessary for the local authority to determine the special educational provision for the child or young person, where the appeal is made under section 51(2)(b);

(e) order the local authority to continue to maintain the EHC Plan in its existing form where the local authority has refused to do so, where the appeal is made under section 51(2)...(f);

(f) order the local authority to continue to maintain the EHC Plan with amendments where the appeal is made under section 51(2)(c), (e) or (f) so far as that relates to either the assessment of special educational needs or the special educational provision and make any other consequential amendments as the First-tier Tribunal thinks fit;

(g) order the local authority to substitute in the EHC Plan the school or other institution or the type of school or other institution specified in the EHC plan, where the appeal is made under section 51(2)(c)(iii) or (iv), (e) or (f);

(h) where appropriate, when making an order in accordance with paragraph (g) this may include naming–

(i) a special school or institution approved under section 41 where a mainstream school or mainstream post-16 institution is specified in the EHC Plan; or

(ii) a mainstream school or mainstream post-16 institution where a special school or institution approved under section 41 is specified in the EHC Plan.

Compliance with the orders of the First-tier Tribunal

44 (1) Subject to paragraph (3) or any direction made by the First-tier Tribunal, if the First-tier Tribunal makes an order requiring a local authority to take any action, the local authority shall take that action within the period specified in paragraph (2).

(2) Where the order–

    (a) dismisses an appeal against a determination to cease an EHC Plan, the local authority shall cease to maintain the EHC Plan immediately;

    (b) requires a local authority to make an assessment or reassessment, the local authority shall within 2 weeks of the order being made notify the child's parent or the young person that it shall make the assessment or reassessment and shall–

        (i) where, following the assessment or reassessment, the local authority decides that it is not necessary for special educational provision to be made for the child or the young person, in accordance with an EHC plan, notify the child's parent or the young person of its decision, giving reasons for it as soon as practicable, and in any event within 10 weeks of the date of the First-tier Tribunal's order; or

        (ii) where, following the assessment or reassessment, it decides that it is necessary for special educational provision to be made for the child or the young person, in accordance with an EHC plan, it must send the finalised plan to the child's parent or the young person under regulation 14(2) and those specified in regulation 13(2) as soon as practicable and in any event within 14 weeks of the date of the First-tier Tribunal's order;

    (c) requires a local authority to make and maintain an EHC Plan, the local authority shall–

        (i) issue a draft EHC Plan within 5 weeks of the order being made; and

        (ii) send a copy of the finalised EHC plan to the child's parent or young person under Regulation 14(2) and to those specified in regulation 13(2), within 11 weeks of the order being made.

    (d) refers the case back to the local authority for it to reconsider, the local authority shall do so within 2 weeks of the order being made and shall either send a copy of the draft EHC Plan as required under Regulation 13 or give notice as required under Regulation 5 of any decision not to maintain an EHC Plan;

    (e) requires a local authority to amend the special educational provision specified in an EHC Plan, the local authority shall issue the amended EHC Plan within 5 weeks of the order being made;

    (f) requires the local authority to amend the name of the school or other institution or the type of school or other institution specified in the EHC plan, the local authority shall issue the amended EHC plan within 2 weeks of the order being made;

    (g) requires the local authority to continue to maintain an EHC Plan in its existing form, the local authority shall continue to maintain the EHC Plan; and

    (h) to continue and amend an EHC Plan, the local authority shall continue to maintain the EHC Plan and amend the EHC Plan within 5 weeks of the order being made.

(3) The local authority need not comply with the time limits specified in paragraph (2)(b) and (c) if it is impractical to do so because–

    (a) exceptional personal circumstances affect the child or their parent, or the young person during that period of time;

    (b) the child or their parent or the young person is absent from the area of the authority for a continuous period of 2 weeks or more during that period of time; or

(c) any of the circumstances referred to in regulation 13(3) apply.

Unopposed appeals

45 (1) This regulation applies where the child's parent or young person has appealed to the First-tier Tribunal and the local authority notifies the First-tier Tribunal that it will not oppose the appeal before it submits a response.

(2) The appeal is to be treated as if it was determined in favour of the appellant and the First-tier Tribunal is not required to make an order.

(3) If the appeal is made under section 51(2)(a) or (d) of the Act, the local authority must, within 2 weeks of the date it notified the First-tier Tribunal under paragraph (1), notify the child's parent or the young person that it must make the EHC needs assessment or reassessment.

(3A) If following the EHC needs assessment or reassessment, the local authority–

(a) decides that it is not necessary for special educational provision to be made for the child or young person in accordance with an EHC plan, the local authority must notify the child's parent or the young person of its decision, giving reasons for it as soon as practicable, and in any event within 10 weeks of the date it notified the First-tier Tribunal under paragraph (1), or

(b) decides that it is necessary for special educational provision to be made for the child or young person in accordance with an EHC plan, it must send the finalised plan to the child's parent or the young person under regulation 14(2) and those specified in regulation 13(2) as soon as practicable and in any event within 14 weeks of the date it notified the First-tier Tribunal under paragraph (1).

(4) If the appeal is made under section 51(2)(c)(i) or (ii), or (e) of the Act, the local authority must issue the amended EHC plan to those specified in regulation 22(3) within 5 weeks of the date it notified the First-tier Tribunal under paragraph (1).

(5) If the appeal is made under section 51(2)(c)(iii) or (iv) of the Act, the local authority must issue the amended EHC plan to those specified in regulation 22(3)–

(a) within 2 weeks of the date it notified the First-tier Tribunal under paragraph (1), or

(b) where the local authority is also required to amend the EHC plan under paragraph (4), within 5 weeks of the date it notified the First-tier Tribunal under paragraph (1).

(6) If the appeal is made under section 51(2)(b) of the Act, the local authority must–

(a) issue a draft EHC plan within 5 weeks of the date it notified the First-tier Tribunal under paragraph (1), and

(b) send a copy of the finalised EHC plan to the child's parent or the young person under regulation 14(2) and to those specified in regulation 13(2), within 11 weeks of the date it notified the First-tier Tribunal under paragraph (1).

(6A) If the appeal is made under section 51(2)(f) of the Act, the local authority must continue to maintain the EHC plan, and where the local authority has also agreed to amend the EHC plan, the local authority must amend it within 5 weeks of the date it notified the First-tier Tribunal under paragraph (1).

(7) The local authority need not comply with the time limits specified in paragraphs (3). . . or (6) if it is impractical to do so because–

(a) exceptional personal circumstances affect the child or their parent or the young person during the relevant period;

(b) the child or their parent or the young person are absent from the area of the local authority for a continuous period of not less than 2 weeks during the relevant period; or

(c) any of the circumstances referred to in regulation 13(3) apply.

Miscellaneous provisions

Academic year

46 (1) For the purposes of section 46 of the Act, an academic year is the period of twelve months which ends–

(a) in relation to a young person attending an institution within the further education sector on 31st July;

(b) in relation to a young person receiving apprenticeship training, on the date that that apprenticeship training finishes, or on the day before the young person attains the age of 26 if earlier;

(c) in all other cases, on the day that the young person's course of education or training is scheduled to end, or on the day before the young person attains the age of 26 if earlier.

(2) In this regulation 'apprenticeship training' has the same meaning as in section 83(5) of the Apprenticeships, Skills, Children and Learning Act 2009.

...

PART 6: PARENTS AND YOUNG PEOPLE LACKING CAPACITY

Where a child's parent lacks capacity

63   In a case where a child's parent lacks capacity at the relevant time references in–

(a) Part 3 of the Act, and

(b) these regulations, except the references in regulation 6(1)(b)(iv) and paragraph 15(b) of Schedule 2,

to a child's parent or the parent of a detained person who is a child are to be read as references to a representative of the parent.

Where a young person lacks capacity

64 (1) In a case where a young person lacks capacity at the relevant time–

(a) references to a young person in the provisions of Part 3 of the Act listed in Part 1 of Schedule 3 are to be read as references to both the young person and the alternative person;

(b) references to a young person or a detained person who is a young person in the provisions of Part 3 of the Act listed in Part 2 of Schedule 3 are to be read as references to the alternative person instead of the young person; and

(c) references to a young person in these regulations listed in Part 3 of

Schedule 3 are to be read as references to both the young person and the alternative person; and

(d) references to a young person in these regulations listed in Part 4 of Schedule 3 are to be read as references to the alternative person instead of the young person.

(2) For the purposes of this regulation, 'the alternative person' means–

(a) a representative of the young person;

(b) the young person's parent, where the young person does not have a representative;

(c) a representative of the young person's parent, where the young person's parent also lacks capacity at the relevant time and the young person does not have a representative.

Mental Capacity Act 2005

65   Regulations 63 and 64 have effect in spite of section 27(1)(g) of the Mental Capacity Act 2005.

...

SCHEDULE 3

PART 1: REFERENCES TO A YOUNG PERSON IN THE ACT THAT ARE TO BE READ AS REFERENCES TO BOTH A YOUNG PERSON AND AN ALTERNATIVE PERSON

Regulation 64(1)(a)

The provisions referred to in regulation 64(1)(a) are–

section 19(a), (b), (c) and (d) (first reference);

section 27(3)(a) and (b);

section 30(6)(a)(i) and (ii);

section 30(8)(d)(i) and (ii);

section 32(1) (first reference) and (2) (first reference);

section 32(3)(c).

PART 2: REFERENCES TO A YOUNG PERSON IN THE ACT THAT ARE TO BE READ AS REFERENCES TO AN ALTERNATIVE PERSON

Regulation 64(1)(b)

The provisions referred to in regulation 64(1)(b) are–

section 33(2)(a);

section 34(5)(c) and (7)(c);

section 36(1) (second reference), (4), (5) (second reference), (7) (opening words and paragraph (b)) and (9) (opening words);

section 38(1) (second reference), (2)(a) and (b), and (5);

section 39(8)(a);

section 40(5)(a);

section 42(5);

section 44(2)(a) and (6);

section 49(1) (second reference), (2) (second reference), (3)(d) and (4)(a);

section 51(1) and (3) (opening words);

section 52(2), (3) and (4) ;

section 53(1)(a), (3)(a) and (4)(a)(i);
section 54(1)(a) and (2)(a);
section 55(1), (3), (4) (opening words and (b)) and (5) (both references);
section 56(1)(f);
section 57(2)(b), (3)(b), (5)(a) and (8)(b);
section 61(3);
section 68(2) (first reference);
section 70(5) (paragraph (b) of the definition of 'appropriate person').

PART 3: REFERENCES TO A YOUNG PERSON IN THE ACT THAT ARE TO BE READ AS REFERENCES TO BOTH A YOUNG PERSON AND AN ALTERNATIVE PERSON

Regulation 64(1)(c)

The provisions referred to in regulation 64(1)(c) are–
regulation 5(4)(c) and (d);
regulation 7(a), (b), (d) and (e);
regulation 8(2)(a) and (b);
regulation 10(4)(c) and (d);
regulation 12(1)(a);
regulation 17(1)(c) (second reference);
regulation 19(a);
regulation 27(3)(c) and (d)
regulation 41(1) (opening words); and the description accompanying 'Travel Costs'
regulation 44(3)(a) and (b);
regulation 45(7)(a) and (b);
regulation 54(1)(a) and (b)
regulation 55 (opening words);
regulation 56(1) (opening words) and (c);
Schedule 2 paragraph 5(d) (second reference) and (e).

PART 4: REFERENCES TO A YOUNG PERSON IN THE ACT THAT ARE TO BE READ AS REFERENCES TO AN ALTERNATIVE PERSON

Regulation 64(1)(d)

The provisions referred to in regulation 64(1)(d) are–
regulation 3 (opening words);
regulation 4(1) (opening words);
regulation 5(1) (opening words) and (3);
regulation 6(1)(a) and (h), (3)(a) and (b) and (4);
regulation 9;
regulation 10 (3);
regulation 13(1) and (2)(a);
regulation 14(2);
regulation 15(3)(b);
regulation 17(1) (second reference in opening words);
regulation 20(2)(a), (10), and (11) (second reference in opening words)
regulation 21(2)(a), (9), and (10) (second reference in opening words);

regulation 22(2)(a) and (b), (3) (opening words and (a)), (4) and (5) (opening words);

regulation 25(1) (first reference);

regulation 27(2)(a);

regulation 31(1)(a) (first reference) and (b), (2) (second reference) and (3) (opening words);

regulation 32;

regulation 33;

regulation 34;

regulation 35;

regulation 36;

regulation 37;

regulation 38(1)(b);

regulation 39;

regulation 44(2)(b) (opening words) (i) (second reference); and (2)(c)(ii);

regulation 45(1);

Schedule 2 paragraph 4(b).

EQUALITY ACT 2010 (DISABILITY) REGULATIONS 2010 SI NO 2128

PART 2: DETERMINATION OF DISABILITY

Other conditions not to be treated as impairments

4 (1) For the purposes of the Act the following conditions are to be treated as not amounting to impairments–

(a) a tendency to set fires,

(b) a tendency to steal,

(c) a tendency to physical or sexual abuse of other persons,

(d) exhibitionism, and

(e) voyeurism.

(2) Subject to paragraph (3) below, for the purposes of the Act the condition known as seasonal allergic rhinitis shall be treated as not amounting to an impairment.

(3) Paragraph (2) above shall not prevent that condition from being taken into account for the purposes of the Act where it aggravates the effect of any other condition.

TRIBUNAL PROCEDURE (FIRST-TIER TRIBUNAL) (HEALTH, EDUCATION AND SOCIAL CARE CHAMBER) RULES 2008 SI NO 2699

PART 1: INTRODUCTION

Citation, commencement, application and interpretation

1 (1) These Rules may be cited as the Tribunal Procedure (First-tier Tribunal) (Health, Education and Social Care Chamber) Rules 2008 and come into force on 3rd November 2008.

(2) These Rules apply to proceedings before the Health, Education and Social Care Chamber of the First-tier Tribunal.

(3) In these Rules–

'the 2007 Act' means the Tribunals, Courts and Enforcement Act 2007;

'applicant' means a person who–

    (a) starts Tribunal proceedings, whether by making an application, an appeal, a claim or a reference;

    (b) makes an application to the Tribunal for leave to start such proceedings; or

    (c) is substituted as an applicant under rule 9(1) (substitution and addition of parties);

'childcare provider' means a person who is a childminder or provides day care as defined in section 19 of the Children and Families (Wales) Measure 2010, or a person who provides childcare as defined in section 18 of the Childcare Act 2006;

'disability discrimination in schools case' means proceedings concerning disability discrimination in the education of a child or young person or related matters;

'dispose of proceedings' includes, unless indicated otherwise, disposing of a part of the proceedings;

'document' means anything in which information is recorded in any form, and an obligation under these Rules or any practice direction or direction to provide or allow access to a document or a copy of a document for any purpose means, unless the Tribunal directs otherwise, an obligation to provide or allow access to such document or copy in a legible form or in a form which can be readily made into a legible form;

'health service case' means a case under the National Health Service Act 2006, the National Health Service (Wales) Act 2006, regulations made under either of those Acts, or regulations having effect as if made under either of those Acts by reason of section 4 of and Schedule 2 to the National Health Service (Consequential Provisions) Act 2006;

'hearing' means an oral hearing and includes a hearing conducted in whole or in part by video link, telephone or other means of instantaneous two-way electronic communication;

'legal representative' means a person who, for the purposes of the Legal Services Act 2007, is an authorised person in relation to an activity which constitutes the exercise of a right of audience or the conduct of litigation within the meaning of that Act;

'mental health case' means proceedings brought under the Mental Health

Act 1983 or paragraph 5(2) of the Schedule to the Repatriation of Prisoners Act 1984;

'nearest relative' has the meaning set out in section 26 of the Mental Health Act 1983;

'party' means–

(a) in a mental health case, the patient, the responsible authority, the Secretary of State (if the patient is a restricted patient or in a reference under rule 32(8) (seeking approval under section 86 of the Mental Health Act 1983)), and any other person who starts a mental health case by making an application;

(b) in any other case, a person who is an applicant or respondent in proceedings before the Tribunal or, if the proceedings have been concluded, a person who was an applicant or respondent when the Tribunal finally disposed of all issues in the proceedings;

'patient' means the person who is the subject of a mental health case;

'practice direction' means a direction given under section 23 of the 2007 Act;

'respondent' means–

(a) in an appeal against an order made by a justice of the peace, the person who applied to the justice of the peace for the order;

(b) in an appeal against any other decision, the person who made the decision;

(c) in proceedings on a claim brought under paragraph 3 of Schedule 17 to the Equality Act 2010 (disabled pupils: enforcement)–

(i) the local authority or the governing body, where the school concerned is a maintained school;

(ii) the proprietor, where the school concerned is an independent school;

(d) [Repealed.]

(da) in an application for, or for a review of, a stop order under the National Health Service (Optical Charges and Payments) Regulations 1997–

(i) the supplier, where the Secretary of State is the applicant;

(ii) the Secretary of State, where the supplier is the applicant;

(db) in any other health service case–

(i) the practitioner, performer or person against whom the application is made, where the National Health Service Commissioning Board or a Local Health Board is, or is deemed to be, the applicant;

(ii) the National Health Service Commissioning Board or Local Health Board that served the notice, obtained the order or confirmation of the order, where any other person is the applicant; or

(e) a person substituted or added as a respondent under rule 9 (substitution and addition of parties);

'responsible authority' means–

(a) in relation to a patient detained under the Mental Health Act 1983 in a hospital within the meaning of Part 2 of that Act, the managers (as defined in section 145 of that Act);

(b) in relation to a patient subject to guardianship, the responsible local social services authority (as defined in section 34(3) of the Mental

Health Act 1983);

(c) in relation to a community patient, the managers of the responsible hospital (as defined in section 145 of the Mental Health Act 1983);

'restricted patient' has the meaning set out in section 79(1) of the Mental Health Act 1983;

'special educational needs case' means proceedings concerning–

(a) an EHC needs assessment within the meaning of section 36(2) of the Children and Families Act 2014,

(aa) a detained person's EHC needs assessment within the meaning of section 70(5) of the Children and Families Act 2014, or

(b) an EHC plan within the meaning of section 37(2) of that Act,

of a child or young person who has or may have special educational needs;

'Suspension Regulations' means regulations which provide for a right of appeal against a decision to suspend, or not to lift the suspension of, a person's registration as a childcare provider;

'Tribunal' means the First-tier Tribunal;

'working day' means any day except a Saturday or Sunday, Christmas Day, Good Friday or a bank holiday under section 1 of the Banking and Financial Dealings Act 1971;

'young person' means, in relation to a special educational needs case or a disability discrimination in schools case, a person over compulsory school age but under 25.

Overriding objective and parties' obligation to co-operate with the Tribunal

2 (1) The overriding objective of these Rules is to enable the Tribunal to deal with cases fairly and justly.

(2) Dealing with a case fairly and justly includes–

(a) dealing with the case in ways which are proportionate to the importance of the case, the complexity of the issues, the anticipated costs and the resources of the parties;

(b) avoiding unnecessary formality and seeking flexibility in the proceedings;

(c) ensuring, so far as practicable, that the parties are able to participate fully in the proceedings;

(d) using any special expertise of the Tribunal effectively; and

(e) avoiding delay, so far as compatible with proper consideration of the issues.

(3) The Tribunal must seek to give effect to the overriding objective when it–

(a) exercises any power under these Rules; or

(b) interprets any rule or practice direction.

(4) Parties must–

(a) help the Tribunal to further the overriding objective; and

(b) co-operate with the Tribunal generally.

...

Case management powers

5 (1) Subject to the provisions of the 2007 Act and any other enactment, the Tribunal may regulate its own procedure.

(2) The Tribunal may give a direction in relation to the conduct or disposal of proceedings at any time, including a direction amending, suspending or setting aside an earlier direction.

(3) In particular, and without restricting the general powers in paragraphs (1) and (2), the Tribunal may–

   (a) extend or shorten the time for complying with any rule, practice direction or direction, unless such extension or shortening would conflict with a provision of another enactment containing a time limit;

   (b) consolidate or hear together two or more sets of proceedings or parts of proceedings raising common issues, or treat a case as a lead case;

   (c) permit or require a party to amend a document;

   (d) permit or require a party or another person to provide documents, information or submissions to the Tribunal or a party;

   (e) deal with an issue in the proceedings as a preliminary issue;

   (f) hold a hearing to consider any matter, including a case management issue;

   (g) decide the form of any hearing;

   (h) adjourn or postpone a hearing;

   (i) require a party to produce a bundle for a hearing;

   (j) stay proceedings;

   (k) transfer proceedings to another court or tribunal if that other court or tribunal has jurisdiction in relation to the proceedings and–

      (i) because of a change of circumstances since the proceedings were started, the Tribunal no longer has jurisdiction in relation to the proceedings; or

      (ii) the Tribunal considers that the other court or tribunal is a more appropriate forum for the determination of the case; or

   (l) suspend the effect of its own decision pending the determination by the Tribunal or the Upper Tribunal of an application for permission to appeal against, and any appeal or review of, that decision.

Procedure for applying for and giving directions

6 (1) The Tribunal may give a direction on the application of one or more of the parties or on its own initiative.

(2) An application for a direction may be made–

   (a) by sending or delivering a written application to the Tribunal; or

   (b) orally during the course of a hearing.

(3) An application for a direction must include the reason for making that application.

(4) Unless the Tribunal considers that there is good reason not to do so, the Tribunal must send written notice of any direction to every party and to any other person affected by the direction.

(5) If a party, or any other person given notice of the direction under paragraph (4), wishes to challenge a direction which the Tribunal has given, they may do so by applying for another direction which amends, suspends or sets aside the first direction.

Failure to comply with rules etc

7 (1) An irregularity resulting from a failure to comply with any requirement in

these Rules, a practice direction or a direction, does not of itself render void the proceedings or any step taken in the proceedings.

(2) If a party has failed to comply with a requirement in these Rules, a practice direction or a direction, the Tribunal may take such action as it considers just, which may include–

(a) waiving the requirement;

(b) requiring the failure to be remedied;

(c) exercising its power under rule 8 (striking out a party's case);

(d) exercising its power under paragraph (3); or

(e) except in mental health cases, restricting a party's participation in the proceedings.

(3) The Tribunal may refer to the Upper Tribunal, and ask the Upper Tribunal to exercise its power under section 25 of the 2007 Act in relation to, any failure by a person to comply with a requirement imposed by the Tribunal–

(a) to attend at any place for the purpose of giving evidence;

(b) otherwise to make themselves available to give evidence;

(c) to swear an oath in connection with the giving of evidence;

(d) to give evidence as a witness;

(e) to produce a document; or

(f) to facilitate the inspection of a document or any other thing (including any premises).

Striking out a party's case

8 (1) With the exception of paragraph (3), this rule does not apply to mental health cases.

(2) The proceedings, or the appropriate part of them, will automatically be struck out if the applicant has failed to comply with a direction that stated that failure by the applicant to comply with the direction would lead to the striking out of the proceedings or that part of them.

(3) The Tribunal must strike out the whole or a part of the proceedings if the Tribunal–

(a) does not have jurisdiction in relation to the proceedings or that part of them; and

(b) does not exercise its power under rule 5(3)(k)(i) (transfer to another court or tribunal) in relation to the proceedings or that part of them.

(4) The Tribunal may strike out the whole or a part of the proceedings if–

(a) the applicant has failed to comply with a direction which stated that failure by the applicant to comply with the direction could lead to the striking out of the proceedings or part of them;

(b) the applicant has failed to co-operate with the Tribunal to such an extent that the Tribunal cannot deal with the proceedings fairly and justly; or

(c) the Tribunal considers there is no reasonable prospect of the applicant's case, or part of it, succeeding.

(5) The Tribunal may not strike out the whole or a part of the proceedings under paragraph (3) or (4)(b) or (c) without first giving the applicant an opportunity to make representations in relation to the proposed striking out.

(6) If the proceedings, or part of them, have been struck out under paragraph (2) or (4)(a), the applicant may apply for the proceedings, or part of them, to be reinstated.

(7) An application under paragraph (6) must be made in writing and received by the Tribunal within 28 days after the date on which the Tribunal sent notification of the striking out to that party.

(8) This rule applies to a respondent as it applies to an applicant except that–

   (a) a reference to the striking out of the proceedings is to be read as a reference to the barring of the respondent from taking further part in the proceedings; and

   (b) a reference to an application for the reinstatement of proceedings which have been struck out is to be read as a reference to an application for the lifting of the bar on the respondent from taking further part in the proceedings.

(9) If a respondent has been barred from taking further part in proceedings under this rule and that bar has not been lifted, the Tribunal need not consider any response or other submission made by that respondent and may summarily determine any or all issues against that respondent.

Substitution and addition of parties

9 (1) The Tribunal may give a direction substituting a party if–

   (a) the wrong person has been named as a party; or

   (b) the substitution has become necessary because of a change in circumstances since the start of proceedings.

(2) The Tribunal may give a direction adding a person to the proceedings as a respondent.

(3) If the Tribunal gives a direction under paragraph (1) or (2) it may give such consequential directions as it considers appropriate.

Orders for costs

10 (1) Subject to paragraph (2), the Tribunal may make an order in respect of costs only–

   (a) under section 29(4) of the 2007 Act (wasted costs) and costs incurred in applying for such costs; or

   (b) if the Tribunal considers that a party or its representative has acted unreasonably in bringing, defending or conducting the proceedings.

(2) The Tribunal may not make an order under paragraph (1)(b) in mental health cases.

(3) The Tribunal may make an order in respect of costs on an application or on its own initiative.

(4) A person making an application for an order under this rule must–

   (a) send or deliver a written application to the Tribunal and to the person against whom it is proposed that the order be made; and

   (b) send or deliver a schedule of the costs claimed with the application.

(5) An application for an order under paragraph (1) may be made at any time during the proceedings but may not be made later than 14 days after the date on which the Tribunal sends–

   (a) a decision notice recording the decision which finally disposes of all issues in the proceedings; or

   (b) notice under rule 17(6) that a withdrawal which ends the proceedings has taken effect.

(6) The Tribunal may not make an order under paragraph (1) against a person

(the 'paying person') without first–
- (a) giving that person an opportunity to make representations; and
- (b) if the paying person is an individual, considering that person's financial means.

(7) The amount of costs to be paid under an order under paragraph (1) may be ascertained by–
- (a) summary assessment by the Tribunal;
- (b) agreement of a specified sum by the paying person and the person entitled to receive the costs ('the receiving person'); or
- (c) assessment of the whole or a specified part of the costs, including the costs of the assessment, incurred by the receiving person, if not agreed.

(8) Following an order for assessment under paragraph (7)(c), the paying person or the receiving person may apply to a county court for a detailed assessment of costs in accordance with the Civil Procedure Rules 1998 on the standard basis or, if specified in the order, on the indemnity basis.

(9) Upon making an order for the assessment of costs, the Tribunal may order an amount to be paid on account before the costs or expenses are assessed.

Representatives

11 (1) A party may appoint a representative (whether a legal representative or not) to represent that party in the proceedings.

(1A) Where a child or young person is a party to proceedings, that child or young person may appoint a representative under paragraph (1).

(2) If a party appoints a representative, that party (or the representative if the representative is a legal representative) must send or deliver to the Tribunal and to each other party written notice of the representative's name and address.

(3) Anything permitted or required to be done by a party under these Rules, a practice direction or a direction may be done by the representative of that party, except–
- (a) signing a witness statement; or
- (b) signing an application notice under rule 20 (the application notice) if the representative is not a legal representative.

(4) A person who receives due notice of the appointment of a representative–
- (a) must provide to the representative any document which is required to be provided to the represented party, and need not provide that document to the represented party; and
- (b) may assume that the representative is and remains authorised as such until they receive written notification that this is not so from the representative or the represented party.

(5) At a hearing a party may be accompanied by another person whose name and address has not been notified under paragraph (2) but who, subject to paragraph (8) and with the permission of the Tribunal, may act as a representative or otherwise assist in presenting the party's case at the hearing.

(6) Paragraphs (2) to (4) do not apply to a person who accompanies a party under paragraph (5).

(7) In a mental health case, if the patient has not appointed a representative, the Tribunal may appoint a legal representative for the patient where–
- (a) the patient has stated that they do not wish to conduct their own case or that they wish to be represented; or

(b) the patient lacks the capacity to appoint a representative but the Tribunal believes that it is in the patient's best interests for the patient to be represented.

(8) In a mental health case a party may not appoint as a representative, or be represented or assisted at a hearing by–

(a) a person liable to be detained or subject to guardianship, or who is a community patient, under the Mental Health Act 1983; or

(b) a person receiving treatment for mental disorder at the same hospital as the patient.

Calculating time

12 (1) An act required by these Rules, a practice direction or a direction to be done on or by a particular day must be done by 5pm on that day.

(2) If the time specified by these Rules, a practice direction or a direction for doing any act ends on a day other than a working day, the act is done in time if it is done on the next working day.

(3) In a special educational needs case or a disability discrimination in schools case–

(a) if the time for starting proceedings by providing the application notice to the Tribunal under rule 20 (the application notice) ends on a day from 25th December to 1st January inclusive, or on any day in August, the application notice is provided in time if it is provided to the Tribunal on the first working day after 1st January or 31st August, as appropriate; and

(b) the days from 25th December to 1st January inclusive and any day in August must not be counted when calculating the time by which any other act must be done.

(4) Paragraph (3)(b) does not apply where the Tribunal directs that an act must be done by or on a specified date.

Sending and delivery of documents

13 (1) Any document to be provided to the Tribunal under these Rules, a practice direction or a direction must be–

(a) sent by pre-paid post or delivered by hand to the address specified for the proceedings;

(b) sent by fax to the number specified for the proceedings; or

(c) sent or delivered by such other method as the Tribunal may permit or direct.

(1A) If the Tribunal permits or directs documents to be provided to it by email, the requirement for a signature on applications or references under rules 20(2), 22(4)(a) or 32(1)(b) may be satisfied by a typed instead of a handwritten signature.

(2) Subject to paragraph (3), if a party provides a fax number, email address or other details for the electronic transmission of documents to them, that party must accept delivery of documents by that method.

(3) If a party informs the Tribunal and all other parties that a particular form of communication, other than pre-paid post or delivery by hand, should not be used to provide documents to that party, that form of communication must not be so used.

(4) If the Tribunal or a party sends a document to a party or the Tribunal by email or any other electronic means of communication, the recipient may request that the sender provide a hard copy of the document to the recipient. The recipient must make such a request as soon as reasonably practicable after receiving the document electronically.

(5) The Tribunal and each party may assume that the address provided by a party or its representative is and remains the address to which documents should be sent or delivered until receiving written notification to the contrary.

Use of documents and information

14 (1) The Tribunal may make an order prohibiting the disclosure or publication of–

(a) specified documents or information relating to the proceedings; or

(b) any matter likely to lead members of the public to identify any person whom the Tribunal considers should not be identified.

(2) The Tribunal may give a direction prohibiting the disclosure of a document or information to a person if–

(a) the Tribunal is satisfied that such disclosure would be likely to cause that person or some other person serious harm; and

(b) the Tribunal is satisfied, having regard to the interests of justice, that it is proportionate to give such a direction.

(3) If a party ('the first party') considers that the Tribunal should give a direction under paragraph (2) prohibiting the disclosure of a document or information to another party ('the second party'), the first party must–

(a) exclude the relevant document or information from any documents that will be provided to the second party; and

(b) provide to the Tribunal the excluded document or information, and the reason for its exclusion, so that the Tribunal may decide whether the document or information should be disclosed to the second party or should be the subject of a direction under paragraph (2).

(4) The Tribunal must conduct proceedings as appropriate in order to give effect to a direction given under paragraph (2).

(5) If the Tribunal gives a direction under paragraph (2) which prevents disclosure to a party who has appointed a representative, the Tribunal may give a direction that the documents or information be disclosed to that representative if the Tribunal is satisfied that–

(a) disclosure to the representative would be in the interests of the party; and

(b) the representative will act in accordance with paragraph (6).

(6) Documents or information disclosed to a representative in accordance with a direction under paragraph (5) must not be disclosed either directly or indirectly to any other person without the Tribunal's consent.

(7) Unless the Tribunal gives a direction to the contrary, information about mental health cases and the names of any persons concerned in such cases must not be made public.

Evidence and submissions

15 (1) Without restriction on the general powers in rule 5(1) and (2) (case management powers), the Tribunal may give directions as to–

(a) issues on which it requires evidence or submissions;

(b) the nature of the evidence or submissions it requires;

(c) whether the parties are permitted or required to provide expert evidence, and if so whether the parties must jointly appoint a single expert to provide such evidence;

(d) any limit on the number of witnesses whose evidence a party may put forward, whether in relation to a particular issue or generally;

(e) the manner in which any evidence or submissions are to be provided, which may include a direction for them to be given–

(i) orally at a hearing; or

(ii) by written submissions or witness statement; and

(f) the time at which any evidence or submissions are to be provided.

(2) The Tribunal may–

(a) admit evidence whether or not–

(i) the evidence would be admissible in a civil trial in England and Wales; or

(ii) the evidence was available to a previous decision maker; or

(b) exclude evidence that would otherwise be admissible where–

(i) the evidence was not provided within the time allowed by a direction or a practice direction;

(ii) the evidence was otherwise provided in a manner that did not comply with a direction or a practice direction; or

(iii) it would otherwise be unfair to admit the evidence.

(3) The Tribunal may consent to a witness giving, or require any witness to give, evidence on oath, and may administer an oath for that purpose.

(4) In a special educational needs case the Tribunal may require–

(a) the parents of the child, or any other person with care of the child or parental responsibility for the child (as defined in section 3 of the Children Act 1989), to make the child available for examination or assessment by a suitably qualified professional person; or

(b) the person responsible for a school or educational setting to allow a suitably qualified professional person to have access to the school or educational setting for the purpose of assessing the child or the provision made, or to be made, for the child.

(5) The Tribunal may consider a failure by a party to comply with a requirement made under paragraph (4), in the absence of any good reason for such failure, as a failure to co-operate with the Tribunal, which could lead to a result which is adverse to that party's case.

Summoning of witnesses and orders to answer questions or produce documents

16 (1) On the application of a party or on its own initiative, the Tribunal may–

(a) by summons require any person to attend as a witness at a hearing at the time and place specified in the summons; or

(b) order any person to answer any questions or produce any documents in that person's possession or control which relate to any issue in the proceedings.

(2) A summons under paragraph (1)(a) must–

(a) give the person required to attend 14 days' notice of the hearing, or such shorter period as the Tribunal may direct; and

(b) where the person is not a party, make provision for the person's necessary expenses of attendance to be paid, and state who is to pay them.

(3) No person may be compelled to give any evidence or produce any document that the person could not be compelled to give or produce on a trial of an action in a court of law.

(4) A summons or order under this rule must–

(a) state that the person on whom the requirement is imposed may apply to the Tribunal to vary or set aside the summons or order, if they have not had an opportunity to object to it; and

(b) state the consequences of failure to comply with the summons or order.

Withdrawal

17 (1) Subject to paragraphs (2) and (3), a party may give notice of the withdrawal of its case, or any part of it–

(a) by sending or delivering to the Tribunal a written notice of withdrawal; or

(b) orally at a hearing.

(2) Notice of withdrawal will not take effect unless the Tribunal consents to the withdrawal except–

(a) in proceedings concerning the suitability of a person to work with children or vulnerable adults;

(b) in proceedings started by a reference under section 67 or 71(1) of the Mental Health Act 1983; or

(c) where a local authority notifies the Tribunal before the expiry of the time limit for submitting a response that it will not oppose the appeal in a special educational needs case.

(3) A party which started a mental health case by making a reference to the Tribunal under section 68, 71(2) or 75(1) of the Mental Health Act 1983 may not withdraw its case.

(4) A party which has withdrawn its case may apply to the Tribunal for the case to be reinstated.

(5) An application under paragraph (4) must be made in writing and be received by the Tribunal within 28 days after–

(a) the date on which the Tribunal received the notice under paragraph (1)(a); or

(b) the date of the hearing at which the case was withdrawn orally under paragraph (1)(b).

(6) The Tribunal must notify each party in writing that a withdrawal has taken effect under this rule.

(7) Where a local authority has notified the Tribunal before the expiry of the time limit for submitting a response that it will not oppose the appeal in a special educational needs case, the notice under paragraph (6) must state the date on which the Tribunal was so notified.

...

The application notice

20 (1) If rule 19 (application for leave) does not apply, an applicant must start proceedings before the Tribunal by sending or delivering an application notice to the Tribunal so that, unless paragraph (1A) applies, it is received–

- (a) if the time for providing the application notice is specified in another enactment, in accordance with that enactment;
- (b) in a case under the Suspension Regulations, within 10 working days after written notice of the decision being challenged was sent to the applicant;
- (c) in a special educational needs case–
    - (i) within 2 months after written notice of the decision being challenged was sent to the applicant; or
    - (ii) within 1 month from the date of issue of the mediation certificate if that date would be a later date than the date calculated by reference to paragraph (i);
- (d) in a case listed in the Schedule, within 3 months after written notice of the decision being challenged was sent to the applicant;
- (e) in any other case, within 28 days after written notice of the decision being challenged was sent to the applicant.

(1A) Where, in a health service case, the Tribunal has contingently removed a practitioner or performer from a list, an application may be made at any time if it is made under–

- (a) section 158(5)(a) of the National Health Service Act 2006;
- (b) section 114(5)(a) of the National Health Service (Wales) Act 2006;
- (c) regulation 15(6)(a) of the National Health Service (Performers Lists) Regulations 2004; or
- (d) regulation 15(6)(a) of the National Health Service (Performers Lists) (Wales) Regulations 2004.

(2) The application notice must be signed by the applicant and must include–

- (a) the name and address of the applicant;
- (b) the name and address of the applicant's representative (if any);
- (c) an address where documents for the applicant may be sent or delivered;
- (d) the name and address of any respondent;
- (e) details of the decision or act, or failure to decide or act, to which the proceedings relate;
- (f) the result the applicant is seeking;
- (g) the grounds on which the applicant relies; and
- (h) any further information or documents required by an applicable practice direction.

(3) The applicant must send with the application notice–

- (a) a copy of any written record of any decision under challenge,
- (b) any statement of reasons for that decision that the applicant has or can reasonably obtain, and
- (c) in a special educational needs case to which section 55(3) of the Children and Families Act 2014 (cases in which an appeal may be made only if a mediation certificate has been issued) applies, a copy of any certificate issued under subsection (4) or (5) of that section, as the case may be.

(4) If the applicant provides the application notice to the Tribunal later than the time required by paragraph (1) or by any extension of time under rule 5(3)(a) (power to extend time)–

- (a) the application notice must include a request for an extension of time and the reason why the application notice was not provided in time; and
- (b) unless the Tribunal extends time for the application notice under rule

5(3)(a) (power to extend time) the Tribunal must not admit the application notice.

(5) In proceedings under Suspension Regulations, the applicant must send or deliver a copy of the application notice and any accompanying documents to the respondent at the same time as it provides the application notice to the Tribunal.

(6) In proceedings other than proceedings under paragraph (5), when the Tribunal receives the application notice it must send a copy of the application notice and any accompanying documents to each other party.

The response

21 (1) When a respondent receives a copy of the application notice, the respondent must send or deliver to the Tribunal a response so that it is received–

    (a) in a case under the Suspension Regulations, within 3 working days after the respondent received the application notice;

    (b) in a health service case, within 21 days after the respondent received the application notice;

    (c) in a special educational needs case or a disability discrimination in schools case to which sub-paragraph (cc) does not apply, within 30 working days after the respondent received the application notice;

    (cc) in a disability discrimination in schools case that includes a claim for the reinstatement of a child young person who has been permanently excluded, within 15 working days after the respondent received the application notice;

    (d) in any other case, within 20 working days after the respondent received the application notice.

(2) The response must include–

    (a) the name and address of the respondent;

    (b) the name and address of the respondent's representative (if any);

    (c) an address where documents for the respondent may be sent or delivered;

    (d) a statement as to whether the respondent opposes the applicant's case and, if so, any grounds for such opposition which are not contained in another document provided with the response;

    (e) in a special educational needs case brought by a parent of a child, the views of the child about the issues raised by the proceedings, or the reason why the respondent has not ascertained those views; and

    (f) any further information or documents required by an applicable practice direction or direction.

(3) The response may include a statement as to whether the respondent would be content for the case to be dealt with without a hearing if the Tribunal considers it appropriate.

(4) If the respondent provides the response to the Tribunal later than the time required by paragraph (1) or by any extension of time under rule 5(3)(a) (power to extend time), the response must include a request for an extension of time and the reason why the response was not provided in time.

(5) The respondent must send or deliver a copy of the response and any accompanying documents to each other party at the same time as it provides the response to the Tribunal.

Chapter 2: Hearings

Decision with or without a hearing

23 (1) Subject to paragraphs (2) and (3), the Tribunal must hold a hearing before making a decision which disposes of proceedings unless–

    (a) each party has consented to the matter being decided without a hearing; and

    (b) the Tribunal considers that it is able to decide the matter without the hearing.

  (2) This rule does not apply to a decision under Part 5.

  (3) The Tribunal may dispose of proceedings without a hearing under rule 8 (striking out a party's case).

Entitlement to attend a hearing

24 Subject to rules 22(7) (exclusion of applicant from proceedings to consider an order under section 166(5) of the Education Act 2002) and 26(5) (exclusion of a person from a hearing)–

    (a) each party is entitled to attend a hearing; and

    (b) in a special educational needs case or a disability discrimination in schools case brought by a parent of a child, the child is entitled to attend a hearing and the Tribunal may permit the child to give evidence and to address the Tribunal.

Notice of hearings

25 (1) The Tribunal must give each party entitled to attend a hearing reasonable notice of the time and place of the hearing (including any adjourned or postponed hearing) and any changes to the time and place of the hearing.

  (2) The period of notice under paragraph (1) must be at least 14 days, except that–

    (a) in proceedings under Suspension Regulations the period of notice must be at least 3 working days;

    (b) the period of notice in respect of a hearing to consider the making of an order under section 166(5) of the Education Act 2002 must be at least 7 days; and

    (c) the Tribunal may give shorter notice–

      (i) with the parties' consent; or

      (ii) in urgent or exceptional circumstances.

Public and private hearings

26 (1) Subject to the following paragraphs, all hearings must be held in public.

  (2) Hearings in special educational needs cases and disability discrimination in schools cases must be held in private unless the Tribunal considers that it is in the interests of justice for a hearing to be held in public.

  (3) Subject to paragraph (2), the Tribunal may give a direction that a hearing, or part of it, is to be held in private.

  (4) Where a hearing, or part of it, is to be held in private, the Tribunal may determine who is permitted to attend the hearing or part of it.

  (5) The Tribunal may give a direction excluding from any hearing, or part of it–

    (a) any person whose conduct the Tribunal considers is disrupting or is likely to disrupt the hearing;

(b) any person whose presence the Tribunal considers is likely to prevent another person from giving evidence or making submissions freely;

(c) any person who the Tribunal considers should be excluded in order to give effect to a direction under rule 14(2) (withholding information likely to cause harm);

(d) any person where the purpose of the hearing would be defeated by the attendance of that person; or

(e) in a special educational needs case or a disability discrimination in schools case brought by a parent of a child or by a young person who lacks capacity to conduct their case, that child or young person, if the Tribunal considers that their presence at the hearing would be adverse to their interests.

(6) The Tribunal may give a direction excluding a witness from a hearing until that witness gives evidence.

Hearings in a party's absence

27 If a party fails to attend a hearing the Tribunal may proceed with the hearing if the Tribunal–

(a) is satisfied that the party has been notified of the hearing or that reasonable steps have been taken to notify the party of the hearing; and

(b) considers that it is in the interests of justice to proceed with the hearing.

Chapter 3: Decisions

Consent orders

29 (1) The Tribunal may, at the request of the parties but only if it considers it appropriate, make a consent order disposing of the proceedings and making such other appropriate provision as the parties have agreed.

(2) Notwithstanding any other provision of these Rules, the Tribunal need not hold a hearing before making an order under paragraph (1), or provide reasons for the order.

Decisions

30 (1) The Tribunal may give a decision orally at a hearing.

(2) Subject to rule 14(2) (withholding information likely to cause harm), the Tribunal must provide to each party as soon as reasonably practicable after making a decision (other than a decision under Part 5) which finally disposes of all issues in the proceedings or of a preliminary issue dealt with following a direction under rule 5(3)(e)–

(a) a decision notice stating the Tribunal's decision;

(b) written reasons for the decision; and

(c) notification of any rights of review or appeal against the decision and the time within which, and the manner in which, such rights of review or appeal may be exercised.

(3) In proceedings under Suspension Regulations, the documents and information referred to in paragraph (2) must be provided at the hearing or sent within 3 working days after the hearing.

(4) The Tribunal may provide written reasons for any decision to which paragraph (2) does not apply.

PART 5: CORRECTING, SETTING ASIDE, REVIEWING AND APPEALING TRIBUNAL DECISIONS

Interpretation

43   In this Part–

'appeal' means the exercise of a right of appeal on a point of law under section 11 of the 2007 Act; and

'review' means the review of a decision by the Tribunal under section 9 of the 2007 Act.

Clerical mistakes and accidental slips or omissions

44   The Tribunal may at any time correct any clerical mistake or other accidental slip or omission in a decision, direction or any document produced by it, by–

(a) sending notification of the amended decision or direction, or a copy of the amended document, to all parties; and

(b) making any necessary amendment to any information published in relation to the decision, direction or document.

Setting aside a decision which disposes of proceedings

45 (1) The Tribunal may set aside a decision which disposes of proceedings, or part of such a decision, and re-make the decision or the relevant part of it, if–

(a) the Tribunal considers that it is in the interests of justice to do so; and

(b) one or more of the conditions in paragraph (2) are satisfied.

(2) The conditions are–

(a) a document relating to the proceedings was not sent to, or was not received at an appropriate time by, a party or a party's representative;

(b) a document relating to the proceedings was not sent to the Tribunal at an appropriate time;

(c) a party, or a party's representative, was not present at a hearing related to the proceedings; or

(d) there has been some other procedural irregularity in the proceedings.

(3) A party applying for a decision, or part of a decision, to be set aside under paragraph (1) must make a written application to the Tribunal so that it is received no later than 28 days after the date on which the Tribunal sent notice of the decision to the party.

Application for permission to appeal

46 (1) A person seeking permission to appeal must make a written application to the Tribunal for permission to appeal.

(2) An application under paragraph (1) must be sent or delivered to the Tribunal so that it is received no later than 28 days after the latest of the dates that the Tribunal sends to the person making the application–

(za) the relevant decision notice;

(a) written reasons for the decision, if the decision disposes of–

(i) all issues in the proceedings; or

(ii) subject to paragraph (2A), a preliminary issue dealt with following a direction under rule 5(3)(e);

(b) notification of amended reasons for, or correction of, the decision following a review; or

(c) notification that an application for the decision to be set aside has been unsuccessful.

(2A) The Tribunal may direct that the 28 days within which a party may send or deliver to the Tribunal an application for permission to appeal against a decision that disposes of a preliminary issue shall run from the date of the decision that disposes of all issues in the proceedings.

(3) The date in paragraph (2)(c) applies only if the application for the decision to be set aside was made within the time stipulated in rule 45 (setting aside a decision which disposes of proceedings) or any extension of that time granted by the Tribunal.

(4) If the person seeking permission to appeal sends or delivers the application to the Tribunal later than the time required by paragraph (2) or by any extension of time under rule 5(3)(a) (power to extend time)–

(a) the application must include a request for an extension of time and the reason why the application was not provided in time; and

(b) unless the Tribunal extends time for the application under rule 5(3)(a) (power to extend time) the Tribunal must not admit the application.

(5) An application under paragraph (1) must–

(a) identify the decision of the Tribunal to which it relates;

(b) identify the alleged error or errors of law in the decision; and

(c) state the result the party making the application is seeking.

Tribunal's consideration of application for permission to appeal

47 (1) On receiving an application for permission to appeal the Tribunal must first consider, taking into account the overriding objective in rule 2, whether to review the decision in accordance with rule 49 (review of a decision).

(2) If the Tribunal decides not to review the decision, or reviews the decision and decides to take no action in relation to the decision, or part of it, the Tribunal must consider whether to give permission to appeal in relation to the decision or that part of it.

(3) The Tribunal must send a record of its decision to the parties as soon as practicable.

(4) If the Tribunal refuses permission to appeal it must send with the record of its decision–

(a) a statement of its reasons for such refusal; and

(b) notification of the right to make an application to the Upper Tribunal for permission to appeal and the time within which, and the method by which, such application must be made.

(5) The Tribunal may give permission to appeal on limited grounds, but must comply with paragraph (4) in relation to any grounds on which it has refused permission.

Application for review in special educational needs cases

48 (1) This rule applies to decisions which dispose of proceedings in special educational needs cases, but not to decisions under this Part.

(2) A party may make a written application to the Tribunal for a review of a decision if circumstances relevant to the decision have changed since the decision was made.

(3) An application under paragraph (2) must be sent or delivered to the Tribunal

so that it is received within 28 days after the date on which the Tribunal sent the decision notice recording the Tribunal's decision to the party making the application.

(4) If a party sends or delivers an application to the Tribunal later than the time required by paragraph (3) or by any extension of time under rule 5(3)(a) (power to extend time)–

    (a) the application must include a request for an extension of time and the reason why the application was not provided in time; and

    (b) unless the Tribunal extends time for the application under rule 5(3)(a) (power to extend time) the Tribunal must not admit the application.

Review of a decision

49 (1) The Tribunal may only undertake a review of a decision–

    (a) pursuant to rule 47(1) (review on an application for permission to appeal) if it is satisfied that there was an error of law in the decision; or

    (b) pursuant to rule 48 (application for review in special educational needs cases).

(2) The Tribunal must notify the parties in writing of the outcome of any review, and of any right of appeal in relation to the outcome.

(3) If the Tribunal takes any action in relation to a decision following a review without first giving every party an opportunity to make representations, the notice under paragraph (2) must state that any party that did not have an opportunity to make representations may apply for such action to be set aside and for the decision to be reviewed again.

Power to treat an application as a different type of application

50   The Tribunal may treat an application for a decision to be corrected, set aside or reviewed, or for permission to appeal against a decision, as an application for any other one of those things.

SEND code of practice: extracts[1]

---

1   *Special educational needs and disability code of practice: 0 to 25 years. Statutory guidance
for organisations which work with and support children and young people who have special
educational needs or disabilities* Department for Education/Department of Health,
January 2015.

9 Education, Health and Care needs assessments and plans

What the chapter covers

This chapter covers all the key stages in statutory assessment and planning and preparing the Education, Health and Care (EHC) plan, and guidance on related topics.

It includes:

- when a local authority **must** carry out an EHC needs assessment, including in response to a request
- who **must** be consulted and provide advice
- the statutory steps required by the process of EHC needs assessment and EHC plan development, including timescales
- how to write an EHC plan
- requesting a particular school, college or other institution
- requesting and agreeing Personal Budgets, including sources of funding
- finalising and maintaining an EHC plan
- transferring an EHC plan
- reviews and re-assessments of an EHC plan
- ceasing an EHC plan
- disclosing an EHC plan

Relevant legislation

Primary

Sections 36 – 50 of the Children and Families Act 2014

The Care Act 2014

Section 2 of the Chronically Sick and Disabled Persons Act 1970

Sections 17, 20 and 47 of the Children Act 1989

Regulations

The Special Educational Needs and Disability Regulations 2014

The Special Educational Needs (Personal Budgets) Regulations 2014

Special Educational Needs (Miscellaneous Amendments) Regulations 2014

The Community Care Services for Carers and Children's Services (Direct Payments) Regulations 2009

The National Health Service (Direct Payments) Regulations 2013

The Special Educational Needs and Disability (Detained Persons) Regulations 2015

Introduction

9.1 The majority of children and young people with SEN or disabilities will have their needs met within local mainstream early years settings, schools or colleges (as set out in the information on identification and support in Chapters 5, 6 and 7). Some children and young people may require an EHC needs assessment in order for the local authority to decide whether it is necessary for it to make provision in accordance with an EHC plan.

9.2 The purpose of an EHC plan is to make special educational provision to meet the special educational needs of the child or young person, to secure the best possible outcomes for them across education, health and social care and, as they get older, prepare them for adulthood. To achieve this, local authorities use the information from the assessment to:

- establish and record the views, interests and aspirations of the parents and child or young person

- provide a full description of the child or young person's special educational needs and any health and social care needs

- establish outcomes across education, health and social care based on the child or young person's needs and aspirations

- specify the provision required and how education, health and care services will work together to meet the child or young person's needs and support the achievement of the agreed outcomes

9.3 A local authority **must** conduct an assessment of education, health and care needs when it considers that it may be necessary for special educational provision to be made for the child or young person in accordance with an EHC plan. The factors a local authority should take into account in deciding whether it needs to undertake an EHC needs assessment are set out in paragraphs 9.14 to 9.15, and the factors a local authority should take into account in deciding whether an EHC plan is necessary are set out in paragraphs 9.53 to 9.56. The EHC needs assessment should not normally be the first step in the process, rather it should follow on from planning already undertaken with parents and young people in conjunction with an early years provider, school, post-16 institution or other provider. In a very small minority of cases children or young people may demonstrate such significant difficulties that a school or other provider may consider it impossible or inappropriate to carry out its full chosen assessment procedure. For example, where its concerns may have led to a further diagnostic assessment or examination which shows the child or young person to have severe sensory impairment or other impairment which, without immediate specialist intervention beyond the capacity of the school or other provider, would lead to increased learning difficulties.

9.4   During the transition period local authorities will transfer children and young people with statements onto the new system (see paragraphs x and xi of the Introduction and paragraph 1.17 in Chapter 1, Principles, for more information on transition and transfer of statements). No-one should lose their statement and not have it replaced with an EHC plan simply because the system is changing.

9.5   EHC plans should be forward-looking documents that help raise aspirations and outline the provision required to meet assessed needs to support the child or young person in achieving their ambitions. EHC plans should specify how services will be delivered as part of a whole package and explain how best to achieve the outcomes sought across education, health and social care for the child or young person.

9.6   An EHC needs assessment will not always lead to an EHC plan. The information gathered during an EHC needs assessment may indicate ways in which the school, college or other provider can meet the child or young person's needs without an EHC plan.

9.7   The statutory processes and timescales set out in this chapter **must** be followed by local authorities. Local authorities should conduct assessments and prepare and maintain EHC plans in the most efficient way possible, working collaboratively with children and young people and their parents. It should be possible to complete the process more quickly than the statutory timescales permit, except in more complex cases or where there is disagreement. It is vital that a timely process is supported by high quality engagement with the child and his or her parents or the young person throughout the assessment, planning and review process.

Requesting an EHC needs assessment

Relevant legislation: Section 36 of the Children and Families Act 2014

9.8   The following people have a specific right to ask a local authority to conduct an education, health and care needs assessment for a child or young person aged between 0 and 25:

143

- the child's parent

- a young person over the age of 16 but under the age of 25, and

- a person acting on behalf of a school or post-16 institution (this should ideally be with the knowledge and agreement of the parent or young person where possible)

9.9   In addition, anyone else can bring a child or young person who has (or may have) SEN to the attention of the local authority, particularly where they think an EHC needs assessment may be necessary. This could include, for example, foster carers, health and social care professionals, early years practitioners, youth offending teams or probation services, those responsible for education in custody, school or college staff or a family friend. Bringing a child or young person to the attention of the local authority will be undertaken on an individual basis where there are specific concerns. This should be done with the knowledge and, where possible, agreement of the child's parent or the young person.

9.10   Children and young people under 19 in youth custodial establishments also have the right to request an assessment for an EHC plan. The child's parent, the young person themselves or the professionals working with them can ask the home local authority to conduct an EHC needs assessment while they are still detained. The process and principles for considering and carrying out an EHC needs assessment and maintaining an EHC plan for children and young people in youth custody are set out in Chapter 10, Children and young people in specific circumstances.

Considering whether an EHC needs assessment is necessary

Relevant legislation: Section 36 of the Children and Families Act 2014 and Regulations 3, 4, and 5 of the SEND Regulations 2014

9.11   Following a request for an EHC needs assessment, or the child or young person having otherwise been brought to its attention, the local authority **must** determine whether an EHC needs assessment is necessary. The local authority **must** make a decision and communicate the decision to the child's parent or to the young person within 6 weeks of receiving the request. The local authority does not have to consider whether an EHC needs assessment is necessary where it has already undertaken an EHC needs assessment for the child or young person during the previous six months, although the local authority may choose to do so if it thinks it is appropriate.

9.12   The local authority **must** notify the child's parent or the young person that it is considering whether an EHC assessment is necessary, and **must** consult the child's parent or the young person as soon as practicable following a request for an EHC needs assessment (or having otherwise become responsible). This is particularly important where the request was not made by the child's parent or the young person, so they have sufficient time to provide their views. In considering whether an EHC needs assessment is necessary, local authorities **must** have regard to the views, wishes and feelings of the child and his or her parent, or the young person. At an early stage, the local authority should establish how the child and his or her parent or the young person can best be kept informed and supported to participate as fully as possible in decision-making. The local authority **must** arrange for the child and his or her parent or the young person to be provided with advice and information relevant to the child or young person's SEN, (for more information, see paragraph 9.21 and Chapter 2).

9.13   Where the local authority considers that special educational provision may need to be made in accordance with an EHC plan and is considering whether an EHC needs assessment is necessary, it **must** notify:

- the child's parent or the young person (and **must** inform them of their right to express written or oral views and submit evidence to the local authority)

- the health service (the relevant Clinical Commissioning Group (CCG) or NHS England where it has responsibility for a child or young person)

- local authority officers responsible for social care for children or young people with SEN

- where a child attends an early years setting, the manager of that setting

- where a child or young person is registered at a school, the head teacher (or equivalent)

- where the young person attends a post-16 institution, the principal (or equivalent)

9.14   In considering whether an EHC needs assessment is necessary, the local authority should consider whether there is evidence that despite the early years provider, school or post-16 institution having taken relevant and purposeful action to identify, assess and meet the special educational needs of the child or young person, the child or young person has not made expected progress. To inform their decision the local authority will need to take into account a wide range of evidence, and should pay particular attention to:

- evidence of the child or young person's academic attainment (or developmental milestones in younger children) and rate of progress

145

- information about the nature, extent and context of the child or young person's SEN

- evidence of the action already being taken by the early years provider, school or post-16 institution to meet the child or young person's SEN

- evidence that where progress has been made, it has only been as the result of much additional intervention and support over and above that which is usually provided

- evidence of the child or young person's physical, emotional and social development and health needs, drawing on relevant evidence from clinicians and other health professionals and what has been done to meet these by other agencies, and

- where a young person is aged over 18, the local authority **must** consider whether the young person requires additional time, in comparison to the majority of others of the same age who do not have special educational needs, to complete their education or training. Remaining in formal education or training should help young people to achieve education and training outcomes, building on what they have learned before and preparing them for adult life.

9.15 A young person who was well supported through the Local Offer while at school may move to a further education (FE) college where the same range or level of support is not available. An EHC plan may then be needed to ensure that support is provided and co-ordinated effectively in the new environment. It may also be the case that young people acquire SEN through illness or accident, or have an existing condition that requires increasing support as they get older.

9.16 Local authorities may develop criteria as guidelines to help them decide when it is necessary to carry out an EHC needs assessment (and following assessment, to decide whether it is necessary to issue an EHC plan). However, local authorities **must** be prepared to depart from those criteria where there is a compelling reason to do so in any particular case and demonstrate their willingness to do so where individual circumstances warrant such a departure. Local authorities **must not** apply a 'blanket' policy to particular groups of children or certain types of need, as this would prevent the consideration of a child's or young person's needs individually and on their merits.

9.17 The local authority **must** decide whether or not to proceed with an EHC needs assessment, and **must** inform the child's parent or the young person of their decision within a maximum of six weeks from receiving a request for an EHC needs assessment (or having otherwise become responsible). The local authority **must** give its reasons for this decision where it decides not to proceed. The local authority **must** also notify the other parties listed in section 9.13 above of its decision.

9.18   If the local authority intends to conduct an EHC needs assessment, it **must** ensure the child's parent or the young person is fully included from the start and made aware of opportunities to offer views and information.

9.19   If the local authority decides not to conduct an EHC needs assessment it **must** inform the child's parents or the young person of their right to appeal that decision and the time limit for doing so, of the requirement for them to consider mediation should they wish to appeal, and the availability of information, advice and support and disagreement resolution services. The local authority should also provide feedback collected during the process of considering whether an EHC needs assessment is necessary, including evidence from professionals, which the parent, young person, early years provider, school or post-16 institution may find useful.

Principles underpinning co-ordinated assessment and planning

Relevant legislation: Section 19 of the Children and Families Act 2014 and Regulations 7 and 9 of the SEND Regulations 2014

9.20   Children, young people and families should experience well co-ordinated assessment and planning leading to timely, well informed decisions. The following general principles underpin effective assessment and planning processes:

Involving children, young people and parents in decision-making

9.21   Local authorities **must** consult the child and the child's parent or the young person throughout the process of assessment and production of an EHC plan. They should also involve the child as far as possible in this process. The needs of the individual child and young person should sit at the heart of the assessment and planning process. Planning should start with the individual and local authorities **must** have regard to the views, wishes and feelings of the child, child's parent or young person, their aspirations, the outcomes they wish to seek and the support they need to achieve them. It should enable children, young people and parents to have more control over decisions about their support including the use of a Personal Budget for those with an EHC plan.

9.22   The assessment and planning process should:

- focus on the child or young person as an individual

147

- enable children and young people and their parents to express their views, wishes and feelings

- enable children and young people and their parents to be part of the decision-making process

- be easy for children, young people and their parents or carers to understand, and use clear ordinary language and images rather than professional jargon

- highlight the child or young person's strengths and capabilities

- enable the child or young person, and those that know them best to say what they have done, what they are interested in and what outcomes they are seeking in the future

- tailor support to the needs of the individual

- organise assessments to minimise demands on families

- bring together relevant professionals to discuss and agree together the overall approach, and

- deliver an outcomes-focused and co-ordinated plan for the child or young person and their parents

9.23   This approach is often referred to as a person-centred approach. By using this approach within a family context, professionals and local authorities can ensure that children, young people and parents are involved in all aspects of planning and decision-making.

9.24   Local authorities should support and encourage the involvement of children, young people and parents or carers by:

- providing them with access to the relevant information in accessible formats

- giving them time to prepare for discussions and meetings, and

- dedicating time in discussions and meetings to hear their views

9.25   In addition, some children and young people will require support from an advocate where necessary (this could be a family member or a professional) to ensure that their views are heard and acknowledged. They may need support in expressing views about their education, their health, the future and how to prepare for it, including where they will live, relationships, control of their finances, how they will

148

participate in the community and how they will achieve greater autonomy and independence. Local authorities should ensure that children and young people who need it have access to this support.

9.26   Practitioners in all services involved in the assessment and planning process need to be skilled in working with children, parents and young people to help them make informed decisions. All practitioners should have access to training so they can do this effectively.

Support for children, young people and parents

9.27   Local authorities should have early discussions with parents or the young person about what the EHC needs assessment process and development of an EHC plan will involve, and the range of options that will be available, such as different types of educational institution and options for Personal Budgets and how these may differ depending on the type of educational institution for which the parents or young person express a preference.

9.28   Local authorities **must** work with parents and children and young people to understand how best to minimise disruption for them and their family life. For example, multiple appointments should be co-ordinated or combined where possible and appropriate.

9.29   Local authorities **must** provide all parents, children and young people with impartial information, advice and support in relation to SEN to enable them to take part effectively in the assessment and planning process. This will include the EHC needs assessment process, EHC plans and Personal Budgets (including the take-up and ongoing management of direct payments). This should include information on key working and independent supporters as appropriate. (See Chapter 2 for more information.)

Co-ordination

9.30   Local authorities are responsible for ensuring that there is effective co-ordination of the assessment and development process for an EHC plan. The co-ordination should include:

- planning the process to meet the needs of children, parents and young people

- timing meetings to minimise family disruption

- keeping the child's parent or young person informed through a single point of contact wherever possible and

149

- ensuring relevant professionals have sufficient notice to be able to contribute to the process

9.31 The EHC needs assessment and plan development process should be supported by senior leadership teams monitoring the quality and sufficiency of EHC needs assessments through robust quality assurance systems. Families should have confidence that those overseeing the assessment process will be impartial and act in their best interests.

Sharing information

9.32 Information sharing is vital to support an effective assessment and planning process which fully identifies needs and outcomes and the education, health and care provision needed by the child or young person. Local authorities with their partners should establish local protocols for the effective sharing of information which addresses confidentiality, consent and security of information (see the References section under Chapter 9 for a link to the DfE advice '*Information sharing for practitioners and managers*'). Agencies should work together to agree local protocols for information collection and management so as to inform planning of provision for children and young people with SEN or disabilities at both individual and strategic levels.

9.33 As far as possible, there should be a 'tell us once' approach to sharing information during the assessment and planning process so that families and young people do not have to repeat the same information to different agencies, or different practitioners and services within each agency.

9.34 Local authorities **must** discuss with the child and young person and their parents what information they are happy for the local authority to share with other agencies. A record should be made of what information can be shared and with whom. (See paragraphs 9.211 to 9.213 for further information on confidentiality and disclosing EHC plans.)

Timely provision of services

9.35 Where particular services are assessed as being needed, such as those resulting from statutory social care assessments under the Children Act 1989 or adult social care legislation, their provision should be delivered in line with the relevant statutory guidance and should not be delayed until the EHC plan is complete. For social care, help and support should be given to the child and family as soon as a need is identified and not wait until the completion of an EHC needs assessment.

Cross-agency working

9.36   Joint working between local authorities and CCGs in the development of an EHC plan supports the provision of effective services for children and young people with SEN. (See Chapter 3, Working together across Education, Health and Care for joint outcomes, for guidance on services working together, and the section later in this chapter on agreeing the health provision in EHC plans.)

9.37   Consideration should be given to:

- the range of professionals across education, health and care who need to be involved and their availability

- flexibility for professionals to engage in a range of ways and to plan their input as part of forward planning

- providing opportunities for professionals to feed back on the process, and its implementation, to support continuous improvement

Looked after children

9.38   Local authorities should be particularly aware of the need to avoid any delays for looked after children and carry out the EHC needs assessment in the shortest possible timescale. Addressing a looked after child's special educational needs will be a crucial part of avoiding breakdown in their care placement.

Timescales for EHC needs assessment and preparation of an EHC plan

Relevant legislation: Sections 36, 37, 38, 39 and 40 of the Children and Families Act 2014 and Regulations 4, 5, 8, 10, and 13 of the SEND Regulations 2014

9.39   The process of EHC needs assessment and EHC plan development **must** be carried out in a timely manner. The time limits set out below are the maximum time allowed. However, steps **must** be completed as soon as practicable. Local authorities should ensure that they have planned sufficient time for each step of the process, so that wherever possible, any issues or disagreements can be resolved within the statutory timescales. Where the child's parent or the young person agrees, it may be possible to carry out steps much more quickly and flexibly. For example, a child's parent or the young person might be happy to agree changes to an EHC plan following a review while at the review meeting, where all parties are content. Under no circumstances should the child's parent or the young person be put under pressure to agree things more quickly than they feel comfortable with, and where there is any doubt or the child's parent or the young person requests more time, local authorities **must** follow the steps and timescales set out in this guidance.

9.40 The whole process of EHC needs assessment and EHC plan development, from the point when an assessment is requested (or a child or young person is brought to the local authority's attention) until the final EHC plan is issued, **must** take no more than 20 weeks (subject to exemptions set out below).

9.41 The following specific requirements apply:

- Local authorities **must** give their decision in response to any request for an EHC needs assessment within a maximum of 6 weeks from when the request was received or the point at which a child or young person was brought to the local authority's attention

- When local authorities request information as part of the EHC needs assessment process, those supplying the information **must** respond in a timely manner and within a maximum of 6 weeks from the date of the request

- If a local authority decides, following an EHC needs assessment, not to issue an EHC plan, it **must** inform the child's parent or the young person within a maximum of 16 weeks from the request for a EHC needs assessment, and

- The child's parent or the young person **must** be given 15 calendar days to consider and provide views on a draft EHC plan and ask for a particular school or other institution to be named in it

9.42 Where there are exceptional circumstances, it may not be reasonable to expect local authorities and other partners to comply with the time limits above. The Special Educational Needs and Disability Regulations 2014 set out specific exemptions. These include where:

- appointments with people from whom the local authority has requested information are missed by the child or young person (this only applies to the duty on partners to comply with a request under the EHC needs assessment process within six weeks)

- the child or young person is absent from the area for a period of at least 4 weeks

- exceptional personal circumstances affect the child or his/her parent, or the young person, and

- the educational institution is closed for at least 4 weeks, which may delay the submission of information from the school or other institution (this does

152

not apply to the duty on partners to comply with a request under the EHC needs assessment process within six weeks)

9.43   The child's parent or the young person should be informed if exemptions apply so that they are aware of, and understand, the reason for any delays. Local authorities should aim to keep delays to a minimum and as soon as the conditions that led to an exemption no longer apply the local authority should endeavour to complete the process as quickly as possible. All remaining elements of the process **must** be completed within their prescribed periods, regardless of whether exemptions have delayed earlier elements.

9.44   The diagram on the following page sets out the statutory timescales and decision points for the process of EHC needs assessment and EHC plan development that local authorities **must** adhere to, subject to the specific exemptions set out in paragraph 9.42. Throughout the statutory process for EHC needs assessment and EHC plan development, local authorities **must** work in partnership with the child and his or her parent or the young person. There is more information earlier in this chapter on the principles of working with parents and young people, and relevant statutory requirements.

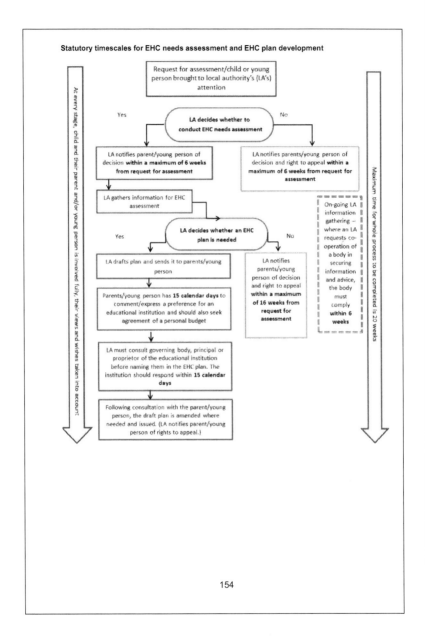

Statutory timescales for EHC needs assessment and EHC plan development

At every stage, child and their parent and/or young person is involved fully, their views and wishes taken into account

Request for assessment/child or young person brought to local authority's (LA's) attention

Yes — **LA decides whether to conduct EHC needs assessment** — No

LA notifies parent/young person of decision **within a maximum of 6 weeks from request for assessment**

LA notifies parents/young person of decision and right to appeal **within a maximum of 6 weeks from request for assessment**

LA gathers information for EHC assessment

Yes — **LA decides whether an EHC plan is needed** — No

LA drafts plan and sends it to parents/young person

LA notifies parents/young person of decision and right to appeal **within a maximum of 16 weeks from request for assessment**

Parents/young person has **15 calendar days** to comment/express a preference for an educational institution and should also seek agreement of a personal budget

LA must consult governing body, principal or proprietor of the educational institution before naming them in the EHC plan. The institution should respond within **15 calendar days**

Following consultation with the parent/young person, the draft plan is amended where needed and issued. (LA notifies parent/young person of rights to appeal.)

On-going LA information gathering – where an LA requests co-operation of a body in securing information and advice, the body must comply **within 6 weeks**

Maximum time for whole process to be completed is 20 weeks

Advice and information for EHC needs assessments

Relevant legislation: Section 36 of the Children and Families Act 2014 and Regulations 6, 7, and 8 of the SEND Regulations 2014

9.45 When carrying out an EHC needs assessment the local authority should seek views and information from the child using appropriate methods, which might include observation for a very young child, or the use of different methods of communication such as the Picture Exchange Communication System.

9.46 The local authority **must** gather advice from relevant professionals about the child or young person's education, health and care needs, desired outcomes and special educational, health and care provision that may be required to meet identified needs and achieve desired outcomes.

9.47 The local authority should consider with the child's parent or the young person and the parties listed under paragraph 9.49 the range of advice required to enable a full EHC needs assessment to take place. The principle underpinning this is 'tell us once', avoiding the child's parent or the young person having to provide the same information multiple times. The child's parent or the young person should be supported to understand the range of assessments available so they can take an informed decision about whether existing advice is satisfactory. The local authority **must not** seek further advice if such advice has already been provided (for any purpose) and the person providing the advice, the local authority and the child's parent or the young person are all satisfied that it is sufficient for the assessment process. In making this decision, the local authority and the person providing the advice should ensure the advice remains current.

9.48 Decisions about the level of engagement and advice needed from different parties will be informed by knowledge of the child or young person held by the early years provider, school or post-16 institution they attend. For example, if the educational provider believes there are signs of safeguarding or welfare issues, a statutory social care assessment may be necessary. If there are signs of an underlying health difficulty, a specialist health assessment may be necessary.

9.49 In seeking advice and information, the local authority should consider with professionals what advice they can contribute to ensure the assessment covers all the relevant education, health and care needs of the child or young person. Advice and information **must** be sought as follows (subject to para 9.47 above):

- Advice and information from the child's parent or the young person. The local authority **must** take into account his or her views, wishes and feelings

- Educational advice and information from the manager, headteacher or principal of the early years setting, school or post-16 or other institution attended by the child or young person. Where this is not available the authority **must** seek advice from a person with experience of teaching children or young people with SEN, or knowledge of the provision which may meet the child's or young person's needs. Where advice from a person with relevant teaching experience or knowledge is not available and the child or young person does not attend an educational institution, the local authority **must** seek educational advice and information from a person responsible for educational provision for the child or young person

- If the child or young person is either vision or hearing impaired, or both, the educational advice and information **must** be given after consultation with a person who is qualified to teach pupils or students with these impairments

- Medical advice and information from health care professionals with a role in relation to the child's or young person's health (see the section later in this chapter on agreeing the health provision in EHC plans)

- Psychological advice and information from an educational psychologist who should normally be employed or commissioned by the local authority. The educational psychologist should consult any other psychologists known to be involved with the child or young person

- Social care advice and information from or on behalf of the local authority, including, if appropriate, children in need or child protection assessments, information from a looked after child's care plan, or adult social care assessments for young people over 18. In some cases, a child or young person may already have a statutory child in need or child protection plan, or an adult social care plan, from which information should be drawn for the EHC needs assessment

- From Year 9 onwards, advice and information related to provision to assist the child or young person in preparation for adulthood and independent living

- Advice and information from any person requested by the child's parent or young person, where the local authority considers it reasonable to do so. For example, they may suggest consulting a GP or other health professional

- Advice from a youth offending team, where the child or young person is detained in a Young Offender Institution. Where the young person is

156

serving their sentence in the community the local authority should seek such advice where it considers it appropriate

- Any other advice and information which the local authority considers appropriate for a satisfactory assessment, for example:

  o   Early Help Assessments

  o   in the case of children of members of the Armed Forces, from the Children's Education Advisory Service

  o   in the case of a looked after child, from the Virtual School Head in the authority that looks after the child and the child's Designated Teacher and the Designated Doctor or Nurse for looked after children

9.50   The local authority **must** give to those providing advice copies of any representations made by the child's parent or the young person, and any evidence submitted by or at the request of the child's parent or the young person.

9.51   The evidence and advice submitted by those providing it should be clear, accessible and specific. They should provide advice about outcomes relevant for the child or young person's age and phase of education and strategies for their achievement. The local authority may provide guidance about the structure and format of advice and information to be provided. Professionals should limit their advice to areas in which they have expertise. They may comment on the amount of provision they consider a child or young person requires and local authorities should not have blanket policies which prevent them from doing so.

9.52   Advice and information requested by the local authority **must** be provided within six weeks of the request, and should be provided more quickly wherever possible, to enable a timely process. (This is subject to the exemptions set out in paragraph 9.42.)

Deciding whether to issue an EHC plan

Relevant legislation: Sections 36 and 37 of the Children and Families Act 2014

9.53   Where, in the light of an EHC needs assessment, it is necessary for special educational provision to be made in accordance with an EHC plan, the local authority **must** prepare a plan. Where a local authority decides it is necessary to issue an EHC plan, it **must** notify the child's parent or the young person and give the reasons for its decision. The local authority should ensure it allows enough time to prepare the draft plan and complete the remaining steps in the process within the 20-week overall time limit within which it **must** issue the finalised EHC plan.

157

9.54 In deciding whether to make special educational provision in accordance with an EHC plan, the local authority should consider all the information gathered during the EHC needs assessment and set it alongside that available to the local authority prior to the assessment. Local authorities should consider both the child or young person's SEN and the special educational provision made for the child or young person and whether:

- the information from the EHC needs assessment confirms the information available on the nature and extent of the child or young person's SEN prior to the EHC needs assessment, and whether

- the special educational provision made prior to the EHC needs assessment was well matched to the SEN of the child or young person

9.55 Where, despite appropriate assessment and provision, the child or young person is not progressing, or not progressing sufficiently well, the local authority should consider what further provision may be needed. The local authority should take into account:

- whether the special educational provision required to meet the child or young person's needs can reasonably be provided from within the resources normally available to mainstream early years providers, schools and post-16 institutions, or

- whether it may be necessary for the local authority to make special educational provision in accordance with an EHC plan

9.56 Where a local authority carries out an EHC needs assessment for a child or young person and

- their circumstances have changed significantly, or

- the child or young person has recently been placed in a new setting, or

- their special educational needs were identified shortly before the EHC needs assessment,

and no comparable special educational provision was being made for the child or young person prior to the EHC needs assessment, then the local authority should consider what new special educational provision is needed, taking into account the points in 9.55 above.

Decision not to issue an EHC plan

Relevant legislation: Section 36 of the Children and Families Act 2014 and Regulation 10 of the SEND Regulations 2014

9.57   Following the completion of an EHC needs assessment, if the local authority decides that an EHC plan is not necessary, it **must** notify the child's parent or the young person, the early years provider, school or post-16 institution currently attended, and the health service and give the reasons for its decision. This notification **must** take place as soon as practicable and at the latest within 16 weeks of the initial request or of the child or young person having otherwise been brought to the local authority's attention. The local authority **must** also inform the child's parent or the young person of their right to appeal that decision and the time limit for doing so, of the requirement for them to consider mediation should they wish to appeal, and the availability of information, advice and support and disagreement resolution services.

9.58   The local authority should ensure that the child's parent or the young person are aware of the resources available to meet SEN within mainstream provision and other support set out in the Local Offer.

9.59   The local authority should provide written feedback collected during the EHC needs assessment process, which the child's parent, the young person, early years provider, school or post-16 institution can understand and may find useful, including evidence and reports from professionals. This information can then inform how the outcomes sought for the child or young person can be achieved through special educational provision made by the early years provider, school or post-16 institution and co-ordinated support from other agencies.

Transparent and consistent decision-making

9.60   It is helpful for local authorities to set up moderating groups to support transparency in decision-making. Such groups can improve the consistency of decision-making about whether to carry out an EHC needs assessment and whether to issue an EHC plan. Through sampling and retrospective comparison, moderating groups can also help local authority practice to become more robust and clearly understood by schools, early years settings, post-16 institutions, young people and parents.

Writing the EHC plan

Relevant legislation: Section 37 of the Children and Families Act 2014 and Regulations 11 and 12 of the SEND Regulations 2014

9.61 The following principles and requirements apply to local authorities and those contributing to the preparation of an EHC plan:

- Decisions about the content of EHC plans should be made openly and collaboratively with parents, children and young people. It should be clear how the child or young person has contributed to the plan and how their views are reflected in it

- EHC plans should describe positively what the child or young person can do and has achieved

- EHC plans should be clear, concise, understandable and accessible to parents, children, young people, providers and practitioners. They should be written so they can be understood by professionals in any local authority

- In preparing the EHC plan the local authority **must** consider how best to achieve the outcomes sought for the child or young person. The local authority **must** take into account the evidence received as part of the EHC needs assessment

- EHC plans **must** specify the outcomes sought for the child or young person. Outcomes in EHC plans should be SMART (specific, measurable, achievable, realistic, time-bound). See the section on 'Outcomes' (paragraph 9.64 onwards) for detailed guidance on outcomes.

- Where a young person or parent is seeking an innovative or alternative way to receive their support services – particularly through a Personal Budget, but not exclusively so – then the planning process should include the consideration of those solutions with support and advice available to assist the parent or young person in deciding how best to receive their support

- EHC plans should show how education, health and care provision will be co-ordinated wherever possible to support the child or young person to achieve their outcomes. The plan should also show how the different types of provision contribute to specific outcomes

- EHC plans should be forward looking – for example, anticipating, planning and commissioning for important transition points in a child or young person's life, including planning and preparing for their transition to adult life

- EHC plans should describe how informal (family and community) support as well as formal support from statutory agencies can help in achieving agreed outcomes

- EHC plans should have a review date (which should link to other regular reviews, including the child in need plan or child protection plan reviews if appropriate)

Content of EHC plans

Relevant legislation: Section 37 of the Children and Families Act 2014 and Regulation 12 of the SEND Regulations 2014

9.62   The format of an EHC plan will be agreed locally, and it is expected that the plan will reflect the principles set out in Chapter 1 of this document. However, as a statutory minimum, EHC plans **must** include the following sections, which **must** be separately labelled from each other using the letters below. The sections do not have to be in the order below and local authorities may use an action plan in tabular format to include different sections and demonstrate how provision will be integrated, as long as the sections are separately labelled.

Section A: The views, interests and aspirations of the child and his or her parents or the young person.

Section B: The child or young person's special educational needs.

Section C: The child or young person's health needs which are related to their SEN.

Section D: The child or young person's social care needs which are related to their SEN or to a disability.

Section E: The outcomes sought for the child or the young person. This should include outcomes for adult life. The EHC plan should also identify the arrangements for the setting of shorter term targets by the early years provider, school, college or other education or training provider.

Section F: The special educational provision required by the child or the young person.

Section G: Any health provision reasonably required by the learning difficulties or disabilities which result in the child or young person having SEN. Where an Individual Health Care Plan is made for them, that plan should be included.

Section H1: Any social care provision which **must** be made for a child or young person under 18 resulting from section 2 of the Chronically Sick and Disabled Persons Act 1970.

Section H2: Any other social care provision reasonably required by the learning difficulties or disabilities which result in the child or young person having SEN. This will include any adult social care provision being provided to meet a young person's eligible needs (through a statutory care and support plan) under the Care Act 2014.

Section I: The name and type of the school, maintained nursery school, post-16 institution or other institution to be attended by the child or young person and the type of that institution (or, where the name of a school or other institution is not specified in the EHC plan, the type of school or other institution to be attended by the child or young person).

Section J: Where there is a Personal Budget, the details of how the Personal Budget will support particular outcomes, the provision it will be used for including any flexibility in its usage and the arrangements for any direct payments for education, health and social care. The special educational needs and outcomes that are to be met by any direct payment **must** be specified.

Section K: The advice and information gathered during the EHC needs assessment **must** be attached (in appendices). There should be a list of this advice and information.

9.63   In addition, where the child or young person is in or beyond Year 9, the EHC plan **must** include (in sections F, G, H1 or H2 as appropriate) the provision required by the child or young person to assist in preparation for adulthood and independent living, for example, support for finding employment, housing or for participation in society.

Outcomes

Relevant legislation: Section 37 of the Children and Families Act 2014 and Regulations 11 and 12 of the SEND Regulations 2014

9.64   EHC plans **must** specify the outcomes sought for the child or young person in Section E. EHC plans should be focused on education and training, health and care outcomes that will enable children and young people to progress in their learning and, as they get older, to be well prepared for adulthood. EHC plans can also include wider outcomes such as positive social relationships and emotional resilience and stability. Outcomes should always enable children and young people to move towards the long-term aspirations of employment or higher education, independent living and community participation. (See Chapter 8 for more details on preparing for adulthood.)

9.65 Long-term aspirations are not outcomes in themselves – aspirations **must** be specified in Section A of the EHC plan. A local authority cannot be held accountable for the aspirations of a child or young person. For example, a local authority cannot be required to continue to maintain an EHC plan until a young person secures employment. However, the EHC plan should continue to be maintained where the young person wants to remain in education and clear evidence shows that special educational provision is needed to enable them to achieve the education and training outcomes required for a course or programme that moves them closer to employment. For example, by accessing a supported internship or apprenticeship.

9.66 An outcome can be defined as the benefit or difference made to an individual as a result of an intervention. It should be personal and not expressed from a service perspective; it should be something that those involved have control and influence over, and while it does not always have to be formal or accredited, it should be specific, measurable, achievable, realistic and time bound (SMART). When an outcome is focused on education or training, it will describe what the expected benefit will be to the individual as a result of the educational or training intervention provided. Outcomes are not a description of the service being provided – for example the provision of three hours of speech and language therapy is not an outcome. In this case, the outcome is what it is intended that the speech and language therapy will help the individual to do that they cannot do now and by when this will be achieved.

9.67 When agreeing outcomes, it is important to consider both what is important *to* the child or young person – what they themselves want to be able to achieve – and what is important *for* them as judged by others with the child or young person's best interests at heart. In the case of speech and language needs, what is important to the child may be that they want to be able to talk to their friends and join in their games at playtime. What is important for them is that their behaviour improves because they no longer get frustrated at not being understood.

9.68 Outcomes underpin and inform the detail of EHC plans. Outcomes will usually set out what needs to be achieved by the end of a phase or stage of education in order to enable the child or young person to progress successfully to the next phase or stage. An outcome for a child of secondary school age might be, for example, to make sufficient progress or achieve a qualification to enable him or her to attend a specific course at college. Other outcomes in the EHC plan may then describe what needs to be achieved by the end of each intervening year to enable him or her to achieve the college place. From Year 9 onwards, the nature of the outcomes will reflect the need to ensure young people are preparing for adulthood. In all cases,

EHC plans **must** specify the special educational provision required to meet each of the child or young person's special educational needs. The provision should enable the outcomes to be achieved.

9.69 The EHC plan should also specify the arrangements for setting shorter term targets at the level of the school or other institution where the child or young person is placed. Professionals working with children and young people during the EHC needs assessment and EHC plan development process may agree shorter term targets that are not part of the EHC plan. These can be reviewed and, if necessary, amended regularly to ensure that the individual remains on track to achieve the outcomes specified in their EHC plan. Professionals should, wherever possible, append these shorter term plans and targets to the EHC plan so that regular progress monitoring is always considered in the light of the longer term outcomes and aspirations that the child or young person wants to achieve. In some exceptional cases, progress against these targets may well lead to an individual outcome within the EHC plan being amended at times other than following the annual review.

What to include in each section of the EHC plan

Section	Information to include
(A) The views, interests and aspirations of the child and their parents, or of the young person	• Details about the child or young person's aspirations and goals for the future (but not details of outcomes to be achieved – see section above on outcomes for guidance). When agreeing the aspirations, consideration should be given to the child or young person's aspirations for paid employment, independent living and community participation • Details about play, health, schooling, independence, friendships, further education and future plans including employment (where practical) • A summary of how to communicate with the child or young person and engage them in decision-making. • The child or young person's history • If written in the first person, the plan should make clear whether the child or young person is being quoted directly, or if the views of parents or professionals are being represented
(B) The child or young person's special educational needs (SEN)	• All of the child or young person's identified special educational needs **must** be specified • SEN may include needs for health and social care provision that are treated as special educational provision

164

Section	Information to include
	because they educate or train the child or young person (see paragraphs 9.73 onwards)
(C) The child or young person's health needs which relate to their SEN	• The EHC plan **must** specify any health needs identified through the EHC needs assessment which relate to the child or young person's SEN. Some health care needs, such as routine dental health needs, are unlikely to be related
	• The Clinical Commissioning Group (CCG) may also choose to specify other health care needs which are not related to the child or young person's SEN (for example, a long-term condition which might need management in a special educational setting)
(D) The child or young person's social care needs which relate to their SEN	• The EHC plan **must** specify any social care needs identified through the EHC needs assessment which relate to the child or young person's SEN or which require provision for a child or young person under 18 under section 2 of the Chronically Sick and Disabled Persons Act 1970
	• The local authority may also choose to specify other social care needs which are not linked to the child or young person's SEN or to a disability. This could include reference to any child in need or child protection plan which a child may have relating to other family issues such as neglect. Such an approach could help the child and their parents manage the different plans and bring greater co-ordination of services. Inclusion **must** only be with the consent of the child and their parents
(E) The outcomes sought for the child or the young person	• A range of outcomes over varying timescales, covering education, health and care as appropriate but recognising that it is the education and training outcomes only that will help determine when a plan is ceased for young people aged over 18. Therefore, for young people aged over 17, the EHC plan should identify clearly which outcomes are education and training outcomes. See paragraph 9.64 onwards for more detail on outcomes
	• A clear distinction between outcomes and provision. The provision should help the child or young person achieve an outcome, it is not an outcome in itself
	• Steps towards meeting the outcomes
	• The arrangements for monitoring progress, including review and transition review arrangements and the arrangements for setting and monitoring shorter term

Section	Information to include
	targets by the early years provider, school, college or other education or training provider
	• Forward plans for key changes in a child or young person's life, such as changing schools, moving from children's to adult care and/or from paediatric services to adult health, or moving on from further education to adulthood
	• For children and young people preparing for the transition to adulthood, the outcomes that will prepare them well for adulthood and are clearly linked to the achievement of the aspirations in section A
(F) The special educational provision required by the child or the young person	• Provision **must** be detailed and specific and should normally be quantified, for example, in terms of the type, hours and frequency of support and level of expertise, including where this support is secured through a Personal Budget
	• Provision **must** be specified for each and every need specified in section B. It should be clear how the provision will support achievement of the outcomes
	• Where health or social care provision educates or trains a child or young person, it **must** appear in this section (see paragraph 9.73)
	• There should be clarity as to how advice and information gathered has informed the provision specified. Where the local authority has departed from that advice, they should say so and give reasons for it
	• In some cases, flexibility will be required to meet the changing needs of the child or young person including flexibility in the use of a Personal Budget
	• The plan should specify:
	○ any appropriate facilities and equipment, staffing arrangements and curriculum
	○ any appropriate modifications to the application of the National Curriculum, where relevant
	○ any appropriate exclusions from the application of the National Curriculum or the course being studied in a post-16 setting, in detail, and the provision which it is proposed to substitute for any such exclusions in order to maintain a balanced and broadly based curriculum
	○ where residential accommodation is appropriate,

166

Section	Information to include
	that fact
	○ where there is a Personal Budget, the outcomes to which it is intended to contribute (detail of the arrangements for a Personal Budget, including any direct payment, **must** be included in the plan and these should be set out in section J)
	• See paragraph 9.131 onwards for details of duties on the local authority to maintain the special educational provision in the EHC plan
(G) Any health provision reasonably required by the learning difficulties or disabilities which result in the child or young person having SEN	• Provision should be detailed and specific and should normally be quantified, for example, in terms of the type of support and who will provide it
	• It should be clear how the provision will support achievement of the outcomes, including the health needs to be met and the outcomes to be achieved through provision secured through a personal (health) budget
	• Clarity as to how advice and information gathered has informed the provision specified
	• Health care provision reasonably required may include specialist support and therapies, such as medical treatments and delivery of medications, occupational therapy and physiotherapy, a range of nursing support, specialist equipment, wheelchairs and continence supplies. It could include highly specialist services needed by only a small number of children which are commissioned centrally by NHS England (for example therapeutic provision for young offenders in the secure estate)
	• The local authority and CCG may also choose to specify other health care provision reasonably required by the child or young person, which is not linked to their learning difficulties or disabilities, but which should sensibly be co-ordinated with other services in the plan
	• See paragraph 9.141 for details of duties on the health service to maintain the health care provision in the EHC plan
(H1) Any social care provision which must be made for a child or young person under 18 resulting from	• Provision should be detailed and specific and should normally be quantified, for example, in terms of the type of support and who will provide it (including where this is to be secured through a social care direct payment)
	• It should be clear how the provision will support achievement of the outcomes, including any provision

Section	Information to include

section 2 of the Chronically Sick and Disabled Persons Act 1970 (CSDPA)	secured through a Personal Budget. There should be clarity as to how advice and information gathered has informed the provision specified
	
	• Section H1 of the EHC plan **must** specify all services assessed as being needed for a disabled child or young person under 18, under section 2 of the CSDPA. These services include:
	
	    ○ practical assistance in the home
	
	    ○ provision or assistance in obtaining recreational and educational facilities at home and outside the home
	
	    ○ assistance in travelling to facilities
	
	    ○ adaptations to the home
	
	    ○ facilitating the taking of holidays
	
	    ○ provision of meals at home or elsewhere
	
	    ○ provision or assistance in obtaining a telephone and any special equipment necessary
	
	    ○ non-residential short breaks (included in Section H1 on the basis that the child as well as his or her parent will benefit from the short break)
	
	• This may include services to be provided for parent carers of disabled children, including following an assessment of their needs under sections 17ZD-17ZF of the Children Act 1989
	
	• See paragraph 9.137 onwards for details of duties on local authorities to maintain the social care provision in the EHC plan

(H2) Any other social care provision reasonably required by the learning difficulties or disabilities which result in the child or young person having SEN	• Social care provision reasonably required may include provision identified through early help and children in need assessments and safeguarding assessments for children. Section H2 **must** only include services which are not provided under Section 2 of the CSDPA. For children and young people under 18 this includes residential short breaks and services provided to children arising from their SEN but unrelated to a disability. This should include any provision secured through a social care direct payment. See chapter 10 for more information on children's social care assessments • Social care provision reasonably required will include any adult social care provision to meet eligible needs for

168

Section	Information to include
	young people over 18 (set out in an adult care and support plan) under the Care Act 2014. See Chapter 8 for further detail on adult care and EHC plans
	• The local authority may also choose to specify in section H2 other social care provision reasonably required by the child or young person, which is not linked to their learning difficulties or disabilities. This will enable the local authority to include in the EHC plan social care provision such as child in need or child protection plans, or provision meeting eligible needs set out in an adult care plan where it is unrelated to the SEN but appropriate to include in the EHC plan
	• See paragraph 9.137 onwards for details of duties on local authorities to maintain the social care provision in the EHC plan
(I) Placement	• The name *and* type of the school, maintained nursery school, post-16 institution or other institution to be attended by the child or young person and the type of that institution (or, where the name of a school or other institution is not specified in the EHC plan, the type of school or other institution to be attended by the child or young person)
	• These details **must** be included only in the final EHC plan, *not* the draft EHC plan sent to the child's parent or to the young person
	• See paragraph 9.78 onwards for more details
(J) Personal Budget (including arrangements for direct payments)	• This section should provide detailed information on any Personal Budget that will be used to secure provision in the EHC plan
	• It should set out the arrangements in relation to direct payments as required by education, health and social care regulations
	• The special educational needs and outcomes that are to be met by any direct payment **must** be specified
(K) Advice and information	• The advice and information gathered during the EHC needs assessment **must** be set out in appendices to the EHC plan. There should be a list of this advice and information

Agreeing the health provision in EHC plans

Relevant legislation: Sections 26 and 37 of the Children and Families Act 2014 and Regulation 12 of the SEND Regulations 2014

9.70 Each CCG will determine which services it will commission to meet the reasonable health needs of the children and young people with SEN or disabilities for whom it is responsible. These services should be described in the Local Offer. Relevant local clinicians, such as community paediatricians, will participate in the development of the child's or young person's EHC plan, advising on the child's needs and the provision appropriate to meet them. CCGs **must** ensure that commissioned services are mobilised to participate in the development of EHC plans. The CCG as commissioner will often have a limited involvement in the process (as this will be led by clinicians from the services they commission) but **must** ensure that there is sufficient oversight to provide assurance that the needs of children with SEN are being met in line with their statutory responsibility. The CCG will have a more direct role in considering the commissioning of a service that does not appear in the Local Offer to meet the complex needs of a specific individual, or in agreeing a Personal Budget.

9.71 The health care provision specified in section G of the EHC plan **must** be agreed by the CCG (or where relevant, NHS England) and any health care provision should be agreed in time to be included in the draft EHC plan sent to the child's parent or to the young person. As part of the joint commissioning arrangements, partners **must** have clear disagreement resolution procedures where there is disagreement on the services to be included in an EHC plan.

9.72 For children and young people in youth custody, the arrangements for carrying out the health part of EHC needs assessments and arranging for the health provision in EHC plans to be made will be slightly different and further guidance for CCGs and relevant health commissioners is set out in Chapter 10.

Responsibility for provision

Relevant legislation: Section 21 of the Children and Families Act 2014

9.73 Health or social care provision which educates or trains a child or young person **must** be treated as special educational provision and included in Section F of the EHC plan.

9.74 Decisions about whether health care provision or social care provision should be treated as special educational provision **must** be made on an individual basis. Speech and language therapy and other therapy provision can be regarded as either education or health care provision, or both. It could therefore be included in an EHC plan as either educational or health provision. However, since communication is so fundamental in education, addressing speech and language impairment should normally be recorded as special educational provision unless there are exceptional reasons for not doing so.

9.75   Agreement should be reached between the local authority and health and social care partners about where provision will be specified in an EHC plan.

9.76   In cases where health care provision or social care provision is to be treated as special educational provision, ultimate responsibility for ensuring that the provision is made rests with the local authority (unless the child's parent has made suitable arrangements) and the child's parent or the young person will have the right to appeal to the First-tier Tribunal (SEN and Disability) where they disagree with the provision specified.

The draft EHC plan

Relevant legislation: Section 38 of the Children and Families Act 2014 and Regulation 13 of the SEND Regulations 2014

9.77   The local authority **must** send the draft EHC plan (including the appendices containing the advice and information gathered during the EHC needs assessment) to the child's parent or to the young person and give them at least 15 days to give views and make representations on the content. During this period, the local authority **must** make its officers available for a meeting with the child's parent or the young person on request if they wish to discuss the content of the draft EHC plan. When the local authority sends the draft EHC plan to the child's parent or the young person the following apply:

- The local authority **must** notify the child's parent or the young person that during this period they can request that a particular school or other institution, or type of school or other institution, be named in the plan. The draft plan **must not** contain the name of the school, maintained nursery school, post-16 institution or other institution or the type of school or other institution to be attended by the child or young person (see below)

- The local authority **must** advise the child's parent or the young person where they can find information about the schools and colleges that are available for the child or young person to attend, for example through the Local Offer

- The local authority should also seek agreement of any Personal Budget specified in the draft plan (see paragraph 9.95 onwards for more information on Personal Budgets)

Requests for a particular school, college or other institution

Relevant legislation: Sections 33 and 39 of the Children and Families Act 2014

9.78   The child's parent or the young person has the right to request a particular school, college or other institution of the following type to be named in their EHC plan:

- maintained nursery school

- maintained school and any form of academy or free school (mainstream or special)

- non-maintained special school

- further education or sixth form college

- independent school or independent specialist colleges (where they have been approved for this purpose by the Secretary of State and published in a list available to all parents and young people)

9.79   If a child's parent or a young person makes a request for a particular nursery, school or post-16 institution in these groups the local authority **must** comply with that preference and name the school or college in the EHC plan unless:

- it would be unsuitable for the age, ability, aptitude or SEN of the child or young person, or

- the attendance of the child or young person there would be incompatible with the efficient education of others, or the efficient use of resources

Efficient education means providing for each child or young person a suitable, appropriate education in terms of their age, ability, aptitude and any special educational needs they may have. Where a local authority is considering the appropriateness of an individual institution, 'others' is intended to mean the children and young people with whom the child or young person with an EHC plan will directly come into contact on a regular day-to-day basis.

9.80   The local authority **must** consult the governing body, principal or proprietor of the school or college concerned and consider their comments very carefully before deciding whether to name it in the child or young person's EHC plan, sending the school or college a copy of the draft plan. If another local authority maintains the school, they too **must** be consulted.

9.81   The local authority **must** also seek the agreement of the nursery, school or post-16 institution where the draft plan sets out any provision to be delivered on their premises which is secured through a direct payment. (See paragraph 9.119 onwards for more information on direct payments). Where this includes a direct payment for SEN provision, it **must** include formal written notice of the proposal specifying:

- the name of the child or young person in respect of whom direct payments are to be made

- the qualifying goods and services which are to be secured by direct payments

- the proposed amount of direct payments

- any conditions on how the direct payments may be spent

- the dates for payments into a bank account approved by the local authority, and

- any conditions of receipt that recipients **must** agree to before any direct payment can be made

9.82   Advice from schools, colleges and other education or training providers will contribute to the development of an EHC plan to ensure that it meets the child or young person's needs, the outcomes they want to achieve and the aspirations they are aiming for.

9.83   The nursery, school or college and, where relevant, the other local authority, should respond within 15 days. Where a nursery, school or college identified at 9.78 above is named on an EHC plan they **must** admit the child or young person.

9.84   The child's parent or the young person may also make representations for places in non-maintained early years provision or at independent schools or independent specialist colleges or other post-16 providers that are not on the list mentioned at 9.78 above and the local authority **must** consider their request. The local authority is not under the same conditional duty to name the provider but **must** have regard to the general principle in section 9 of the Education Act 1996 that children should be educated in accordance with their parents' wishes, so long as this is compatible with the provision of efficient instruction and training and does not mean unreasonable public expenditure. The local authority should be satisfied that the institution would admit the child or young person before naming it in a plan since these providers are not subject to the duty to admit a child or young person even if named in their plan.

173

9.85 Children with EHC plans can attend more than one school under a dual placement. Dual placements enable children to have support from a mainstream and a special school. This can help to prepare children for mainstream education and enable mainstream and special schools to share and develop their expertise in supporting children with different types of SEN. In order for a child with SEN who is being supported by a dual placement to be deemed as being educated at a mainstream school they should spend the majority of their time there.

9.86 Where appropriate, a young person with an EHC plan can attend a dual placement at an institution within the further education sector and a special post-16 institution. The local authority should work with the young person, post-16 provider and independent specialist college to commission such a placement where that will achieve the best possible outcome for the young person. To be deemed as being educated in a mainstream further education institution, young people should spend the majority of their time there.

9.87 The local authority should consider very carefully a request from a parent for a denominational school, but denominational considerations cannot override the requirements of the Children and Families Act 2014.

Where no request is made for a particular school or college or a request for a particular school or college has not been met

Relevant legislation: Sections 33 and 40 of the Children and Families Act 2014

9.88 Where a parent or young person does not make a request for a particular nursery, school or college, or does so and their request is not met, the local authority **must** specify mainstream provision in the EHC plan unless it would be:

- against the wishes of the parent or young person, or

- incompatible with the efficient education of others

9.89 Mainstream education cannot be refused by a local authority on the grounds that it is not suitable. A local authority can rely on the exception of incompatibility with the efficient education of others in relation to maintained nursery schools, mainstream schools or mainstream post-16 institutions taken as a whole only if it can show that there are no reasonable steps it could take to prevent that incompatibility. Where a parent's or young person's request for a particular mainstream school or mainstream post-16 institution has not been met, the school or post-16 institution in question becomes a possible candidate for consideration by the local authority according to the conditions in the above paragraph.

9.90   Where the local authority considers a particular mainstream place to be incompatible with the efficient education of others it **must** demonstrate, in relation to maintained nursery schools, mainstream schools or mainstream post-16 institutions in its area taken as a whole, that there are no reasonable steps that it, or the school or college, could take to prevent that incompatibility. Efficient education means providing for each child or young person a suitable, appropriate education in terms of their age, ability, aptitude and any special educational needs they may have. Where a local authority is considering whether mainstream education is appropriate (as opposed to considering the appropriateness of an individual institution) the term 'others' means the children or young people with whom the child or young person with an EHC plan would be likely to come into contact on a regular day-to-day basis. Where a parent or young person wants mainstream education and it would not be incompatible with the efficient education of others, the local authority has a duty to secure that provision.

Reasonable steps

9.91   What constitutes a reasonable step will depend on all the circumstances of the individual case. The following are some of the factors that may be taken into account:

- Whether taking the step would be effective in removing the incompatibility

- The extent to which it is practical for the early years provider, school, college or local authority to take the step

- The extent to which steps have already been taken in relation to a particular child or young person and their effectiveness

- The financial and other resource implications of taking the step, and

- The extent of any disruption that taking the step would cause

9.92   The following are examples of reasonable steps that might be taken in different circumstances:

- Reasonable steps to ensure that the inclusion of a child with challenging behaviour in a mainstream primary school setting is not incompatible with the efficient education of others may include:

  o addressing factors within the class that may exacerbate the problem, for example using circle time to discuss difficult relationships and identify constructive responses

  o teaching the child alternative behaviour, for example by taking quiet time in a specially designated area at times of stress

175

- ○ providing the child with a channel of communication, for example use of peer support

- ○ using a carefully designed system of behaviour targets drawn up with the child and linked to a reward system which, wherever possible, involves parents or carers

- ○ ensuring that all staff coming into contact with the child are briefed on potential triggers for outbursts and effective ways of heading off trouble at an early stage

- ○ drawing up a contingency plan if there is an outburst in class, for example, identifying with the child a key helper who can be called to remove the child from the situation, and

- ○ ensuring that if there is any possibility that positive handling may need to be used to prevent injury to the child, young person or others or damage to property, relevant staff have had training in appropriate techniques, that these have been carefully explained to the child and that the circumstances in which they will be used are recorded in a written plan agreed with and signed by the child and their parents or carers

- Reasonable steps taken to ensure that the inclusion of a child with autistic spectrum disorder who is distracting and constantly moves around in a mainstream secondary school is not incompatible with the efficient education of others may include:

  - ○ ensuring all possible steps are taken to provide structure and predictability to the child's day, for example by the use of visual timetables, careful prior explanation of changes to routines and clear instructions for tasks

  - ○ ensuring that the child is taught a means of communicating wants and needs using sign, symbol or spoken language

  - ○ working with a member of staff on a structured programme of activities designed to prepare him or her for joining in class or group activities, for example by using 'social scripts' to rehearse appropriate behaviour

  - ○ having an individual workstation within a teaching space where distractions can be kept to a minimum and everything needed for the work to be done can be organised in sequence, and

- ○ ensuring that all staff are briefed on the warning signs which may indicate potential behaviour challenge and on a range of activities which provide effective distraction if used sufficiently early

- Reasonable steps taken to ensure that the inclusion of a young person with a learning disability who does not use verbal communication in a mainstream course at a further education college is not incompatible with the efficient education of others may include:

  - ○ the involvement of staff from the college's learning support team in the school-based transition reviews

  - ○ an orientation period during the summer holidays, to enable the student to find his or her way around the college campus and meet the learning support staff

  - ○ opportunities to practise travelling to and from college

  - ○ the development of an individual learning programme outlining longer term outcomes covering all aspects of learning and development, with shorter term targets to meet the outcomes

  - ○ supported access to taster sessions over a first year in college

  - ○ a more detailed assessment of the young person's needs and wishes provided by learning support tutors during a 'taster' year

  - ○ staff development to ensure an understanding of the student's particular method of communication

  - ○ use of expertise in access technology to identify appropriate switches or communication boards to facilitate the student's involvement in an entry-level course, and

  - ○ courses normally covered in one year planned over two years to meet the young person's learning needs

9.93   There may be a range of reasons why it may not always be possible to take reasonable steps to prevent a mainstream place from being incompatible with the efficient education of others – for example, where the child or young person's behaviour systematically, persistently or significantly threatens the safety and/or impedes the learning of others.

9.94   A decision not to educate a child or young person in a mainstream setting against the wishes of the child's parent or the young person should not be taken lightly. It is important that all decisions are taken on the basis of the circumstances of each case and in consultation with the parents or young person, taking account of the child or young person's views. Local authorities should consider reasonable steps that can be taken for mainstream schools and mainstream post-16 institutions generally to provide for children and young people with SEN and disabled children and young people.

Requesting a Personal Budget

Relevant legislation: Section 49 of the Children and Families Act 2014, the Special Educational Needs (Personal Budgets) Regulations 2014, the Community Care, services for Carers and Children's Services (Direct Payments) Regulations 2009 (the 2009 regulations will be replaced by those made under the Care Act 2014), and the National Health Service (Direct Payments) Regulations 2013

9.95   A Personal Budget is an amount of money identified by the local authority to deliver provision set out in an EHC plan where the parent or young person is involved in securing that provision (see 'Mechanisms for delivery of a Personal Budget' below).

9.96   Local authorities **must** provide information on Personal Budgets as part of the Local Offer. This should include a policy on Personal Budgets that sets out a description of the services across education, health and social care that currently lend themselves to the use of Personal Budgets, how that funding will be made available, and clear and simple statements of eligibility criteria and the decision-making processes.

9.97   Personal Budgets are optional for the child's parent or the young person but local authorities are under a duty to prepare a budget when requested. Local authorities **must** provide information about organisations that may be able to provide advice and assistance to help parents and young people to make informed decisions about Personal Budgets. Local authorities should use the information on Personal Budgets set out in the Local Offer to introduce the idea of Personal Budgets to parents and young people within the person-centred approach described in paragraphs 9.21 to 9.26.

9.98   The child's parent or the young person has a right to request a Personal Budget, when the local authority has completed an EHC needs assessment and confirmed that it will prepare an EHC plan. They may also request a Personal Budget during a statutory review of an existing EHC plan.

9.99   Personal Budgets should reflect the holistic nature of an EHC plan and can include funding for special educational, health and social care provision. They should be focused to secure the provision agreed in the EHC plan and should be designed to secure the outcomes specified in the EHC plan.

9.100 Further resources on Personal Budgets are available through the DfE-funded 'Making it Personal' project. This includes guidance for parents, commissioners and suppliers and is available on the Kids website – a link is provided in the References section under Chapter 3.

Mechanisms for delivery of a Personal Budget

9.101 There are four ways in which the child's parent and/or the young person can be involved in securing provision:

- Direct payments – where individuals receive the cash to contract, purchase and manage services themselves

- An arrangement – whereby the local authority, school or college holds the funds and commissions the support specified in the plan (these are sometimes called notional budgets)

- Third party arrangements – where funds (direct payments) are paid to and managed by an individual or organisation on behalf of the child's parent or the young person

- A combination of the above

Setting and agreeing the Personal Budget

9.102 The child's parent or the young person should be given an indication of the level of funding that is likely to be required to make the provision specified, or proposed to be specified in the EHC plan. An indicative figure can be identified through a resource allocation or banded funding system. As part of a person-centred approach to the development of the EHC plan, the local authority should agree the provision to be made in the plan and help the parent or young person to decide whether they want to take up a Personal Budget. Local authorities should be clear that any figure discussed at this stage is indicative and is a tool to support the planning process including the development of the draft EHC plan. The final allocation of funding budget **must** be sufficient to secure the agreed provision specified in the EHC plan and **must** be set out as part of that provision.

9.103 Details of the proposed Personal Budget should be included in section J of the draft EHC plan and, where the proposed budget includes direct payments for special educational provision, this section must include the SEN and outcomes to be met by the payment. Local authorities must also provide written notice of the conditions for receipt of any direct payment for special educational provision and can do this alongside the draft EHC plan. The child's parent or the young person should confirm their decision and agreement of the budget. Where appropriate, this **must** include their agreement, in writing, of the conditions for receipt of the direct payment, alongside any request for a particular school, college or other institution to be named in the EHC plan. Where the child's parent or the young person has nominated a person to receive payments on their behalf, the agreement must come from the proposed recipient.

9.104 Where a direct payment is proposed for special educational provision, local authorities **must** secure the agreement of the early years setting, school or college, if any of the provision is to be delivered on that institution's premises. Local authorities should usually do this when they consult the institution about naming it on the child or young person's EHC plan. The local authority should also seek assurance from the child's parent, young person or nominee that any person employed by the child's parent or young person, but working on early years, school or college premises, will conform to the policies and procedures of that institution and may write such an assurance into the conditions for receipt of the direct payment.

9.105 Where agreement cannot be reached with the early years setting, school or college, the local authority **must not** go ahead with the direct payment. However, they should continue to work with the child's parent or the young person and the school, college or early years setting to explore other opportunities for the personalisation of provision in the EHC plan. Local authorities may wish to discuss the potential for arrangements whereby the local authority, the early years setting, school or college, holds a notional budget with a view to involving the child's parent or the young person in securing the provision. The broader purpose of such arrangements is to increase the participation of children, their parents and young people in decision-making in relation to special educational provision

9.106 Local authorities **must** consider each request for a Personal Budget on its individual merits and prepare a Personal Budget in each case unless the sum is part of a larger amount and disaggregation of the funds for the Personal Budget:

- would have an adverse impact on services provided or arranged by the local authority for other EHC plan holders, or

- where it should not be an efficient use of the local authority's resources

In these circumstances, the local authority should inform the child's parent or the young person of the reasons it is unable to identify a sum of money and work with them to ensure that services are personalised through other means. Demand from parents and young people for funds that cannot, at present, be disaggregated should inform joint commissioning arrangements for greater choice and control (see Chapter 3, Working together across education, health and care for joint outcomes, paragraphs 3.38 and 3.39).

9.107 If the local authority refuses a request for a direct payment for special educational provision on the grounds set out in regulations (see paragraphs 9.119 to 9.124 below) the local authority **must** set out their reasons in writing and inform the child's parent or the young person of their right to request a formal review of the decision. The local authority **must** consider any subsequent representation made by the child's parent or the young person and notify them of the outcome, in writing, setting out the reasons for their decision.

9.108 Where the disagreement relates to the special educational provision to be secured through a Personal Budget the child's parent or the young person can appeal to the First-tier Tribunal (SEN and Disability), as with any other disagreement about provision to be specified in an EHC plan.

9.109 Decisions in relation to the health element (Personal Health Budget) remain the responsibility of the CCG or other health commissioning bodies and where they decline a request for a direct payment, they **must** set out the reasons in writing and provide the opportunity for a formal review. Where more than one body is unable to meet a request for a direct payment, the local authority and partners should consider sending a single letter setting out the reasons for the decisions.

Scope of Personal Budgets

9.110 The Personal Budget can include funding from education, health and social care. However, the scope of that budget will vary depending on the needs of the individual, the eligibility criteria for the different components and the mechanism for delivery. It will reflect local circumstances, commissioning arrangements and school preference. The scope of Personal Budgets should increase over time as local joint commissioning arrangements provide greater opportunity for choice and control over local provision.

9.111 Local authority commissioners and their partners should seek to align funding streams for inclusion in Personal Budgets and are encouraged to establish arrangements that will allow the development of a single integrated fund from which a single Personal Budget, covering all three areas of additional and individual support, can be made available. EHC plans can then set out how this budget is to be used including the provision to be secured, the outcomes it will deliver and how health, education and social care needs will be met.

Education

9.112 The special educational provision specified in an EHC plan can include provision funded from the school's budget share (or in colleges from their formula funding) and more specialist provision funded wholly or partly from the local authority's high needs funding. It is this latter funding that is used for Personal Budgets, although schools

181

and colleges should be encouraged to personalise the support they provide and they can choose to contribute their own funding to a Personal Budget (this will usually be an organised arrangement managed by the setting, but some schools and colleges, including specialist settings, have made innovative arrangements with young people, giving them direct (cash) payments).

9.113 High needs funding can also be used to commission services from schools and colleges, including from special schools. In practice, this will mean the funding from the local authority's high needs budget for the SEN element of a Personal Budget will vary depending on how services are commissioned locally and what schools and colleges are expected to provide as part of the Local Offer. The child's parent or the young person should be made aware that the scope for a Personal Budget varies depending on their school preference. For example, as part of their core provision, special schools and colleges make some specialist provision available that is not normally available at mainstream schools and colleges. The particular choice of a special school, with integrated specialist provision, might reduce the scope for a Personal Budget, whereas the choice of a place in a mainstream school that does not make that particular provision could increase the opportunity for a Personal Budget.

Health

9.114 Personal Health Budgets for healthcare are not appropriate for all of the aspects of NHS care an individual may require. Full details of excluded services are set out in guidance provided by NHS England and include primary medical (i.e. GP services) and emergency services.

9.115 In principle, other than excluded services a Personal Health Budget could be given to anyone who needs to receive healthcare funded by the NHS where the benefits of having the budget for healthcare outweigh any additional costs associated with having one.

9.116 Since April 2014, everyone receiving NHS Continuing Healthcare (including children's continuing care) has had the right to ask for a Personal Health Budget, including a direct payment. From October 2014 this group will benefit from 'a right to have' a Personal Health Budget.

9.117 The mandate to NHS England sets an objective that from April 2015 Personal Health Budgets including direct payments should be an option for people with long-term health needs who could benefit from one. This includes people who use NHS services outside NHS Continuing Healthcare.

Social Care

9.118 The Care Act 2014 mandates, for the first time in law, a Personal Budget as part of the care and support plan for people over 18 with eligible care and support needs, or where the local authority decides to meet needs. The Act also clarifies people's right to request a direct payment to meet some or all of their care and support needs, and covers people with and without capacity to request a direct payment. For children and young people under 18, local authorities are under a duty to offer direct payments (see paragraph 9.123 below) for services which the local authority may provide to children with disabilities, or their families, under section 17 of the Children Act 1989.

Use of direct payments

9.119 Direct payments are cash payments made directly to the child's parent, the young person or their nominee, allowing them to arrange provision themselves. They **must** be set at a level that will secure the provision specified in the EHC plan. If a direct payment is not set at a suitable level, it **must** be reviewed and adjusted. Local authorities **must not** make direct payments for the purpose of funding a school place or post-16 institution.

9.120 Local authority and health commissioning body duties to secure or arrange the provision specified in EHC plans are discharged through a direct payment only when the provision has been acquired for, or on behalf of, the child's parent or the young person and this has been done in keeping with regulations. Funding **must** be set at a level to secure the agreed provision in the EHC plan and meet health needs agreed in the Personal Health Budget Care Plan (see paragraph 9.124 below for the additional information that needs to be included in an EHC plan to meet the requirements for a Care Plan).

9.121 Direct payments for special educational provision, health care and social care provision are subject to separate regulations. These are:

- The Community Care, services for Carers and Children's Services (Direct Payments) Regulations 2009 (the 2009 regulations will be replaced by those made under the Care Act 2014)

- The National Health Service (Direct Payments) Regulations 2013

- The Special Educational Needs (Personal Budgets) Regulations 2014

9.122 The regulations have many common requirements including those covering consent, use of nominees, conditions for receipt, monitoring and review of direct payments and persons to whom direct payments **must not** be made (such as those subject to certain rehabilitation orders). Detailed arrangements for direct payments should be set out in section J of the EHC plan.

9.123 Local authorities **must** offer direct payments for social care services. For both education and social care the local authority **must** be satisfied that the person who receives the direct payments will use them in an appropriate way and that they will act in the best interests of the child or young person. Regulations governing the use of direct payments for special educational provision place a number of additional requirements on both local authorities and parents before a direct payment can be agreed. These include requirements to consider the impact on other service users and value for money and to seek agreement from educational establishments where a service funded by a direct payment is delivered on their premises.

9.124 Direct payments for health require the agreement of a Care Plan between the CCG and the recipient. This requirement can be fulfilled by sections G and J of the EHC plan as long as it includes the following information:

- the health needs to be met and the outcomes to be achieved through the provision in the plan

- the things that the direct payment will be used to purchase, the size of the direct payment, and how often it will be paid

- the name of the care co-ordinator responsible for managing the Care Plan

- who will be responsible for monitoring the health condition of the person receiving care

- the anticipated date of the first review, and how it is to be carried out

- the period of notice that will apply if the CCG decides to reduce the amount of the direct payment

- where necessary, an agreed procedure for discussing and managing any significant risk, and

- where people lack capacity or are more vulnerable, the plan should consider safeguarding, promoting liberty and where appropriate set out any restraint procedures

Finalising and maintaining the EHC plan

Relevant legislation: Sections 39, 40 and 43 of the Children and Families Act 2014 and Regulations 13 and 14 of the SEND Regulations 2014

9.125 When changes are suggested to the draft EHC plan by the child's parent or the young person and agreed by the local authority, the draft plan should be amended and issued as the final EHC plan as quickly as possible. The final EHC plan can differ from the draft EHC plan only as a result of any representations made by the child's parent or the young person (including a request for a Personal Budget) and decisions made about the school or other institution (or type of school or other institution) to be named in the EHC plan. The local authority **must not** make any other changes – if the local authority wishes to make other changes it **must** re-issue the draft EHC plan to the child's parent or the young person (see paragraph 9.77). The final EHC plan should be signed and dated by the local authority officer responsible for signing off the final plan.

9.126 Where changes suggested by the child's parent or the young person are not agreed, the local authority may still proceed to issue the final EHC plan. In either case the local authority **must** notify the child's parent or the young person of their right to appeal to the Tribunal and the time limit for doing so, of the requirement for them to consider mediation should they wish to appeal, and the availability of information, advice and support and disagreement resolution services. The local authority should also notify the child's parent or the young person how they can appeal the health and social care provision in the EHC plan.

9.127 The child's parent or the young person may appeal to the Tribunal against the description of SEN in the EHC plan, the special educational provision, and the school or other provider named, or the fact that no school or other provider is named.

9.128 Mediation and appeals for children and young people whose EHC plans are finalised while they remain in custody are covered in Chapter 10.

9.129 As well as the child's parent or the young person, the final EHC plan **must** also be issued to the governing body, proprietor or principal of any school, college or other institution named in the EHC plan, and to the relevant CCG (or where relevant, NHS England).

9.130 Where a nursery, school or college (of a type identified in paragraph 9.78) is named in an EHC plan, they **must** admit the child or young person. The headteacher or principal of the school, college or other institution named in the EHC plan should ensure that those teaching or working with the child or young person are aware of their needs and have arrangements in place to meet them. Institutions should also ensure that teachers and lecturers monitor and review the child or young person's

185

progress during the course of a year. Formal reviews of the EHC plan **must** take place at least annually. If a child or young person's SEN change, the local authority should hold a review as soon as possible to ensure that provision specified in the EHC plan is appropriate.

Maintaining special educational provision in EHC plans

Relevant legislation: Section 42 of the Children and Families Act 2014

9.131 When an EHC plan is maintained for a child or young person the local authority **must** secure the special educational provision specified in the plan. If a local authority names an independent school or independent college in the plan as special educational provision it **must** also meet the costs of the fees, including any boarding and lodging where relevant.

9.132 The local authority is relieved of its duty to secure the special educational provision in the EHC plan, including securing a place in a school or college named in the plan, if the child's parent or the young person has made suitable alternative arrangements for special educational provision to be made, say in an independent school or college or at home.

9.133 Where the child's parent or the young person makes alternative arrangements, the local authority **must** satisfy itself that those arrangements are suitable before it is relieved of its duty to secure the provision. It can conclude that those arrangements are suitable only if there is a realistic possibility of them being funded for a reasonable period of time. If it is satisfied, the authority need not name its nominated school or college in the EHC plan and may specify only the type of provision. This is to avoid the school or other institution having to keep a place free that the child's parent or the young person has no intention of taking up.

9.134 If the local authority is not satisfied that the alternative arrangements made by the child's parent or the young person are suitable, it could either conclude that the arrangements are not suitable and name another appropriate school or college, or it could choose to assist the child's parent or the young person in making their arrangements suitable, including through a financial contribution. But the local authority would be under no obligation to meet the costs of those arrangements.

9.135 Where the child's parent or the young person makes suitable alternative arrangements for educational provision the health commissioning body is still responsible for arranging the health care specified in the child or young person's EHC plan. If the child's parent or the young person makes alternative arrangements for health care provision then the health commissioning body would need to satisfy itself that those arrangements are suitable. If the arrangements are not suitable the health commissioning body would arrange the provision specified in the plan or, if

186

they felt it appropriate, assist the child's parent or the young person in making their own arrangements suitable.

9.136 These arrangements ensure that local authorities meet their fundamental responsibility to ensure that children and young people with EHC plans get the support they need whilst enabling flexibility to accommodate alternative arrangements made by the child's parent or the young person.

Maintaining social care provision in EHC plans

9.137 For social care provision specified in the plan, existing duties on social care services to assess and provide for the needs of disabled children and young people under the Children Act 1989 continue to apply. Where the local authority decides it is necessary to make provision for a disabled child or young person under 18 pursuant to Section 2 of the Chronically Sick and Disabled Person Act (CSDPA) 1970, the local authority **must** identify which provision is made under section 2 of the CSDPA. The local authority **must** specify that provision in section H1 of the EHC plan. It **must** secure that provision because under Section 2 of the CSDPA there is a duty to provide the services assessed by the local authority as being needed.

9.138 Where the young person is over 18, the care element of the EHC plan will usually be provided by adult services. Under the Care Act 2014, local authorities **must** meet eligible needs set out in an adult care and support plan (as set out in the Care Act 2014). Local authorities should explain how the adult care and support system works, and support young people in making the transition to adult services. Local authorities should have in place arrangements to ensure that young people with social care needs have every opportunity to lead as independent a life as possible and that they are not disadvantaged by the move from children's to adult services.

9.139 However, where it will benefit a young person with an EHC plan, local authorities have the power to continue to provide children's services past a young person's 18th birthday for as long as is deemed necessary. This will enable the move to adult services to take place at a time that avoids other key changes in the young person's life such as the move from special school sixth form to college.

9.140 The Care Act 2014 requires local authorities to ensure there is no gap in support while an individual makes the transition from children's to adult services on or after their 18th birthday. Children's services **must** be maintained until a decision on adult provision is reached and where it is agreed that adult services will be provided, children's services **must** continue until the adult support begins. Young people will also be able to request an assessment for adult care in advance of their 18th birthday so they can plan ahead knowing what support will be received. See Chapter 8 for further details on young adults over 18 with social care needs, and Chapter 10 for further details on children and young people with social care needs.

187

Maintaining health provision in EHC plans

Relevant legislation: Section 42 of the Children and Families Act 2014

9.141 For health care provision specified in the EHC plan, the CCG (or where relevant NHS England) **must** ensure that it is made available to the child or young person. The joint arrangements underpinning the plan will include agreement between the partners of their respective responsibilities for funding the arrangements, to ensure that the services specified are commissioned. CCGs will need therefore to satisfy themselves that the arrangements they have in place for participating in the development of EHC plans include a mechanism for agreeing the health provision, which would usually be delegated to the relevant health professionals commissioned by the CCG. CCGs may however wish to have more formal oversight arrangements for all EHC plans to which they are a party.

Specific age ranges

All children under compulsory school age

9.142 Children under compulsory school age are considered to have SEN if they have a learning difficulty or disability which calls for special educational provision to be made and when they reach compulsory school age are likely to have greater difficulty in learning than their peers, or have a disability which prevents or hinders them from making use of the facilities that are generally provided. There is an additional precautionary consideration, that they are considered to have a learning difficulty or disability if they would be likely to have a learning difficulty or disability when they are of compulsory school age if no special educational provision were made for them. The majority of children with SEN are likely to receive special educational provision through the services set out in the Local Offer. A local authority **must** conduct an EHC needs assessment for a child under compulsory school age when it considers it may need to make special educational provision in accordance with an EHC plan (see paragraphs 9.11 to 9.19 for details of the process for deciding whether to undertake an EHC needs assessment). Where an EHC plan may be needed, the local authority should involve fully the child's parent and any early years or school setting attended by the child in making decisions about undertaking an EHC needs assessment and whether provision may need to be made in accordance with an EHC plan.

Children aged under 2

9.143 Parents, health services, childcare settings, Sure Start Children's Centres or others may identify young children as having or possibly having SEN. For most children under two whose SEN are identified early, their needs are likely to be best met from locally available services, particularly the health service, and for disabled children, social care services provided under Section 17 of the Children Act 1989. The Local

Offer should set out how agencies will work together to provide integrated support for young children with SEN, and how services will be planned and commissioned jointly to meet local needs.

9.144 For very young children local authorities should consider commissioning the provision of home-based programmes such as Portage, or peripatetic services for children with hearing or vision impairment. Parents should be fully involved in making decisions about the nature of the help and support that they would like to receive – some may prefer to attend a centre or to combine home-based with centre-based support. Children and their parents may also benefit from Early Support, which provides materials and resources on co-ordinated support. Further information about the programme can be found on the GOV.UK website – a link is given in the References section under Chapter 2.

9.145 Special educational provision for a child aged under two means educational provision of any kind. Children aged under two are likely to need special educational provision in accordance with an EHC plan where they have particularly complex needs affecting learning, development and health and are likely to require a high level of special educational provision which would not normally be available in mainstream settings. A decision to issue an EHC plan may be made in order to allow access to a particular specialist service that cannot otherwise be obtained, such as home-based teaching. The factors a local authority should take into account in deciding whether an EHC plan is necessary are set out in paragraphs 9.53 to 9.56.

Children aged 2 to 5

9.146 Where young children are attending an early years setting, the local authority should seek advice from the setting in making decisions about undertaking an EHC needs assessment and preparing an EHC plan. Local authorities should consider whether the child's current early years setting can support the child's SEN, or whether they need to offer additional support through an EHC plan, which may include a placement in an alternative early years setting. Chapter 5 sets out more detail on SEN support for children in early years settings.

9.147 Where a child is not attending an early years setting the local authority should collect as much information as possible before deciding whether to assess. The local authority will then consider the evidence and decide whether the child's difficulties or developmental delays are likely to require special educational provision through an EHC plan. The local authority **must** decide this in consultation with the child's parent, taking account of the potential for special educational provision made early to prevent or reduce later need.

9.148 Following an assessment, the local authority **must** decide whether to make special educational provision in accordance with an EHC plan. For children within one to two

189

years of starting compulsory education who are likely to need an EHC plan in primary school, it will often be appropriate to prepare an EHC plan during this period so the EHC plan is in place to support the transition to primary school.

9.149 Parents of children under compulsory school age can ask for a particular maintained nursery school to be named in their child's plan. The local authority **must** name the school unless it would be unsuitable for the age, ability, aptitude or SEN of the child, or the attendance of the child there would be incompatible with the efficient education of others or the efficient use of resources. The child's parents may also make representations in favour of an independent, private or voluntary early years setting for their child. If the local authority considers such provision appropriate, it is entitled to specify this in the plan and if it does, it **must** fund the provision. However, it cannot require an independent, private or voluntary setting to admit a child, unless the setting agrees. The local authority should ensure that parents have full information on the range of provision available within the authority's area and may wish to offer parents the opportunity to visit such provision.

Young people aged 19 to 25

9.150 It is important to ensure young people are prepared effectively for adulthood and the decision to provide or continue an EHC plan should take this into account, including the need to be ambitious for young people (see paragraph 8.51). The outcomes specified in the EHC plan should reflect the need to be ambitious, showing how they will enable the young person to make progress towards their aspirations. The local authority, in collaboration with the young person, his or her parent where appropriate, and relevant professionals should use the annual review process to consider whether special educational provision provided through an EHC plan will continue to enable young people to progress towards agreed outcomes that will prepare them for adulthood and help them meet their aspirations.

Young people turning 19 who have EHC plans

9.151 In line with preparing young people for adulthood, a local authority **must** not cease an EHC plan simply because a young person is aged 19 or over. Young people with EHC plans may need longer in education or training in order to achieve their outcomes and make an effective transition into adulthood. However, this position does not mean that there is an automatic entitlement to continued support at age 19 or an expectation that those with an EHC plan should all remain in education until age 25. A local authority may cease a plan for a 19- to 25-year-old if it decides that it is no longer necessary for the EHC plan to be maintained. Such circumstances include where the young person no longer requires the special educational provision specified in their EHC plan. In deciding that the special educational provision is no longer required, the local authority **must** have regard to whether the educational or

190

training outcomes specified in the plan have been achieved (see the section on Outcomes, paragraphs 9.64 to 9.69).

9.152 The local authority should also consider whether remaining in education or training would enable the young person to progress and achieve those outcomes, and whether the young person wants to remain in education or training so they can complete or consolidate their learning. In both cases, this should include consideration of access to provision that will help them prepare for adulthood. Young people who no longer need to remain in formal education or training will not require special educational provision to be made for them through an EHC plan.

Reviewing and re-assessing EHC plans

9.153 Where an EHC plan will still be maintained for a young person aged 19 or over, it **must** continue to be reviewed at least annually. The plan **must** continue to contain outcomes which should enable the young person to complete their education and training successfully and so move on to the next stage of their lives, including employment or higher education and independent living. This will happen at different stages for individual young people and EHC plans extended beyond age 19 will not all need to remain in place until age 25.

9.154 Local authorities should ensure that young people are given clear information about what support they can receive, including information about continuing study in adult or higher education, and support for health and social care, when their plan ceases. See paragraphs 9.199 to 9.210 for guidance on the process for ceasing an EHC plan.

New requests for EHC needs assessments for 19- to 25-year-olds

9.155 Young people who do not already have an EHC plan continue to have the right to request an assessment of their SEN at any point prior to their 25th birthday (unless an assessment has been carried out in the previous six months).

9.156 Where such a request is made, or the young person is otherwise brought to the attention of the local authority as being someone who may have SEN, the local authority **must** follow the guidance earlier in this chapter for carrying out EHC needs assessments. In addition, when making decisions about whether a plan needs to be made for a 19- to 25-year-old, local authorities **must** consider whether the young person requires additional time, in comparison to the majority of others of the same age who do not have SEN, to complete his or her education or training.

Transfer of EHC plans

Relevant legislation: Section 47 of the Children and Families Act 2014 and Regulations 15 and 16 of the SEND Regulations 2014

Transfers between local authorities

9.157 Where a child or young person moves to another local authority, the 'old' authority **must** transfer the EHC plan to the 'new' authority. The old authority **must** transfer the EHC plan to the new authority on the day of the move, unless the following condition applies. Where the old authority has not been provided with 15 working days' notice of the move, the old authority **must** transfer the EHC plan within 15 working days beginning with the day on which it did become aware.

9.158 The old authority should also transfer any opinion they have received under the Disabled Persons (Services, Consultation and Representation) Act 1986 that the child or young person is disabled. Upon the transfer of the EHC plan, the new authority becomes responsible for maintaining the plan and for securing the special educational provision specified in it.

9.159 The requirement for the child or young person to attend the educational institution specified in the EHC plan continues after the transfer. However, where attendance would be impractical, the new authority **must** place the child or young person temporarily at an appropriate educational institution other than that specified – for example, where the distance between the child or young person's new home and the educational institution would be too great – until the EHC plan is formally amended. The new authority may not decline to pay the fees or otherwise maintain the child at an independent or non-maintained special school or a boarding school named in an EHC plan unless and until they have amended the EHC plan.

9.160 The new authority may, on the transfer of the EHC plan, bring forward the arrangements for the review of the plan, and may conduct a new EHC needs assessment regardless of when the previous EHC needs assessment took place. This will be particularly important where the plan includes provision that is secured through the use of a direct payment, where local variations may mean that arrangements in the original EHC plan are no longer appropriate. The new authority **must** tell the child's parent or the young person, within six weeks of the date of transfer, when they will review the plan (as below) and whether they propose to make an EHC needs assessment.

9.161 The new authority **must** review the plan before one of the following deadlines, whichever is the later:

- within 12 months of the plan being made or being previously reviewed by the old authority, or

- within 3 months of the plan being transferred

9.162 Some children and young people will move between local authority areas while they are being assessed for a plan. The new authority in such cases should decide whether it needs to carry out an EHC needs assessment themselves and it **must** decide whether to undertake an EHC needs assessment if it receives a request from the child's parent or the young person. The new authority should take account of the fact that the old authority decided to carry out an EHC needs assessment when making its decision. If it decides to do so then it should use the information already gathered as part of its own EHC needs assessment. Depending on how far the assessment had progressed, this information should help the new authority complete the assessment more quickly than it would otherwise have done.

Transfers between clinical commissioning groups

9.163 Where the child or young person's move between local authority areas also results in a new CCG becoming responsible for the child or young person, the old CCG **must** notify the new CCG on the day of the move or, where it has not become aware of the move at least 15 working days prior to that move, within 15 working days beginning on the day on which it did become aware. Where for any other reason a new CCG becomes responsible for the child or young person, for example on a change of GP or a move within the local authority's area, the old CCG **must** notify the new CCG within 15 working days of becoming aware of the move. Where it is not practicable for the new CCG to secure the health provision specified in the EHC plan, the new CCG **must**, within 15 working days of becoming aware of the change of CCG, request the (new) local authority to make an EHC needs assessment or review the EHC plan. The (new) local authority **must** comply with any request.

9.164 For looked after children moving between local authorities, the old CCG retains responsibility for provision in the new local authority – for example, commissioning the provision from the new CCG as required.

9.165 Where a child or young person with an EHC plan moves to Northern Ireland, Wales or Scotland, the old authority should send a copy of the child or young person's EHC plan to the new authority or board, although there will be no obligation on the new authority or board to continue to maintain it.

193

Reviewing an EHC plan

Relevant legislation: Section 44 of the Children and Families Act 2014 and Regulations 2, 18, 19, 20, and 21 of the SEND Regulations 2014

9.166 EHC plans should be used to actively monitor children and young people's progress towards their outcomes and longer term aspirations. They **must** be reviewed by the local authority as a minimum every 12 months. Reviews **must** focus on the child or young person's progress towards achieving the outcomes specified in the EHC plan. The review **must** also consider whether these outcomes and supporting targets remain appropriate.

9.167 Reviews should also:

- gather and assess information so that it can be used by early years settings, schools or colleges to support the child or young person's progress and their access to teaching and learning

- review the special educational provision made for the child or young person to ensure it is being effective in ensuring access to teaching and learning and good progress

- review the health and social care provision made for the child or young person and its effectiveness in ensuring good progress towards outcomes

- consider the continuing appropriateness of the EHC plan in the light of the child or young person's progress during the previous year or changed circumstances and whether changes are required including any changes to outcomes, enhanced provision, change of educational establishment or whether the EHC plan should be discontinued

- set new interim targets for the coming year and where appropriate, agree new outcomes

- review any interim targets set by the early years provider, school or college or other education provider

9.168 Reviews **must** be undertaken in partnership with the child and their parent or the young person, and **must** take account of their views, wishes and feelings, including their right to request a Personal Budget.

9.169 The first review **must** be held within 12 months of the date when the EHC plan was issued, and then within 12 months of any previous review, and the local authority's decision following the review meeting **must** be notified to the child's parent or the young person within four weeks of the review meeting (and within 12 months of the

194

date of issue of the EHC plan or previous review). Professionals across education, health and care **must** co-operate with local authorities during reviews. The review of the EHC plan should include the review of any existing Personal Budget arrangements including the statutory requirement to review any arrangements for direct payments. For looked after children the annual review should, if possible and appropriate, coincide with one of the reviews in their Care Plan and in particular the personal education plan (PEP) element of the Care Plan.

9.170 Local authorities **must** also review and maintain an EHC plan when a child or young person has been released from custody. The responsible local authority **must** involve the child's parent or the young person in reviewing whether the EHC plan still reflects their needs accurately and should involve the youth offending team in agreeing appropriate support and opportunities.

9.171 When reviewing an EHC plan for a young person aged over 18, the local authority **must** have regard to whether the educational or training outcomes specified in the EHC plan have been achieved.

9.172 The local authority should provide a list of children and young people who will require a review of their EHC plan that term to all headteachers and principals of schools, colleges and other institutions attended by children or young people with EHC plans, at least two weeks before the start of each term. The local authority should also provide a list of all children and young people with EHC plan reviews in the forthcoming term to the CCG (or, where relevant, NHS England) and local authority officers responsible for social care for children and young people with SEN or disabilities. This will enable professionals to plan attendance at review meetings and/or provide advice or information about the child or young person where necessary. These lists should also indicate which reviews **must** be focused on transition and preparation for adulthood.

Reviews where a child or young person attends a school or other institution

9.173 As part of the review, the local authority and the school, further education college or section 41 approved institution attended by the child or young person **must** co-operate to ensure a review meeting takes place. This includes attending the review when requested to do so. The local authority can require the following types of school to convene and hold the meeting on the local authority's behalf:

- maintained schools

- maintained nursery schools

- academy schools

- alternative provision academies

- pupil referral units

- non-maintained special schools

- independent educational institutions approved under Section 41 of the Children and Families Act 2014

9.174 Local authorities can request (but not require) that the early years setting, further education college or other post-16 institution convene and hold the meeting on their behalf. There may be a requirement on the post-16 institution to do so as part of the contractual arrangements agreed when the local authority commissioned and funded the placement.

9.175 In most cases, reviews should normally be held at the educational institution attended by the child or young person. Reviews are generally most effective when led by the educational institution. They know the child or young person best, will have the closest contact with them and their family and will have the clearest information about progress and next steps. Reviews led by the educational institution will engender the greatest confidence amongst the child, young person and their family. There may be exceptional circumstances where it will be appropriate for the review meeting to be held by the local authority in a different location, for example where a young person attends programmes of study at more than one institution.

9.176 The following requirements apply to reviews where a child or young person attends a school or other institution:

- The child's parents or young person, a representative of the school or other institution attended, a local authority SEN officer, a health service representative and a local authority social care representative **must** be invited and given at least two weeks' notice of the date of the meeting. Other individuals relevant to the review should also be invited, including youth offending teams and job coaches where relevant

- The school (or, for children and young people attending another institution, the local authority) **must** seek advice and information about the child or young person prior to the meeting from all parties invited, and send any advice and information gathered to all those invited at least two weeks before the meeting

- The meeting **must** focus on the child or young person's progress towards achieving the outcomes specified in the EHC plan, and on what changes might need to be made to the support that is provided to help them achieve those outcomes, or whether changes are needed to the outcomes themselves. Children, parents and young people should be supported to engage fully in the review meeting

- The school (or, for children and young people attending another institution, the local authority) **must** prepare and send a report of the meeting to everyone invited within two weeks of the meeting. The report **must** set out recommendations on any amendments required to the EHC plan, and should refer to any difference between the school or other institution's recommendations and those of others attending the meeting

- Within four weeks of the review meeting, the local authority **must** decide whether it proposes to keep the EHC plan as it is, amend the plan, or cease to maintain the plan, and notify the child's parent or the young person and the school or other institution attended

- If the plan needs to be amended, the local authority should start the process of amendment without delay (see paragraph 9.193 onwards)

- If the local authority decides not to amend the plan or decides to cease to maintain it, they **must** notify the child's parent or the young person of their right to appeal that decision and the time limits for doing so, of the requirements for them to consider mediation should they wish to appeal, and the availability of information, advice and support and disagreement resolution services

Reviews where a child or young person does not attend a school or other institution

9.177 The following requirements apply to review meetings where a child or young person does not attend a school or other institution:

- The child's parent or the young person, a local authority SEN officer, a health service representative and a local authority social care representative **must** be invited and given at least two weeks' notice of the date of the meeting. Other individuals relevant to the review should also be invited, including youth offending teams and job coaches where relevant, and any other person whose attendance the local authority considers appropriate

- The local authority **must** seek advice and information about the child or young person prior to the meeting from all parties invited and send any advice and information gathered to all those invited at least two weeks before the meeting

197

- The meeting **must** focus on the child or young person's progress towards achieving the outcomes specified in the EHC plan, and on what changes might need to be made to the support provided to help them achieve those outcomes, or whether changes are needed to the outcomes themselves. Children, parents and young people should be supported to engage fully in the review meeting

- The local authority **must** prepare and send a report of the meeting to everyone invited within two weeks of the meeting. The report **must** set out recommendations on any amendments required to the EHC plan, and should refer to any difference between the local authority's recommendations, and those of others attending the meeting

- Within four weeks of the review meeting, the local authority **must** decide whether it proposes to keep the plan as it is, amend the plan, or cease to maintain the plan, and notify the child's parent or the young person

- If the plan needs to be amended, the local authority should start the process of amendment without delay (see paragraph 9.193 onwards)

- If the local authority decides not to amend the plan or decides to cease to maintain it, they **must** notify the child's parent or young person of their right to appeal that decision and the time limit for doing so, of the requirement for them to consider mediation should they wish to appeal, and the availability of information, advice and support, and disagreement resolution services

Reviews of EHC plans for children aged 0 to 5

9.178 Local authorities should consider reviewing an EHC plan for a child under five at least every three to six months to ensure that the provision continues to be appropriate. Such reviews would complement the duty to carry out a review at least annually but may be streamlined and not necessarily require the attendance of the full range of professionals, depending on the needs of the child. The child's parent **must** be fully consulted on any proposed changes to the EHC plan and made aware of their right to appeal to the Tribunal.

Transfer between phases of education

9.179 An EHC plan **must** be reviewed and amended in sufficient time prior to a child or young person moving between key phases of education, to allow for planning for and, where necessary, commissioning of support and provision at the new institution.

The review and any amendments **must** be completed by 15 February in the calendar year of the transfer at the latest for transfers into or between schools. The key transfers are:

- early years provider to school

- infant school to junior school

- primary school to middle school

- primary school to secondary school, and

- middle school to secondary school

9.180 For young people moving from secondary school to a post-16 institution or apprenticeship, the review and any amendments to the EHC plan – including specifying the post-16 provision and naming the institution – **must** be completed by the 31 March in the calendar year of the transfer.

9.181 For young people moving between post-16 institutions, the review process should normally be completed by 31 March where a young person is expected to transfer to a new institution in the new academic year. However, transfers between post-16 institutions may take place at different times of the year and the review process should take account of this. In all cases, where it is proposed that a young person is to transfer between one post-16 institution and another within the following 12 months, the local authority **must** review and amend, where necessary, the young person's EHC plan at least five months before the transfer takes place.

9.182 In some cases, young people may not meet the entry requirements for their chosen course or change their minds about what they want to do after the 31 March or five-month deadline. Where this is the case, local authorities should review the EHC plan with the young person as soon as possible, to ensure that alternative options are agreed and new arrangements are in place as far in advance of the start date as practicable.

9.183 Note: For those moving from secondary school to a post-16 institution or apprenticeship starting in September 2015, any amendments to the EHC plan – including specifying the post-16 provision and naming the institution – **must** be completed by 31 May 2015. For those moving between post-16 institutions at other times of year prior to March 2016, these amendments must be made three months before the transfer takes place. Thereafter, the deadlines set out above **must** be adhered to in all cases.

Preparing for adulthood in reviews

9.184 All reviews taking place from Year 9 at the latest and onwards **must** include a focus on preparing for adulthood, including employment, independent living and participation in society. This transition planning **must** be built into the EHC plan and where relevant should include effective planning for young people moving from children's to adult care and health services. It is particularly important in these reviews to seek and to record the views, wishes and feelings of the child or young person. The review meeting organiser should invite representatives of post-16 institutions to these review meetings, particularly where the child or young person has expressed a desire to attend a particular institution. Review meetings taking place in Year 9 should have a particular focus on considering options and choices for the next phase of education.

9.185 As the young person is nearing the end of their time in formal education and the plan is likely to be ceased within the next 12 months, the annual review should consider good exit planning. Support, provision and outcomes should be agreed that will ensure the young person is supported to make a smooth transition to whatever they will be doing next – for example, moving on to higher education, employment, independent living or adult care. For further guidance on preparing for adulthood reviews, see Chapter 8, Preparing for adulthood from the earliest years.

Re-assessments of EHC plans

Relevant legislation: Section 44 of the Children and Families Act 2014 and Regulations 23, 24, 25, 26 and 27 of the SEND Regulations 2014

9.186 The review process will enable changes to be made to an EHC plan so it remains relevant to the needs of the child or young person and the desired outcomes. There may be occasions when a re-assessment becomes appropriate, particularly when a child or young person's needs change significantly.

Requesting a re-assessment

9.187 Local authorities **must** conduct a re-assessment of a child or young person's EHC plan if a request is made by the child's parent or the young person, or the governing body, proprietor or principal of the educational institution attended by the child or young person, or the CCG (or NHS England where relevant). A local authority may also decide to initiate a re-assessment without a request if it thinks one is necessary. A re-assessment may be necessary when a young person with care support specified in their EHC plan turns 18. Adult care services will need to carry out an assessment to identify what support adult services may need to provide, and ensure the assessment is timely so that services are in place when needed.

9.188 A local authority can refuse a request for a re-assessment (from the child's parent, young person or educational institution attended) if less than 6 months have passed since the last EHC needs assessment was conducted. However the local authority can re-assess sooner than this if they think it is necessary. A local authority may also decide to refuse a request for re-assessment (from the child's parent, young person or educational institution attended) if it thinks that a further EHC needs assessment is not necessary, for example because it considers the child or young person's needs have not changed significantly.

9.189 When deciding whether to re-assess an EHC plan for a young person aged 19 or over, the local authority **must** have regard to whether the educational or training outcomes specified in the EHC plan have been achieved.

9.190 The local authority **must** notify the child's parent or the young person of its decision as to whether or not it will undertake a re-assessment within 15 calendar days of receiving the request to re-assess. If the local authority decides not to re-assess, it **must** notify the child's parent or the young person of their right to appeal that decision and the time limit for doing so, of the requirement for them to consider mediation should they wish to appeal and the availability of information, advice and support and disagreement resolution services.

The re-assessment process

9.191 The process for re-assessment will be the same as the process for a first assessment (once the decision to carry out an assessment has been taken). Re-assessments **must** follow the same process as for the first EHC needs assessment and drawing up of the EHC plan, set out earlier in this chapter, with the same timescales and rights of appeal for the child's parent or the young person.

9.192 The overall maximum timescale for a re-assessment is 14 weeks from the decision to re-assess to the issuing of the final EHC plan, subject to the exemptions set out in paragraph 9.42. However, the local authority **must** aim to complete the process as soon as practicable. Following a re-assessment, the EHC plan **must** be reviewed within 12 months of the date that the finalised EHC plan is sent to the child's parent or the young person and subsequently reviewed every twelve months from the date the EHC plan was last reviewed.

Amending an existing plan

Relevant legislation: Sections 37 and 44 of the Children and Families Act 2014 and Regulations 22 and 28 of the SEND Regulations 2014

9.193 This section applies to amendments to an existing EHC plan following a review, or at any other time a local authority proposes to amend an EHC plan other than as part of a re-assessment. EHC plans are not expected to be amended on a very frequent basis. However, an EHC plan may need to be amended at other times where, for example, there are changes in health or social care provision resulting from minor or specific changes in the child or young person's circumstances, but where a full review or re-assessment is not necessary.

9.194 Where the local authority proposes to amend an EHC plan, it **must** send the child's parent or the young person a copy of the existing (non-amended) plan and an accompanying notice providing details of the proposed amendments, including copies of any evidence to support the proposed changes. The child's parent or the young person should be informed that they may request a meeting with the local authority to discuss the proposed changes.

9.195 The parent or young person **must** be given at least 15 calendar days to comment and make representations on the proposed changes, including requesting a particular school or other institution be named in the EHC plan, in accordance with paragraphs 9.78 to 9.94 of this chapter.

9.196 Following representations from the child's parent or the young person, if the local authority decides to continue to make amendments, it **must** issue the amended EHC plan as quickly as possible and within 8 weeks of the original amendment notice. If the local authority decides not to make the amendments, it **must** notify the child's parent or the young person, explaining why, within the same time limit.

9.197 When the EHC plan is amended, the new plan should state that it is an amended version of the EHC plan and the date on which it was amended, as well as the date of the original plan. Additional advice and information, such as the minutes of a review meeting and accompanying reports which contributed to the decision to amend the plan, should be appended in the same way as advice received during the original EHC needs assessment. The amended EHC plan should make clear which parts have been amended. Where an EHC plan is amended, the following review **must** be held within 12 months of the date of issue of the original EHC plan or previous review (not 12 months from the date the amended EHC plan is issued).

9.198 When sending the final amended EHC plan, the local authority **must** notify the child's parent or the young person of their right to appeal and the time limit for doing so, of the requirement for them to consider mediation should they wish to appeal, and the availability of information, advice and support and disagreement resolution services.

Ceasing an EHC plan

Relevant legislation: Section 45 of the Children and Families Act 2014 and Regulations 29, 30 and 31 of the SEND Regulations 2014

9.199 A local authority may cease to maintain an EHC plan only if it determines that it is no longer necessary for the plan to be maintained, or if it is no longer responsible for the child or young person. As set out in the Introduction (paragraph xi.), the legal definition of when a child or young person requires an EHC plan remains the same as that for a statement under the Education Act 1996. The circumstances in which a statement can be ceased or not replaced with an EHC plan during the transition period are the same as that for ceasing an EHC plan.

9.200 The circumstances where a local authority may determine that it is no longer necessary for the EHC plan to be maintained include where the child or young person no longer requires the special educational provision specified in the EHC plan. When deciding whether a young person aged 19 or over no longer needs the special educational provision specified in the EHC plan, a local authority **must** take account of whether the education or training outcomes specified in the EHC plan have been achieved. Local authorities **must not** cease to maintain the EHC plan simply because the young person is aged 19 or over.

9.201 The circumstances where a local authority is no longer responsible for the child or young person include where any of the following conditions apply (subject to paragraphs 9.202 and 9.203 below):

- A young person aged 16 or over leaves education to take up paid employment (including employment with training but excluding apprenticeships)

- The young person enters higher education

- A young person aged 18 or over leaves education and no longer wishes to engage in further learning

- The child or young person has moved to another local authority area

9.202 Where a young person of compulsory school or participation age – i.e. under the age of 18 – is excluded from their education or training setting or leaves voluntarily, the local authority **must not** cease their EHC plan, unless it decides that it is no longer necessary for special educational provision to be made for the child or young person in accordance with an EHC plan. The focus of support should be to re-engage the young person in education or training as soon as possible and the local authority **must** review the EHC plan and amend it as appropriate to ensure that the young person continues to receive education or training.

9.203 Where a young person aged 18 or over leaves education or training before the end of their course, the local authority **must not** cease to maintain the EHC plan unless it has reviewed the young person's EHC plan to determine whether the young person wishes to return to education or training, either at the educational institution specified in the EHC plan or somewhere else. If the young person does wish to return to education or training, and the local authority thinks it is appropriate, then the local authority **must** amend the EHC plan as necessary and it **must** maintain the plan.

The local authority should seek to re-engage the young person in education or training as soon as possible.

9.204 A local authority will not be able to cease an EHC plan because a child or young person has been given a custodial sentence. The local authority will have to keep the plan while the child or young person is in custody. Details of the local authority's duties in those circumstances are set out in Chapter 10, Children and young people in specific circumstances.

9.205 Where a local authority is considering ceasing to maintain a child or young person's EHC plan it **must**:

- inform the child's parent or the young person that it is considering this

- consult the child's parent or the young person

- consult the school or other institution that is named in the EHC plan

9.206 Where, following the consultation, the local authority decides to cease to maintain the child or young person's EHC plan, it **must** notify the child's parent or the young person, the institution named in the child or young person's EHC plan and the responsible CCG of that decision. The local authority **must** also notify the child's parent or the young person of their right to appeal that decision and the time limit for doing so, of the requirement for them to consider mediation should they wish to appeal, and the availability of information, advice and support, and disagreement resolution services.

9.207 Support should generally cease at the end of the academic year, to allow young people to complete their programme of study. In the case of a young person who reaches their 25th birthday before their course has ended, the EHC plan can be maintained until the end of the academic year in which they turn 25 (or the day the apprenticeship or course ends, or the day before their 26th birthday if later). It is important that a child or young person's exit from an EHC plan is planned carefully, to support smooth transitions and effective preparation for adulthood. See paragraphs 8.77 to 8.80 of Chapter 8 on 'Leaving education or training' for more information.

9.208 Where a young person aged 18 or over is in receipt of adult services, the local authority should ensure that adult services are involved in and made aware of the decision to cease the young person's EHC plan.

9.209 Where the child's parent or the young person disagrees with the local authority's decision to cease their EHC plan, they may appeal to the Tribunal. Local authorities

must continue to maintain the EHC plan until the time has passed for bringing an appeal or, when an appeal has been registered, until it has been concluded.

9.210   Where the care part of an EHC plan is provided by adult services under the Care Act 2014 because the person is 18 or over, the Care Plan will remain in place when the other elements of the EHC plan cease. There will be no requirement for the young person to be re-assessed at this point, unless there is reason to re-assess him or her for health and social care because their circumstances have changed.

Disclosure of an EHC plan

Relevant legislation: Regulations 17 and 47 of the SEND Regulations 2014

9.211   A child or young person's EHC plan **must** be kept securely so that unauthorised persons do not have access to it, so far as reasonably practicable (this includes any representations, evidence, advice or information related to the EHC plan). An EHC plan **must not** be disclosed without the consent of the child or the young person, except for specified purposes or in the interests of the child or young person. If a child does not have sufficient age or understanding to allow him or her to consent to such disclosure, the child's parent may give consent on the child's behalf. The specified purposes include:

- disclosure to the Tribunal when the child's parent or the young person appeals, and to the Secretary of State if a complaint is made to him or her under the 1996 Act

- disclosure on the order of any court or for the purpose of any criminal proceedings

- disclosure for the purposes of investigations of maladministration under the Local Government Act 1974

- disclosure to enable any authority to perform duties arising from the Disabled Persons (Services, Consultation and Representation) Act 1986, or from the Children Act 1989 relating to safeguarding and promoting the welfare of children

- disclosure to Ofsted inspection teams as part of their inspections of schools or other educational institutions and local authorities

- disclosure to any person in connection with the young person's application for a Disabled Students Allowance in advance of taking up a place in higher education, when requested to do so by the young person

- disclosure to the principal (or equivalent position) of the institution at which the young person is intending to start higher education, when requested to do so by the young person, and

- disclosure to persons engaged in research on SEN on the condition that the researchers do not publish anything derived from, or contained in, the plan which would identify any individual, particularly the child, young person or child's parent. Disclosure in the interests of research should be in accordance with the Data Protection Act 1998 and wherever possible should be with the knowledge and consent of the child and his or her parent or the young person

9.212 The interests of the child or young person include the provision of information to the child or young person's educational institution. It is important that teachers or other educational professionals working closely with the child or young person should have full knowledge of the child or young person's EHC plan. School governing bodies should have access to a child or young person's EHC plan. Disclosure in the interests of the child or young person also includes disclosure to any agencies other than the local authority which may be referred to in the plan as making educational, health or social care provision.

9.213 Disclosure of the EHC plan, where the local authority considers this necessary in the interests of the child or young person, can be in whole or in part. Local authorities should consider carefully when disclosing an EHC plan whether there are parts of the EHC plan that do not need to be disclosed in the interests of the child or young person, for example sensitive health or social care information. All those who have access to the EHC plan should always bear in mind the need to maintain confidentiality about the child or young person in question.

Transport costs for children and young people with EHC plans

Relevant legislation: Section 30 of the Children and Families Act 2014 and Schedule 2(14) of the SEND Regulations 2014

9.214 The parents' or young person's preferred school or college might be further away from their home than the nearest school or college that can meet the child or young person's SEN. In such a case, the local authority can name the nearer school or college if it considers it to be appropriate for meeting the child or young person's SEN. If the parents prefer the school or college that is further away, the local authority may agree to this but is able to ask the parents to provide some or all of the transport funding.

9.215 Transport should be recorded in the EHC plan only in exceptional cases where the child has particular transport needs. Local authorities **must** have clear general arrangements and policies relating to transport for children and young people with SEN or disabilities that **must** be made available to parents and young people, and these should be included in the Local Offer. Such policies **must** set out the transport arrangements which are over and above those required by section 508B of the Education Act 1996.

9.216 Where the local authority names a residential provision at some distance from the family's home, the local authority **must** provide reasonable transport or travel assistance. The latter might be reimbursement of public transport costs, petrol costs or provision of a travel pass.

9.217 Transport costs may be provided as part of a Personal Budget where one is agreed and included in the EHC plan as part of the special educational provision.

11 Resolving disagreements

Children and young people in youth custody

Please see Chapter 10, paragraphs 10.76 to 10.78.

Registering an appeal with the Tribunal

11.39 Parents and young people have two months to register an SEN appeal with the Tribunal, from the date when the local authority sent the notice containing a decision which can be appealed or one month from the date of a certificate which has been issued following mediation or the parent or young person being given mediation information, whichever is the later. In some cases parents and young people will not register the appeal within the two-month limit. Where it is fair and just to do so the Tribunal has the power to use its discretion to accept appeals outside the two-month time limit.

11.40 The Tribunal will not take account of the fact that mediation has taken place, or has not been taken up, nor will it take into account the outcome of any mediation. Parents and young people will not be disadvantaged at the Tribunal because they have chosen not to go to mediation.

Parents' and young people's right to appeal to the Tribunal about EHC needs assessments and EHC plans

The First-tier Tribunal (SEN and Disability)

11.41 The Tribunal forms part of the First-tier Tribunal (Health, Education and Social Care Chamber). Tribunals are overseen by Her Majesty's Courts and Tribunals Service.

The role and function of the Tribunal

11.42 The Tribunal hears appeals against decisions made by the local authorities in England in relation to children's and young people's EHC needs assessments and EHC plans. It also hears disability discrimination claims against schools and against local authorities when the local authority is the responsible body for a school.

11.43 The Tribunal seeks to ensure that the process of appealing is as user friendly as possible, and to avoid hearings that are overly legalistic or technical. It is the Tribunal's aim to ensure that a parent or young person should not need to engage legal representation when appealing a decision. Parents and young people may find it helpful to have support from a voluntary organisation or friend at a hearing.

Who can appeal to the Tribunal about EHC needs assessments and plans

11.44 Parents (in relation to children from 0 to the end of compulsory schooling) and young people (over compulsory school age until they reach age 25) can appeal to the Tribunal about EHC needs assessments and EHC plans, following contact with a mediation adviser in most cases (see paragraph 11.18). Young people can register an appeal in their name but can also have their parents' help and support if needed. Chapter 8, paragraphs 8.15 to 8.18 , gives further guidance on the rights of young people under the Children and Families Act 2014 and the involvement and support of parents.

What parents and young people can appeal about

11.45 Parents and young people can appeal to the Tribunal about:

- a decision by a local authority not to carry out an EHC needs assessment or re-assessment

- a decision by a local authority that it is not necessary to issue an EHC plan following an assessment

- the description of a child or young person's SEN specified in an EHC plan, the special educational provision specified, the school or other institution or type of school or other institution (such as a mainstream school/college) specified in the plan or that no school or other institution is specified

- an amendment to these elements of the EHC plan

- a decision by a local authority not to amend an EHC plan following a review or re-assessment

- a decision by a local authority to cease to maintain an EHC plan

The Tribunal does not hear appeals about Personal Budgets, but will hear appeals about the special educational provision to which a Personal Budget may apply (see paragraph 9.108).

11.46 Parents and young people who are unhappy with decisions about the health and social care elements of an EHC plan can go to mediation (see paragraphs 11.31 to 11.35). They can also complain through the health and social care complaints procedures, set out in paragraphs 11.101 to 11.104 and 11.105 to 11.111.

Conditions related to appeals

11.47 The following conditions apply to appeals:

- the parent or young person can appeal to the Tribunal when the EHC plan is initially finalised, following an amendment or a replacement of the plan

- appeals **must** be registered with the Tribunal within two months of the local authority sending a notice to the parent or young person of the decision about one of the matters that can be appealed to the Tribunal or within one month of a certificate being issued following mediation or the parent or young person being given mediation information

- the right to appeal a refusal of an EHC needs assessment will be triggered only where the local authority has not carried out an assessment in the previous six months

- when the parent or young person is appealing about a decision to cease to maintain the EHC plan the local authority has to maintain the plan until the Tribunal's decision is made

Decisions the Tribunal can make

11.48 The Tribunal has prescribed powers under the Children and Families Act 2014 to make certain decisions in relation to appeals. The Tribunal can dismiss the appeal, order the local authority to carry out an assessment, or to make and maintain an EHC plan, or to maintain a plan with amendments. The Tribunal can also order the local authority to reconsider or correct a weakness in the plan, for example, where necessary information is missing. Local authorities have time limits within which to comply with decisions of the Tribunal (see the Special Educational Needs Regulations 2014).

11.49 In making decisions about whether the special educational provision specified in the EHC plan is appropriate, the Tribunal should take into account the education and training outcomes specified in Section E of the EHC plan and whether the special educational provision will enable the child or young person to make progress towards their education and training outcomes. The Tribunal can consider whether the education and training outcomes specified are sufficiently ambitious for the child or young person. When the Tribunal orders the local authority to reconsider the special educational provision in an EHC plan, the local authority should also review whether the outcomes remain appropriate.

How parents and young people can appeal

11.50 When appealing to the Tribunal parents and young people **must** supply a copy of the decision that they are appealing against and the date when the local authority's decision was made, or the date of the mediation certificate. The parent or young person who is appealing (the appellant) will be required to give the reasons why they are appealing. The reasons do not have to be lengthy or written in legal language but should explain why the appellant disagrees with the decision. Parents and young people have to send all relevant documents, such as copies of assessments, to the Tribunal.

11.51 Once the appeal is registered the local authority will be sent a copy of the papers filed and will be given a date by which they **must** respond and asked to provide details of witnesses – this will apply to all parties. The parties will also be told of the approximate hearing date. Hearings are heard throughout the country at Her Majesty's Courts and Tribunals Service buildings. The Tribunal will try to hold hearings as close to where the appellant lives as possible. Appeals are heard by a judge and a panel of Tribunal members who have been appointed because of their knowledge and experience of children and young people with SEN or disabilities. The local authority will provide a bundle of papers for each of the panel members and the parent, including any document requested by the parent. Advice on making SEN appeals to the Tribunal is available from the Ministry of Justice website – a link is given in the References section under General.

11.52 A video is available from the Ministry of Justice website which gives appellants some guidance on what happens at a hearing – a link to it is given in the References section under Chapter 11. A DVD of this video can be requested from the Tribunal by writing to:

First-tier Tribunal (Special Educational Needs and Disability)
Darlington Magistrates Court
Parkgate
Darlington
DL1 1RU

Disability discrimination claims

11.53 The parents of disabled children and disabled young people in school have the right to make disability discrimination claims to the Tribunal if they believe that their children or the young people themselves have been discriminated against by schools or local authorities when they are the responsible body for a school. Claims **must** be made within six months of the alleged instance of discrimination. The parents of disabled children, on behalf of their children, and disabled young people in school can make a claim against any school about alleged discrimination in the matters of exclusions, the provision of education and associated services and the making of reasonable adjustments, including the provision of auxiliary aids and services. They can also make claims to the Tribunal about admissions to independent and non-maintained special schools. Claims about admissions to state-funded schools are made to local admissions panels.

11.54 Disability discrimination claims by young people against post-16 institutions, and by parents about early years provision and about their treatment as a parent in being provided with an education service for their child, are made to the county courts. Claims by parents and young people against local authorities about the policies the authorities have adopted also go to the county courts.

11.55 Guidance on how to make a disability discrimination claim to the Tribunal is available from the Ministry of Justice website, via the link to information about the Tribunal given in the References section under General.

Exclusion

11.56 The Government issues statutory guidance on school exclusion, which can be found on the GOV.UK website – a link is given in the References section under Chapter 11.

11.57 The guidance sets out details of the permanent exclusion review panel process, including parents' right to ask for an SEN expert to attend. In addition, claims for disability discrimination in relation to permanent and fixed-period exclusions may be made to the Tribunal.

11.58 Local authorities have a duty to arrange suitable, full-time education for pupils of compulsory school age who would not otherwise receive such education, including from the sixth day of a permanent exclusion. Schools have a duty to arrange suitable, full-time education from the sixth day of a fixed period exclusion (see Chapter 10, paragraphs 10.47 to 10.52 on alternative provision). Suitable education means efficient education suitable to a child's age, ability and aptitude and to any SEN the child may have.

Please note that the following figure shows the maximum time it would take to register an appeal at the Tribunal both with and without mediation and have the appeal heard. Most registrations of an appeal, even where the case goes to mediation will take a far shorter time than this. The top half the diagram is for appeals after receipt of a finalised EHC plan.

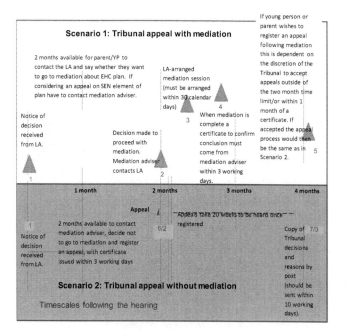

11.59 The young person or parent making the appeal and the local authority should both receive a copy of the Tribunal's decision and reasons by post within 10 working days of the hearing. Along with the decision notice the Tribunal will send a leaflet which will explain the application process for permission to appeal the Tribunal decision to the Upper Tribunal, if the appellant considers that the decision made was wrong in law. Local authorities can also appeal to the Upper Tribunal on the same grounds.

11.60 Step-by-step guidance on the process of appealing to the Tribunal and what it involves can be found at the Ministry of Justice website – a link is given in the References section under General.

Index